ECONOMIC GROWTH AND DISPARITIES

A WORLD VIEW

SIDNEY R. JUMPER
University of Tennessee

THOMAS L. BELL
University of Tennessee

BRUCE A. RALSTON
University of Tennessee

Prentice-Hall, Inc., Englewood Cliffs, New Jersey 07632

Library of Congress Cataloging in Publication Data

Jumper, Sidney R
  Economic growth and disparities.

  Includes bibliographical references and index.
    1. Economic development. 2. Economic history —
1945- I. Bell, Thomas L., joint author;
II. Ralston, Bruce A., joint author. III. Title.
HD82.J85   330.9'047   79-23728
ISBN 0-13-225680-0

059603

© 1980 by Prentice-Hall, Inc., Englewood Cliffs, N.J. 07632

Printed in the United States of America

10 9 8 7 6 5 4 3 2 1

HD
82
.J85
1980

Editorial/production supervision
  and interior design by Ian M. List
Chapter opening design by Suzanne Behnke
Cover design by Suzanne Behnke
Manufacturing buyer: Tony Caruso

Prentice-Hall International, Inc., *London*
Prentice-Hall of Australia Pty. Limited, *Sydney*
Prentice-Hall of Canada, Ltd., *Toronto*
Prentice-Hall of India Private Limited, *New Delhi*
Prentice-Hall of Japan, Inc., *Tokyo*
Prentice-Hall of Southeast Asia Pte. Ltd., *Singapore*
Whitehall Books Limited, *Wellington, New Zealand*

CONTENTS

PREFACE

INTRODUCTION

This book is intended for use in one- or two-semester courses designed to introduce students to selected geographic dimensions of world economic activities. The basic emphasis is upon differential characteristics of economic development and the striking contrasts that exist among peoples residing in the affluent and the poor nations of the world. These contrasts, and the historical, cultural, political, and physical circumstances that have influenced their development, appear to have been substantially neglected in the learning experiences of most American students. The central objective of the book, therefore, is to aid students in comprehending those important world issues which are certain to affect the choices available to them in their future lives.

APPROACH

Throughout the book emphasis is given to an understanding of real world differences in levels of human development. Theory and sophisticated analytical procedures receive relatively minor attention, although broad generalizations are often used as bases for discussions of problems and relationships. In some instances the opinions and biases of the authors will become readily apparent, and they may be in sharp contrast to the opinions, biases, and understandings of instructors and students. Rather than detracting from the value of the book, however, the human foibles of the authors may be used as points of departure which stimulate lively discussions and raise interest levels concerning the issues being addressed. The world scope of the subject matter prohibits anything resembling exhaustive treatment of any of the topics, leaving instructors a wide latitude for drawing upon their own areas of special knowledge for purposes of illustration and explanation.

ORGANIZATION

The book's content is organized into seven parts, the first of which introduces geography and its major concepts. Part II establishes the underlying themes for the remainder of the book by setting forth the fundamental characteristics, philosphies, relationships, and problems affecting world scale variations in developmental activities, and some of the major strategies that may be employed in efforts toward modernization. Part III focuses upon world food supplies, the geographic dimensions of hunger, systems of farming, and factors affecting variations in production, consumption, and marketing of agriculatural products. Part IV deals with world energy resources and the non-energy minerals. Emphasis is given to patterns of their development and consumption, and to the influences of their relative availability upon the economic and political stability of nations and alliances. Part V describes and analyzes the factors affecting differing intensities of manufacturing development, using selected industries to illustrate specific geographic characteristics and problems. Part VI examines the service industries, including communications, service centers, and the role of multinational corporations in economic development. Part VII, "Geography in an Unstable World," is an effort to summarize some of the issues affecting differential developmental patterns and problems and the roles that geographers can and do play in attempting to help resolve some of the major problems facing humankind.

LEVELS OF PRESENTATION

A concerted effort has been made to present major concepts, important relationships, and broad generalizations in simple and direct language. The book is designed to enable students, most of whom will not become professional geographers, to recognize the value of geographical understandings within the broad spectrum of knowledge. The intention is to open the door to intellectual curiosity with a gentle push, and thereby to stimulate in those who read the book a splendid curiosity about the geography which touches their lives.

ACKNOWLEGEMENTS

The authors are indebted to many persons in and out of the field of geography whose ideas were drawn upon in the preparation of the text. Special thanks are owed to members of the geography faculty at the University of Tennessee, Knoxville, whose valuable insights and suggestions contributed significantly to the book's content. Gratitude must also be expressed to the department's secretaries, Beth Hilgert, Pam Sharpe, and Laconna Flynn, who labored for countless hours to convert the penciled scribblings of the authors into typed copy.

A major vote of thanks is extended to Janet Ralston, who prepared the maps for the book. The care and skill that she exercised in her work are largely responsible for any measure of attractiveness the book may have to professors and students.

Most of all, the authors are indebted to the patience and understanding of their families. Thus for all the times during which you were inconvenienced, frustrated, and ignored by your husbands and fathers, we thank you Mickey and Kim, Linda, Brian, and Leia, and Janet.

University of Tennessee

Sidney R. Jumper
Thomas L. Bell
Bruce A. Ralston

PART ONE
MAJOR GEOGRAPHICAL CONCEPTS

CHAPTER ONE

the scope and concepts of economic geography

INTRODUCTION

A primary concern of geography is understanding and explaining the locational arrangements of phenomena over the earth's surface. This includes identification, measurement, and analysis of specific dimensions of human and physical phenomena and how various groups have organized the use of the earth's surface for their own benefit.

Each portion of the earth's surface possesses its own unique character, with physical and human ingredients not precisely repeated anywhere else on earth. On the other hand, basic similarities occur in the physical processes at work over broad and widely separated areas and in the responses of different groups to those processes and to needs which are perceived in accordance with cultural conventions.

Virtually all thoughts and acts leading to decisions about *where* something is to take place or about the *character* of an *area* reflect unconscious use of "commonsense" geographic knowledge. *Professional* geographers, as well, focus much of their attention upon the same types of commonsense geographical knowledge. The professional geographer, however, systematically collects, organizes, and analyzes information about particular types of locational or distributional problems or about particular areas or service functions.

Because virtually all human and physical things and functions have measurable geographic dimensions, the subject matter of geography is enormously rich and diverse. So immense are the problem areas and data sources which are relevant to geographic analysis that no individual can develop expertise in more than a small segment of the whole. For that reason those who adopt geography as a professional field specialize in one or two topics or regions. Possible topical specializations include economic, urban, cultural, physical, marketing, resource, agricultural, rural, industrial, behavioral, and population geography. This does not mean, of course, that an urban or any other specialist can ignore physical, cultural, population, or industrial geography. Each specialist normally considers the other topical specialties within the context of his or her own area of particular interest. The study of each special topic may include the entire world, or its scope may be narrowed to a particular area such as the San Joaquin Valley, the American Midwest, the Soviet Union, or Asia. The scope of this book is the world, and the emphasis is upon the broad field of economic geography.

ECONOMIC GEOGRAPHY

Economic geography is primarily concerned with the distributional aspects of goods and services and with seeking explanations for the myriad ways in which humans utilize earth resources and organize their economic activities. A study of the geography of economic activity may be justified on the premise that people have a strong desire to create order in their world so that they might have reasonably secure and satisfying lives. Through studying the geographic dimensions of economic activities, geographers hope to discover ways through which use of the earth's surface can be made more efficient and more satisfying. Improvements in the efficiency with which surface space is utilized, for example, is of central importance to private and public efforts to solve problems ranging from energy shortages and inept governmental administration to ineffective transportation systems and control over air and water pollution.

Each of us, acknowledged geographer or not, employs certain concepts of economic geography in making decisions about things such as where to live, vacation, work, attend school, and seek entertainment. All decisions involve choices among existing alternatives based upon consideration of such factors as distance, time, and cost of movement. Conflicts frequently develop over the most economically desirable versus the most socially or environmentally desirable places to locate such facilities as new roads, sewage treatment plants, shopping centers, schools, massage parlors, and public housing projects. Positions taken on problems created by the flight of city residents and jobs to suburban locations or on how much of the nation's energy needs should be met by domestic as opposed to foreign sources are examples of ways in which we utilize our knowledge of local and world economic geography.

In literally thousands of ways the lives of us all are affected by events which occur next door or halfway around the world. A cantankerous neighbor can lower the value or the satisfaction of living in otherwise pleasant surroundings. A drought in the Soviet Union can lead to increased foreign demand for American wheat and cause higher bread prices in the United States. Conflicts within the Middle East can affect the supply and the price of gasoline. The widely varying opinions held by individuals and groups concerning major local, national, and world issues are related in part to their different levels of knowledge and understanding of the geographical dimensions of things.

Relatively deprived peoples as well as those from advanced areas use geographical knowledge in making economic decisions, but this is usually at a more local scale. Land must be allocated for specific uses, crops must be selected which can be marketed through local facilities, and plans must be made for local production of most goods needed by the family or by the immediate community. Housing for people and animals must be located with access to dependable water supplies, and provisions must be made for obtaining fuel and fiber. Whether a family or a community goes hungry or is well-fed may depend in large part on how correctly the land allocations are made.

MAJOR QUESTIONS AND CONCEPTS

Every discipline operates within the limits of certain key concepts and basic questions. The questions asked serve to focus the line of attack upon a particular problem and to define the scope (or the boundaries) of an investigation. A concept is a notion, an idea, or a way of thinking. Concepts provide the framework within which a discipline functions and they define its range of operation.

The basic questions asked by geographers in studying the spatial characteristics of phenomena include not only *where* they occur but *how* they came to be there; *what processes* were involved in their occurrences; *why* they remain there; *what factors* in the social and physical environments have affected their spatial character; and *where, when,* and to *what extent* changes in their spatial character can be expected to occur in the future. All of these questions focus upon area, or surface space.

The concepts utilized by geographers are often shared with other disciplines, but the geographer employs them with particular respect to their spatial applications. The following discussion of concepts is necessarily brief and incomplete, but it includes many of the "big ideas" which form the foundation stones of economic geography.

Distance and Orientation. Distance and orientation are core concepts to an understanding of systems for organizing space to meet human needs. Distance, in economics, is usually measured by the cost, in both money and time, required to overcome it. These costs are frequently referred to as *friction of distance*. Any product can be transported only a certain distance before the cost of movement threatens to exceed the value of the commodity being transported. A good rule of thumb to use here is that, all other factors being equal, *the higher the value of a commodity per unit weight, the greater the distance that it can be profitably transported*. This rule normally works well in a general sense because high-valued commodities usually carry larger profit margins than low-valued goods. An ounce of gold, with a value of $200.00, would normally carry a larger profit in a business transaction than an ounce of coal, with a value of about a penny.

The friction, or the handicap, of distance also depends on what modes are available for and the kinds of obstacles to the movement of peoples and commodities. When modern and well-managed systems of transportation, such as railroads, highways, airways, and pipelines, are abundantly available, almost any commodity can be moved over much longer distances than where modes of movement are limited to human porters, pack animals, and animal-drawn wagons. Goods that can be economically moved for hundreds of miles in the United States may be able to move only a few miles at the same cost in India or Zaire. At the same time, movement of a product over 5 miles of highway in a traffic-clogged city may be more costly than moving the same product over several times that distance on a sparsely traveled expressway or interstate highway. The variable effect of distance as a handicap in movement of commodities is one of the major factors differentiating one part of the world from another.

The importance of correctly orienting activities toward each other is perhaps largely self-evident. All of us recognize how essential it is to know our right from our left sides and, in traveling over a modern interstate highway, to know the cardinal directions of north, south, east, and west. It is also important that manufacturing plants choose locations which provide correct orientation relative to raw materials, markets, energy sources, labor supplies, and other factors which are locationally vital to the production and marketing structures of the industries. Businesses should be correctly oriented toward sources of supplies and toward customers, just as farmers must orient their plans for producing particular crops toward the availability of markets for those crops.

Size and Shape. The size and shape of a city, a nation, the market area for a manufacturing company, or the service area for a public utility are of substantial importance in determining the relative efficiency with which the area can be managed and in defining the strategies that may be employed in supplying the area with goods and services. Both terms are frequently used as a basis for comparing one area with another. In contrasting the Soviet Union with Switzerland, for example, one of the most obvious differences is in relative size — the Soviet Union is the largest nation on earth and Switzerland is one of the smallest. Any mention of Chile brings to mind the long narrow shape of the country. Thoughts of India call forth the image of a triangle and of Italy, a boot.

Precisely how size affects the spatial organization of an area depends on a great many factors. A large, sparsely populated area may have difficulty in building a good network of roads, power lines, and the like because of the distances that must be covered and the high per capita costs of covering those distances. In a small nation or in a city, on the other hand, competition for land may push its price so high as to eliminate the possibility that it might be used for producing certain goods or for providing certain services. Who would seriously consider, for example, buying 100 acres of Manhattan Island for the purpose of raising wheat? Smallness and compactness may also increase the military vulnerability of a nation in light of the enormous destructive capability of nuclear weapons. Likewise, small size reduces the chance that an area will possess the variety and quantity of natural resources needed by a modern industrial economy.

Shape, like size, has many economic implications. Chile's shape, for example, creates special problems in communication, travel, and national unity. It has an extremely long border to defend; the transport network is an elongated linear system; and its relatively small population is stretched out over a wide range of climatic and soil conditions.

Most cities in the affluent regions of the world are roughly star-shaped, with the points of the star following major routeways outward from the central city. In this case shape is influenced by the initial design of the transport system, which once set in motion offers strong resistance to change.

Shapes of farms and fields influence the types and sizes of mechanical equipment farmers may use most profitably. Huge tractors, for example, require a great deal of space for turning around, and they are used where field sizes tend to be long and relatively narrow so that the number of turn-arounds required is small relative to the amount of land being cultivated. In cases where overhead irrigation systems are employed, round fields may be most desirable.

Scale. Closely associated with the concepts of size and distance is the concept of scale, which refers to proportionate relationships. This concept is particularly important in economic geography because the scale at which a problem is observed or studied may strongly influence the nature of conclusions drawn or decisions made concerning its solution. Think of yourself as a space traveler from a distant galaxy, visiting the solar system for the first time. Suppose that your first landing place is the earth's moon, about 240,000 miles from earth. As you look around from your point of observation on the moon, the earth looms as the largest and brightest planet in the sky. You record your observation of and conclusions about the earth from your position on the moon and then, out of curiosity, decide to move in to a distance of about 1,000 feet above the earth's surface for a closer look. At 1,000 feet you again record your observations and conclusions about the earth. How would observations and conclusions made at 1,000 feet differ from those made at 240,000 miles? Recordings made from the moon would respresent a *small-scale* view of the earth, where visual detail is lacking and much of what we consider to be vitally important to our lives would be entirely obscured from the observer's vision. Observations made at 1,000 feet would contain comparatively large amounts of detail, and the *scale* of observation is much *larger*.

In somewhat the same way, economic decisions reflect the peculiar scales of observation and responsibility of the decision makers. The mayor of a small town where the primary source of employment is a textile mill, for example, may favor high tariffs against imported textiles if imported fabrics are reducing the market for the town's plant and causing production cutbacks, factory layoffs, and reduced taxable income for the town's treasury. The President of the United States, however, may strongly oppose imposition of high tariffs upon foreign textiles because the overall American economy benefits from trade arrangements with foreign nations and this might be negatively affected by such tariffs. The perspectives of the town mayor and the President are at variance, partly because of differences in their scales of observation.

Scale concepts also apply to the size and efficiency of the operation of a firm. A manufacturer may achieve certain *economies of scale*, for example, when increasing the productive capacity of the plant results in lowering per-unit production costs. On the other hand, if enlarged plant capacity causes increased per unit production costs, the plant is experiencing *diseconomies of scale*. The same may be true of a farmer who, by acquiring additional land and machinery, is able to lower unit production costs and achieve economies of scale in his operation. If the farmer purchases so much machinery and land that added expenditures for management, labor, and maintenance cause unit production costs to rise, the result is one of diseconomies of scale.

Locational Significance. The concepts of distance, orientation, size, shape, and scale are used by almost all of us in developing plans for organizing the use of space. This holds true whether we are planning the layout of a factory, the landscaping of a yard, the arrangement of furnishings in a room, a national network of roads, or locations for a chain of restaurants. In all these cases and many others we are directly concerned with *locational significance*, or the importance of *relative* and *absolute* location. Proper arrangement of furnishings in a room requires that each piece be located in just the right place relative to other pieces and to such absolute (fixed in location) objects as walls, doorways, and windows. A successful plan for developing a chain of restaurants requires that each restaurant be correctly located relative to other restaurants in the chain and to competing restaurants. The precise locational design should be based upon a set of objectives, such as the intended use of a room or the specific market sought for the restaurants. Moreover, the value of a particular location may change through time. Adding an additional piece of furniture to the room may require relocating all pieces so that they will have a compatible arrangement with the new piece. Introduction of a competing restaurant or a major change in a highway routeway may require reevaluation of a location previously selected for one of the units in the chain of restaurants. Revising plans for the location of one restaurant could, in turn, force a revision in locational strategy for the entire chain.

Success or failure of almost any type of business depends in part on the wisdom used in selecting its location. A city's growth, stagnation, or decline may hinge upon how well it is served by its location. The sales potential of a gasoline station will probably depend in part on choosing the correct side of the street for its location. Locational significance is probably the most central concept in economic geography. All other concepts are refinements of this overriding principle.

Comparative Advantage. Whether a location is good or bad for a particular activity depends on the comparative (or competitive) advantage of that location relative to other possible locations for the same activity. Essentially, the concept asserts that an area that enjoys several alternative production opportunities tends to develop the opportunity in which it has a comparative advantage over other areas or which offers the most productive possible use of the area. Comparative advantage, therefore, offers the basic rationale for areal specialization of production. Although the corn belt of the United States obtains higher per acre wheat yields than the wheat belt, for example, corn production has a comparative advantage — all things such as physical conditions, markets, and production alternatives considered — over the production of wheat. Again, considering all factors affecting the production and marketing of corn, the corn belt has a comparative advantage over all other regions in the United States as a corn growing area.

That an area possesses a comparative advantage in output of some product at one point in time does not mean that the advantage is permanent. Changes in technology, markets, transportation networks, labor costs, or skills, for example, often result in the transfer of comparative advantage for producing a particular product from one area to another.

A discussion of comparative advantage, in space and in time, leads naturally into consideration of four additional concepts used by geographers to explain patterns of location, interactions among various locations, and the special advantages of particular places for production of certain commodities. These concepts are (1) complementarity, (2) intervening opportunity, (3) transferability, and (4) inertia [1].

Complementarity. Interactions among places occur because one place can supply certain goods or services which are in demand somewhere else. Automobile assembly plants in Detroit have complementary relationships with dozens of nearby places which manufacture the thousands of parts that are put together to form a finished motor vehicle. Low-sulfur coal is moved all the way from Wyoming for burning in thermoelectric power plants in the eastern United States because of federal and state requirements which limit emissions of sulfur dioxide, a major pollutant, into the atmosphere. Climatic adversities often result in low wheat yields in the Soviet Union, which leads to complementary relationships between the Soviet Union and surplus wheat-producing areas in the United States, Canada, and Australia.

Intervening Opportunity. Potentially complementary relationships among places are often modified, made improbable, or eliminated because of the existence of intervening opportunities. In the case of low-sulfur coal moving from Wyoming to Pennsylvania, for example, the complementarity of Wyoming coal and Pennsylvania power plants could be eliminated if adequate supplies of low-sulfur coal are found in Pennsylvania or if processes are developed which make it less expensive to remove the sulfur from Appalachian coal prior to burning. On the other hand, if low-sulfur coal deposits are found in Pennsylvania but quantities are inadequate to supply all local power plants, the complementary relationships between Wyoming and Pennsylvania may be maintained at a reduced level. As another example, consider an automobile dealer in Columbus, Georgia, who obtains automobiles from Detroit. If an assembly plant is opened in Atlanta, the dealer is likely to take advantage of the intervening opportunity offered by Atlanta as a source of cars. In effect, therefore, creation of an intervening opportunity represents an alteration in the complementarity of places.

Transferability. Transferability refers to the relative ease with which a good can be moved from one place to another. The capacity to move goods, even when demand is present, varies enormously from region to region depending on the availability of transportation facilities, the degree to which movement is encouraged or restricted by domestic and international transportation and trade regulations, and the financial capabilities of potential trading partners. Whether or not interchange of goods will actually occur between any two areas is ultimately determined by transfer costs in most instances, although emergency situations can cause exceptions to this generalization.

In a larger sense, the concept of transferability can also be applied to movement of industries from one place to another. Industries with large fixed-capital investments, such as the steel industry, are less able to transfer production facilities from one place to another than industries with smaller investments in more mobile plants and equipment, such as a shoe manufacturing plant. The textile industry was able to transfer most of its production facilities from southern New England to the Southeast because savings from lower labor and other production costs in the Southeast exceeded the costs of relocation.

Inertia. Inertia refers to an indispositon toward change. This may take the form of a low propensity to transfer from one location to another or to a low propensity to cease a long-standing practice which might involve frequent locational transfer. Because the steel industry is restrained from locational changes by the high costs involved in moving its production facilities, its locational pattern may be described as strongly influenced by inertia. Any function which resists change from established patterns is affected by inertia, but in geography that concept is normally applied to problems of location.

Time–Space Relationships. Factors that influence the manner in which activities are organized over space are subject to change through time. The degree of complementarity of one place with another and the transferability of goods may be positively or negatively altered by improvements in or deterioration of transportation facilities, increases or decreases in transport costs, acquisition or loss of intervening opportunities, new technical achievements, and many other factors. Spatial arrangements of the present should be thought of as only one phase in a long continuum of change.

Improvements in transportation and communication have brought nearly all parts of the world closer together in time and cost of movement. This is often referred to as *time–space convergence.* The convergence of places in time and in cost of movement has led to a vast growth in the interchange of goods, ideas, and services among areas and to a great expansion in the availability of external resources. External resources (those obtained from foreign areas) have become increasingly vital to most affluent societies as their own high quality and cheaply obtainable reserves have been used up and as their appetites for larger quantities and a greater variety of resources have mushroomed. The resulting growth in trade and the decline of local and national self-sufficiency have led to a *progressive interdependence* among nations and regions of the world. While allowing regions to augment their access to an accelerating variety of resources temporarily, however, dependence on external supplies has also added to their vulnerability. Foreign suppliers, by reducing or shutting off exports of vital materials, especially when several exporters are able to act in concert, have the potential for creating severe economic, social, and political problems within the importing regions. A prime example of this concept is the increasing dependence of Western Europe, Japan, and the United States on the importation of oil from the Middle East. The potential of this dependence for interruption of economic activities was clearly demonstrated during the oil embargo of 1973. Just as the importing nations are dependent on the Middle East for oil, however, the Middle East is dependent on the importers for money, food, and the technology to operate their oil fields and to support their economic development. Thus the potential for economic problems among importers of materials is held in check by the equal dependence among exporters for supplies of food, manufactured goods, technology, and money from the areas where their resources are being marketed. Furthermore, a nation threatened with economic deterioration because of embargoed supplies of vital materials may be tempted to use force in reopening its supply lines. At the same time, however, when two or more areas are equally interdependent for equally vital materials, the stimulus for conflict is reduced and the interchange of goods, ideas, and peoples can result in improved understanding among different cultures. The paradox in such an eventuality is that increased vulnerability produces increased international security.

Spatial Variation and Spatial Association. All the concepts heretofore discussed are related in one degree or another to two additional concepts: (a) *spatial variation* and (b) *spatial association.* It is common knowledge that parts of the earth's surface differ from one another. Some of these differences are physical, or natural; others are primarily of a cultural (induced by people) nature. In studying patterns of variation among areas, however, it is often found that two or more phenomena have a high frequency of locational association. When such associations are discovered, it is the task of the researcher to determine whether the association is *causal* or coincidental. Carelessness in interpreting associations among phenomena can lead to spectacular errors. When comparing levels of air pollution with life expectancy among the world's nations, for example, the researcher is likely to find that as the amount of pollution increases, so does life expectancy. The positive association between pollution and life expectancy might even by proved by statistical procedures. To conclude that pollution is healthy and that life expectancy can be increased through raising levels of atmospheric pollutants, however, would be foolhardy. Here, as in most cases, the value of a set of facts depends largely on the skill, knowledge, and wisdom of the interpreter.

CONCLUSIONS

The basic purpose for offering the concepts outlined in this chapter is to present a geographical framework within which economic growth and economic disparities, the two major themes of this book, can be analyzed and interpreted. Additional concepts will be presented in the chapters which follow, although the authors have no intention of attempting to cover the entire range of concepts in economic geography.

Similarly, the purpose of this book is to provide a particular kind of framework through which some of the world's major problems can be analyzed, understood, and interpreted. Again, the purpose is not to present all the facts, situations, or places wherein these problems occur. Facts, in themselves, whether about economics, history, places, chemicals, rocks, or whatever, have limited value unless the possessor of those facts is able to understand and interpret them within a larger framework of knowledge. This larger framework includes the values, objectives, and substantive dimensions of all or some portion of humankind. The more complete the framework within which facts are viewed and analyzed, the more likely that their true meanings will be discovered and that actions taken to remedy the problems to which they pertain will be successful. The objective of this book, therefore, is to add to, or strengthen, the geographical portion of the knowledge framework of those individuals into whose hands the book is placed.

REFERENCE

[1] Edward L. Ullman, "The Role of Transportation and the Bases for Interaction," in William L. Thomas (ed.), *Man's Role in Changing the Face of the Earth* (Chicago: University of Chicago Press, 1956), pp. 862–880.

PART TWO
SOME DEVELOPMENTAL AND CONCEPTUAL ASPECTS OF ECONOMIC DISPARITIES

CHAPTER TWO

disparities in wealth

INTRODUCTION

Differences in levels of economic development and in the generation and accumulation of wealth are readily observable at scales ranging from small communities to the world as a whole. During most of human history, economic disparities have been more pronounced within than among major world regions. Each region had a small contingent of rich and powerful rulers, landlords, and merchants, but the vast majority of people everywhere was locked into recurrent malnutrition and squalor. During and after the eighteenth century, however, the peoples around the North Atlantic began to achieve affluence. Since that time their affluence has increased appreciably, whereas most of the peoples of Africa, Asia, and Latin America have made comparatively little economic progress. Thus with achievement of affluence by most nations bordering the North Atlantic, major disparities in wealth *among* nations were set in motion and these disparities are growing (Fig. 2-1). Internal disparities in wealth have continued, and they seem to widen with some consistency from nation to nation as overall wealth decreases [1].

Wealth refers to objects of economic utility (primarily property and money) and to human capital (skills, knowledge, and attitudes). Many aspects of national wealth, such as attitudes toward work, health, social and political stability and the quality of the physical environment, are difficult to measure or to be assigned precise values in national currencies.

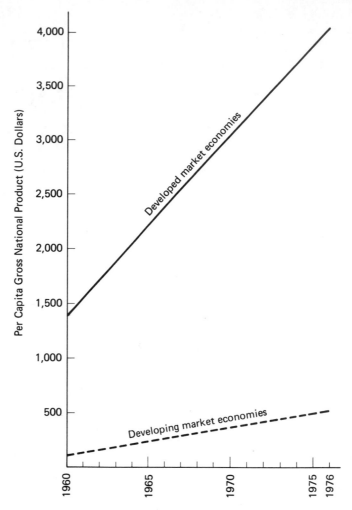

Fig. 2-1. Per capita gross domestic product in developed and in developing market economies: 1960-1976. [Generalized from data in *Statistical Yearbook, 1977* (New York: United Nations, 1978).]

EQUITY, EQUALITY, AND SOCIAL JUSTICE

Equity and equality are fundamental philosophical concepts that have spawned a wide range of political, economic, and social theories and debates. Although these concepts are too complex to be dealt with adequately in this book, it is important to note that the manner in which they are interpreted by a particular society strongly influences its policies and programs and its perception of social justice.

Although equity and equality have certain similarities in meaning, they are at the same time distinctly different. Equality, as applied to the state of being of humankind, implies that all peoples are equal and that they should have equal status, wealth, and influence. Equity, on the other hand, refers primarily to the equal application to all peoples of a fair set of rules. Thus justice is achieved under equality only when all peoples have exactly equal amounts of everything, whereas under equity justice may be achieved as long as all people operate under the same sets of fairly applied rules.

Equity rather than equality is the basic operating concept of most of the world's major political and economic systems, including democracy, capitalism, and socialism. Inequality, therefore, is an accepted feature of these systems. Differences do exist, however, in the extent and kinds of inequalities which are acceptable. Differences also exist in the extent to which and the areas in which social intervention by government is considered desirable in order to eliminate or to reduce inequalities. During most of American history not only were vast inequalities overlooked, but inequities were openly permitted in the application of justice. Rules by which society operated were applied unequally according to differences in wealth, race, sex, and ethnic origin. Since World War II, however, Americans have moved rapidly to extend equity to all persons regardless of race, sex, size of bank account, or national origin. Yet inequities still exist. Those who suffer the most from inequities tend to be the poor; those who are segregated into racial, ethnic, religious, or ideological minorities; and those who lack educational and technical skills.

Inequities exist in every nation and among virtually all groups of peoples. Inequities often compound inequalities in such areas as income, health care, nutrition, education, housing, and social opportunities. Thus inequities and inequalities have geographic dimensions. They vary in intensity from region to region and from time to time within a particular region.

Inequities and inequalities are also related to the concept of *social justice.* Justice involves a fair and impartial administration of law or of the principles of equity. Social justice involves an equitable dealing of peoples with each other. In some societies social justice is interpreted to mean "free market competition," in which all members of a society and all places within that society compete for rewards on an equal basis according to their abilities and their willingness to work. Under such a system peoples and areas which have the greater natural assets or who devise the best means for using their assets achieve the greatest rewards. Another concept of social justice focuses upon a system for distribution of rewards according to need, toward the common good, or in some measure according to the degree to which a person or a region suffers natural, cultural, or economic handicaps. On the one hand the emphasis is upon equity of opportunity; the other focuses upon equity of outcome [2]. The vigor with which particular concepts of equity, equality, and social justice are pursued influences the manner in which the wealth of the world is distributed as well as attitudes toward economic growth.

MEASURES OF DISPARITIES IN WEALTH

Measures of disparities in the distribution of wealth are difficult to obtain and to interpret. The problem presents a particular quandry on a world scale because of international differences in units of currency, tax rates, standards of living, employment structures, governmental and private charities or welfare programs, and the like. Even if one could obtain an accurate measure of the relative values of different units of currency (United States' dollars compared with Turkish liras, Saudi Arabian riyals, Philippine pesos, Indian rupees, Soviet roubles, etc.), the problem of interpreting levels of wealth in different areas remains unsolved. The real purchasing power of a particular unit of currency varies from one nation to another and from place to place within the same nation. A farm family with an income of $1,000 may have a considerably higher standard of living than an urban family with twice that income because the farm family may obtain all or much of its food, fuel, and building supplies from the farm (goods which are often not reportable as income), whereas the urban family must purchase all such supplies out of reportable income. That per capita incomes in the United States are 52 times larger than per capita incomes in India, for example, does not necessarily mean that the average American is 52 times wealthier than the average Indian nor that the standard of living of the American is 52 times higher than that of the Indian. India is a predominantly agricultural nation, whereas the United States is predominantly urban and industrial. Incomes within poor societies, therefore, are often undervalued in international reporting schemes. It is also difficult to interpret real values of currencies which are used for the purchase of materials beyond those required to sustain life. How much real wealth does $1,000 represent, for example, when it is expended by a poor family for food or by a wealthy family for a seashore vacation? Wealthy families normally have substantial amounts of *discretionary income* (income which they can spend as they choose), whereas the incomes of poor families are often committed entirely to the purchase of food, shelter, and clothing needed for survival. Wealthy families, likewise, may engage in *conspicuous consumption* (in the highly noticeable purchase of goods and services beyond actual needs).

Additional difficulties in comparing international levels of wealth involve problems in measuring regional differences in capabilities for managing money, assessing the values of cultural factors such as attitudes toward work and toward education, and measuring the real worth of experiences and skills held by those in the labor force.

A modern building rises amidst the squalor of slum housing in a developing country. (Reprinted from *Finance and Development*, a publication of the International Monetary Fund and the World Bank Group.)

FACTORS ASSOCIATED WITH DISPARITIES IN WEALTH

The following discussion of factors associated with disparities in wealth is in many ways oversimplified and incomplete. The causes of wealth disparities are extremely complex, involving hundreds of physical, political, economic, cultural, and historical variables, as well as a good share of chance or luck. Items selected for discussion are those which seem to the authors to have been particularly strong influences upon the economic history of the world during the last two centuries.

Although the major patterns of disparities in wealth have not changed appreciably during the last hundred years or more, many of the attitudes and conditions affecting economic growth have changed. In the more highly developed nations, attention has shifted measurably toward concern for human rights and welfare and for solving problems caused by economic growth. Reorienting their massive fixed-capital investments and their entrenched economic and political systems to facilitate economic efficiency and to protect or to improve environmental quality has become a constant struggle. The relatively stable populations of affluent nations have further encouraged a slowdown in economic growth, for rapid population growth has traditionally served as one of the more significant mechanisms for promoting market expansion, increased demand, and rising production.

In contrast to the skepticism with which some of the more affluent nations are approaching future economic growth, most of the developing nations are pursuing growth with vigorous abandon. Concerns about the quality of the environment are overshadowed by desires for higher standards of living, greater security against unemployment and hunger, and in some instances a nationalistic desire for military strength. Economic growth in such areas is encouraged by the lack of a need to perform the costly task of tearing down or drastically altering preexisting infrastructures and by the opportunity to put into immediate use the vast assortment of technical know-how developed by the more affluent nations through decades of costly research and experimentation. Because the economic gap between affluent and poor societies is increasing, however, it seems apparent that certain elements essential to economic growth are not yet available to most of the developing nations.

Savings

Most of the factors affecting the abilities of areas to generate wealth involve their relative capacities to accumulate and to utilize savings effectively. Savings may represent capital investments in stocks, bonds, and the means of production. They may be held in the form of precious metals (gold, for example), foreign exchange, or international credits. Savings may also accrue to an area in the form of a favorable physical environment or as a rich and varied natural resource base, and they may be represented by institutional forms such as educational and health care facilities which encourage the development of human resources. The most effective utilization of savings normally occurs in areas which have achieved greatest success in development of human resources and where the cultural characteristics of the people include favorable attitudes toward work and a high degree of optimism that living conditions can be positively altered through individual and collective effort.

Contrasts in living styles of Filipinos in Manila. (Reprinted from *War on Hunger*, a publication of the Agency for International Development.)

Because combinations of circumstances associated with the generation of and utilization of savings vary so widely from place to place, persons who perform identical work and who are equally productive may be rewarded quite differently in different areas. Differences in labor productivity and in the extent to which labor is rewarded for effort give rise to internal and international trade and to shifts in the location of production. Because of substantially lower wage rates for equal productivity in Asia than in the United States, for example, electronics, textile, and other industries have shifted much of their productive capacities from the United States to such areas as Taiwan, Hong Kong, and Japan. Shifts in the location of production, however, also involve transfers in savings. Such transfers may be encouraged or discouraged by national policies concerning tariffs, subsidies, trade agreements, and aid programs and by policies of business organizations such as multinational corporations.

Importance of Being First

One of the most crucial factors associated with current inequities in wealth distribution is that once inequities are established, they tend toward permanence. Those who *initially* acquire large amounts of wealth possess advantages in the generation of additional wealth over those of more modest means. They can outbid the poor for needed goods and services. They have greater ability than the poor to provide high-quality education and health care for their peoples, develop and implement new technologies, and exploit their own and other physical resources.

Capacity for Sectorial Transfers of Labor

Wealthy nations also have the ability to execute sectorial transfers in demand for and supply of labor. By mechanizing agriculture, for example, the affluent, urban, industrial nations have encouraged the transfer of agricultural workers to industrial jobs. By mechanization of manufacturing, workers are enabled to transfer from that sector into employment in education, health care, research, and other service functions.

Rapid rates of economic growth are encouraged in areas which have accumulated substantial savings and where a surplus of labor is available or can be made available for secondary and tertiary employment [3]. In poor nations where agricultural productivity per worker is low and where capital for mechanization and other methods of improving productivity is not available, the labor force must often remain primarily in agricultural employment just to meet the basic food requirements of the population. A limit exists even within relatively rich nations, however, beyond which the labor force in a particular occupational sector cannot be appreciably reduced without a decline in productivity. When this point is reached, potentials for further economic growth and for increases in affluence are obtainable primarily through development of more efficient production processes and an increase in productivity per worker. The United Kingdom is a case in point, for its agricultural labor force is no longer of sufficient size to supply large numbers of workers for other types of employment. Because the British have also failed to invest heavily in modernization of manufacturing, their industrial productivity and rates of growth in per capita gross domestic product have been lower than those of most other affluent nations during recent years.

Knowledge

Of all the factors responsible for disparities in wealth, different levels of knowledge are probably most important. Knowledge is "the mother of all other resources" [4]. Without knowledge, other resources have no purpose and no value. The greater the amount of knowledge, the wider the purposes for, utility of, and value of resources. Knowledge makes its greatest contribution to overall wealth and human well-being when it is utilized to generate new knowledge. Here again the nations which already possess wealth have an advantage over poor nations. Only the affluent nations can afford to employ and equip large numbers of skilled scientists and technicians to conduct *basic research* (research which has no immediate prospect for yielding tangible benefits but which forms the basis for later research which does) or to develop and implement innovative methods and processes. Nor can poor nations match affluent nations in funding the kinds of educational and training institutions and programs required for developing large supplies of skilled and innovative workers. Knowledge, like many other factors related to disparities in wealth, is unevenly distributed and difficult to measure. Education may be used as a surrogate for knowledge, but 1 year or 10 years of education may mean vastly different things in different areas.

The quality of education programs probably diminishes in some proportion to decreases in national wealth. In one area anyone who can read or write may be thought of as an "educated person," whereas the same person in another area may be considered "functionally illiterate." Standards also vary from one area to another in how much knowledge, or education, is required to qualify persons for skilled occupations such as technicians and medical practitioners. In most instances, however, standards increase with increases in relative wealth and with higher stages of economic development.

By whatever methods of measurement one might choose, major differences in knowledge and in educational attainment occur among the regions of the world. Approximately one-third of the world's population is considered illiterate, with highest rates of illiteracy occurring in Africa,

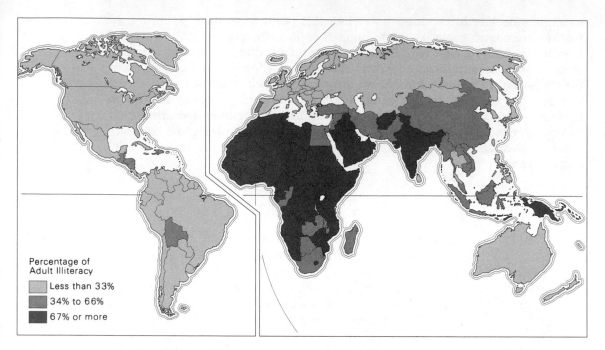

Fig. 2-2. Adult illiteracy rates, about 1970. [From "World Population Growth and Illiteracy Patterns," *Literacy and World Population* (Washington, D.C.: Population Reference Bureau, Inc.), 30, No. 2.]

southern and eastern Asia, and parts of Middle and South America (Fig. 2-2). Although the percentage of illiterates among the world's adult population declined from 44 to 34 percent between 1950 and 1970, the number of illiterates increased from about 700 to 783 million because population growth in many poor areas outran the ability of governments to provide new schools and teachers [5].

Illiteracy rates are twice as high in rural as in urban areas and about half again as high for females as for males. In contrast to the decrease in the rate of illiteracy which occurred for males between 1960 and 1970, the rate for females rose from 58 to 60 percent [6].

High rates of illiteracy are encouraged by the multitude of languages used by the peoples of the world, many of which have no written form. Some religious and political groups oppose literacy for fear that exposure of the people to written ideas will encourage defections from the faith or revolutions against the current power structure. Schools are virtually inaccessible to millions of the world's children, whose daily lives are entirely occupied with the struggle to survive [7].

A positive relationship exists between literacy, or educational level, and the receptivity of peoples toward change, including innovativeness and new ideas [8]. Thus low levels of literacy serve as a constraint against economic development and against the establishment of educational programs. Without educational (literacy) advancement, the receptivity of a population to change and its capacity to innovate are likely to stagnate at the lowest possible levels. The stagnation may continue indefinitely unless some exterior impulse is introduced to induce change. Meanwhile, those with wealth, high educational status, and a strong degree of innovativeness continue to add economic and knowledge distance between themselves and those of lesser knowledge.

Capacity for Change

How rapidly economic growth occurs depends in large part on the pace at which a society *can* change. The pace of change depends on the willingness and the skill employed in the destruction of the old order, old facilities, old equipment, old skills, and old processes and their replacement by a new order, new equipment, new skills, and new processes that are more efficient and more productive. In nearly all cases the poor nations have proved less capable than affluent societies of uprooting or destroying old habits, old skills, obsolete facilities, outmoded geographical divisions, and antiquated social and economic structures. The key factor in explaining development of economic disparities in the world, therefore, is probably the differential abilities of societies to produce or to induce rational change. Economic growth is encouraged when the changes occurring within a society operate to deplete or to frustrate the formalization of institutions, when excessive procedural limitations upon the capacity of an area to implement opportunities for change can be avoided and when the changes which occur result in the shifting of resources toward increasingly productive uses. A decline in the capacity of a society to respond promptly to opportunities for promoting increased efficiency and productivity, however, will result in underrealization of growth potential.

Innovation and Diffusion

The two basic elements producing cultural change are *innovation* and *diffusion*. Both of these elements, which involve the creation and marketing of new products and new and better methods for accomplishing work, occur most widely and with greatest intensity within affluent areas. High levels of creativity, productivity, and consumption are closely associated with an intense degree of labor specialization. Specialization of labor evolves from improvements in the quality of human resources or through making superior systems of education and health care available to all segments of a population.

During recent years major efforts have been made to launch several poor societies onto the paths of modernization by transplanting into them certain of the trappings of the highly specialized, high technology societies. The results have rarely produced lasting benefits except to those who were already well-off. Economic disparities *within* the poor societies have thus been increased. There is reason to believe, however, that given adequate time the benefits which first accrue to the upper classes will filter downward to the poor.

Effective Demand

The primary expression of world economic disparities is through differences in effective demand (i.e., differences in real purchasing power). Factors which are likely to determine how rapidly demand can be created in any area include the size and age of the stock of capital goods; the amount and quality of managerial talent; the size, health, and skills of the labor force; the level of technology; the character of systems of transportation and communication; and the amount and quality of available physical resources. When a nation allows its stock of capital goods to become old and outmoded, employment of new technology becomes increasingly difficult, the relative productivity of labor declines, economic efficiency deteriorates, and effective demand is likely to diminish. Herein lies a significant paradox. As industries become larger and more automated, with greater fixed-capital investments per worker in order to gain efficiencies in output, costs of re-tooling and modernization rise. With rising costs of modernization the managers of industry are likely to engage in short-term profit taking in preference to long-term capital improvements. Thus the factors which create high levels of effective demand, unless carefully monitored, may have inherrent characteristics that serve as a braking system toward sustaining those demand levels.

Within developing nations levels of effective demand are low, which makes it difficult to generate the necessary ingredients for efficient production. Lack of efficient production systems has a negative effect upon demand, producing a situation often referred to as *circular causation*.

Political Factors

Political factors which are direct or indirect causes of disparities in wealth include quality of leadership, type of political system employed, kinds of relationships which exist among nations, and degree of stability of the political system. Political stability, whatever the system, is of particular importance as a contributor to economic progress. Between 1950 and 1975, for example, most of the fastest growing economies were politically stable and many of the slowest growers were not [9].

Plantation opulence. Madewood Plantation House built in 1840, Ascension Parish, Louisiana. (Courtesy, John B. Rehder.)

Political leaders in many of the developing nations are largely of two types: (1) those with little training or experience in management of complex political–economic systems or in international negotiations or (2) those who have achieved wealth and status through subservience to a system of international inequalities and who work to perpetuate that system [10]. Likewise, the populations of many developing nations have had only brief experience with political independence. Their own lack of education and of access to information leaves them ill-prepared for the responsibilities of self-government or for deciding which of several political factions to support. The result is often either political instability or the creation of some form of totalitarian regime, or both.

Whatever the state of development of an area, the political system may pursue one of several emphases, including

1. democratic, market-oriented
2. totalitarian, market-oriented
3. democratic, centrally planned
4. totalitarian, centrally planned

Under any of the emphases above, decisions must be made concerning the degree of the nation's involvement in international political and economic activities. Some leaders view international involvement as a mechanism through which the rich nations maintain their advantages over the poor. Other leaders see participation in international politics and trade as a necessary means toward economic development and political independence.

Physical Factors

Disparities in the physical characteristics of nations, including their sizes, shapes, climates, landforms, surface and ground water supplies and their mineral resources, are significant influences upon differing potentials for economic development. Large size, a variety of climates favorable to production of numerous agricultural commodities, substantial areas of well-watered and well-drained plains, and a variety of mineral resources offer the most attractive physical circumstances for obtaining national affluence.

Modern technology has enabled some societies to overcome, in part, the disadvantages of their natural environments. Plants are bred to produce in previously uninviting climates; resources are moved long distances into areas where they do not occur naturally; and water is transferred from wet to dry areas. Only a few nations, however, have been able to reach beyond their own boundaries to tap large amounts of physical resources from other nations. Most of the relatively poor nations are restricted primarily to their own resources, and they lack the technology to make the most effective use even of the resources they possess. Whether the advantage of the high technology nations is more apparent than real and more short-term than long-run, however, remains for the future to reveal.

MANIFESTATIONS OF DISPARITIES

The primary manifestations of disparities in wealth are the huge gaps in human welfare which permeate the earth's surface. About two-thirds of the world's people live in poverty, with little chance of improving their lots in life. The remaining one-third live in relative comfort, most of them within societies where further improvements in life styles are quite possible. Affluence like poverty, however, does not occur without risks. Affluent nations possess the greatest capability for self-destruction, as they have developed and amassed the most terrifying military capabilities. They have created enormous environmental problems because of their haste to accumulate wealth through exploiting natural resources. Their tendency to promote specialization of all forms of labor and production leaves them highly vulnerable to economic and social chaos should any major part of the system break down over an extended period of time. They have become dependent on such massive transportation, communication, and energy infrastructures that the task of modifying those infrastructures to meet future needs may

American poverty. A two room cabin in southern Applalachia. (Courtesy, John B. Rehder.)

well be overwhelming. When such problems occur, the affected nations may be characterized as *overdeveloped.*

The poor societies, on the other hand, are stifled by entrenched tradition, lack of capital, lack of human skills, and burgeoning populations. Population pressures and ignorance rather than the rush to accumulate wealth have often led to types of environmental degradation similar to those within advanced societies. The sets of risks poor societies face differ significantly from those of the affluent nations, but they are often just as dangerous to survival. Problems tend to be more localized than those of the advanced nations, but because of inadequate infrastructural development the chances that exterior sources of aid can be obtained are substantially lower. Meaningful responses even to critical problems are slow to develop and may never occur. Whereas the affluent societies are often strangled by their fixed-capital investments, the poor societies are strangled by tradition, population expansion, and ignorance. Under such circumstances the condition may be described as a problem of *underdevelopment.*

Waste

Waste is a significant characteristic of developed and developing societies. In affluent areas waste usually takes the form of intemperate use of materials such as energy resources and other minerals. In the poor societies waste is most vividly displayed in undeveloped human resources.

Intolerance

Almost all peoples are intolerant in some degree toward groups to which they do not belong. Intolerance, or prejudice, is a barrier to objective assessment of the qualities, capabilities, and deficiencies of those whose color, language, customs, and traditions are different from our own. Intolerance is both a cause of and a consequence of disparities in social and economic well-being in the world. It is a major cause of conflict, both physical and intellectual.

Intolerance has played a major role in the conflicts among tribal groups in Africa, between blacks and whites in the United States, between Catholics and Protestants in Northern Ireland, between Arabs and Jews in the Middle East, and between the Chinese and the Soviets along the Russian-Chinese border. Such conflicts disrupt international trade, prevent cooperative exchanges of science and technology, and hamper the flow of capital. Such disruptions also divert attention, energy, money, and materials from developmental efforts. The greater burdens of intolerance and disruption normally fall most heavily upon the poor. The poor usually lack the political and economic power to control the direction of events. Thus they become the victims not only of the intolerances of the privileged classes but of their own intolerances as well.

A subtle form of intolerance is the *paternalistic* attitudes held by affluent peoples toward those who are poor [11]. Paternalism by nature implies inferior status to those toward whom it is directed and aristocratic status for those who hold paternalistic views. Disparities are enhanced by these views, for not only do the affluent often look upon the poor as inferior but the poor often view themselves as inferior beings.

Immobility

One of the more pronounced expressions of the existence of disparities in wealth concerns differences in mobility. Affluent peoples have the means through which to construct facilities which provide for high levels of mobility. Poor peoples often do not. The relative immobility of the poor precludes them from exposure to cultural conditions, beliefs, experiences, and associations other than those found within a short radius of their home villages. Immobility tends to perpetuate traditional ways, intolerances, and beliefs or to depress opportunities for innovation and for diffusion of goods and ideas. Thus spatial immobility contributes powerfully to social and economic immobility and to a broadening of disparities in wealth.

Social Unrest

Social unrest is both a cause and a result of disparities in wealth. Unrest normally occurs because one group feels that it has been victimized by another group. The offending group may be represented by landowners, police, businesses, government, the military, or the church. Unrest is frequently suppressed by the forceful actions of those in the privileged classes. Once the power of the privileged class is shown to have a weakness, however, unrest may erupt into violence. The unrest of peoples living under colonial rule in Africa and Asia, for example, erupted following World War II. The effectiveness of European dominance had been weakened by the war, allowing local leadership and feelings of nationalism to emerge. Within 10 years after the war ended, the colonial era in world history had been brought virtually to a close.

Hunger

Hunger is perhaps the most catastrophic and loathsome of the several manifestations of disparities in wealth. Until recent decades, however, hunger was such a common phenomenon that it was considered an inevitable part of the human condition and little attention was directed toward its alleviation. Even today, sympathy for the world's hungry peoples may be regarded largely as a luxury among those who are affluent enough to provide some degree of aid to the afflicted.

Lack of attention to the problem of hunger is somewhat paradoxical in view of the enormous calamities that hunger has produced. There is little doubt, for example, that "the human waste resulting from hunger is considerably greater than that from wars and epidemics put together" [12]. Even when per capita food production increases, the very poor are usually the last to benefit. Much of the increased output is absorbed in the production of high-quality foods, such as meat, for the affluent. Rural areas are likewise often deprived in favor of funneling available surpluses of imported foods into the more accessible and politically powerful cities. Hunger is undoubtedly the most pervasive of the issues which could serve as unifying bonds for the poor peoples of the world.

War

Just as hunger is probably the most loathsome manifestation of disparities in wealth, war is certainly the most violent. Economic disparities are not always direct causes of war, but frequently they are major contributing factors. The outcomes of conflicts over ownership of or accessibility to resources and territories may have great positive or negative economic consequences for the competing parties. In some instances such conflicts develop out of emotional issues involving national pride. In other situations possession of some resource or parcel of territory may be considered vital to the security of two or more nations. The Arab–Israeli conflict, for example, stems from a long tradition of antagonism between two major cultures which have spawned three of the world's great religions: Judaism, Christianity, and Islam [13]. More recently, the conflict has been intensified by disputes over certain parcels of territory which both Israel and its neighbors consider vital to their respective securities.

In many instances disparities in wealth have contributed to the outbreak of civil wars. The Communist revolutions in Russia and China were fueled in part by resentments held by the poor against the wealthy and privileged classes. Lenin rallied support for his cause from the peasant classes during the 1918 revolution by promising peace, food, and land. Mao Tse-tung, during the Communist Revolution in China, promised to free his people from the threat of starvation. The desire for economic and political equality was also instrumental in the rise of nationalism and the revolutionary movements which ended colonialism in Africa, Asia, and Latin America. These two goals are major stimulants, as well, of the internal revolutions now festering in such areas as Rhodesia and South Africa.

It seems apparent that internal, or civil, war is most likely when a bipolarization of wealth occurs (when the society consists of a very large group of very poor peoples and a very small group of very rich peoples) and when socioeconomic mobility (the opportunity to improve one's socioeconomic status) is extremely difficult. Awareness of relative socioeconomic status is not equally developed among all peoples, but such awareness is increasing. Still, millions of people appear unmindful of their own poverty, or they are unwilling or unable to conceive of themselves under circumstances other than those which they have experienced.

THE SPATIAL DISTRIBUTION OF WEALTH

Despite its considerable disadvantages, per capita gross national product (GNP) is probably the best available measure of the comparative distribution of wealth in the world (see Chapter 3 for further discussion of GNP). A general picture of the distribution of wealth in the world may be acquired by assigning each nation to one of three classes, according to per capita GNP (Fig. 2-3):

1. *Affluent Regions.* Those with a per capita GNP which is at least twice the world average.
2. *Regions of Moderate Means.* Those with a per capita GNP between one-half and twice the world average.
3. *Poor Regions.* Those with a per capita GNP which is less than one-half the world average.

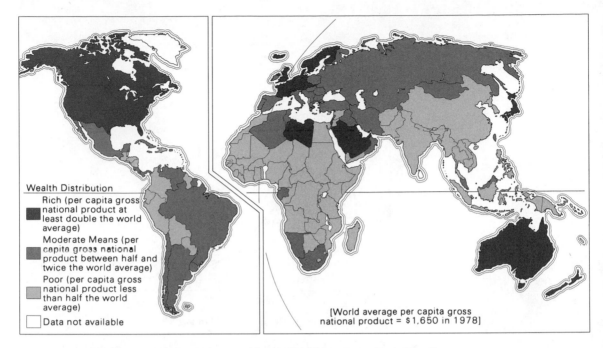

Fig. 2–3. Relative wealth: 1978. [From "World Population Data Sheet" (Washington, D.C.: Population Reference Bureau, Inc., 1978).]

Affluent Regions

Most of the affluent nations border the North Atlantic Ocean and its adjoining seas. Such nations include the United States, Canada, the United Kingdom, and the nations of northern and western Europe. Australia and New Zealand, as outposts of European (primarily British) settlement, are also included among the affluent nations. Nations which have recently joined the ranks of the affluent include Japan and the oil-exporting nations of Kuwait, the United Arab Emirates, Qatar, and Libya. The nations around the North Atlantic are those which were first to acquire affluence, and they have used their initial advantages to enhance and safeguard their superior positions. The oil-exporting nations have recently tapped their savings in the form of energy resources and Japan has utilized exceptional business acumen and its capacity to make sectorial labor transfers to enhance wealth.

The internal distribution of wealth in most of the affluent nations is somewhat similar to that which would occur in a *normal* distribution (a normal curve) (Fig. 2–4). This means that relatively small percentages of the

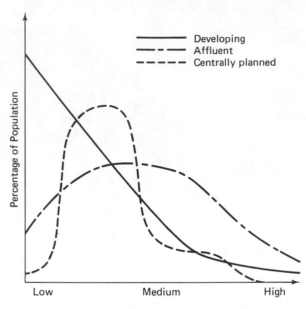

Per Capita Gross National Product

Fig. 2-4. Generalized model of comparative internal distribution of personal incomes within affluent market economies, developing market economies, and centrally planned economies. [Income curve for affluent market economies was generalized from data in D. G. Champernowne, *The Distribution of Income Between Persons*, (Cambridge University Press, 1973) and from the *Statistical Abstract of the United States*, 1977. Income curve for developing market economies was generalized from data in *National Income and its Distribution in Under-Developed Countries*, United Nations Statistical Papers, Series E, No. 3, 1951. Income curve for centrally planned economies was generalized from theoretical constructs reflecting the administrative nature of wage determination in centrally planned economies and that wage differentials in such economies are smaller than those in market economies. From Stanislaw Wellisz, *The Economies of the Soviet Bloc* (New York: McGraw-Hill Book Co., 1964).]

population are either poor or affluent and that most of the population is in the middle-income (middle-class) category. In nations which have most recently acquired affluence, income distribution tends to be more skewed toward large numbers of poor, a relatively small middle class, and modest numbers of very rich peoples than in nations with long histories of affluence. The narrowest range of income distribution occurs within the centrally planned economies where wages are controlled by the state and where accumulation of extremely large amounts of wealth by individuals is made virtually impossible because of restrictions against the ownership of private property. In the centrally planned economies, therefore, the gap between the poorest and the richest elements of society is smaller than that within nations which possess market economies (Fig. 2-4).

Poor Regions

The poor nations are found predominantly in Africa and in southern and eastern Asia, although a few Latin American nations are also poor (Fig. 2-3). The only nations in Africa which are *not* poor are those with substantial mineral wealth which has been developed for export. Libya and Algeria are oil and gas exporters. Gabon exports oil, uranium, and other minerals, and South Africa exports gold, diamonds, chromite, and a variety of other minerals. Nigeria, Zambia, Zaire, Rhodesia, and Morocco appear to have the best opportunities to raise per capita GNP significantly in the near future because of their considerable reserves and exports of oil, gas, copper, and phosphate. These nations are representative of those with substantial capital savings stored in the form of natural resources.

The poor nations in southern and eastern Asia are handicapped largely by huge populations which, like those of Africa and Latin America, are growing rapidly. In all the poor nations and in some of those with a moderate per capita GNP, a large percentage of the population is very young. In Africa, for example, approximately 44 percent of the population is under 15 years of age; in Asia, 38 percent; and in Latin America, 42 percent. This compares with 24 percent in the United States, 23 percent in northern Europe, 23 percent in western Europe, and 25 percent in the Soviet Union (Fig. 2-5). In most areas with a high percentage of the population under 15 years, life expectancy is relatively short, ranging from 42 years in western Africa to 66 years in eastern Asia. By contrast, life expectancy in all the affluent areas exceeds 70 years.

No major region of the world which had in excess of 30 percent of its population under 15 years of age in 1978 had a per capita GNP above $2,000 (Fig. 2-5). On the other hand, all major regions with less than 30 percent of the population under 15 years of age had per capita incomes above $2,000 (Fig. 2-5). This is evidence of the drain placed upon a region's capital resources by rapidly growing populations where the percentage of the total population in the most productive working years (roughly 16 to 65) is relatively small.

Regions of Moderate Means

Regions of moderate means are located primarily in eastern and southern Europe, northern and southwestern Asia, and Latin America. The moderately affluent nations of southwest Asia (around the Persian Gulf), Africa, and Latin America have accumulated savings through the export of minerals and

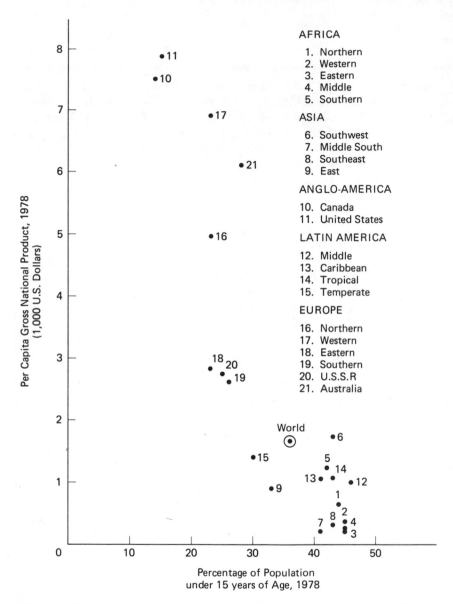

Fig. 2-5. Percentage of population under 15 years of age compared with per capita gross national product: 1975. [From "World Population Data Sheet" (Washington, D.C.: Population Reference Bureau, Inc., 1977).]

agricultural commodities, and most of them have relatively low population densities. Southern and eastern Europe have amassed savings through exploitation of natural resources, development and utilization of human skills, and sectorial transfers of labor. From the mid-1920s until the early 1950s the Soviet Union embarked upon a program of forced industrialization, involving complete control of the economy by the state and the transfer of capital and labor from agriculture to mining and manufacturing. With its incorporation into the Soviet Bloc of nations following World War II, eastern Europe became subject to many of the same policies that had been applied to the Soviet economy.

DISPARITIES IN WEALTH: WHAT ARE THE RISKS?

It seems apparent that wealth begets wealth and that in large measure a direct relationship exists between wealth and the quantities of goods produced and consumed. Increases in wealth and in production and consumption are also paralleled by increases in social and economic complexity, increases in work specialization, a proliferation in types of goods available for consumption, and increases in distances over which commodities are transported. All of these changes require increased consumption of energy.

As the affluent nations vest ever larger amounts of social and economic capital into their complex, specialized, consumptive system, the sheer mass of the system is apparently becoming an increasingly overpowering inertial force. To alter the basic direction of the system significantly would involve staggering economic costs and quite possibly overwhelming pressures from those who stand to lose wealth or stature as a result of change. Thus the more we invest and the further we progress, the greater is our commitment toward more growth and more change of the same type as before [14]. Whether they wish to or not, the poor nations appear to be caught up increasingly in the overall direction of change established by the inundating power of the affluent societies. Progress is everywhere associated with rising levels of consumption, the application of technology to production, higher levels of worker productivity, and the "westernization" of modes of behavior. The desire for manufactured soft drinks, convenience foods, and automobiles, for example, seems to have penetrated to every corner of the world. Every nation desires to industrialize, mechanize, and contemporize its economic and social systems. The result of the direction of change in which the world is moving has been to increase rather than to decrease disparities in wealth between rich nations and poor nations. Although whether the overall direction of change yields good or bad results is largely a value judgement, it does entail certain risks to the affluent as well as to the poor. The risks lead to a series of questions concerning wealth and possible consequences of disparities in the distribution of wealth:

1. What are the risks to the affluent and to the poor alike of constant growth of and increasing disparities in the distribution of wealth?
2. How much wealth *should* a people possess; how much *should* they produce; and how much *should* they consume?
3. How much *can* production and consumption be increased, and how much growth in production and consumption can occur before the dangers in such growth begin to outweigh potential gains?
4. What is the nature of the opportunities that may be lost if too much attention is focused upon dangers of wealth and growth and too little upon potential gains?
5. What is the prospect that the numerically superior poor will revolt against the affluent minority?
6. To what extent is the human habitat (the earth environment) threatened by wealth and by continued economic growth, and to what extent are solutions to environmental problems dependent on the growth of affluence?
7. How long can the world's natural resource base — especially of nonrenewable resources — support growth of or even a continuation of current levels of production and consumption?
8. What are the prospects for a significant redistribution of the world's wealth and for narrowing the gap between the rich and the poor — primarily by an upgrading of life-styles in the poor areas?
9. What is the probability that a redistribution of wealth (and thus of consumption) would result in a decrease in production?
10. To what extent can wealth and economic growth be channeled toward development of human rather than material resources, including a reduction in disparities in knowledge?
11. What are the implications to present social, economic, and political systems of the problems associated with growth in wealth and in wealth disparities?

These are some of the great unanswered, and perhaps unanswerable, questions of our time. They involve extremely complex social, economic, political, environmental, and moral issues, and it is likely that none of the problems outlined has a single solution. Much of the attention of subsequent chapters is directed toward providing an informational base upon which these questions can be analyzed and discussed.

REFERENCES

[1] H. F. Lydall, "Theories of the Distribution of Earnings," in A. B. Atkinson (ed.), *The Personal Distribution of Incomes* (London: George Allen and Unwin, Ltd., 1976), p. 30.

[2] For more information concerning equality, equity, and social justice, see the following references:

Geographical Perspectives on American Poverty, Monographs in Social Geography, No. 1 (Worcester, Mass.: Clark University, Department of Geography, 1972).

J. Drewnowski, *On Measuring and Planning the Quality of Life* (The Hague: Mouton, 1974).

B. E. Coates, R. Johnston, and P. Knox, *Geography and Inequality* (Oxford: Oxford University Press, 1977).

[3] N. Kaldor, *Causes of the Slow Rate of Economic Growth of the United Kingdom* (London: Cambridge University Press, 1966). See also, T. F. Cripps and R. J. Tarling, *Growth in Advanced Capitalist Economies: 1950-1970* (London: Cambridge University Press, 1976).

[4] Erich W. Zimmerman, *World Resources and Industries* (New York: Harper and Row, 1951), p. 10. The expression is paraphrased from Wesley C. Mitchell, "Conservation, Liberty, and Economics," in *The Foundations of Conservation Education* (New York: National Wildlife Federation, 1941), pp. 1 and 2.

[5] *Literacy and World Population* (Washington, D.C.: Population Reference Bureau Inc.), **30**, No. 2, p. 3.

[6] *Ibid.*

[7] Camillo Bonanni, "The Autodafe of an Adult Literacy Worker," in *Convergence*, Ontario Institute for Studies in Education, 4, No. 1, pp. 23-25.

[8] John M. Villaume, "Theory-Informed Middle-Range Evaluation of Literacy Programs," in *Literacy Discussion*, **5**, No. 3, p. 45.

[9] David Morawitz, "Twenty-five Years of Economic Development," *Finance and Development*, 14, No. 3, September, 1977, p. 13.

[10] Paul Streeten, "Changing Perceptions of Development," *Finance and Development*, 14, No. 3, September, 1977, p. 15.

[11] Pierre L. Van deu Berghe, "Paternalistic Versus Competitive Race Relations," in Bernard E. Segal (ed.), *Racial and Ethnic Relations* (New York: Thomas Y. Crowell Co., 1966), pp. 53-69.

[12] Josue de Castro, *The Geography of Hunger* (Boston: Little, Brown & Co., 1952), p. 5.

[13] Preston E. James, *One World Perspective* (New York: Blaisdell Publishing Co., 1965), p. 86.

[14] Michael Treshow, *The Human Environment* (New York: McGraw-Hill Book Co., 1976), p. 356.

CHAPTER THREE
the growth-
no growth
controversy

INTRODUCTION

The "goodness" of growth has been a prevailing dogma among western societies during most of modern history. That growth is "supposed to happen" comes naturally to us from childhood when we look forward to "growing up" and later in life as we expect to grow in wealth, knowledge, and influence. An accepted advantage of living within societies that emphasize individual freedom and welfare has been the existence of the "ladder of success." This is the concept that any individual, through hard work, thrift, and motivation, can rise in socioeconomic status. The type of ladder which exists, conceptually, within the developed democracies is one where the rungs of the ladder are closely spaced, so that even the most humble citizen might advance toward its top. Elsewhere, rungs between the bottom and the top of the ladder either are nonexistent (making the ladder impossible to climb) or are so widely spaced that only the strongest individuals can progress from a lower to a higher level. It must also be presumed, of course, that movement on the ladder is two-directional — those above the bottom rung may descend the ladder to a lower socioeconomic status.

ELEMENTS OF GROWTH

Growth can occur only when certain ingredients are brought together for that purpose. These ingredients include a sufficient variety, quantity, and quality of natural resources; an adequate supply of labor with appropriate skills; ample amounts of capital; technical and research support commensurate with the degree of sophistication of the growth which is planned; and a political and economic environment favorable to growth. Growth is most commonly expressed in terms of income, population, living standards, employment, production, education, and life expectancy. Precisely what kind of growth occurs depends on the manner in which the ingredients of growth are brought together and managed toward what ends.

MEASURING ECONOMIC GROWTH

Although the concept of economic growth is relatively simple, its measurement is not. Lack of data, differences in quality of data, and lack of comparability of data collected by various sources make it difficult to compare growth among different areas or for different periods of time. Such as they are, however, measurements of growth may be given in either relative or absolute magnitudes. *Relative* growth refers to the rate or percentage of growth of a particular area, industry, or service during a particular period of time or to the growth of one region or one factor compared with another during the same period of time. *Absolute* growth refers to the actual number of dollars, production units, or people added during the period. Because the type of growth measure used normally depends on the objectives of the user, interpreters of growth measures would do well to look carefully into the purpose for which the measures were prepared. If rapid growth is considered a political asset, for example, a state governor would be likely to report growth in measures which make his or her record look most impressive. Suppose, for example, the governor's state had a total employed labor force of 100,000 at the beginning of the term and 110,000 by the time the governor had to run for reelection 4 years later. This represents a relative growth of 10 percent and an absolute growth of 10,000. The governor may wish to compare the state with an adjacent state, whose employed labor force rose from 1,000,000 to 1,080,000 during the same period. This represents a relative growth of 8 percent but an absolute growth of 80,000. The governor's state, compared to the one ajoining, enjoyed a higher *rate* of growth but only one-eighth the *absolute* growth of the neighbor. Which measure of growth do you think the governor would use?

The most commonly available and frequently used measure of economic growth among the world's nations is *gross national product* (GNP). To compare the GNP of the United States with that of Canada would be meaningless, however, because of the vast difference in population between the two countries. For that reason, per capita GNP is a more valid measure of comparative economic well-being or growth than total GNP (Fig. 2–1). To have high validity, however, comparative studies of growth in per capita GNP

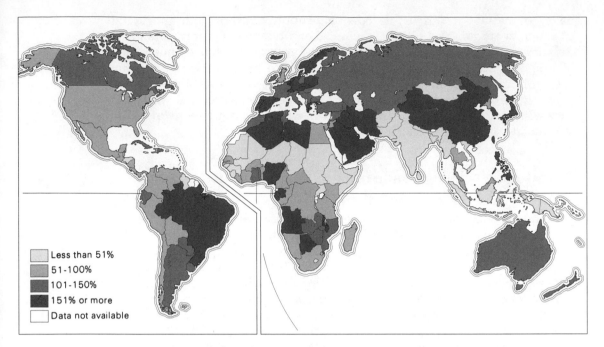

Less than 51%
51-100%
101-150%
151% or more
Data not available

Fig. 3-1. Rate of growth in per capita gross national product: 1971–1976. [From "World Population Data Sheet, 1971 and 1976" (Washington, D.C.: Population Reference Bureau, Inc.).]

would require that the data be given in the same currency values, that all the data be collected and compiled with the same levels of care and accuracy, that time-sequence data be properly discounted for inflation, and that the period of time covered by the data be the same. A growth in per capita GNP from $2,000 in 1965 to $2,200 in 1975 would not represent real growth (growth in purchasing power), for example, if the annual rate of inflation during that period was 10 percent. At an annual 10 percent rate of inflation a person making $2,000 in 1970 would have to make approximately $5,000 in 1980 just to stay even in purchasing power.

It is also true that world patterns of economic growth differ significantly when they are measured in absolute and in relative values. When the *rate* of growth in per capita GNP is mapped, a number of the developing nations in South America, Africa, and Asia as well as several European nations appear as growth leaders (Fig. 3-1). Growth patterns differ substantially, however, when the *absolute* growth in per capita GNP is mapped (Fig. 3-2). The leading nations in absolute growth are, for the most part, the highly developed, affluent, industrialized nations of Anglo–America and western Europe, plus Japan, Australia, and New Zealand. Oil-rich Saudi Arabia, Kuwait, and Libya are also among the growth leaders in absolute and relative growth, with oil-rich Iran, Iraq, Algeria, and Nigeria joining the leaders in rate of growth.

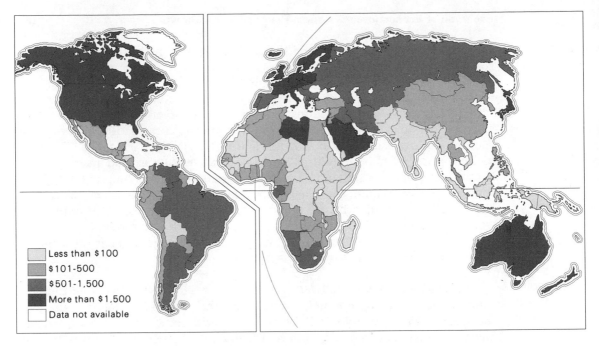

Fig. 3-2. Absolute growth in per capita gross national product: 1971-1976.
[From "World" Population Data Sheet, 1971 and 1976" (Washington, D.C.:
Population Reference Bureau, Inc.).]

World patterns of *absolute* growth, therefore, compare more favorably than
patterns of *rate* of growth, with the distribution of per capita gross national
product (compare fig. 2-3, 3-1, and 3-2).

THE GROWTH CONCEPT

Among the bases underlying development of the "growth cult" in western societies are the Judeo-Christian tradition; the expansionist impetus
emanating from the Age of Exploration and the existence of a land frontier;
the scientific, industrial, and democratic revolutions; and the rise of capitalism. From the Judeo-Christian tradition comes the premise that mankind
is superior to and was created to have dominion over all other forms of creation. [1] If the premise is interpreted to mean that mankind has free reign
to exploit everything in nature for its own enjoyment, a basis has been
provided for justifying growth in all its forms. Because economic growth
during the last several hundred years reached greatest heights in areas of
European (Western) cultural influence, the following discussion is limited
primarily to events reflecting Western attitudes, ideas, and actions.

Evolution of Economic and Technical Frameworks for Growth

During most of human history the major control over human actions was social. Tribal and religious taboos, military tyrants, and powerful priests and princes kept all but a small minority of peoples under rigid control. Despite the permissiveness afforded the growth concept by Judaism and Christianity, these two religions existed as a major influence upon western culture for hundreds of years without appreciable rates of population or economic growth actually occurring. During most of the long saga of human history prior to about 1500 A.D. virtually all resources had been in short supply. The spectre of starvation hung constantly over the masses. Opportunities for economic and social advancement were virtually nonexistent. Nearly all land and other resources were held by a wealthy nobility and were unobtainable by the poor. Christianity and other religions offering rewards after death for those who "keep the faith" attracted converts among those who had no hope for rewards in life.

The Age of Discovery: 1400-1600. The first major event in establishing a framework for rapid economic growth was the Age of Discovery. Whatever the reasons that prompted the event, whether from a search for wealth and adventure, from a desire to spread Christianity, or from advances in ship design and the science of navigation, the period from about 1400 to 1600 saw Europeans enhance their knowledge of world geography at an unprecedented rate. Vast new areas were opened to settlement and trade; supplies of land, forests, and minerals in the Americas, Africa, and Asia appeared inexhaustible; and new commercial adventures generated enormous wealth. Most of the benefits of this newfound wealth were fed into European coffers, where per capita wealth began to escalate. It was difficult for Europeans to conceive of a time when the land frontier would end or when the abundance of known resources would diminish.

The stimulus to trade provided by the Age of Discovery also led to development of the first national or international systems of economic thought. Prior to the fifteenth century little organized attention had been given to economics. No basis had been established through which economic growth could be promoted beyond the level of a single firm, estate, or plantation. The few broad economic controls that did exist had been enacted primarily for the collection of taxes and to protect game on estates of aristocrats. The expansion of knowledge about the world offered by the Age of Discovery, however, along with improvements in navigation and the transfer of riches from newfound lands into Europe gave rise to a class of wealthy merchants. By the 1500s many merchants had attained great economic and political power. The importance of trading as a means for promoting economic growth during the 1500s and 1600s is shown by the designation of that period by historians as the "Age of Mercantilism." The mercantilists believed that governments should regulate economic activities so as to protect private enterprise and to control trade in a way that would ensure a surplus of exports over imports — thus stimulating national economic growth and adding to individual wealth.

In summary, the most significant aspects of growth–promoting events which arose from the Age of Discovery are as follows:

1. The funneling of great amounts of wealth into Europe.
2. The beginning of a change in perception of resources from one of scarcity to one of abundance.
3. Development of a new class of wealthy entrepreneurs, the mercantilists.
4. Emergence of the first organized systems of economic thought applicable at the nation scale.

The Age of Revolution. Literally, and figuratively, the period from 1600 to 1850 was an age of highly significant revolution in government, science, technology, and economics. The democratic revolution had been simmering in the minds of intellectuals since the Athenian experiment in democracy between 600 and 400 B.C. Democracy, however, is a system which requires that its adherents have faith in their future and hope for an improved condition for mankind. Hope for improvements in life came during and following the Age of Discovery with the growth of wealth in Europe, the opening of new opportunities for settlement and trade and for the establishment of new political units, and development of an expansionist attitude toward resources. During the 1600s the British made many advances toward the achievement of democracy. The American style of democracy was born in the late 1700s, after which democratic institutions spread into France and other areas. It was in the United States, however, that the philosophy of the pioneer spirit, self-reliance, and individualism achieved peak development.

The significance of the democratic revolution in promoting the growth concept is that for the first time in human history large segments of the world's population became concerned with extending individual rights and promoting the welfare of the masses. Privileges of ownership and exploitation of resources were opened to all individuals. In the United States, especially, transmission of land and other resources to private hands became a matter of urgent national policy [2].

Coinciding roughly with the American Revolution, the industrial revolution began to rise out of new discoveries and applications in science and technology. The key invention, the one which put the industrial revolution in motion, was development of the first successful steam engine by James Watt in 1769. The steam engine and the other machines which followed provided humankind with "robot" power and with the mechanical energy required to lift, dig, and transport materials in quantities and at speeds far exceeding those of which humans and animals were capable.

As the scientific, industrial, and democratic revolutions emerged during the late 1700s and early 1800s, accompanied by mechanization and rapidly rising output per worker, production began to compete with and even to supplant trade as the chief means for acquiring wealth and for promoting economic growth. The importance of trade did not diminish; rather it grew at unprecedented rates because of the complementary relationships between production and trade. Growth of agricultural and industrial production and the rise of large-scale production enterprises, however, were also unprecedented in size and in effect. Owners of the means of production (capital) accumulated huge fortunes and their economic influence grew accordingly.

The growth of democracy and the ascendancy of production as the dominant mechanism for generating wealth stimulated a significant change in economic thought. It was during this period that capitalism, or free enterprise, emerged as a dominant economic philosophy. In his *Wealth of Nations*, published in 1776, Adam Smith set forth the basic principles of *laissez-faire* economics. Smith outlined the concept of the "invisible hand," whereby the greatest good for the greatest number is achieved when individual goals are pursued in a spirit of free competition without governmental interference. Laissez-faire capitalism, as a form of *economic democracy*, reflected the growing belief among western peoples in political freedom. According to the laissez-faire economists, free competition and free trade were the best means through which to promote economic growth.

Beyond Laissez-Faire. Because unregulated economic growth often resulted in the exploitation of workers by those who owned the means of production, a body of economic theory soon emerged to counter laissez-faire capitalism. The best known and the most influential of the anticapitalist economists was Karl Marx. Marx viewed history as a class struggle between workers and capitalists (those who owned the means of production). Capitalism, according to Marx, enslaved the workers and would eventually lead to violent revolution. He called for government ownership of all property and, therefore, of all means of production. His theories, along with those of Friederick Engels, formed the bases for modern socialism and communism.

In the meantime, economists who wished to preserve many of the basic features of capitalism began to question the idea that unregulated enterprise offered the best means toward economic growth and individual prosperity. The result was a number of theories which proposed varying degrees of governmental control over private enterprise. John Maynard Keynes and others advocated enactment of legislation to encourage collective bargaining between workers and employers, income redistribution to weaken class divisions, and government spending to reduce unemployment and to counteract the cycles of economic growth and depression which had characterized capitalistic systems.

Following World War II, with the rise of *service industries* (industries

The huge ship in this photograph is the supertanker "Batillus," with a capacity of 550,000 tons. The smaller ship alongside the "Batillus" is representative of tanker sizes in common use at about the beginning of World War II.
(Courtesy, Chantiers de l'Atlantique, Saint Nazaire, France.).

that do not produce tangible goods but which provide research, transportation, repair, instruction, sales, and other beneficial functions for producers
and consumers) as the dominant sources of employment in the advanced
nations, a new body of economic theory emphasizing *welfare economics*
emerged which combined certain elements of capitalism, socialism, and
social justice. The movement toward welfare economics, often referred to as
social democracy or *democratic socialism*, had gained strength during the
Great Depression of the 1930s, especially in Europe. Although leaders of the

movement toward welfare economics had at first favored elimination of private property, the dominant train of thought which surfaced during the 1950s and 1960s emphasized retention of maximum reliance upon private ownership and the market economy but under the umbrella of extensive governmental planning and control to ensure an equitable distribution of the benefits of economic growth. Such systems, as they have been implemented, stress full employment, guaranteed incomes, and availability of certain services such as medical care and education to all elements of the population regardless of ability to pay for those services.

The Ecological Revolution: 1960–?

Just as most of the ingredients for rapid economic growth originated in Europe and Anglo-America, so was growth itself confined primarily to those areas. In the rush toward growth, increasing individual and national wealth, and higher levels of living, Europeans and Anglo-Americans came to depend more and more on resources and markets in the less developed parts of the world. In pursuing growth they neglected to consider its adverse effects in the form of air and water pollution, resource depletion, waste, scenic and widelife destruction, and the hazards that were being created for human health and survival. Although several conservation movements surfaced during the late 1800s and in the first half of the twentieth century, each movement was directed primarily toward saving or reducing the depletion of a particular resource or set of resources. Not until the 1960s was there a general awakening in Europe and in Anglo-America to the ecological concept — or to the idea that the earth's environment is an interrelated, interacting, and interdependent system. A change in any part of the system leads to changes in other parts of the system through processes of adaptation which are required to maintain equilibrium, or balance, in the system as a whole. The danger to mankind is that through the headlong pursuit of growth, material prosperity, and economic efficiency without regard to the damage such pursuits are exacting upon the natural environment the processes which function to maintain equilibrium in nature may so alter the natural environment as to make it untenable for human survival. In the discussion which follows, some of the principal arguments offered by groups opposed to and in favor of growth are presented.

THE REVOLT AGAINST GROWTH

Although sporadic warnings of the dangers of growth had been raised by ecologists and conservationists prior to World War II, the attention of economists and political leaders was confined almost entirely to the benefits of growth. In the 1960s, however, a widespread, consistent and organized effort was mounted against growth. The major stimulus for the revolt against growth was the development during and after World War II of a variety of technical and chemical products and processes with particularly severe potentials for degrading the environment and for adversely affecting human health. The worst offenders appeared to be a noxious group of pesticides and herbicides with long-lasting toxic effects on the environment, such as DDT, Kepone, and Mirex.

Searching examinations were also made of the *external costs* (costs borne by the environment and not reflected in the selling price of a commodity) of growth in production and consumption. Energy and other minerals were being exploited at unprecedented rates to support what appeared to be an insatiable demand for new cars; air conditioners; convenience items such as disposable diapers, throwaway bottles, chemically treated fabrics; and high-energy foods. Not only were resources being depleted and the environment damaged, but urban areas were finding it increasingly difficult and expensive to dispose of mushrooming quantities of wastes. Water quality was deteriorating rapidly as lakes, rivers, and even the near-shore areas of the oceans were recipients of growing quantities or urban and industrial wastes and agricultural chemicals. Air quality was also deteriorating, especially over urban areas, because of emissions from automobiles, power plants, factories, and other sources. Many environmental scientists feared that the deterioration of the environment, if not stopped, would soon become irreversible. Doomsday warnings were commonplace, and environmental issues became matters of widespread public concern.

Much of the blame for environmental problems was directed primarily against growth. Although some experts focused most of the blame for environmental degradation upon one or another or the various aspects of growth, such as population or technology, it was widely agreed that there were definite limits to growth and that those limits had already been reached or would be reached within the near future. Some forecasters predicted an end not only to economic progress but also to the growth of knowledge. Whatever the limits to growth, it was thought that the more rapid the occurrence of growth, the sooner those limits would be reached.

The No-Growth Concept

Policies of zero growth, a steady-state economy, and even economic and technical de-development have been advocated for the United States and other affluent societies so that the world might avoid the disastrous consequences of growth. Suggestions were made by leading environmentalists such as Paul Ehrlich that the United States, as the richest nation on earth, should lead the way toward no growth, or de-development, and encourage other

Removal of junked cars in Anderson County, Tennessee. (Courtesy, Tennessee Valley Authority.)

affluent nations to do likewise while promoting "ecologically feasible" development within presently undeveloped societies [3]. Others have suggested that the goals of economic and technological strategies should be a global equilibrium based upon the concept of the earth as a spaceship [4]. The objective is to view the earth as a closed system offering no imputs beyond those we already have. Once something is used up, or destroyed, there is no opportunity for replacement. Reserves of raw materials must be preserved through recycling and through guarding against the negative externalities (such as air and water pollution) of production and consumption. At the same time, demands against the environment must be held in check by stabilizing or reducing population, minimizing use of nonrenewable resources, and holding economic growth—if it is to occur at all—to nonmaterial goods and services. Economic practices such as those which encourage maximization of production through planned obsolesence must be abandoned. Ultimately, the amount of matter and energy taken from the environment must be returned to it in forms where they would eventually become reusable.

Technical progress as a solution to environmental problems caused by growth is largely rejected by advocates of no growth. Technology has contributed to past environmental deterioration and proponents of no growth believe that it will prove inadequate to cope with future environmental and economic problems if growth policies are maintained. The rate of technical development required to support continued exponential growth in population, production, and consumption will probably involve excessively high costs, and the speed with which new technology must be implemented in order to provide for protecting the environment under policies of continued growth would allow too little time for its testing against potentially disastrous consequences for humankind.

Modern proponents of no growth, steady-state economics, spaceship earth policies, and de-development are echoing the same basic predictions made by classical economists such as Malthus, Ricardo, and Mills. Although they differ in certain specifics concerning how and when diminishing returns for effort will occur, all have centered their ideas around the concept of the inevitability of natural resource scarcity and all have predicted that resource scarcity will eventually cause an end to economic growth.

Growth Revisited

Those who favor continued economic growth argue that failure to make full utilization of resources promotes scarcity. They point to the record of recent decades during which advances in technology have made increasing quantities of resources available to more and more people. Moreover, the threat of scarcity encourages discovery of alternative or substitute resources which are often superior to the resources being replaced. The substitutes are frequently more common or more widely found than the resources originally used. Knowledge, however, is seen as the ultimate resource and its development can be maximized only under conditions of economic growth which both feed and are fed by growth of knowledge. Through growth of knowledge the range of available resources has been enormously expanded and humankind has been liberated from a narrow range of resource alternatives.

Technology is seen by most advocates of growth as an inseparable component of humankind's efforts to win a decent living. Heretofore it has extended the limits to growth and if properly used it can do so indefinitely. Although much of the environmental damage of recent decades has resulted from technical applications, improved technology also offers the best opportunity for solving those problems without seriously disrupting world social and economic order. Technological solutions to many of the most severe environmental problems, moreover, are relatively inexpensive compared with their benefits.

Proponents of growth argue that many proposals of those who advocate no growth or de-development are unrealistic and unworkable. Growth has become a dogma of western culture, and it is unlikely that this dogma will be reversed within the near future. To do so would require that the basic optimism of western society, that levels of living can be raised through work, education, or frugality, must be largely eliminated along with the concept that a prime responsibility of government is to promote improvements in individual economic welfare and political freedom. Realistically it seems doubtful that a de-developmental or no-growth catalyst can be found short of the abandonment of democratic institutions and the imposition by government of severe restrictions upon family sizes and levels of production and consumption, together with unyielding enforcement of rigid standards of environmentally related behavior.

It is also highly doubtful that the end product of de-development or no growth would actually produce a high-quality environment. The only peoples who have made conscious efforts to protect and improve their environments and to reduce population growth and who have demonstrated a willingness to make sacrifices in order to achieve a high-quality environment are those from the more affluent societies. Investments in efforts to protect the environment inevitably require the diversion of funds from other economic and technical ventures, and such diversions are more likely to take place under conditions of growth and optimism than under conditions of economic stagnation and lack of confidence in the future. Affluent societies are in a much better position than those which are impoverished to improve the aesthetic qualities of natural surroundings, control commercial development, and channel funds into technologies that enhance environmental protection. New factories can more economically incorporate environmental protection into their facilities than old factories. New machines constructed under new standards offer better protection for the environment than old machines.

That improvements in environmental quality are linked to growth rather than no growth is well-illustrated by the delays in implementation of governmental regulations intended to raise environmental quality during the major economic recession of the early and middle 1970s. The recession brought a significant decline in public interest and public pressure for environmental protection as jobs, earnings, inflation, and decreased purchasing power became the primary issues of the period.

Zero growth and de-development approaches to solving environmental problems often ignore the complex social consequences of such policies and fail to distinguish between growth which is good and that which is bad for the environment. Antigrowth policies, therefore, are likely to have their most negative impacts upon those who are already disadvantaged. Economists have long noted that during periods when per capita GNP stagnated or declined, unemployment levels have risen. Those most adversely affected during these periods are the poor, least well-educated, young, and minorities. Under policies of no growth, only the largest and strongest businesses would be likely to survive, with wealth becoming more and more concentrated into the hands of a few powerful families and huge corporations. At the same time the slowdown or cessation of innovativeness and technical development resulting from zero growth in the more affluent societies would rob developing areas of the backlog of technology and ideas which they have drawn upon to stimulate their own efforts to provide for the basic needs of their peoples.

AN ALTERNATIVE: SELECTIVE GROWTH

It can be seen from the previous discusson that neither unrestrained growth nor zero growth is without significant problems for the future of humanity. That limits exist to certain types of growth can hardly be seriously doubted. Science and technology are not cure-alls for human problems. Precisely what the limits to growth really are, however, and what types of growth must or should be curtailed are more matters of speculation and opinion than they are of scientific knowledge. Policies which prohibit all growth may have negative results for humanity which are equally as serious as policies which permit unrestrained growth. It is possible, therefore, that consideration should be given to another option, that of selective growth.

Even within democratically oriented societies governments have enormous powers to influence growth. Because funds for research and development are supplied largely by governments, priorities established by governments become the priorities of publicly supported research efforts and also of many private organizations. Through tax incentives, grants, budget allocations, and control of interest rates and money supplies, governments have powerful weapons to encourage or to discourage growth in particular segments of the economy or in particular regions. By utilizing such powers responsibly, governments can encourage shifts in growth from waste-producing economic sectors and from regions where the environment is most seriously threatened or most vulnerable to damage into sectors such as environmental protection and human development and into regions which are most compatible to specific types of development.

Although many of the most serious environmental problems are worldwide in scope, efforts to solve them are handicapped by strong divisions among nations and culture groups. Undeveloped nations, in particular, are concerned that economic slowdowns in affluent areas will adversely affect their own efforts to achieve higher standards of living through loss of trade and economic aid. As long as the majority of the world's people occupying the majority of the world's land surface are determined to pursue growth at whatever cost to the environment, policies of no growth or de-development among the affluent nations are unlikely to produce desired environmental improvements. On the other hand, the world's environment is likely to benefit significantly in the long run through the diffusion into undeveloped areas of innovations to protect the environment which have resulted from policies of selective growth in affluent societies.

Selective growth within affluent areas may also offer the most feasible long-term means for moderate advances among undeveloped societies. As demand for resources in affluent nations outruns domestic production, new sources of supply will usually be sought in undeveloped areas. The resulting capital transfers not only serve as a mechanism for the redistribution of wealth on a world scale but they have the potential for reducing purchasing power and consumption within affluent societies in response to national goals for maintaining favorable balances of trade.

CONCLUSIONS

The history of humankind is laced with threats to its survival, some more and some less serious. Pestilence, famine, plague, and war have been the traditional villains, and growth of knowledge, science, technology, and wealth have been looked upon as weapons to strike the villains down. With seeming suddenness, however, the image of growth began to change from one of hope to one of despair.

It is now the task of human civilization to describe, measure, and analyze this newfound villain. Adjustments in economic and political policies and programs in response to specific problems have occurred in the past, and because economics and politics are not exact sciences, the adjustments have often occurred through a process of trial and error over extended periods of time. Time itself was not so much an enemy when the human capacity to build or to destroy and the consequences of error were not so great. The margin for error in current society is considerably narrower than before. New products are being developed, produced, and marketed more rapidly than facilities to monitor and test them. When errors occur, their results could be far-reaching and long-lasting. The "Golden Age" of luxury, plenty, and security is threatened with turning into an "Age of Fear."

Whatever happens relative to problems of growth depends largely on how these problems are perceived by the general public and by those in decision-making capacities. All persons have an imperfect knowledge of the world, and the manner in which any individual perceives of problems of growth or the environment may have little relationship to reality. For practical purposes, however, perceived conditions are the "realities" upon which decisions are based.

Perceptions of the relative importance of problems and of the actions required to solve them depend largely on the perspective from which each problem is viewed. Variations in perception of the same problem comes primarily from differences in the extent to which each individual or group feels personally involved or threatened by the problem or by proposals for its solution. An ecology professor may favor worldwide prohibition against the use of chemical pesticides, which he views as a threat to the world environment, whereas the mother of a child in Guatemala believes that continued use of the pesticide is the only means through which her children can be protected against the debilitating and often fatal disease of malaria.

It is also important to recognize that the problems of growth and environment are not of the same magnitude in all parts of the world. Most problems have a particular geographic bias, and all forms of production and consumption are constrained in one degree or another by considerations of cost, space utility, and politics. Resource shortages, for example, rarely occur because of a miserly physical environment. They occur because the spatial structures of resource distributions are unfavorable relative to markets, national boundaries, legislation, or the costs of producing, processing, and marketing the resources.

The problem of growth itself is also in the process of significant geographical reorientation. Growth of material production and consumption seems to have lost some of its attractiveness in the more affluent parts of the world where, since World War II, capital investments have shifted strongly toward human rather than natural resources. Among developing nations, on the other hand, desires for economic growth and for high levels of material consumption appear stronger than ever. Investments in human resources remain relatively small, and low levels of education, health, and technical skills among the populations have often made such investments discouragingly unproductive.

It could be, as G. E. Hutchinson has stated, that an effort should be made to find the level of consumption which produces an optimum amount of happiness and satisfaction among the population [5]. Hutchinson pointed to the possibility that some of our attitudes toward resources might need changing so that one type of desire could be substituted for another. He concluded: "It ought to be possible to show that it is as much fun to repair the biosphere and the human societies within it as it is to mend the radio or the family car" [6].

REFERENCES

[1] L. A. White, *The Science of Culture* (New York: Farrar, Straw, and Young, 1949), pp. 121–145.

[2] L. W. Moncrief, "The Cultural Basis for Our Environmental Crises," *Science*, **170**, October, 1970, pp. 508–512.

[3] Paul Ehrlich, Ann Ehrlich, and John P. Holdren, *Human Ecology* (San Francisco: W. H. Freeman Co., 1973), p. 10.

[4] K. E. Boulding, "The Economics of the Coming Spaceship Earth," H. Jarrett (ed.), *Environmental Quality In A Growing Economy* (Baltimore: Johns Hopkins University Press, 1966). G. Tyler Miller, *Replenish the Earth* (Belmont, Calif.: Wadsworth Publishing Co., 1972).

[5] G. E. Hutchinson, "On Living in the Biosphere," *Scientific Monthly*, **67**, December, 1948, pp. 393--397.

[6] *Ibid.*, p. 397.

CHAPTER FOUR

population growth

INTRODUCTION

Population problems are not new to the world. Throughout history there have been concerns about too many people, too few people, too many old people, too many or too few young people, and other problems related to the military, political, economic, and social fortunes and aspirations of particular areas. Recently, however, concerns about population have centered around mounting population growth in the world. Each hour of every day some 13,765 babies are born and about 5,517 people die, leaving a surplus of 8,248 births over deaths.

Population growth did not reach such explosive proportions until the last few decades (Fig. 4-1). It wasn't until approximately 1825 that the world population reached 1 billion persons. During the next 135 years (1825-1960), 2 billion more were added and the fourth billion required only 15 years (1960-1975). Since the 1960s the rate of growth has declined slightly, primarily because of falling birth rates among the relatively affluent inhabitants of Europe, the Soviet Union, and the United States, where rates of growth were already comparatively low, and a declining birth rate in China. In most of the less developed areas of Africa, Asia, and Latin America, however, growth rates have continued at levels of 2 to 3 percent or more annually and few signs point to a major drop in rates of increase, at least until near the end of the twentieth century.

How many people can the earth support—at what standard of living?

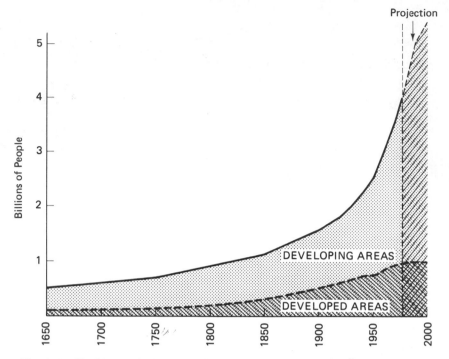

Fig. 4-1. World population growth, 1650-2000. [From Quentin H. Stanford (ed.), *The World's Population: Problems of Growth* (New York: Oxford University Press, 1972), Table 4, p. 19; and recent estimates of population growth by the Population Reference Bureau, Inc.]

What are the likely short-term and long-term consequences to the natural environment from efforts to produce enough food, fiber, and other materials to nourish, clothe, and house the more than 70 million people being added to the world's population each year? What social, economic, and political consequences are likely to emerge from increased densities of people and a growing competition for scarce resources? How will rapid population growth affect the life-styles of the affluent peoples of the earth or the aspirations of impoverished masses in the less developed areas to raise their levels of living and increase their security against hunger, disease, and environmental hazards? These are some of the most critically important questions of our age.

WORLD PATTERNS OF POPULATION
DISTRIBUTION AND DENSITY

About 60 percent of the world's people live within four large regions of the northern hemisphere which contain less than 10 percent of the dry land. These regions are (1) northeastern United States and southeastern Canada,

(2) non-Soviet Europe, (3) India, and (4) eastern China and Japan (Fig. 4-2). Additional pockets of high population density occur on all the continents and on a few islands, notably the Nile Valley in Egypt, the Los Angeles Basin of California, several river plains in southeast Asia, and the island of Java. By contrast, most of the northern and western interior portions of North America; interior South America, Africa, and Australia; and northern and interior Asia are sparsely populated. Substantial variations in density also occur within both sparsely and densely populated regions.

China contains the largest population among the nations, with about 22 percent of the world's people. China is followed by India, with more than 15 percent; the Soviet Union, with nearly 7 percent; and the United States, with slightly more than 5 percent. Whereas the Soviet Union and the United States have population densities of only 30 and 60 persons per square mile of land area, respectively, densities exceed 225 per square mile in China and more than 500 per square mile in India. The Netherlands has a population density of nearly 1,000 persons per square mile; and Taiwan, nearly 1,200. Because the capacity of the earth to support life varies so dramatically from place to place, data offering only the density of population per square mile of surface area have little meaning as a basis for understanding complex population problems. In some densely populated areas, such as The Nether-

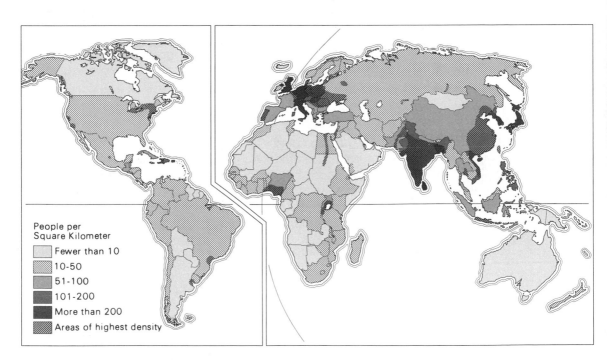

People per
Square Kilometer

Fewer than 10
10-50
51-100
101-200
More than 200
Areas of highest density

Fig. 4-2. Population density per square kilometer of surface area, 1976. [From *Statistical Yearbook, 1977* (New York: United Nations, 1978).]

lands, people live in affluence and comfort, whereas in others, such as India, they live in squalor and are frequently hungry. At the same time, people in many sparsely populated areas, such as Chad in north central Africa, are among the most impoverished on earth. Overall population densities offered for large areas such as the Soviet Union, China, and Egypt are particularly meaningless. Most of the land area in each of these countries is virtually empty. In Egypt, nearly the entire population is crowded into the Nile Valley, most of the Soviet population lives in about 10 percent of the national territory, and the bulk of China's people are found in the eastern third of the country.

Any good measure of the capacity of land to support people should consider the quality of the land for agricultural production, subsurface mineral content, and the characteristics of the political, economic, and social institutions which humans have created to deal with their natural advantages or disadvantages. Creativeness, skill, entrepreneurship, capital, and technology are at least equal in importance to soils and minerals in determining the human carrying capacity of the land. Further, few regions today are entirely self-sufficient. Through trade, they draw portions of their support from and contribute to the support of nearby and distant regions. In all these respects, positions of peoples, regions, and nations change through time. Whereas England once exported coal and iron ore and commanded a far-flung empire from which it drew minerals and foodstuffs for an expanding population, it is now hampered by shortages of the minerals once exported and its favored position in world trade has declined dramatically. The capacity of any area to support a given population at a given level must, therefore, be constantly redefined in light of changing conditions.

Density Related to Arable Land

A detailed assessment of the land's human carrying capacity is clearly beyond the scope of this work. Some light can be shed upon the ability of an area to produce enough food for its people, however, by basing density calculations upon available quantities of arable land (land suitable for producing cultivated crops).

No specific relationship exists between the number of people living in an area and the availability of arable land. Several of the more populous nations have had large populations for centuries and the number of inhabitants has grown roughly in proportion to the food supply or to the ingenuity of local inhabitants to extract larger quantities of food from available land. Ability to transport food in quantity over long distances, especially over land routes, is a recent development. Through most of history the population of a particular locality grew or declined with fluctuations in *local* food output. Even in modern times the capability of nations to supplement domestically produced food depends largely on their relative wealth and technical ability and on the existence of a surplus supply of food somewhere else in the world. Wealthier nations can normally outbid poor nations for available surpluses, meaning that the poor nations are more effectively restricted to supplies that can be produced domestically. Because poor nations are more locally dependent than wealthy nations, the ratio between population and quantity of arable land is more significant to the poor than to the rich nations. This is emphasized in that the limited wealth, limited technical ability, and cultural resistance against new methods of crop production in poor lands are reflected in lower per acre and per worker yields than in wealthier and more technically advanced areas.

In China, only 11 percent of the surface is arable, and most of that is in the eastern one-third of the country (Table 4-1). In the United States 19 percent of the land surface is arable, and again the majority is within the eastern half of the country. Moreover, whereas China's population is roughly *four* times that of the United States, her population density of more than 2,000 people per square mile of arable land is greater than *six* times the approximately 300 persons per square mile of arable land in the United States. China, therefore, has only about one-third acre of arable land per person compared with more than 3 acres per person in the United States. About half of India's land is arable, giving her almost as much arable land as the United States although she has only one-third of the surface area. Because of her larger population, however, India has three times as many people per square mile of arable land as the United States. In Japan there are approximately 4,500 people per square mile of arable land, or more than 7 people for every arable acre in the country.

Some areas which appear to have very low population densities when the number of people is measured against total land area are among the most densely populated parts of the earth when number of people is calculated per square mile of arable land (Compare Fig. 4-2 with Fig. 4-3). Many nations in Africa and most of those in Asia, Europe, and Latin America have more people per square mile of arable land than the United States, Canada, or Australia. These last three nations are also the world's major sources of surplus foods. Saudi Arabia, which has only about 8 persons per square mile of total land area has nearly 4,000 persons per square mile of arable land. This is more than four times the arable land density in India and twice that of China.

The quality and productivity of arable land varies substantially. Much of the more marginal arable land is in wheat and other small grains and is lacking in adequate moisture, or the growing season is too short for the land to be highly productive. The vast wheat lands of the Soviet Union suffer from both moisture deficiencies and short growing seasons, and much of the wheat- and cotton-growing portion of India is marginally arable. Although amount of arable land is a better indicator of potential productivity than total land area, considerations of productivity must also include the qualities

TABLE 4–1. Percentage of Land Which Is Arable — Selected Nations

Nation	Percentage of Land Which Is Arable[a]	Nation	Percentage of Land Which Is Arable[a]
AFRICA		**LATIN AMERICA**	
Nigeria	23.6	Brazil	3.5
Egypt	2.7	Mexico	12.1
Ethiopia	10.3	Argentina	7.0
South Africa	9.9	Colombia	4.4
Congo, Dem. Rep.	1.8	Venezuela	5.7
Sudan	2.8	Chile	6.1
Algeria	3.0	Ecuador	10.7
Tanzania	12.7	Bolivia	2.8
Uganda	16.0	El Salvador	30.3
Ghana	10.7	Honduras	7.3
Angola	0.7	Paraguay	2.2
Rhodesia	4.7		
Ivory Coast	6.4	**EUROPE**	
Zambia	2.6	Germany (West)	33.4
Niger	11.5	United Kingdom	30.7
Libya	1.9	USSR	10.3
		Italy	50.8
ASIA		France	33.1
China	11.2	Spain	40.8
India	49.6	Poland	50.3
Japan	16.2	Romania	44.1
Thailand	21.9	Germany (East)	46.3
Turkey	33.5	Czechoslovakia	42.5
Korea (South)	22.9	The Netherlands	28.8
Burma	23.4	Hungary	60.7
Vietnam (North)	12.7	Greece	29.2
Vietnam (South)	17.2	Sweden	7.1
Malaysia	18.9	Austria	20.6
Saudi Arabia	0.2	Denmark	60.9
Syria	35.9	Finland	8.1
Iran	7.0	Norway	2.6
		Switzerland	16.2
ANGLO-AMERICA			
United States	19.8		
Canada	4.2		

[a]Includes orchard land.

SOURCE: *Oxford World Atlas* (New York: Oxford University Press, 1973), p. xi.

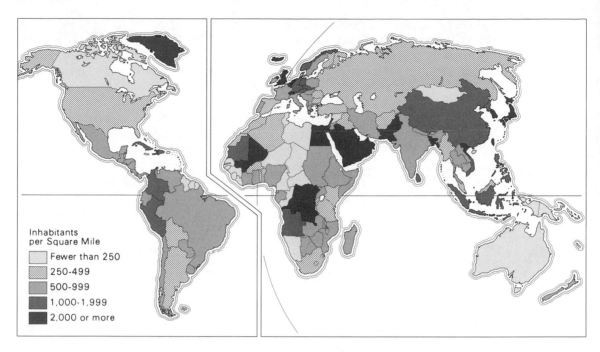

Fig. 4-3. Population density per square mile of arable land. [From *Oxford World Atlas* (New York: Oxford University Press, 1973), p. xi; and "World Population Data Sheet" (Washington, D.C.: Population Reference Bureau, Inc., 1976).]

of soils and climates as well as the cultural characteristics of those who live upon and work the land.

WORLD PATTERNS OF POPULATION GROWTH

The growth of population has been described as a "bomb" and as an "explosion." The intensity of the explosion or the length of the fuse on the bomb, however, varies significantly from place to place over the earth. Predictions of future population growth are handicapped by inadequate data and the inability of forecasters to know precisely what events will influence growth. The only forecasts included here, therefore, are based upon current rates of growth, and they are made for purposes of illustration rather than prognostication.

In describing population growth, demographers (population specialists) use terms such as the *crude birth rate* (number per thousand people in the total population), the *crude death rate*, the *crude rate of natural increase* (number of births minus the number of deaths), *rate of growth* (percent increase in the total population in one year), the *infant mortality rate* (number of infants dying, per thousand born, during the first year of life), and *life expectancy* (mean number of years of expectation of life at birth). Rates of growth are affected not only by births and deaths but also by emigration and immigration and by the age and sex composition of a population.

World population has grown geometrically (exponentially) during recent decades, with numbers of people doubling in shorter and shorter periods of time (Fig. 4-1). Among the larger regions of the world, growth rates are highest in Middle America, tropical South America, and northern and eastern Africa (Fig. 4-4). Lowest growth rates are in Europe, North America, and the Soviet Union (Table 4-2). At rates of growth prevailing during 1978, the world population would double in only 41 years. The doubling time averages only about 27 years in South America, 26 years in Africa, and 36 years in Asia. In Europe, on the other hand, the doubling time exceeds 100 years in many nations and in the United Kingdom, Austria, Belgium, and East and West Germany, either zero or negative growth rates have been reached. In North America the doubling time is approximately 116 years, and it is 77 years in the Soviet Union.

The share of the world's population living in the developed nations increased from about 22 percent in 1800 to a peak of approximately 34 per-

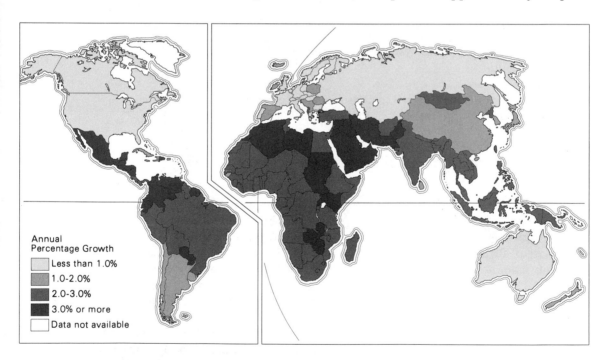

Fig. 4-4. Rates of population growth, 1978. (Courtesy, Washington, D.C.: Population Reference Bureau, Inc., 1978.)

TABLE 4–2. Population Data for Major World Regions, 1978

Area	Estimated Size of Population (Millions)	Crude Birth Rate[a]	Crude Death Rate[a]	Growth Rate (%)	Years to Double Population	Infant Mortality Rate	Life Expectancy (in Years)	Per Capita Gross National Product (U.S. Dollars)
WORLD	4,219	29	12	1.7	41	99	60	$1,650
Africa	436	46	19	2.7	26	147	46	440
Asia	2,433	30	12	1.9	36	105	58	610
Anglo–America	242	15	9	0.6	116	15	73	7,850
Middle America	87	42	8	3.3	21	68	63	1,000
Tropical South America	188	37	9	2.8	25	98	61	1,090
Temperate South America	40	23	9	1.4	50	57	66	1,400
Northern Europe	82	13	12	0.1	693	13	72	4,910
Western Europe	153	12	11	0.1	693	14	72	6,900
Eastern Europe	108	18	11	0.7	99	25	70	2,820
Southern Europe	137	17	9	0.8	87	24	71	2,620
USSR	261	18	9	0.9	77	28	69	2,760
Oceania	22	21	9	1.2	58	41	68	4,730

[a]Crude rates of births and deaths refer to number of births or deaths per thousand persons in the total population.

SOURCE: "World Population Data Sheet," (Washington, D.C.: Population Reference Bureau, Inc. 1978).

cent in 1920. During this period birth rates remained relatively high in the developed areas even though death rates were declining. The major drop in death rates (especially in infant mortality) occurred after 1900, however, and a substantial decline in birth rates took place during the 1920s and 1930s. The sharp rise in birth rates that followed World War II was apparently temporary, for during the 1950s birth rates again declined, and they have continued to decline since that time. Because of their falling birth rates, the proportion of the world's population living in the developed nations dropped from about 33 percent in 1940 to approximately 29 percent in 1978.

Factors Associated with Variable Growth Rates

The most obvious difference between areas of high and low rates of population growth is in relative affluence. Lowest rates of growth occur among the wealthiest; best educated; and most urbanized, industrialized, optimistic, and materialistic peoples where health care standards are good to excellent and where old age security is provided through state plans.

Highest rates of growth occur among the poorest; least educated; and most rural, agricultural, and fatalistic peoples where health care standards are low and where old age security is provided by children.

The influence upon population growth rates of philosophical, economic, and attitudinal differences among various culture groups was illustrated in the Gallup International Research Institute's first survey of global public opinion in 1976 [1]. The results of the poll indicated that only 11 percent and 17 percent of persons living in Anglo-America and western Europe, respectively, wished that their countries had larger populations, compared with 38, 49, and 82 percent of those living in the Far East, Latin America, and Africa, respectively. The same poll showed that as many as four or more children were considered desirable for a young married couple by 9 and 18 percent of those living in western Europe and Anglo-America but by 31, 33, and 79 percent of those living in the Far East, Latin America, and Africa, respectively. A substantial majority of those in western Europe and Anglo-America considered two, one, or no children as the ideal number compared to only 4 percent of Africans and 31 percent of those in Latin America and the Far East.

Basic Philosophical Differences.   At the risk of oversimplification, we might group the world's peoples into two classes: those who welcome change and those who resist change. Those who resist change we shall call *fatalists*, and those who welcome change we shall call *optimists*. Fatalism, basically, is the belief that individual lives are preordained by supernatural forces. Optimism, on the other hand, is the belief that, through their own acts or through working in concert with God, people can positively alter conditions of adversity. These two basic philosophies are discussed more fully in Chapter 7. Suffice it to say here that people who feel that they have no control over their destinies have no incentive to practice birth control or to attempt to limit the sizes of their families. Where optimism is the basic philosphy, however, limiting family size may be seen as a means through which individual welfare can be enhanced. If the financial and other resources of a family or of a nation are distributed to a relatively small number of people, a larger share of wealth is available to each individual than when the wealth is distributed to a large number. Fatalism, therefore, is a prevailing characteristic among the poor, high-growth populations of the world, whereas optimism has found its greatest expression among the most affluent peoples where growth rates are low.

Health Care and Old Age Security.   A good surrogate for comparing relative levels of health care among the nations of the world is the infant mortality rate (Fig. 4–5). The most significant factor of all those which have produced the high rates of population growth during recent decades has been the decline in infant mortality associated with widespread adoption of modern

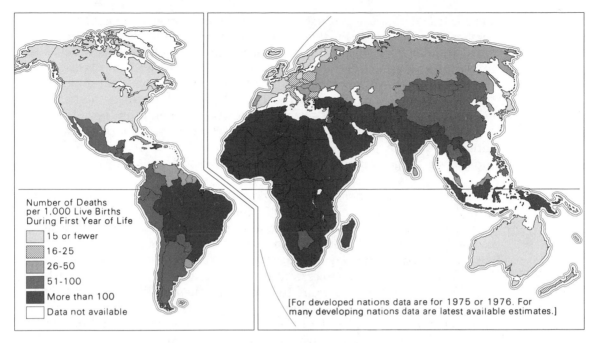

Number of Deaths
per 1,000 Live Births
During First Year of Life

☐ 15 or fewer
▨ 16-25
▧ 26-50
▨ 51-100
■ More than 100
☐ Data not available

[For developed nations data are for 1975 or 1976. For many developing nations data are latest available estimates.]

Fig. 4-5. Infant mortality rates. (Courtesy, Washington, D.C.: Population Reference Bureau, Inc., 1978.)

methods of immunization and sanitation. Although infant mortality remains relatively high in many parts of Africa, Latin America, and non-Soviet Asia, it has dropped significantly in nearly all parts of the world during the present century. The decline in infant mortality has diminished the need for a large number of births to ensure survival of a family or of a race. In most affluent areas, therefore, birth rates have been reduced substantially. Demands created by each child for food, clothing, schooling, and the amenities of the "good life" are much higher than in poor societies and are best obtained if families are small. In most poor societies, on the other hand, birth rates have remained about as they were when infant mortality rates were much higher. Children are often the only luxuries available to families; they provide labor for work in the fields, and they provide the only old age security their parents are likely to obtain. Furthermore, within underdeveloped societies birth control devices are little understood and they are often prohibitively expensive. Even "the pill" has frequently been ineffective in reducing the number of births because the peoples of many undeveloped areas have not learned the discipline of following regular schedules. Sterilization as a means to reduce birth rates requires medical services not normally available, and incentives must be offered to obtain voluntary submission to the sterilization procedures. When India offered transistor radios to men who volunteered for

sterilization during the 1960s, the country's relatively small electronics industry became overtaxed. Further, with fewer than 30,000 physicians to serve a
population in excess of 600 million, the number of sterilizations which could
be performed was hardly adequate to bring about a significant reduction in
the birth rate. More recently, along with a move to strengthen the powers of
the central government and in the face of past failures of democratic processes to reduce population growth, laws were enacted in India which posed
the threat of fines and jail sentences for parents who had more than two or
three children. A few months following passage and attempts to enforce
those laws, the government which passed them was toppled.

Education, Urbanization, and Industrialization. Lowest rates of population
growth occur among the most highly educated, urbanized, and industrialized
societies (Fig. 4-4). Education, urbanization, and industrialization are in
themselves positively associated, and each of these factors is positively associated with rising socioeconomic aspirations. Among well-educated, urbanized, or industrialized peoples, status is acquired largely through knowledge,
position, and wealth. The desire to perpetuate the family through large numbers of children gives way to aims such as promoting the education, health,
and material welfare of each of a small number of children. Laws prohibiting
the use of child labor in most types of urban employment and therefore
prohibiting the use of children to enhance family income have further
eroded the advantage of large families in urban areas.

In theory most relatively poor nations are in a "transitional" stage between a primitive subsistence economy and a modern, complex, industrialized economy. How long this transition will require, or how long it will
take to "make a 'baby grand' seem more desirable than a 'grand baby'" is
not clear [2]. Efforts to educate and to provide urban industrial jobs for
the population of undeveloped societies face severe obstacles. The multi-
tudes of peoples involved, linguistic diversity, the large percentage of those
in such societies who are of school age, the lack of qualified teachers, lack
of capital, deficiencies in food production, the lag in cultural adjustment to
new life-styles, lack of skills among workers, limited purchasing power,
credit restrictions, and limited ability to purchase or to develop essential raw
materials and processing facilities are virtually overwhelming obstacles to
rapid advancement.

ECONOMIC CONSEQUENCES OF POPULATION GROWTH

The economic consequences of population growth are extensive, affecting the quality of the physical environment as well as the social and economic
welfare of current and future generations. Some economic consequences of

rapid growth are negative, and some are positive. Some economic aspects of slow growth or no growth are positive, and some are negative. Whether population growth should be encouraged or discouraged in any area depends in theory on whether or not that area has surpassed or has yet to reach an *optimum population*. A precise definition of optimum population is illusive, however, and if a meaningful definition is given, its application must reflect a particular set of objectives for a given population group at a given time. The objectives must include the level of living sought for the population, what standards of environmental quality are desired, the extent to which knowledge and technology have been developed and can be made available to the population, and the variety and quality of the available resource base. Because of changes in knowledge, technology, the relative values of particular resources, and national goals, the number of people considered optimum for any area requires constant reevaluation. Despite its abstract and illusive nature, however, the concept of an optimum population, which we shall

Indian women being instructed in family planning. (Reprinted from *War on Hunger*, a publication of the Agency for International Development.)

loosely define as the number of people required to maximize long-term and short-term welfare, provides a useful basis against which to evaluate population growth.

In developing nations with meager absolute economic growth, a high rate of population increase will likely result in the following problems:

1. Total output of goods and total wealth generated must be spread over a rapidly increasing number of people, with smaller shares available per person than if the growth rate was smaller. Raising living standards under these circumstances is especially difficult.
2. A large proportion of the population will consist of young people, creating heavy demands upon the economic resources of such areas to provide educational and other services for the young.
3. Major difficulties are encountered in providing jobs for the large number of people entering the labor force each year.
4. Demand for new resources and pressures upon the land are likely to increase in some proportion to the increase in the population.
5. If the population increases faster than domestic food production, scarce funds may have to be diverted from domestic developmental programs and from the purchase of technology and talent to the purchase of imported foods. Balance of payments problems and increased scarcity of investment capital are likely to diminish already low levels of living further in the poorest nations.
6. Lack of rural employment opportunities and the inability of the land held by individual families to provide food for their growing number of members may force large numbers of people who are ill-prepared for urban employment into cities which are ill-prepared to receive them. Employment in cities in poor nations is not characteristically industrial but is menial service jobs offering low pay. Urban residents, on the other hand, are much larger consumers of energy and other resources than rural residents, and they often demand sophisticated goods and services that must be imported from more affluent areas with consequent losses of investment capital and foreign exchange needed for development.

A low rate of population growth, or zero growth, carries its own set of problems, including

1. A population of increasing age, with a rising percentage of the total population having been removed from the labor force as a result of age or because of infirmities that come with age. The strain upon the labor force to provide facilities and services for an aging population may equal or exceed the strain of providing education and other services to youth in a rapidly growing population.

2. Older people tend toward conservative economic and political viewpoints; they tend to resist change more vigorously than the young; and as they gain strength through numbers, they may be able to block needed social, economic, and political reforms.
3. Funds are likely to be diverted from research and other developmental programs into nonregenerating areas associated with the needs of the aged.
4. An aging population where a relatively small percentage of people are in the younger age groups may find that its potential military strength is being eroded because of the reduced number of youths available for military service. This may be seen as a particularly serious problem by small or sparsely populated nations.

Problems associated with an aging population are already visible in many of the more affluent parts of the world where growth rates have been declining for several decades. At the same time, problems associated with a rapidly growing population are well-established within most of the world's poor societies. Where population is growing faster than economic output, levels of living tend to deteriorate and the economic and social advancements which may lead to changes in attitudes toward large families are postponed, perpetuating high rates of growth.

CONCLUSIONS

For the most part, those portions of the world which have made the least progress during recent times are also the most crowded and most malnourished, with high rates of population increase and economies which are agriculturally based. Although the poorest areas have made some economic progress during recent decades, much greater absolute economic growth has occurred in the rich nations and the gap between rich and poor peoples has widened (Fig. 2-1). The widening gap may be explained in large part in that poor peoples must expend several times as much effort as the rich to accomplish similar absolute levels of achievement. It also seems apparent that the capital, ideas, innovations, technology, and managerial skills required to solve the problems of poor nations — if they are to be solved at all — must come primarily from the affluent societies.

Apparently the rate of world population increase reached its peak during the 1960s (at about 2.0 percent per year) and may decline to approximately 1.5 percent or lower prior to the end of the twentieth century. The explosive rates of growth occurring during the three decades following World War II reflected the rapid decline in infant mortality rates during that period. Eventually those prevented from dying during infancy will die of old age;

death rates will rise; and the rate of growth should decline. The absolute increase in numbers of people is more important than the relative, or rate of, increase, however, and the total number of people added to the world's population will probably increase each year at least until the end of the twentieth century. At growth rates prevailing in 1978 it is estimated that approximately 72 million people were being added to the world's population each year. Because of the larger population base, however, that number should rise to some 90 million people annually by the year 2000 even if the rate of increase drops to 1.5 percent per year. To feed an annual increment of 75 million people requires an increase in grain output of approximately 20 million tons per year, an amount greater than the Canadian wheat crop [3].

At the same time that population has been increasing by 1.7 to 2.0 percent annually, production of food and industrial commodities has been increasing at an annual rate of approximately 5 percent [4]. Whereas the bulk of the increase in population is occurring in the less developed nations (about 85 percent), however, the bulk of the increase in production of wealth and goods is taking place in the developed nations. If we assume that about 30 percent of the world's people are relatively affluent, that the remaining 70 percent are poor, and that the purchasing power of each affluent person is approximately five times that of each poor person, the total impact of the affluent upon world resources is more than double that of the poor. Data such as these offer the spectre of a raped and devastated planet within the near future, with any increase in numbers of affluent in the world simply hastening the process of destruction. At the same time, inhabitants of the poor nations are straining to improve their life-styles and to catch up with the affluent peoples of Europe and Anglo-America. Herein is one of the great paradoxes of our time. To provide the necessary incentives to the poor peoples of the world to reduce family sizes and therefore to lower rates of population growth will apparently require that methods be found for substantially raising the living standards of the poor. But by raising living standards and levels of material consumption we run the risk of placing such severe strains upon the world's resource base, and indeed upon the entire physical environment, as to seriously damage the human habitat. It is likely that only through maximum efforts to advance the state of knowledge and understanding in all spheres of human intellect can the most serious consequences to humanity be blunted or avoided.

REFERENCES

[1] George Gallup, "Population Explosion Is Likely to Continue," *The Knoxville News-Sentinel*, November 11, 1976, p. C-2.

[2] Erich W. Zimmerman, *World Resources and Industries* (New York: Harper and Row, Publishers, 1951), p. 110.

[3] Nathan Keyfitz, "World Resources and the World Middle Class," *Scientific American*, **235**, 1976, p. 28.

[4] *Ibid.*, p. 29.

CHAPTER FIVE

disparities in urban development

INTRODUCTION

The human condition is increasingly being shaped by cities. To be civilized is, by its strict Latin definition, to live in cities. The percentage of the world's population living in cities (urbanization) is increasing at a much faster pace than general population growth. Even within developing nations the pace of urbanization is accelerating. Hundreds of thousands of migrants from rural areas within developing nations pour into overcrowded cities in search of a better life than they can find in the countryside. Many become disillusioned because the rate of urban job formation, even in economies that are rapidly developing, cannot keep pace with the swelling city populations. Whether they are called shantytowns, favellas, bustees, or bideonvilles, the most recent arrivals to the city often end up living in squatter slums at the periphery of the city. Many of these squatter settlements do not have adequate or safe water, sanitary facilities, or decent housing.

In developed societies, such as the United States or western Europe, urban areas are also troubled. There is an increasing polarization between the poor, often minority, population living in the central city and the relatively affluent suburbanites at the periphery of the more densely settled central areas. The search for residential living space at low densities has created a sprawl of settlements unparalleled in human history. Development of such "low-slung and far-flung" cities has been encouraged by the tremendous mobility afforded by the automobile.

The problems of the cities in the developed and developing world have elements of communality but the disparities are more striking. The purpose of this chapter is to describe patterns of urban settlement at the world scale. The internal structure of modern cities and the relationship of those cities to the surrounding countryside in the developed and developing world will be examined so that the processes causing structural disparities can be understood. Modern urban ills will be reviewed, and a prognosis about the urban future will be attempted.

Shakespeare once wrote, "What is a city but the people?" Indeed, the combined talents and creative genius of humankind are best revealed in cities, as is the worst in human nature. As we shape our cities, so they, in turn, shape our lives. One of the most important ways in which cities shape our lives is through their role as job providers. Cities are magnets which attract manufacturing and service activities. Agglomeration of businesses sustain cities and give them function. Are our twentieth-century cities functioning properly? Are present cities the hope for future society or an outmoded legacy of an earlier era sadly in need of restructuring?

BASIC DEFINITIONS

The term *urban*, as used here, refers to any settlement of at least 20,000 inhabitants. This minimum cutoff value is a commonly though by no means universally accepted figure. The United States Bureau of the Census, for example, defines an urban place as a settlement with no less than 2,500 inhabitants. Demographic data provided by the United Nations, the most accurate source of information for many of the developing nations, record the number of people living in urban places of 20,000 or greater. The United Nations relies heavily upon the percentage of a country's population living in urban places of at least 20,000 as a key indicator of economic development [1]. In 1976 this percentage was 58 in North America, whereas in most of Asia it was less than 15; in tropical Africa, less than 8 (Fig. 5-1).

The percentage of a country's population living in urban areas is referred to as that nation's degree of *urbanization*. Urbanization is a process that has a beginning and an end (i.e., the urban population cannot exceed 100 percent of the total population). When a nation's cities are growing but the rural population is growing at a comparable or faster rate than urban population, level of urbanization will not increase [2]. The concomitants of becoming urban include changing life-styles, a decreased emphasis upon the family as an integrating force, increased occupational division of labor, and social heterogeneity [3].

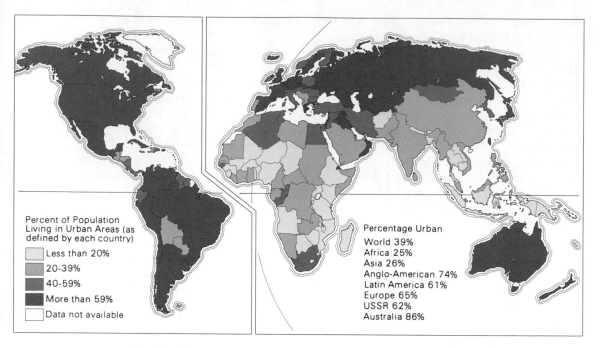

Fig. 5-1. Percentage of population living in urban areas, 1978.* [From "World Population Data Sheet" (Washington, D.C.: Population Reference Bureau, Inc., 1978).]

PATTERNS AND CHARACTERISTICS OF URBAN GROWTH

Today approximately 43 percent of the world's population lives in urban areas of at least 20,000, and the growth of urban dwellers is increasing at a faster annual rate (3 percent) than their rural counterparts (1 percent). The urban growth rate is 4 percent in the developing world and 2 percent in the developed countries.

If current growth trends continue, Europe's total population will be 23 percent larger by the year 2000, whereas its *urban* population will have grown by 62 percent. In the developing world the rate of urbanization will be nothing short of spectacular. By 2000 the number of people living in cities will increase fourfold in East Africa, fivefold in South Asia and northern and southern Africa, sixfold in Asia (excluding South Asia), sevenfold in Latin America, and more than ninefold in tropical Africa.

Large cities will bear the brunt of this massive growth. In 1975, for example, 23 percent of the population of the United Kingdom lived in

*Percentage of population living in urban areas as defined by each country.

London, 16 percent of all Frenchmen lived in Paris, 14 percent of the Japanese were in Tokyo–Yokohama, and 32 percent of all Americans lived in the urban agglomeration along the northeastern seaboard from Boston, Massachusetts, to Richmond, Virginia [4]. Increasingly, large urban places are coalescing into multimetropolitan conurbations or *megalopolises* such as the Rhine–Ruhr Basin in West Germany and the seven cities of the Randstad in The Netherlands.

HISTORICAL DEVELOPMENT OF URBAN AREAS

Preindustrial Urban Development

The city as a form of human organization has its antecedents in the rural agricultural village of more than 5,000 years ago. It was not until livestock were domesticated and crops were planted that societies could at last end their nomadic existence and become sedentary. By applying advancing technologies such as irrigation and the use of draft animals, wheeled vehicles, and metal implements, agricultural productivity increased beyond the level needed for subsistence. Some labor, therefore, could be freed to engage in activities such as the production of artistic and utilitarian articles which could be bartered or traded for other needed goods. Scholars debate whether the production of an agricultural surplus enabled cities to develop or whether the natural growth of trade between complementary regions allowed the accumulation of surpluses and enhanced the opportunities for agricultural innovation. Such innovation increased productivity and allowed even greater numbers of people to leave the land and seek alternative urban employment. Whatever the temporal sequence of development, the earliest cities differed in significant ways from their modern counterparts. By contemporary standards most of the ancient cities were small. Rome, during the reign of Caesar Augustus, had about 300,000 residents and most cities were much smaller. Perhaps less than 3 percent of the world's population lived in cities at that time. Although the degree of urbanization was not large, the impacts of cities upon the economy and social structure of early civilizations were unmistakable. Cities were the points of articulation for trade, often strategically located for defense against enemies and to enable interaction among trading allies. City-based civilizations flourished first in fertile river valleys such as the Tigris and Euphrates in present day Iraq, the Indus valley of India, the Yellow River (Yangtze) of China, and the Nile Valley of Egypt. The functions of the early cities are not completely understood. One urban expert contends that most of these "cities" were centers for religious ceremonies. These ceremonial centers also served as the foci for social, economic, and political organization within the regions in which they were located [5]. The resource base limited the degree of urbanization in

Two solutions to providing housing for rapidly growing urban populations. The top photograph represents a spontaneous settlement in a developing nation. Reprinted from *Agenda*, a publication of the Agency for International Development. The bottom photograph is the Habitat '67 Apartment Complex for Expo '67 in Montreal. (Reprinted from *Finance and Development*, a publication of the International Monetary Fund and the World Bank Group.)

early societies. In modern societies there is a complementary division of labor between city and surrounding countryside whereby the hinterland produces some of the food for the city while the city supplies goods and services for its tributary area. Some urban scholars suggest that ancient cities were more exploitive of their hinterlands, depending on rural residents to supply them with food and tribute [6].

With the invasion of Rome by Teutonic tribes, urban-based civilization in western Europe came to a temporary end. Urbanization continued to flourish in the Byzantine Empire with its capital city of Constantinople and in the civilizations of the Far East during the "Dark Ages" of western Europe.

Feudalism during the Middle Ages of western Europe was based upon personal oaths of loyalty (fealty) of knights to the nobility which dominated the upper classes of European society, whereas the vast majority of the population cked out a living as peasant farmers (serfs). Only when a noble-man wished to finance a war against an enemy did control over a given territory and the taxing privileges that went with that control become an important consideration. As the Middle Ages waned, jurisdictional boundaries became more important, as did centrally located administrative cities. With the Renaissance, urban-based society, especially in northern Italy, once again flourished in powerful city-states such as Venice and Genoa.

The Industrial City. The accumulation of capital in European nations, brought about by the Age of Exploration, also helped to transform urban centers. Large European cities became the nerve centers of an expanding network of finance, trade, and commerce on a theretofore unknown scale. Economic expansion was accompanied by a population explosion in the cities. For centuries the filth and squalor of the compact, densely settled urban places had discouraged high rates of natural increase in urban areas. Communicable diseases were easily transmitted in these unsanitary urban environments and urban areas had higher death rates than surrounding countrysides. Coupled with high death rates were lowered fertility rates as families adapted to urban life-styles which were less family-centered than rural villages. In many cities the net effect of high death rates and low fertility rates was a negative rate of natural increase. Only by rural migrants entering into urban occupations were such cities able to grow at all, and then only slowly. Bubonic plague, the infamous "Black Death" that was the scourge of western Europe, is estimated to have killed between one-fourth and one-third of the entire European population during the Middle Ages. Cholera, smallpox, and similar diseases kept the rate of natural increase low.

New agricultural innovations and rising health standards resulted in over-populated rural areas with high unemployment rates. Many of these people were pushed into the cities in search of alternative employment. The growth of manufacturing spurred by the industrial revolution provided jobs for

millions of others seeking improved job opportunities. The rate of urbanization was unparalleled in human history. The populations of England's largest
cities (100,000 and above) grew almost ninefold between 1800 and 1900.
London grew from less than 800,000 to more than 4 million. The rapid
growth of urban places created severe social disruption. The working class
districts of Europe and the ethnic ghettos of American cities were almost
intolerable. Severe housing shortages forced families to live together in tene-
ment structures at extremely high densities.

The push of landless peasants into the burgeoning industrial European
cities of the nineteenth century bears a resemblance to what is happening
today in many of the developing nations. The major difference is that the
urban economies of today's developing nations are not always expanding
quickly enough to absorb the new arrivals. Industrial jobs were the lure and
the hope of many European rural migrants of the nineteenth century. As
wave after wave of rural migrants and immigrants arrived at these industrial
behemoths in search of new opportunity, their lives were changed by the
experience. Some groups were easily assimilated into the acquisitive capitalistic system. For example, immigrants from northern Europe were accul-
turated into the mainstream of American economic life within a generation;
for southern Europeans and other ethnic groups the process was longer. For
blacks, visibly distinct and a target of racial prejudice, the process seemed
interminable. The disparities of income were so pronounced that a reaction
was needed. Social reform programs were instituted to help the destitute.
Many charitable organizations are legacies of the early social reformers who
responded to the relative deprivation of urban slum dwellers.

The Postindustrial Metropolis. Although capitals and major port cities in
the third world have the outward trappings of modernity, it is largely in the
developed world where large cities have progressed until they have become
handlers of capital, dispensers of information, organizers of corporate institutions, and molders of opinion on a huge scale. The most viable cities
have changed their economic bases (i.e., their predominant economic activities) as the structures of regional, national, and international markets have
changed. For example, Chicago first grew to preeminence as a center for
meat-packing, agricultural implement manufacture, and steelmaking. The
meat-packing function has declined significantly in the last few years as
technology in the industry increasingly favors locations closer to sources
of cattle in the West. During 1954-1963, Chicago led all other cities in the
United States in the development of corporate office headquarters. The shift
from manufacturing to tertiary economic activity, illustrated by Chicago's
transition, is by no means an isolated example of such a change. Rather,
Chicago's changed economic base is symptomatic of a shift in emphasis that

occurred in most large cities in economically advanced societies. Commercial, office, banking, scientific, and intellectual endeavors have become the major economic bases of modern cities as manufacturing technology has spread into hinterland areas of developed nations. When methods of production became standardized, manufacturers were often able to substitute a higher percentage of semiskilled and unskilled workers for more costly skilled labor. As transportation linkages increased, central location in a major metropolis was no longer a great advantage and, in fact, in cases of extremely congested cities, became a detriment to industrial location. Some manufacturing enterprises moved to areas of the country offering cheaper labor. The vacuums created by such departures are filled by service-related industries.

Cities are becoming increasingly interdependent as the transportation and communication networks bind them into a national and even international community. The locational freedom allowed by the quantum leap in political and economic integration that has taken place in the last quarter century has allowed cities to coalesce so that the suburbs of one central city blend into the suburban sprawl of another. Sprawl is possible because of improved transportation technology and the lessened need for residences to be close to jobs. The "spread city" is by no means confined to the United States, although the megalopolis (600-mile strip city from Boston to Washington) along the Eastern seaboard is the archetypal example. The Randstand in The Netherlands (centering upon Rotterdam and Amsterdam), the Ruhr district of West Germany (heavy industrial and thriving commercial centers), and the industrial conglomeration around Tokyo Bay from Tokyo to Osaka are but a few examples of such spread development.

In the United States, corporate city limits are usually inadequate to express the area over which the city's influence is most directly felt. The suburbs from which a large percentage of the city's workers are drawn are also included in the government's accounting of urban areas. The major metropolitan measurement unit used in United States government statistics on population and housing is called the *Standard Metropolitan Statistical Area* (SMSA). The SMSA consists of a central city (or cities) of at least 50,000 population and also includes adjacent counties if they are essentially metropolitan in character and functionally integrated into the economic structure of the principal city. More than 280 such SMSA's existed in 1977 (Fig. 5-2).

In some cases even the SMSA is inadequate to express the influence of metropolitan dominance. The city of New York, for example, has vast influence over large sections of the state of New York as well as over suburbs in southwestern Connecticut and northeastern New Jersey. The New York SMSA had a 1970 population of more than 15 million, whereas the central city of New York had a population of only about half that amount.

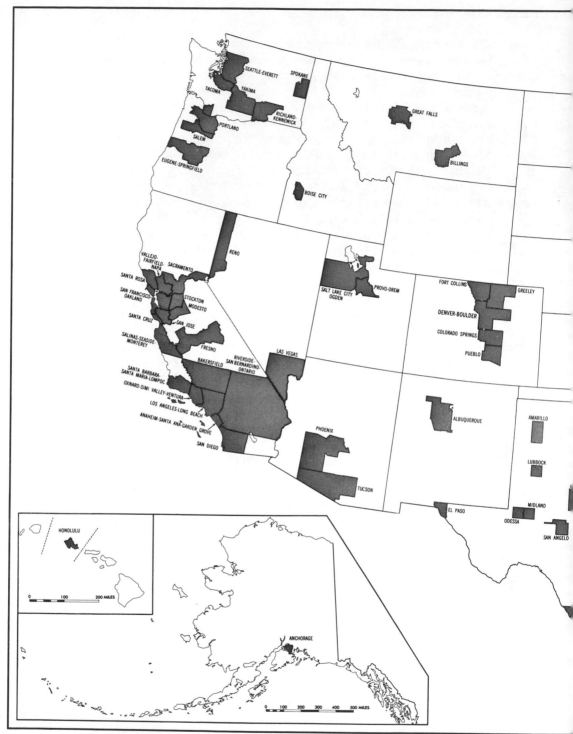

Fig. 5-2. Standard metropolitan statistical areas in the United States, 1977. (Courtesy, Washington, D.C.: Geography Division, Bureau of the Census, U.S. Department of Commerce.)

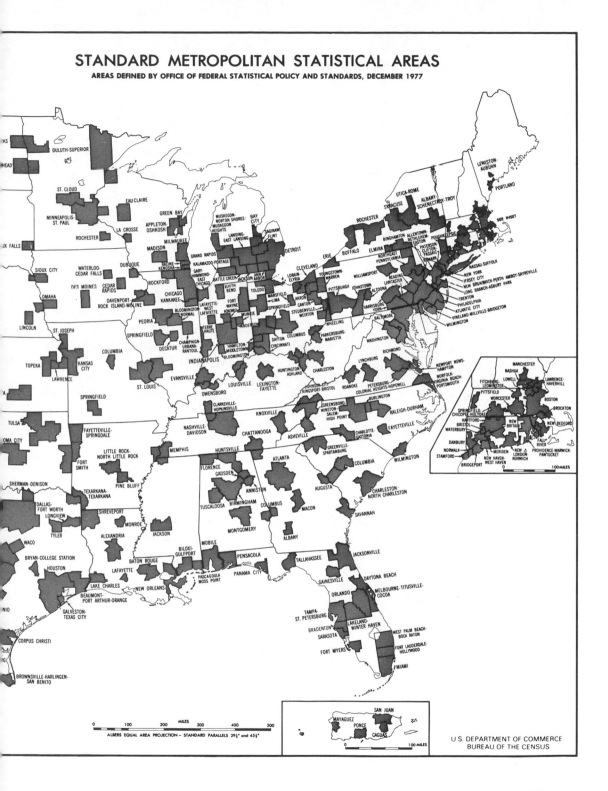

STANDARD METROPOLITAN STATISTICAL AREAS
AREAS DEFINED BY OFFICE OF FEDERAL STATISTICAL POLICY AND STANDARDS, DECEMBER 1977

U.S. DEPARTMENT OF COMMERCE
BUREAU OF THE CENSUS

DISPARITIES IN URBAN MORPHOLOGY

Although it is difficult to generalize about the structural form (morphology) of cities, certain distinctions can be drawn between cities located in developed nations and those in the developing countries. These differences can be classified into three types—land-use mixtures, density differences, and poverty concentrations.

Land-Use Mixtures. In most cities of the developing world, residential, commercial, and industrial land uses are intermingled, whereas in most developed nations these land uses are separated into specialized functional districts. Separation of land uses in developed cities is largely a twentieth-century phenomenon. Intermingled land uses in the cities of the developing countries are almost identical to the morphology of cities in the developed world before the arrival of trams and trolleys in the late nineteenth century. The major factor contributing to these land-use differences is the availability of low-cost, intracity transportation. When the public transportation system consists of pedicabs and other crude or relatively expensive modes, as in most developing nations, a constraint is placed upon the choice of residential location. Merchants often reside in the rear of their shops or in small apartments above them. People of different means and backgrounds reside near the center of the city with very little evident differentiation in their social status. The social caste system in many Arab countries and in Hindu areas of India is based upon sharp *individual* class distinctions, but when the aggregated residential structures of such cities are examined, these social differences are less evident.

Improved intraurban transportation in developed nations allows individuals to separate themselves according to social class, producing a pattern of homogeneous neighborhoods which might be called a modern "spatial caste system." The outward movement of the wealthy, and later of the middle class, started before the twentieth century and increased as modes of transportation changed from the horse-drawn omnibus to the cable car, street car, and electric intraurban railway. Spatial separation between workplace and residence increased tremendously when private automobiles became accessible to the majority of the population in the post-World War II era.

Density Differences. Along with outward expansion of the cities in the developed nations came a lowering of population density. In the non-Western city, densities are still high, peaking around the central core because the core is the area of maximum accessibility. In most developed nations daytime activity in the city's core is intensive, but few people live in the area. High land values in central cities exclude nearly all residential land uses except high-rise apartment buildings. The landscape is normally dominated by commercial establishments and office structures.

The absence of resident populations in the central business district is most noticeable in the United States where tax structures and governmental policies have encouraged sprawl. Some authors have drawn an analogy between the lack of central city population and the crater of a volcano. The point at which residential population densities in such cities is greatest is within the inner city neighborhoods of the poor which are located adjacent to the commercial and office "crater" or core.

Poverty Concentrations. In Western cities residences sorted themselves out by economic status as land-use competition in the city intensified. A residential turnover process known as *filtering* is present in most Western societies. With the exception of a few fashionable inner city neighborhoods (e.g., Beacon Hill in Boston), former residences of the wealthy are purchased by the most upwardly mobile of the next lower status group. The wealthy often move away from the congestion and life-styles of the center city into new housing constructed on the city's outskirts. The filtering or trickling down of housing continues as long as home construction occurs at the periphery of the city. In most developed nations many more families are poor than wealthy. Because of this social class structure the filtering process is often not sufficient to provide enough housing to meet the demands of each progressively lower status group. The functioning of the filtering mechanism is further exacerbated by the zoning regulations imposed by many suburban municipalities which attempt to perpetuate the socioeconomic homogeneity of their populations. When demand for housing outstrips available supply, governments often intervene by building low-cost public housing for the poor. Demand for the relatively few houses made available through the filtering process may be so great that the homes are subdivided into multiple family units. Deterioration of housing quality can be rapid when such density adjustments take place.

In non-Western societies the poor, such as the landless and homeless street people who often spend much of their lives on the sidewalks of teeming cities like Calcutta, may be located in the central city. Larger numbers of the poor are, however, found in the shantytown slums of the city's periphery. Accessible locations near high-quality urban services make central location a desirable asset in such developing societies. Landless peasants from the countryside arriving in the city cannot afford the high rents in the accessible urban core. Residence in the core seems reserved for merchants, government workers, and professional people.

The question could be legitimately asked: "If conditions in the slums of large non-Western cities are so bad, why do peasants continue to migrate to the cities?" The question has no simple answer. Where already small land parcels are further subdivided among several heirs or where the firstborn is sole heir to any available land (primogeniture), excessive pressures are strong among those who do not inherit economically viable parcels of land to leave

An urban slum in India. (Courtesy, Agency for International Development.)

the rural areas (i.e., an economic push). The city is viewed as a place where life is better than the rural area left behind. Essential services, though barely available in many squatter settlements, are better than those available in the countryside. The slums may be settlements of hope rather than despair as the former village dwellers seek to improve their lot in life. Even if the chances of such improvements are slim, they may perceive their opportunities in the city to be better than the poverty of the countryside.

SYSTEMATIC DIFFERENCES BETWEEN THE CITIES OF THE DEVELOPED AND DEVELOPING NATIONS

The internal morphologies of cities in the developing nations differ in significant ways from those in the advanced nations. The manner in which cities function as integrated systems also varies greatly. In the third world, a few "islands" of modernity normally occur in the major cities surrounded by a "sea" of traditional subsistence agriculture and peasants living in rural villages. Economists refer to this disparity in modernization as a *dual economic structure*. Most of the teeming millions in India are not residing in

Calcutta, Bombay, or Madras but in more than 500,000 rural villages of less than 5,000 population.

In many countries the disparities between the few large cities and rural countryside is a legacy from the colonial era when European powers poured their resources unevenly into capitals and ports. The poor nations may contain only one very large city (sometimes referred to as a *primate city*) and many very small cities. Intermediate-sized centers which might serve as regional capitals of a fully integrated national economy are notably absent. Residents of small towns and villages often have limited choices as to where they might receive urban goods and services. This pattern of village trade domination in the distribution system stifles competition and the growth of needed intermediate-sized distribution centers [7].

Large developed countries with complex economic and social structures usually contain a full complement of cities which are functionally integrated into a national system. If the city system were ideally integrated, the population of any city in the country would bear a particular systematic relationship to the largest city in the country [8]. The interrelationship between cities of different size in such large developed nations indicates that growth in any city is transmitted throughout the urban system and changes in the urban system impinge upon each city as well.

URBAN PROBLEMS CAUSED BY GROWTH

Some urban ills can be traced directly to the inability of cities to cope with their rates of growth [9]. Cities have rarely grown according to orderly plans, although strides continue to be made in that direction as the interrelationships between growth and the quality of modern urban life are recognized. Excessive population growth places so much stress upon the quality of urban services, the physical environment, and human coping mechanisms that deterioration in the quality of life becomes perceptible to the urban residents. The consequences of uncontrolled growth are increased costs of services, loss of community identity, and deterioration of environmental quality.

Increasing Costs of Public Services. Costs of services are normally higher in dispersed, low density urban areas than within compact settlements. Recently, the costs of maintaining our largest and most densely settled cities have escalated. The infrastructure of these metropolitan areas was, for the most part, constructed during an era of abundant cheap energy. As energy costs continue to climb, so too does the cost of maintaining many of these energy-inefficient structures. The relationship between density of the settlement pattern and the cost of providing most urban public services is U-shaped (Fig. 5-3). The U-shape of the cost curve can be related to econ-

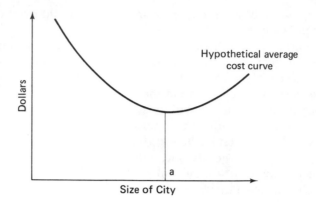

Fig. 5-3. Hypothetical costs of providing urban services as a function of city size.

omies of scale. The average cost declines out to point *a* as scale of the public facilities increases. Beyond a certain population or density level (point *a* in Fig. 5-3), diseconomies begin to occur. The population level at which economies of scale begin to occur will differ depending on the characteristics of the service in question. There may be no ideal size for an urban area, but the cost of maintaining the largest world cities may be more than their residents can bear. If the rural migration streams to the large cities of the third world continue unabated without a commensurate increase in job opportunities, the quality of life will probably erode. Whereas the largest cities in 1975 were located in the developed nations, by 2000 the largest cities are likely to be located in the developing countries, especially in Latin America which is experiencing high rates of natural increase in urban areas. Mexico City is projected to be the world's largest city by 2000, with over 31 million residents [10]. Most of those residents will be recently displaced campesinos from rural areas, who are without jobs and often without hope.

Urban policy makers have often failed to comprehend the relationship between the impact of investments in urban services and land-use patterns. Growth is not created by the installation of new infrastructure; the infrastructure merely influences the concentration of growth which might otherwise have occurred elsewhere in the region [11]. Federal subsidies in the United States, for example, have indirectly encouraged the sprawl that characterizes American cities. The availability of subsidized highways for commuting from single-family dwellings subsidized by federally guaranteed mortgages encouraged returning servicemen and others to build in the suburbs after World War II. The pattern has since been especially aggravated by expansion of the transportation infrastructure. Federal monies fund 90 percent of interstate highway construction, up to 80 percent of mass transit investments, 75 percent of the cost of interceptor sewers and treatment plants, and 70 percent of noninterstate highways. Many of these federally funded projects actually stimulate further dispersion of urban populations.

Substantial excess capacity is normally built into many of these infra-structural facilities. Recent studies have shown that it may be cheaper to add capacity to existing systems as demands arise rather than to design excess capacity into the system from the beginning [11]. As a result of such findings, future federal policies in the United States may discourage funding designed to promote growth. By holding construction of transit lines, sewers, and highways to areas under actual development, new growth may occur in a more compact manner.

Loss of Community Identity. In the compact city of the preindustrial era most people could comprehend much of their urban environment. Most of these cities could be traversed in about 20 minutes of walking time and for this reason are sometimes called *pedestrian cities.* As cities grew in popula-tion and area the familiarity of residents with the cities declined. Some planners claim that the new scale of urban activities has led to a loss of community identity. Plans to integrate residential, commercial, and in-dustrial land uses within compact development clusters, while simultane-ously preserving open spaces between the clusters, are used in many new towns of Anglo–America and western Europe. Much of this planning effort has been focused upon reconstructing a human scale of activity that has been lost since the era of the pedestrian city [12].

Other urban experts contend that humans need not have familiarity with all the city's structural elements to maintain a sense of community identity. Identity, they claim, is based upon common interests with others rather than place [13]. A growing number of suburban residents in the United States avoid contact with central cities altogether. The community of interest for many suburbanites revolves around suburban jobs and shopping centers. The need for commuting to the central city has diminished as industry and com-mercial facilities continue to suburbanize. Fairfield County, Connecticut, for example, was once composed of many exclusively residential suburbs of New York, but now it is rapidly attracting corporate headquarters. Fairfield County may soon surpass Chicago as the second most popular corporate address for the 500 largest corporations in America, with only New York housing the headquarters of more large corporations [14].

Affluent urban communities in the developed world are likely to be composed of dispersed communities of interest which have become almost totally unhitched from the local neighborhood [15]. In cities of the devel-oping world and in poor areas of cities in the developed world, sense of community is still distance-based. Within ethnic neighborhoods of America's largest cities, for example, neighborhood ties are especially strong. One author has called such ethnic enclaves of the working class *urban vil-lages* [16]. Although the housing quality in such areas is often poor and overcrowded, the reinforcing support of like neighbors recreates a close acquaintanceship network similar to the rural villages that many of these recent immigrants left behind when they came to America. Even when residential quality approaches slum conditions, a great deal of residential satisfaction can be generated by linguistic, cultural, and familial ties. Urban renewal programs in the United States have often failed to consider the tragic effect of spatial disruption upon the evicted tenants of slum neighborhoods. In an attempt to rectify the symbolic feelings of the community with the needs and goals of the city, the views of neighborhood residents are now being solicited on proposed construction projects which might disrupt the community.

Deterioration of Environmental Quality. Pollution is often a by-product of urban concentration; it is fostered by uncontrolled growth, the industrial structure, and the climatic conditions in which a city finds itself. Much of the congestion that occurs periodically on the urban arterials arises from spatial separation of the functional elements of the modern city. Pollution and congestion are but two elements which influence the quality of life in modern urban areas. A paper about the air pollution problem in New York stated that "breathing the polluted air of New York is equivalent to smoking 38 cigarettes a day and the effect on human respiratory systems is just as destructive" [17]. Residents of Tokyo, a city notorious for a lack of land-use zoning, must frequently take oxygen breaks from sidewalk machines in order to prevent respiratory problems caused by polluted air. Modern cities, however, have cleaner air and cleaner water now than 150 years ago. Cities of Europe and America during the industrial revolution were typified by overcrowded and unsanitary living conditions, plumes of thick smoke bellowing from coal-fired industrial boilers and homes, and disease and pestilence which ravaged the urban populace.

Conditions in the poorest sections of cities in the developing world would be found intolerable by most people in the developed nations. Few of the squatter slums that are so numerous in many of the developing world's cities have piped water, sewerage disposal systems, or electricity. Cholera and other diseases spread by unsanitary conditions are endemic in such settlements.

The Arab oil embargo of late 1973 demonstrated how vulnerable the ravenous energy-consuming cities of North America, western Europe, and Japan really are. Tough choices will need to be made between degradation of air and water quality and the quest for less costly domestic energy supplies. One of the greatest of all polluters is the automobile. Major cities throughout the world grind to a halt twice a day as automobiles, which consume almost a quarter of the energy in the developed world, clog the overtaxed capacity of highways. Excess highway capacity encourages an increase in nonwork trips. Newly installed highway capacity will divert people from alternative routes that they otherwise would have traveled. As soon as capacity is reached on the new route, more capacity is demanded by users. The answer to improved transportation planning is normally not construction of more capacity but better management of the existing infrastructure. Sharing rides to work is one alternative to the driver-only automobile for reducing congestion, pollution, and energy consumption, but pooling arrangements require the user to give up some scheduling flexibility.

Cleaning up the environment has become a global problem and the cost of restoration to a pristine state will be exorbitantly high if not impossible.

In all the world's great cities the effects of urban population have spread into the surrounding countryside. The city region is the pollution fall-out zone [18].

Declaring clean-air days or temporarily restraining a particular factory from emitting pollutants are piecemeal measures. The breadth of environmental degration includes noise, air and water pollution, solid waste disposal, and sanitation and sewerage disposal problems.

In the future, urban areas should give greater attention to the physical environment as a constraint to development. Approval of a high-rise apartment complex on a particular land parcel, for example, should be contingent upon the structural qualities of the underlying rock strata, the possible degradation of the groundwater supply and the erosion potential of the land as well as the social and economic impact of the proposed development upon the surrounding neighborhood. The choice between uncontrolled growth and a more aesthetically pleasing environment will not be easy to make and the costs of wasteful consumption by modern urban society will be high.

PROBLEMS OF URBAN DISPARITY

It is within urban areas that the contrasts between the haves and the have-nots are brought into sharpest focus. The most important urban disparities concern income, density, and accessibility. The implications of each of these disparities will be considered in turn.

The Consequences of Income Disparities. The differentiation between rich and poor is as striking within cities as it is between the cities and countrysides in developed and in developing nations. Urban societies are not egalitarian allocators of wealth. In the United States, for example, it has been estimated that the lowest 20 percent of the population receives only 5 percent of the total national income, whereas the highest 20 percent of the population receives 45 percent of the income [19]. As the middle classes in the United States flee to the affluent suburbs, America's large cities become polarized both by race and by available financial resources. The central city has become the domain of the poor and the racial minorities. The city is becoming socially isolated from the surrounding suburbs. Cultural attractions, shopping opportunities, offices, and manufacturing plants continue to move to the suburbs. The image of the American suburb as a bedroom community with a sterile cultural life-style is no longer appropriate (if such an atmosphere ever really existed).

The frustrations of inner city dwellers sometimes result in violent attacks against the groups and policies they feel are responsible for their lot in life. The Watts riots in Los Angeles, the Notting Hill riots in London, and attacks against the Turkish community in Central Rotterdam are evidence that racial and economic strife are not confined to a single country. Sociologists looking for explanations of such outbursts often explain them as a result of the relative deprivation of the urban poor. The poor have always been with us, but they are now influenced by rising expectations. Advertising creates a demand for consumer items. When people of little economic means become cognizant of the income disparity between themselves and the affluent, anger and frustration often result. The poor find their opportunity for advancement seemingly blocked at every turn by a combination of a deprived environment, poor education, and lack of employment opportunities through which the person may advance.

In many cases the poor attempt to migrate to places which they believe will offer them better opportunities for advancement. Although national boundaries often constrain migrants seeking improved employment opportunities, the problem of the alienated in cities is international in scope. In spite of immigration quotas, barriers to entry, and discriminatory practices against aliens, workers from the poorer nations of the world continue to enter (either legally or illegally) the more affluent countries in search of economic advancement. The immigration into the United States from Mexico and into the United Kingdom from former British dependencies in Asia, Africa, and the Caribbean are well-publicized examples.

Even within a region of relative wealth, such as continental Europe, substantial migration occurs. Thousands of southern Europeans from the poor regions of Italy, Greece, Yugoslavia, Portugal, and Turkey seek jobs in the cities of West Germany, northern Italy, and the Benlux countries. These "guest workers" (as they are called in Germany) are often discriminated against; and they are given the menial positions that citizens of the host country often refuse to take. Differences in affluence within the countries of Europe influence the magnitudes of these migrations. In recent years many of the immigrants to developed European cities have begun to return to their homelands because of tighter immigration quotas, discrimination in the host country, and disillusionment with the economic advancement that can be obtained elsewhere.

In South Africa, thousands of African males from Lesotho and other enclaves of the region have left their families behind for work in the mines, fields, and cities of a country in which they are treated as second-class citizens under the racist policy of *apartheid*. As more of the Bantu home-land areas set aside by the white minority government in South Africa are given "independence," the international migrations of laborers to South Africa are likely to increase.

Economic deprivation has an impact upon the psychological makeup of the urban poor. Durkheim suggests that when people become urbanized, the bonds that held them together in the rural village (kinship and acquaintance-ship ties) break down to be replaced by a new order based upon formal institutions such as government, churches, and labor unions [20]. The occupational division of labor and new life-styles of the city require that relationships become formalized. The dehumanizing effects of urbanization may in its most severe form cause *anomie*, a feeling that the established urban social norms are not relevant to the achievement of one's goals and that life has no meaning. The "punk rock" craze which started in working class sections of British industrial cities may be yet another manifestation of anomie, the lack of belief in established norms.

Disparities in Density. Examples of anomie have been related to variables other than poverty in the city. A close degree of association between rates of crime and the density of population has been demonstrated [21]. In some societies, privacy and a sense of personal territoriality are important regula-tors of behavior.

In non-Western cultures the purported relationship between high popula-tion density and high crime rates are not supported by the facts. Hong Kong has one of the highest densities of any city in the world (well over 90,000 persons per square mile in many neighborhoods) and yet the rate of crime and violence is low. Research has shown cross-cultural differences in the way in which individuals react to lack of privacy and overcrowdedness [22]. In Western cities, poverty, high density, and overcrowded living conditions overlap to such a great extent that it is difficult to separate which variable or combination of variables is most likely to cause criminal behavior.

Disparities in Accessibility. Inaccessibility and poverty of a population are frequently highly interrelated. Development experts have often blamed the inaccessibility of many of India's rural villages to larger cities as a major stumbling block to India's economic advancement. More than one-third of the 11,000 villages in the Kanpur region of India, for example, have no road whatsoever and another one-third are served by unsurfaced roads which are virtually impassable during the monsoon season [23].

As a group the transportation disadvantaged (usually broadly defined as the poor, elderly, and handicapped) have less mobility than their more affluent and mobile counterparts. These disadvantaged individuals are sometimes the victims of the recent suburbanization of job opportunities.

Prior to the rapid escalation of land prices in central cities, which began during the modern industrial era, activities concentrated in central cities. New industries, older factories whose facilities have become obsolete, and activities wishing to relocate because of the crowded and congested conditions of these central activity centers look upon suburban land as a logical locational alternative. Suburban land in most Western cities is less expensive per parcel, allowing industries to be built on one level. Separate industrial operations can usually be integrated in a more cost effective manner when the factory is located in a single-storied structure rather than in the obsolete multi-storied structures present in the central city. Industrial suburbanization adversely affects the central city poor to a greater degree than in any other group. These individuals have a low degree of accessibility to private automobiles and are heavily dependent on modes of public transportation which were not designed to serve dispersed, low density suburban development patterns. Few bus routes serve new industrial parks and other suburban activity centers. Access by urban inner city poor to expanding suburban jobs is decreasing, and the job opportunities in the central city are declining. In metropolitan Chicago, for example, 337,000 new jobs were created in the metropolitan area between 1960 and 1970. The net figure masks the fact that the increase in the suburbs of 548,000 jobs was offset by a decrease of 211,000 jobs in the central city [24].

The commuting pattern of urban residents throughout the developed nations reflects the shifting pattern of commercial and industrial activities. Formerly the greatest single traffic stream was that of suburban white-collar employees commuting to their central city jobs. During the last few years the commuting pattern that has grown the fastest is the "reverse commuting" trip (i.e., the movement of blue-collar central city residents to suburban manufacturing work locations). Modern postindustrial cities in the United States have become less centrally focused as urban sprawl and changing life-styles have resulted in creation of numerous centers of activity within metropolitan regions. The epitome of this amorphous undirected growth is found in California. Los Angeles has been described as a "hundred suburbs in search of a central business district" [25]. Gertrude Stein, describing a trip to Oakland, wrote that, "when you get there, there isn't any there there" [26]. Crosstown movement between suburbs, a movement pattern poorly served by existing public transportation, is the most important commuting pattern in the United States. It has been estimated that almost three-fourths of the suburbanites in the New York metropolitan region live and work in the suburbs [27].

Patterns of accessibility discrimination exist in the developing nations as well. An economic premium is placed upon central location in developing area cities, so that the urban poor are often forced to live on the less accessible peripheries of cities. Such a settlement pattern has been depicted as a spontaneous response to lack of an adequate housing stock in most developing cities [28]. The governments of most developing nations have placed relatively little emphasis on the provision of housing in their development priorities. Squatter slums on the edge of the city represent the only housing available to thousands of migrants who arrive seeking urban jobs.

The peripheral settlements often grow without control or functional efficiency. Urban services such as water, sewerage, and fire and police protection are usually inadequate or nonexistent. Jobs that might be obtained in the central city are unavailable to peripheral slum dwellers because of either lack of transportation to reach the job or lack of funds to obtain such transportation. The service sector in such communities is unusually large, for the jobs most easily obtained are those selling merchandise or performing menial service tasks.

ALTERNATIVE URBAN GROWTH PATTERNS

Urban areas in developed nations are now losing population to rural areas, reversing a centuries-old agglomerative trend of continued urbanization. The percentage of England's population that lived in cities of 20,000 or more peaked in 1960 and has subsequently declined. Part of this trend is simply a definitional problem, as suburbanization of a population that is essentially urban in character continues almost unabated. In the United States, however, entire SMSA's have lost population since 1970. At least two-thirds of the recent nonmetropolitan growth may be attributed to rural population increases outside the commuting radii of the 250 largest urban areas. A significant portion of the new nonmetropolitan residents are undoubtedly within the commuting radius of rapidly expanding suburban employment opportunities. Since 1970, suburbs in the United States have grown 9 percent and rural areas (including exurban communities outside the commuting radii of large central cities) have increased by 5 percent, whereas central cities have lost more than 2 percent of their population. Between 1970 and 1975 rural areas grew two and one-half times faster than urban places [29].

Such growth trends have led some urban experts to suggest that just as we are beginning to understand what makes a city tick, the age of cities is drawing to a close to be replaced by an entirely new settlement fabric [30]. The argument is based upon the diminishing need for face-to-face contact in order to exchange information and commodities. Telecommunication technology has advanced to such a state that it is now feasible for some individuals to accomplish work tasks through remote computer terminals in their homes rather than commuting to work. For the vast bulk of the labor force, however, commuting to work centers will still be required for decades to come. Dispersion may become a concomitant of the urban growth process. As the older central portions of American cities become technologically obsolete, large parts of the central city may undergo changes in land use to lower density dispersed activity centers [31].

Webber foresees a world society that is integrated by an ever-expanding network of communications. The largest cities need to be no larger than about 100,000 population, and such settlements will be interconnected by a system of efficient corridors to expedite movement that must be accommodated [32]. Although information processing industries are the fastest growing sectors of the postindustrial metropolis, the need to move commodities and raw materials for processing and ultimate distribution remains. Some ecologists suggest that the physical resource bases of city hinterlands will eventually act as limits to expansion of city regions [33].

Many urban experts feel that recent population redistribution in the United States will have important economic consequences. Fundamental population movements in American society may be evidence of a changing comparative areal advantage of some regions at the expense of others. It is now the resource-endowed former hinterland areas (e.g., coal-rich and well-watered Appalachia) of the country that are enjoying some of the most rapid economic growth in a society increasingly tied to a higher priced energy, whereas these same regions were economic backwaters a few years ago.

Recent demographic and economic stabilization in America indicate that profound changes in the regional structure of American society may be taking place. Population growth is now at replacement levels or

The Congress Building in Brasilia, Brazil. (Courtesy, Consulate of Brazil.)

below. America's rate of economic expansion relative to the developing nations has slowed down as well. These changes have definable geographic consequences. If the *national* growth rate stabilizes, each *region's* share of the aggregate output produced and income generated depends on the relative economic growth of the other regions in the country. If one region well-endowed with important natural resources begins to expand, it may do so at the expense (or economic contraction) of another region [34]. The recent (post 1970) growth of the "Sunbelt" in the United States has been largely at the expense of the industrial Northeast and North Central states. A coalition of Northeastern governors was formed in the late 1970s to seek ways in which the economic viability of their regions might be maintained.

The United States and many other economically advanced nations have achieved low rates of natural increase and their economies are increasing at slow or modest rates compared to the remainder of the world even though their absolute growth remains much greater. These developed nations have begun to achieve a convergence of economic development among their regions. The former economic backwaters are expanding and the overdeveloped and overconcentrated regions are declining such that parity of development among the regions may someday be obtained. A myriad of factors might prevent such a regional convergence from ever becoming a reality. Changing energy sources, new technologies, and changing life styles could all be shocks to a national city system that might channel development in directions not presently anticipated.

The view of future urban societies as consisting of low density cities spread widely over the landscape with telecommunication as the connective tissue holding it all together is not a universally held viewpoint. Some authors argue that continued agglomeration will be humankind's destiny. The agglomerative tendencies that have lead to the development of megalopoli around the world are likely to continue so that more and more of the world's population will be concentrated into these urban giants. The urban planner Constantinos Doxiadis foresaw 12 such agglomerations for the United States by the next century, each with a name that reflects the amalgamation of the former cities (e.g., Ciloubustonis — an agglomeration of Cincinnati, Louisville, Columbus, Dayton, and Indianapolis) (Fig. 5-4) [35]. Architects such as Paolo Soleri, Buckminister Fuller, and Louis Kahn believe a single structure might someday replace the city's buildings as we have come to know them [36]. These *megastructures* would contain commercial, office, residential, and industrial functions. Recent construction of Peachtree Center in Atlanta, Renaissance Center in Detroit, and the Galleria in Houston demonstrate the megastructure concept on a limited scale. Solid waste generated by such a structure could, for example, be burned in a central incinerator and the heat produced as a by-product be used to supply the residential units. Soleri is building a prototype megastructure called Two Suns *Arcology* (a shortened version of architecture and ecology) in Arizona.

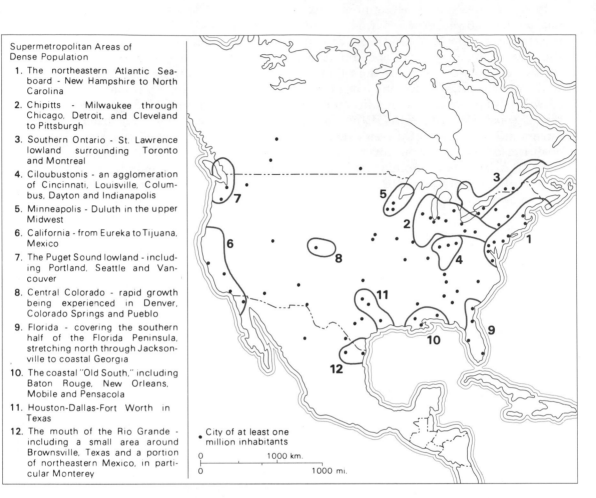

Supermetropolitan Areas of
Dense Population

1. The northeastern Atlantic Sea-board - New Hampshire to North Carolina

2. Chipitts - Milwaukee through Chicago, Detroit, and Cleveland to Pittsburgh

3. Southern Ontario - St. Lawrence lowland surrounding Toronto and Montreal

4. Ciloubustonis - an agglomeration of Cincinnati, Louisville, Columbus, Dayton and Indianapolis

5. Minneapolis - Duluth in the upper Midwest

6. California - from Eureka to Tijuana, Mexico

7. The Puget Sound lowland - including Portland, Seattle and Vancouver

8. Central Colorado - rapid growth being experienced in Denver, Colorado Springs and Pueblo

9. Florida - covering the southern half of the Florida Peninsula, stretching north through Jacksonville to coastal Georgia

10. The coastal "Old South," including Baton Rouge, New Orleans, Mobile and Pensacola

11. Houston-Dallas-Fort Worth in Texas

12. The mouth of the Rio Grande - including a small area around Brownsville, Texas and a portion of northeastern Mexico, in particular Monterey

• City of at least one million inhabitants

0   1000 km.

0   1000 mi.

Fig. 5-4. Doxiadis' view of United States metropolitan areas in the year 2060. [From Constantinos A. Doxiadis, *Urban Renewal and the Future of the American City* (Chicago: Public Service Administration, 1966), Figure 49.]

The structure when completed will provide housing for 3,000 people, will be heated by solar power and waste heat, and will use photosynthesis to supply food and oxygen.

Megastructures and sophisticated telecommunication devices seem as distant as another galaxy to many urban experts who are more concerned about the problems of today's cities. What alternative growth patterns are being implemented to alleviate the problems that face today's societies? The presently utilized palliatives in the affluent world include the development of new towns, the channelization of growth into corridors, central city revitalization, and development of regional-level governmental structures that better represent our present dispersed living patterns than current organizations do.

In the developing nations the major problem of urban growth has centered upon job creation to stem the tide of rural-to-urban migration and upon reducing the population growth rate. Two methods are most frequently utilized to provide a viable alternative to migration. First, labor-intensive rural projects such as irrigation and road construction have been developed to provide nonagricultural rural employment. Secondly, redistribution policies have attempted to channel growth away from the largest cities into regional capitals in areas that lag behind the economic expansion of the rest of the country.

New Towns. Entirely new urban areas have been created in England, the United States, and the Scandinavian countries. Public and private development funds have been used in an effort to build communities where none previously existed. Reston, in Virginia, Irvine, in California, and Columbia and Greenbelt, in Maryland, are but a few examples of such developments. The new town is not intended to be a suburb of a larger city, although in many instances that is exactly what it is. New towns are usually designed to be independent, freestanding communities. In order to achieve such a goal, industry and commerce must be developed as well as an attractive living environment. When the slate is clean, innovative design concepts can be built into such towns at the outset. Clustered housing, green space, control over signs, separation of pedestrian and vehicular traffic, and mixed income and racial neighborhoods are the ideal characteristics that new towns are designed to incorporate. Seldom are all of these features included in a single new town. Some new towns have, in fact, simply become homogeneous, upper middle-class suburban communities without a viable independent economic base; others are showcases of urban design. Täby, in Sweden, may be one of the best designed new towns, although residents often find the environment too sterile and yearn for the excitement and visual stimulation of cities which have "grown like Topsy." Although most new-town developments in the United States have thus far been financed by private investors, the government may need to take a more active role if such planning concepts are to be widely diffused. It is difficult for private developers to purchase suitable land parcels of a size sufficient to develop a large community and all the ancillary facilities near a large established urban center. Housing in the private sector is typically constructed for fast turnover and maximum profits with little concern for the aesthetics or the functional viability of the development as a true community.

Corridor Development. The recent emphasis on energy efficiency has convinced many planners that land uses must be developed only along designated corridors. In this way sprawl might be controlled, density of development would increase, and services could be provided more efficiently as long as average costs of service provision continued to decrease. Coupled with the desire to increase energy efficiency of the urban area is the growing concern about environmental degradation. Control over the extension of urban services is viewed as a powerful planning tool to channel growth in ecologically desirable patterns. The "no sewer, no subdivision" policy has, for example, been an effective deterrent to continual urban sprawl in suburban northern Virginia, outside Washington, D.C. [37].

Corridor development is not, however, a new concept. The typical developed urban center of the 1920s resembled a starfish. The urban area spread out like tenacles along mass transportation lines and commuter suburbs developed at ever-increasing distances from the central city. Profound land-use changes emerged with the advent of the private automobile. The interstices between the corridors of suburbs began to fill up. The mobility afforded to urban dwellers who owned an automobile allowed them more flexibility than had theretofore been possible. The influence of mass transportation as a shaper of land-use patterns reached its zenith prior to World War II.

Many planners still feel that mass transit may be used to shape American cities, although only 3 percent of the population uses mass transit as a mode of transportation. The automobile now conveys over 90 percent of the labor force (either as a passenger or the driver) to work each day [38]. Fixed-guideway systems (subways) costing billions of dollars are nonetheless being constructed in the San Francisco Bay area (BART), Atlanta (MARTA), and Washington, D.C. (METRO).

Enthusiasts for fixed rail systems point to the success of the Toronto subway [39]. The subway system in Toronto is fairly recent, has added capacity only as demand has been generated, and serves a high density compact settlement pattern. Unlike the United States, Canada does not offer tax relief for homeowners on the interest portion of their mortgage payment. This, coupled with the exorbitant price of single-family dwelling units in Toronto, has forced many families to reside in densely settled apartment complexes close to the center of the city. Such high density development is the forte of fixed-guideway systems.

Fixed-guideway systems channeling movement along high density corridors are impractical except in the largest of metropolitan areas. Commuting patterns have been diffused throughout the urban region. The monocentric city where movement patterns focus upon the central business district exists only in the models of location theorists. Today's cities are polycentric with commuting patterns that are so complex as to defy generalization.

Central City Revitalization. There is a small but growing movement of middle-class people back into the central city. These individuals are usually young couples without children or older couples who have already raised their children ("empty nesters"). Central cities look at such individuals as a major bright spot for revitalization efforts. The property taxes these middle-class people pay support urban services. The number of former suburbanites moving into the central city is, however, a trickle in comparison to the outward movement into the suburbs.

Private redevelopment of deteriorating neighborhoods has restored architecturally valuable homes in many American cities. The results of such revitalization are not viewed with favor by every economic segment of the central city population. Poor central city residents may become resentful of such redevelopment efforts because property taxes on their own homes begin to increase as neighborhoods are upgraded. The poor may find themselves unable to afford the taxes on their own homes.

Lack of residential maintenance and improvements (called *disinvestment*) is a major problem in slum areas. The reasons for disinvestment are often economic. Financial institutions consider older housing in inner city neighborhoods a poor loan risk and they may be unwilling to loan money to property investors in those areas. Investors are then forced to pay the full purchase price for residences in such neighborhoods. In order to receive a reasonable economic return, investors often pursue a short-run strategy of extracting maximum rent with a minimum of operating costs [40]. Maintenance is minimal or nonexistent, and deterioration is the result.

Some of the inner city housing units fall into such a state of disrepair that the owners refuse to pay taxes on them. Governmental agencies thereby acquire liens on numerous housing units in slum neighborhoods. The Federal Housing Administration in the United States, for example, holds the title to over 40,000 units in Philadelphia's inner city. The government has allowed private citizens (but not speculators) to obtain such deteriorated units for a nominal fee under the proviso that the unit be restored within a reasonable amount of time. The program is called *urban homesteading* because of the strong resemblance it bears to the Homestead Acts which opened up the western United States to farm settlement [41]. In those earlier acts, potential settlers were given quarter sections (160 acres) of western land if they agreed to establish a farm. As innovative as this urban homesteading program is, it will appeal to only a few people unless the quality of urban services (especially police protection and public school systems) is noticeably improved.

Regional Level Government. An increasing number of urban problems extend beyond the jurisdictional boundaries of individual municipalities. Problems of the postindustrial city are metropolitan in scale and yet the structure and mechanism of most local governments have not yet adjusted to accommodate this new reality. Notable exceptions to fragmented local control include the Greater London plan, the Toronto metropolitan plan, the Minneapolis–St. Paul regional Council of Governments, and city–county consolidation in Jacksonville, Miami, Nashville, and Indianapolis. Regional governmental structures may mean that a local municipality must voluntarily relinquish a degree of jurisdictional power. Such a procedure is not likely to be undertaken unless the political integrity of the local community is assured. In the United States, all federal funds allocated to large urban areas must now be channeled through a regional level planning authority to make sure that the monetary requests from local municipalities are consistent with defined regional goals [42].

THE CITY AS A CATALYST FOR REGIONAL DEVELOPMENT

Cities have been used by developing nations as catalysts around which to develop economically lagging regions. Brazil, for example, made a conscious decision to develop the Mato Grosso and Amazonian interior regions of the country to stem some of the migration to the coastal cities of São Paulo and Rio de Janeiro. The new capital city, Brasilia, was constructed 600 miles inland from the coast. The cost of the project was staggering and almost bankrupted Brazil's treasury. At first the new city was a viable entity only on working days. Many government employees chose to commute by plane back to Rio on weekends. Within the last few years, however, evidence is mounting that Brasilia has become a viable urban center. A large market-place has developed along some of the alleyways of the beautifully designed new city and informal squatter settlements have arisen on the city's outskirts [43].

CONCLUSIONS

Development resources are most often mobilized, directed, and co-ordinated from cities. This is how cities have historically functioned in developed societies that have passed from a traditional way of life through the industrial era and beyond. In developing countries, cities can become cancerous growths on national economic viability unless rates of population growth and rural-to-urban migration are slowed. Paradoxically, however, cities offer the greatest hope for the development of modern economic systems. Cities do not exist in isolation and should be considered as a part of an integrated system of national development. Cities are the main articulation points in the distribution system and the major allocators of economic benefits to their surrounding interdependent hinterlands.

Cities are not without their share of problems as these agglomerations of people linked by social and economic ties exacerbate pollution, congestion, and social disorders such as crime and alienation. The problems of urban areas have been with us as long as cities have existed.

Cities are the nerve centers for economic impulses as they are transmitted throughout the world even though some feel that cities as an organization form have outlived their usefulness. Countervailing trends in urban growth patterns have divided urban futurists into two camps. Some urban scholars see suburbanization of population, commerce, and industry as only the first stage in an ever more dispersed, low density pattern of development. Others studying urbanization and the coalesence of formerly separable urban entities into polycentric megalopoli foresee even greater levels of urbanization at higher levels of human density. The ultimate urban form of the future would be a single megastructure encompassing all human needs.

Planners have offered many innovative solutions to the plethora of urban problems. Some solutions, such as new town developments, would build an entire community from a formerly rural area. Other solutions start from present urban realities and attempt to renew and revitalize those parts that can be salvaged and abandon those parts that have outlived their usefulness. All of these plans involve choices and trade-offs between competing goals. Is it desirable to upgrade an inner city neighborhood if poor people are displaced in the process? Should an industry seek new suburban land for expansion if inner city employment opportunity would be adversely affected? The answers to these questions require knowledge of the geographical impact of investment decisions.

REFERENCES

[1] *Demographic Yearbook 1975* (New York: United Nations, 1976).

[2] Kingsley Davis, *World Urbanization 1950-70* (Berkeley: University of California Press, 1969).

[3] Louis Wirth, "Urbanism as a Way of Life," *American Journal of Sociology*, 44, 1938, pp. 1-24.

[4] *Demographic Yearbook 1975, op. cit.*

[5] Paul Wheatley, *The Pivot of the Four Corners* (Edinburgh: Edinburgh University Press, 1971).

[6] Thomas L. Blair, *The International Urban Crisis* (New York: Hill and Wang, 1974), pp. 27-28.

[7] E. A. J. Johnson, *The Organization of Space in Developing Countries* (Cambridge, Mass.: Harvard University Press, 1970).

[8] Brian J. L. Berry, "City Size Distribution and Economic Development," *Economic Development and Cultural Change*, 9, 1961, pp. 573-588.

[9] Alvin Toffler, *Future Shock* (New York: Bantam Books, 1974).

[10] Frederick C. Turner, "The Rush to the Cities in Latin America," *Science*, 192, June 4, 1976, pp. 955–962.

[11] John A. Busterud, "Planning by Accident: The Land Use Impacts of Infrastructure Investments," address to the Urban Planning Lecture Series, Stanford University, Stanford, Calif., January, 1977.

[12] Kevin Lynch, "The Possible City" in E. W. Ewald, Jr. (ed.), *Environment and Policy: The Next Fifty Years* (Bloomington, Ind.: University of Indiana Press, 1968).

[13] Melvin J. Webber, "Order in Diversity: Community Without Propinquity," in Lowdon Wingo, Jr. (ed.), *Cities and Space* (Baltimore: Resources for the Future, 1963), pp. 23–54.

[14] "Bedroom to Board Room," *Time*, August 28, 1978.

[15] Amos Hawley and Basil Zimmer, *The Metropolitan Community* (Beverly Hills, Calif.: Sage Publications, 1970).

[16] Herbert Gans, *The Urban Villagers* (Glencoe, Ill.: The Free Press, 1962).

[17] Environmental Protection Agency, "38 Cigarettes a Day" (Washington, D.C., 1971).

[18] Blair, *op. cit.*, p. 107.

[19] Economic and Social Data Division, World Bank, *World Economic and Social Indicators* Report No. 700/77/09, November–December 1977, Table XI.

[20] Emile Durkheim, *The Division of Labor in Society*, George Simpson, transl., (New York: Macmillan, 1933).

[21] David M. Smith, *The Geography of Social Well Being* (New York: McGraw-Hill Book Co., 1973).

[22] Edward T. Hall, *The Hidden Dimension* (Garden City, N.Y.: Anchor Books, 1966).

[23] Johnson, *op. cit.*, p. 194.

[24] Brian J. L. Berry, et al., *Chicago: Transformations of an Urban System* (Cambridge, Mass.: Ballinger Press, 1977).

[25] Gordon J. Fielding, *Geography as Social Science* (New York: Harper and Row, 1974).

[26] Gertrude Stein, as quoted in D. Stea and R. M. Downs, *Maps in Minds* (New York: Harper and Row, 1977) p. 135.

[27] Edward F. Bergman, *Modern Political Geography* (Dubuque, Iowa: W. C. Brown, 1975), pp. 89–90.

[28] J. F. C. Turner, "Uncontrolled Urban Settlement: Problems and Policies," in Gerald Breese (ed.), *The City in Newly Developing Countries* (Englewood Cliffs, N.J.: Prentice-Hall, 1969), pp. 507–534.

[29] Brian J. L. Berry, *The Changing Shape of Metropolitan America* (Cambridge, Mass.: Ballinger Press, 1977).

[30] Melvin J. Webber, "The Post-City Age," *Daedalus*, 97, No. 4, Fall 1968, pp. 1093–1099.

[31] David Birch, "From Suburb to Urban Place," *Annals of the American Academy of Political and Social Science*, No. 422, 1975.

[32] Webber, *op. cit.*, 1968.

[33] Lester R. Brown, "City Limits," *Man Not Apart*, 6, No. 16, September, 1976.

[34] Brian J. L. Berry, "Transformation of the Nation's Urban System: Small City Growth as a Zero-Sum Game," Policy Note P77-1 Harvard University, (Cambridge, Mass.: Department of City and Regional Planning, April, 1977).

[35] Constantinos A. Doxiadis, *Urban Renewal and the Future of the American City* (Chicago: Public Administration Service, 1966).

[36] Nilo Lindgren, "Soleri's Archologies," *IEEE Spectrum* 13, No. 7, July, 1976, pp. 42–45.
Buckminister Fuller, "The Prospects of Humanity," *Ekistics*, 107, October, 1964, pp. 232–242.
Gordon D. Friedlander, "In Support of Megastructures," *IEEE Spectrum*, 13, No. 7, July, 1976, pp. 37–41.

[37] Population Reference Bureau, "Suburban Growth: A Case Study," *Population Bulletin*, 28, No. 1, February, 1972.

[38] Alan Altshuler, "The Politics of Urban Transportation Innovation," *Technology Review*, May, 1977, pp. 51–58.

[39] Melvin Webber, "The BART Experience: What Have We Learned?" *The Public Interest*, No. 45, Fall, 1976, pp. 79–108.

[40] Maurice Yeates and Barry Garner, *The North American City*, 2nd ed. (New York: Harper and Row, 1976), Chapter 17.

[41] James W. Hughes and Kenneth D. Bleakly, Jr., *Urban Homesteading* (New Brunswick, N.J.: Rutgers Center for Urban Policy Research, 1977).

[42] Edward F. Bergman, *Modern Political Geography* (Dubuque, Iowa: W. C. Brown, 1975), Chapter 5.

[43] "Brazil: Future Shock," *Newsweek*, September 16, 1974, p. 44.

CHAPTER SIX

disparities in transportation development

INTRODUCTION

No inventions have played greater roles in world economic and social changes than those which have given the world modern methods of transportation and communication. Where modern systems of transportation and communication have not developed, social and economic changes have been slow to occur and local self-sufficiency is not so much a choice as a necessity. Peoples in such areas are severely limited in exposure to new ideas and in access to information and goods. Because the choice of materials to satisfy needs is restricted primarily to those which can be produced within the immediate locality, production processes are often highly inefficient and the goods obtained may be of low quality. The range of opportunities for economic development is small, as is the variety of foods and fibers available for consumption.

Peoples living in areas which possess well-developed systems of modern transportation and communication have access to a much wider range of ideas, information, and goods. Because they have access to resources scattered over a large area, they can select those of highest quality. Output of local resources is restricted to commodities which can be produced with great efficiency and at a competitive advantage in comparison to other areas.

Production tends to become highly specialized and consumption highly diversified. Modern communications systems make possible almost instant provision of information concerning such factors as quality, quantity, and price of goods available in numerous localities. Buyers are able to choose goods which best meet their needs from several alternative sources and they can often place orders, obtain confirmation, and have shipment initiated within a matter of minutes, hours, or a few days.

Because well-developed transportation and communication systems stimulate specialization in production and an increase in the variety of commodities consumed, they generate constant demands for improvements in the quantity, quality, efficiency, flexibility, and area of coverage of the systems. In the process of such development, localities tend to decline in self-sufficiency and to become increasingly dependent for supplies on a greater number of more distant areas. Because goods can be moved only at a certain cost, one might expect prices to rise as distances of movement increase. For example, it might be expected that locally produced potatoes would sell for substantially lower prices than those brought in from a distance of 500 miles. If local production costs exceed those in the distant area by more than the cost of transporting the potatoes for 500 miles, however, consumers may benefit by using supplies from the distant source.

Modern transportation and communication is not without disadvantages. The decline in local self-sufficiency and the increasing interaction with distant sources experienced by areas possessing modern facilities also make these areas increasingly vulnerable to disruption by strikes, wars, or the imposition of controls over trade. Because modern transportation systems are heavy users of energy, they can also be shut down or seriously curtailed by fuel shortages which result from internal or international problems not directly related to the transportation systems themselves. Moreover, modern transportation and communications facilities are costly to develop, and to provide and maintain them requires diversion of funds from other possible uses such as for health care or education.

On the other hand, modern transportation and communication have liberated many of the world's peoples from the narrow constraints of local goods, services, and knowledge. They have contributed heavily to production efficiencies by encouraging economies of scale in output; they have removed many former restrictions upon settlement; and they have provided increased opportunities for acquiring firsthand and secondhand knowledge of the world. Their development has coincided with major improvements in living standards and in the quantity and variety of goods and services available to peoples and with the urbanization of a large percentage of the world's population.

FACTORS AFFECTING ROUTEWAY AND NETWORK DEVELOPMENT AND SPACING

Effective Demand

Construction of transportation and communication networks and the particular routeways selected are stimulated primarily by *effective demand.* Some areas produce surpluses of goods which are in demand somewhere else (complementary areas). Surplus creates an impetus for movement, but the direction in which the goods move is determined by the locations of areas providing effective demand. Not all demand is effective, as many peoples who wish to obtain goods and services do not have adequate purchasing power to acquire them. Ineffective demand, in turn, retards full development of areas with a potential for surplus production. For transportation and communication actually to develop, one area must have the ability to purchase surpluses produced by other areas. The greater the purchasing power possessed by the people of an area, the greater is their effective demand for goods and for communications services and the more intensive and far-reaching are the transport and communications facilities built to serve them.

How closely routes are spaced and how much they are used reflect factors such as *demand per unit area, size of area* to be served, *types of goods*

Road maintenance gang preparing for ditch-clearing work in Ethiopia. (Courtesy, Agency for International Development.)

to be moved, governmental and industry *regulations*, amount of *industry competition*, type of *ownership*, conditions of *weather* and *climate*, availability of *capital* and *technology*, and *land surface characteristics*. Place-to-place variations in these factors influence decisions concerning how demand is to be met, what levels of service will be made available, and what modes of transportation or communication are to be utilized. Moreover, *changes* in factors affecting demand and supply, modes of movement, and ownership of equipment and routeways lead to changes in network densities and use.

Demand per Unit Area

Generally, the higher the demand per unit area, the more closely spaced the routeways. In some instances, however, routeways are maintained or developed to meet social needs. Many urban areas in the United States operate unprofitable transit lines to provide service for elderly and disadvantaged residents who lack alternative means of transportation. Freight lines are also frequently operated at losses where their discontinuance is likely to produce adverse socioeconomic conditions within the areas served. Closest routeway spacings, however, are ordinarily associated with areas of high population density and affluence.

Competition

Intense competition among carriers may lead to development of a dense network of lightly used routes, whereas absence of competition, even where effective demand is high, may produce a low density network of heavily used routes. In the Soviet Union, for example, an authoritarian government owns and manages the transportation system and depends primarily on railroads for moving goods. Without significant competition among different modes, or among different rail lines, there is little incentive to provide more convenient routes or to offer other services to attract additional business. Moreover, users of the transport network have limited ability to influence governmental leaders to improve services. The result is a relatively low density network of heavily traveled routes. Although the Soviet rail network contains only about one-third the track mileage of United States' railroads, for example, it carries more than twice as much freight and 20 times as many passengers. On the other hand, in several western European nations, where transportation systems are publicly controlled, there is a much higher route density than in the Soviet Union. This has occurred partly because users exert considerable influence upon political leaders through their voting powers, partly because population densities are higher, and partly because the smaller and more effectively occupied national territories permit construction of numerous routeways at relatively low cost per ton-mile of goods hauled.

Land Surfaces

Land surfaces which are hilly, mountainous, swampy, or laced with streams add to the cost of routeway development. Because such areas are often ill-suited to human habitation, they usually contain fewer routeways than densely inhabited and well-drained plains. Hills and mountains also cause reductions in speed and increases in fuel consumption for land vehicles. Inland water transport is handicapped by shallow channels, sand bars, and other channel obstacles.

Weather and Climate

Conditions of weather and climate often create problems for land, sea, and air transportation. Icebergs endanger vessels in the North Atlantic, and storms, wherever they occur, are a major hazard. Fog also endangers movement even though modern radar equipment aids in avoiding collisions and in making correct approaches to docking or landing facilities.

View of the Port of Rotterdam in the Netherlands. (Courtesy, Consulate General of the Netherlands.)

Railroads, highways, and aircraft runways are difficult to build and maintain in extremely cold regions where subsoils are permanently frozen. Surface thawing in summer creates boggy conditions and the weight of roadbeds may cause thawing of subsurface ice with the result that the beds sink below the surface or become uneven. In rainy tropical regions wooden crossties rot or they are devoured by termites so quickly that steel ties must be used. Vegetation grows so rapidly that roadways become overgrown unless they are under constant use and maintenance. In desert regions the expansion and contraction of materials caused by wide differences between daytime and nighttime temperatures results in weakening and cracking of steel and concrete. High daytime temperatures cause engines to overheat and blowing sand obscures routes and damages equipment. Railroads are able to operate better than other carriers under adverse weather conditions and the greatest danger posed by severe winds and storms is to aircraft.

Congestion is a severe problem in many urban areas, around airports of large cities and along highway arteries connecting large nearby population concentrations. In most urban areas congestion is greatest from 7:00 to 9:00 A.M. and 4:00 to 6:00 P.M. when workers are commuting to and from work. Efforts to relieve congestion by construction of additional highways have been only partially successful. During recent years many cities have promoted use of mass transit, car pooling, van pooling, and other systems of multiple-occupancy vehicles in an effort to reduce traffic congestion as well as to reduce energy consumption and air pollution.

THE MAJOR MODES

The major modes of transportation include railroad, highway, pipeline, waterway, and air movement. Each mode has certain advantages and disadvantages involving such factors as cost of routeway construction and maintenance, equipment costs, speed of movement, amount of government regulation, and rates of technological change. Because of the early importance of water transportation, patterns of settlement developed along seacoasts and navigable streams. This settlement pattern, in turn, influenced subsequent routes for railroads, highways, pipelines, and air carriers. International movements of commodities are primarily by water and air, whereas internal movements are by a variety of carriers with the major carrier differing from country to country and from place to place within countries depending on the particular set of circumstances faced in each area.

Railroads

Although much of the technology for early railroad development was produced in England, the greatest achievements in construction occurred in the United States. The first American railroad consisted of 13 miles of track opened in Maryland in 1830. By 1860 the railroad network east of the Mississippi River was approximately as it is today. Chicago had become the world's greatest rail center, and the railroads had triumphed over competing forms of movement. Costs of moving goods had been reduced to only about 5 percent of prerailroad levels. After 1860 the great transcontinental routes were built, and all parts of the nation were connected by 1900 although development in the South lagged behind the rest of the country.

Railroads are best suited for long-distance movement of low-value bulky items such as unprocessed agricultural commodities, minerals, building materials, and chemicals. Commodities which are perishable, high in value, or destined for short trips (generally under 200 miles) are usually best moved by other carriers. The superiority of railroads for movement of passengers between and among cities disappeared in the United States with the coming of motorcars, buses, and airplanes, although railroads have continued to carry large numbers of passengers in the smaller and more densely populated nations of Europe. During recent years the United States Congress has heavily subsidized an organization called AMTRAK, which is attempting to revive rail passenger service. Although it has had some success, AMTRAK is handicapped by low speeds caused largely by poor track conditions, competition from other modes, and equipment shortages and failures.

The amount of fixed capital required for railroad development and maintenance is high compared to other forms of commercial transportation. Besides rolling stock, railroads must also purchase routeways and build roadbeds. Motortrucks bear routeway costs only indirectly, and airlines not at all. Initial construction of many railroads was subsidized through land grants from the public domain, but maintenance costs and taxes along the rights-of-way demand huge expenditures annually.

Profitability of railroads depends on how intensively the roads are used. In the United States less than 40 percent of the track turns a profit and about 10 percent of the network accounts for approximately half of total railroad freight movement.

Disadvantages of railroads include their fixed (inflexible) routeways, delays in movement because of fragmented ownership, and high terminal costs. To improve the flexibility of their service, and to provide door-to-door pick up and delivery, railroads have adopted a "piggyback" system whereby truck trailers are rolled onto flatbed cars, moved by rail between general points of origin and destination, and then removed from the flatbeds by motortruck for delivery to precise destinations. In the United States fragmented control has often resulted in delays of movement as cars are transferred and reassembled from one railroad line to another. Terminal costs arise from loading and unloading cars and assembling carloads of commodities for delivery along particular routeways. The costs are relatively high for railroads, compared with motortrucks, because goods moved by truck require less handling and because smaller volumes are required for a specific trip by truck. Unitized trains, those hauling a single commodity such as coal or iron ore from a single origin to a single destination, are the most efficient carriers and are used whenever possible.

Another problem for the railroads in some areas is the number of different rail gauges (width of track separation) in use. World gauge widths range from 1 foot, 3 inches to 5 feet, 6 inches. When the track gauge changes along a routeway, goods being hauled must bear the costs of transfer from one carrier to another. Gauges have been standardized within most nations, but changes at international borders are not uncommon. Some 52 break-of-gauge points in the rail network of India reduce the efficiency normally gained with increasing length of haul.

Waterways

Waterways furnished the primary avenues for movement of freight prior to development of railroads. Water movement was easy and inexpensive compared to land transportation. Its chief problem was the limited availability of navigable waterways. Settlement was concentrated along coastlines and along streams capable of providing passage for boats. After the War of 1812 in the United States, and several decades earlier in Europe, a major canal-building era occurred, spurred on by use of steam-powered boats. Steamboats, first successfully developed in 1786, became the leading mode of travel in the United States during the early 1800s. This event, combined with the enormous success of the Erie Canal, connecting Lake Erie with the Hudson River and New York, led to development of a system of canals which by 1850 provided some 4,500 miles of relatively fast and low-cost transportation. Steamboats reduced the time and cost of transportation by 80 percent on the Mississippi River between 1815 and 1860, and New Orleans during these years grew faster than New York. The coming of the railroads shortly after the beginning of the canal era, however, made many canals obsolete even before they were completed.

The major advantage of water transportation is its ability to move goods long distances at low cost per ton-mile. Its chief disadvantage is low speed (barges on inland waterways move an average of only 5 miles per hour). Because internal water transportation is slow, it is used primarily to move low-value, bulky, nonperishable commodities such as sand, gravel, oil, and grain over relatively long distances. Barge transportation costs in the United States are normally only one-fifth to one-tenth that of rail transport per ton-mile, but the barge may require ten or more times longer to make the trip than a train.

Other disadvantages of inland water transportation, compared with movement by faster modes, are that shippers and receivers must maintain larger inventories and investment funds are tied up in goods which are in transit over longer periods. Ships and barges are also more vulnerable than trains to adverse weather conditions and terminal costs are comparatively high. Frozen or flooded rivers can halt movement over long periods, strong winds may damage vessels directly or cause them to run aground, and fog is a distinct threat to navigation.

Ocean ships carry a much larger percentage of finished and semifinished goods than inland vessels. Handling costs are high — sometimes exceeding actual movement costs for distances equal to an Atlantic crossing. Use of containerized freight, however, is an increasingly popular means for lowering handling costs. Another major advance in ocean transport has been development of huge supertankers, whose capacities of several hundred thousand barrels of petroleum have lowered the cost and the amount of energy required for transporting petroleum.

Because oceangoing vessels are expensive, require considerable amounts of time to construct, and have a use expectancy of 20 years or more, overall load capacities do not normally change rapidly, and innovations are slow to be widely adopted. Shortages in capacities are usually reflected in higher prices charged for shipping, whereas overcapacity can lead to exceptionally low rates because costs of operating a fully loaded ship are little more than for one which is empty.

Motortruck

Although land roads formed important links between various centers of population even prior to the coming of the railroads, it was not until development of the internal combustion engine that roads became major carriers of freight.

Motortruck transportation has developed primarily since 1920 and has become most important in North America and in western Europe. Since 1920 much faster improvements have occurred in roads and in motor vehicles than in railroads, trains, or marine transportation. A dense network of roadways has been built to cover all sections of the United States, western Europe, and many other parts of the world, and most of the construction has been at public expense as a convenience to automobile traffic rather than at the direct expense of the trucking companies.

The primary advantages of motortrucks are speed, low terminal costs, and flexibility of movement, which gives them a competitive edge over other modes for short hauls and often for transporting perishable or high-value goods over long distances. Operating costs are high, but the trucking business is highly competitive. Capital requirements for entering the business, as well as profit margins, are relatively low. Large trucking firms have little advantage over small firms. Economies of scale are limited because of the small capacity of each carrier. The rapid wearing out of equipment is a disadvan-

Bridge construction in a Philippine Village. (Courtesy, Agency for International Development.)

tage in that replacement is required about every 4 years but an advantage in that technical innovations are quickly diffused throughout the industry — a definite advantage for trucks over railroads and water transportation.

Air Transportation

From its inception, the fate of commercial air transportation has been tied largely to direct or indirect governmental support. The United States industry was launched following World War I with surplus governmental airplanes and former military pilots. Authorization to carry the mail gave the industry a much needed boost in 1925, and governmental subsidization of the fledgling airlines was one of the first programs of Federal aid to private industry. Airports were first constructed in the United States largely with state and local funds, but the Federal role increased during the "great depression" and following World War II. Advances in aircraft design and performance have resulted primarily from governmentally sponsored research, and the widespread exposure of civilian and military personnel to the convenience, comfort, speed, and relative safety of air travel during World War II provided the basis for the rapid growth of air transportation following the war. Government efforts to maintain military air superiority and the Korean and Vietnam Wars have continued to provide equipment and trained personnel for an industry whose share of commercial intercity passenger traffic rose from 1.7 percent in 1944 to 75 percent in the early 1970s.

Air transportation specializes in passenger traffic, although its use in moving high-value, light-weight, and perishable items has increased substantially since World War II. As larger aircraft are brought into service, costs per unit weight are reduced and the competitive position of air cargo service improves. Most cargo is transported on passenger planes, but increasing numbers of strictly cargo carriers are providing regular service between major cities.

The primary advantage of air transportation is speed of movement over long distances. For short hauls the time savings over other modes are relatively minor, and costs per ton-mile or per passenger-mile are high because takeoffs and landings, the most expensive aspect of aircraft operation, are frequent. The utilization rate is vitally important to the profitability of air transportation, as operating costs are about the same whether aircraft are full or empty. The shorter the haul, the greater the need for operation at full capacity. On flights of 300 miles or under, for example, 80 to 90 percent of craft capacity must be filled just to cover operating expenses. With longer flights, the cost per passenger- or per ton-mile decreases rapidly. Competition among airlines is primarily in advertising, quality of aircraft, service, and network design. Because of the high cost of short hauls the service network must be designed so that short flights are minimized and operate near full capacity.

Pipelines

Pipelines are a highly specialized, low-cost, but relatively slow, form of transportation. They carry mostly liquids and gases but have a potential for transporting solids — including dry-bulk commodities in specially designed containers.

The first major commercial pipeline in the United States was completed in 1879 between the oil fields around Titusville, Pennsylvania, and the Reading Railroad about 110 miles away. Most pipelines extend between major oil and gas fields and the chief markets for these products and have been built almost entirely with private funds. About 70 percent of United States' energy resources move through a million-mile pipeline network.

Pipeline efficiency increases with size, as doubling pipe diameter more than quadruples carrying capacity at less than double the cost of construction. Because of the economies gained by large-diameter pipes, competing oil and gas companies seldom build their own pipelines. They share both costs of construction and utilization of large-diameter pipes.

The major advantage of pipelines is their ability to transport liquids and gases over long distances at relatively low cost across almost any type of terrain, with virtually no ill effects from any kind of climatic or weather conditions. In most instances land costs can be minimized by leasing rather than buying rights-of-way and by burying the pipe. Notable exceptions occur in areas of permafrost and frequent and severe earthquake activity. In such instances pipelines may have to elevated and specially designed to prevent melting of the permafrost and to withstand earth movements. Disadvantages of pipelines include their inflexibility, and the large amounts of materials which are stored in the lines. Maximum efficiency is gained when pipes are operated at full capacity. They are ordinarily designed to meet average or less than average demands for commodities being shipped, with facilities provided at the destination for storing excess supplies during minimum demand.

Recent experiments with long-distance transportation of coal in slurry pipelines indicated that substantial savings may be possible over alternative transport modes. Slurry movement involves grinding the coal into a consistency of fine sand and mixing it with water so that it moves as a liquid. Demand for lengthy shipments has increased since enaction of legislation regulating sulfur dioxide (SO_2) emissions from steam electric-generating plants. Most coal reserves in the eastern United States are relatively high in sulfur content, whereas western deposits are not. Two legitimate arguments against the slurry pipeline are that needed business will be diverted from an already depressed railroad industry and, perhaps most important, the water required for pipeline movement of the coal will greatly intensify water shortages in western states where water problems are already epidemic.

WORLD PATTERNS OF ROUTEWAY DEVELOPMENT: THE MAJOR MODES

Routeways of the major transportation modes are extremely uneven in development density from one region to another. Areas with a dense network of routeways of one mode normally have a dense network of the other modes, with the possible exception of inland waterways and pipelines. Where routeways are of low density, the primary transport mode is likely to be railway or highway, with the two modes existing together in areas of moderate and high routeway density. Generally, highest routeway densities have developed in western Europe, Japan, and the northeastern United States. Lowest routeway densities occur in Africa, Latin America, and eastern and southern Asia (Fig. 6-1 and 6-2).

Railways

Approximately 750,000 miles of railway lines are in current service in the world. Anglo–America and Europe, combined, contain about 70 percent

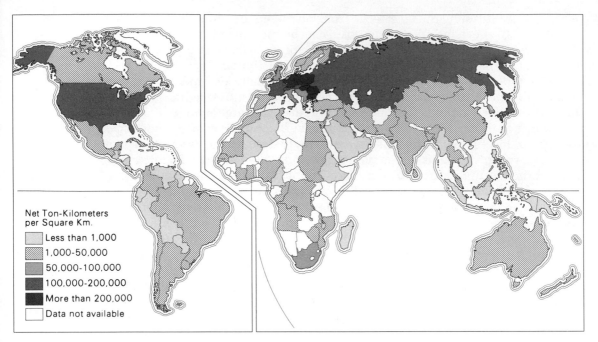

Fig. 6-1. Rail freight density: Net ton-kilometers of rail freight moved per square kilometer of surface area, 1974. Interpretation of this map should take into consideration the substantial differences in population density from nation to nation and within nations. Most of the Canadian population and rail traffic, for example, occur within the southeastern portion of the nation where the rail density is quite high. Similarly, the Pampas area of Argentina and Sao Paulo State in Brazil have much higher traffic densities than other portions of those nations. [From *Statistical Yearbook: 1975* (New York: United Nations, 1976), Tables 18 and 156.]

of this mileage; Asia, less than 12 percent; South and Central America, around 10 percent; Africa, slightly more than 5 percent; and Australia and New Zealand, approximately 4 percent (Table 6-1).

In the United States and Canada highest railroad densities occur in the area between the Great Lakes-St. Lawrence Seaway and the Ohio River. The southeastern United States possesses a rail network of moderate density, whereas the western portion of the nation is served by a few major lines. The density of rail lines is closely related to population density and the spacing of large cities.

Because of the high degree of industrialization within the northeastern quarter of the United States, and the region's agricultural wealth, dense population, and strong export trade, a dense pattern of railways was built prior to 1900 to haul raw and finished goods within, into, and out of the region. In building a system to maximize service, virtually every population

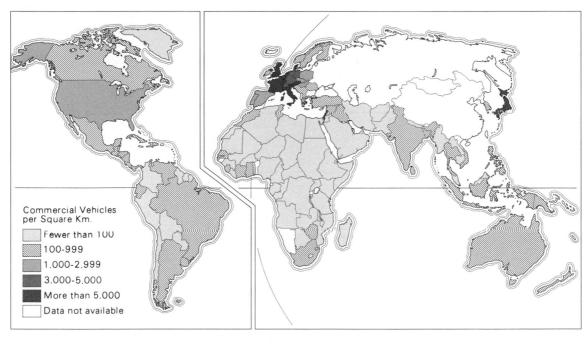

Fig. 6-2. Commercial motor vehicles in use per square kilometer of surface area. Generally, areas with the highest densities of commercial vehicles move the greatest quantities of freight by motor vehicle and have the highest densities of roads. As in Fig. 9-1, however, the averaging of densities for entire nations obscures certain high density road networks such as those in southeastern Canada, the eastern United States, and southeastern Australia. [From *Statistical Yearbook, 1975* (New York: United Nations, 1976), Tables 18 and 157.]

center of any size within the region was served by at least one rail line (Fig. 6-3). As long as there was little competition along east–west routes, the railroads prospered. With the coming of modern highways and motortrucks, completion of the Great Lakes–St. Lawrence Seaway, and development of an extensive network of pipelines to move petroleum products, however, a great deal of the high-revenue freight and most short-haul freight began to move by motortruck and pipeline. In addition, substantial quantities of goods formerly transported by rail from the southern Great Lakes areas to Atlantic ports began moving directly to overseas markets from inland ports such as Chicago. With much of their trade siphoned away, many rail routes became unprofitable. Governmental regulations, however, required that service be maintained on some of the unprofitable lines. Funds for upkeep of tracks and for purchase and repair of equipment were reduced because of falling profits, and the quality of tracks and rolling stock began a long deterioration which further reduced the attractiveness of the railroads as prime movers of

TABLE 6-1. Rail Traffic, Selected Countries: 1976

Country	Passenger Kilometers (Millions)	Freight Net-Ton Kilometers (Millions)
USSR	315,061	3,295,399
United States	15,688	1,146,492
China	NA	301,000[a]
Canada	3,090	195,642
India	148,916	134,874
Poland	42,799	130,857
France	57,168	68,508
Czechoslovakia	17,910	70,748
Germany (West)	36,451	59,219
South Africa	NA	69,336
Japan	322,911	47,550
Romania	22,380	67,560
Germany (East)	21,955	58,181
Norway	1,997	2,709
Mexico	4,058	34,821
United Kingdom	36,840	20,400

[a]1971

SOURCE: *Statistical Abstract of the United States, 1978.*

goods (Fig. 6-4). Passenger service, faced with competition from private automobiles, airlines, and buses, was drastically curtailed, and the frequency of freight service was reduced on many routes (Tables 6-2 and 6-3). The loss of business by the railroads finally resulted in bankruptcy for several major companies and a gradual assumption of responsibility for their operation by the United States Government — first through subsidizing an expanded passenger service (AMTRAK) and second through establishment of a subsidized freight service called CONRAIL.

Railroads in the Southeast have never experienced the heavy demand for traffic that existed in the Northeast. The southeastern network was a minimum-cost system of much lower density, connecting the largest urban centers without development of extensive feeder lines (short routes connecting minor sources of traffic with main lines). In part because southern lines were not burdened with such heavy maintenance costs and with extensive service over unprofitable routes, they did not experience financial difficulties as severe as those affecting the northeastern lines.

In northwestern Europe the network of rail lines is even more closely spaced than in the northeastern United States. Higher fuel prices and lower personal incomes in Europe than in the United States have discouraged motor vehicle traffic, and the relatively small size of European countries makes internal movement by pipeline less desirable than in the United States.

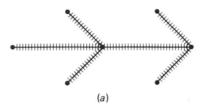

(a)

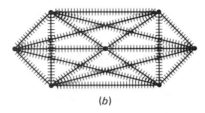

(b)

Fig. 6-3. Minimum cost and maximum service transport networks. (*a*) Minimum cost transport system. All centers are connected, but not necessarily by the most direct routes. This type of system was employed in railroad services to the southeastern United States, and is used in areas where demand for transportation is relatively low. (*b*) Maximum service transport system. All centers are connected by direct routes. This type of system is used in areas where demand for transport is high. A network approximating a maximum service system was built by the railroads to service the northeastern United States, with most construction occurring between 1850 and 1920, prior to the development of motor trucks.

The rail network of the Soviet Union is of greatest density between Moscow and the Black Sea where most of the Soviet population is located. To the east of the Urals railroad service is confined primarily within a wedge-shaped area which narrows toward Lake Baikal. Alternative systems of transport have not been highly developed, with the exception of oil and gas pipelines which now reach most major population centers in the country. The Trans-Siberian Railway is one of the most spectacular engineering accomplishments in the world, stretching more than 5,000 miles between Moscow in the west and Vladivostok on the Pacific Coast.

Extensive railroad development has also occurred in Japan, São Paulo State in Brazil, the Pampas Region of Argentina, central Chile, South Africa, northern India, and in eastern, southeastern, and southwestern Australia. Most of these railroads, as well as those in other regions where line densities

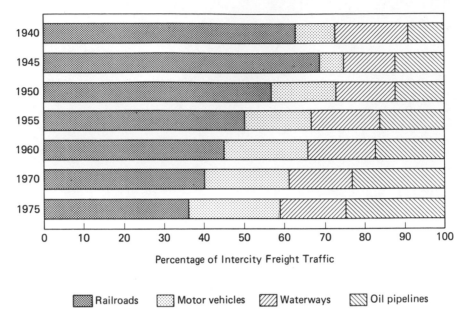

Fig. 6-4. Percentage distribution of ton-miles of intercity freight traffic in the United States by type of transportation: 1940–1975. (Courtesy, Washington D.C.: Bureau of the Census, U.S. Interstate Commerce Commission.)

are lower, were constructed with European capital or at the direct influence of European colonial governments. Exceptions to this generalization have occurred in Manchuria and Korea where railroads were built largely by the Japanese.

Highways

Whereas dense railway networks are confined largely to the most highly developed and densely populated areas of the earth, highway networks are somewhat more uniformly distributed. Developing nations, especially when they are of relatively small size and when the greatest need is for short hauls, normally find that their transportation needs can be more economically and more quickly met through construction of a network of highways than of railways. Roads and motor vehicles are vital to local movements of peoples and goods within urban centers, and they provide a basic stock of equipment which can be used and expanded to service a more extensive transportation network as it develops. Highways also provide routeways for privately owned pleasure and business vehicles which, even in the poorest nations, may be acquired by wealthy and influential individuals and businesses.

TABLE 6-2. Percentage of Intercity Freight Traffic in the United
States, by Type of Transport: 1940 and 1976

Year	Rail	Motor Vehicle	Inland Waterway	Oil Pipelines
1940	63.24	9.53	18.13	9.10
1976	36.52	22.31	16.09	23.90

SOURCE: *Statistical Abstract of the United States, 1975,* p. 547. *Statistical Abstract of the United States, 1978,* p. 639.

Capital requirements for roads of moderate quality and for purchase of motortrucks, buses, and automobiles are normally lower than for building railways and for purchasing railway rolling stock. Because of their ability to move over surfaces which require little skill or equipment to prepare, motortrucks offer a more flexible and extensive transportation system at lower cost than fixed-route railroads within areas where transport systems are in initial stages of development. Furthermore, in many of the least developed areas, roads are more likely to resemble rough trails rather than the long ribbons of smooth concrete and asphalt so familiar in the affluent areas.

Highest highway densities occur in the eastern United States and in northwestern Europe. Few people in these areas live more than a few hundred yards from some sort of road or major highway. On the other hand, the sparsely populated subpolar areas of Canada and the Soviet Union, the tropical Amazonian Lowland of interior Brazil, the Congo Basin, the southeastern one-third of the Arabian Desert, and the desert areas of west–central Australia, interior China, and northern and southern Africa are virtually without roads. The subpolar areas depend largely on air transportation, whereas the Amazon and Congo Basins depend on water transportation. Most remaining areas are served with a sparse network of roads which are often spaced 50 to 300 miles apart.

TABLE 6-3. Percentage of Intercity Passenger Traffic in the United
States, by Type of Transport: 1950 and 1976

Year	Auto	Air	Bus	Rail	Inland Waterway
1950	86.20	01.98	05.20	06.39	00.23
1976	85.77	11.45	01.73	00.76	00.28

SOURCE: *Statistical Abstract of the United States, 1978,* p. 639.

Pipelines

Pipelines have been used primarily to transport oil and natural gas over relatively long distances and are most extensive in the United States, the Soviet Union, Canada, the Middle East, northern Africa, and Venezuela. In the United States, pipelines extend primarily between the major oil- and gas-producing regions in Texas, Oklahoma, and along the Gulf Coast, toward market areas in the eastern, northeastern, and middle western states. In Alaska, an oil pipeline extends from the North Slope Fields at Prudhoe Bay to the southern coast, crossing some of the most difficult terrain on earth. Soviet pipelines have been built from the Caspian Sea, Volga–Urals Field, and the oil and gas fields on the eastern side of the Urals to most sizable cities within the country and into the satellite countries of eastern Europe. Middle East lines extend from the Persian Gulf and from the Kirkuk region in interior Iraq to the eastern Mediterranean. In Canada, the principal line extends from Alberta into eastern Canada, dipping into the United States through Minnesota, Wisconsin, and Michigan. Venezuelan lines are designed to move oil to export points along the coast, as are the pipelines that have been built in Algeria and Libya.

Europe does not possess an extensive pipeline system although several lines have been constructed during recent years between large ports capable of handling supertankers and cities which have large oil refining capacities. An example is the movement of crude oil by pipeline from the "superport" of Rotterdam, The Netherlands, to oil refineries in Antwerp, Belgium.

Air Transportation

Air transportation is designed primarily to move passengers rather than freight, although as larger aircraft are built, their importance as cargo carriers increases. Excluding private automobiles, aircraft were responsible for more than 80 percent of all intercity passenger movement in the United States in 1976, compared to less than 15 percent in 1950 (Table 6-3).

Number of passengers carried and number of flights arriving and departing a city are closely related to that city's relative affluence and economic structure. The general circulation pattern is roughly the same as that for railroads, except that air routes extend into remote areas that are not reached by railways nor at times by highways, and a dense net of routes crisscrosses the North Atlantic and several other ocean areas.

Inland Water Transportation

The most extensive system of heavily used inland waterways is in western Europe, centering upon the coastal areas of northern France, Belgium, The

Traveling to market by oxcart in a developing area. Note the Volkswagen advertisement alongside the road. (Reprinted from *War on Hunger,* a publication of the Agency for International Development.)

Netherlands, and Germany and extending into central France and Germany. In the United States, the Great Lakes provide the finest inland waterway system in the world. The lakes are connected with the Atlantic Ocean through the St. Lawrence River, the New York Barge Canal and Hudson River, and the Mississippi River. The longest waterway system comprises the Mississippi River and its major tributaries, including the Ohio, the Tennessee, and the Missouri Rivers. An extensive system of canals has also been constructed along the Atlantic and Gulf Coasts, known as the Intracoastal Waterway. The Intracoastal Waterway is unbroken from southern New England to the southern tip of Florida, but there are several gaps in its development along the Gulf Coast.

In Latin America, the greatest potential for water transportation is along the Amazon River and its tributaries, but demand for movement of goods along most of the system is small. The Rio de la Plata and the Rio Parana in Argentina and Paraguay also provide a navigable channel reaching from Brazil to the Argentine port city of Buenos Aires.

Inland waterways are relatively rare in Africa, which is a plateau continent with most of the land surface (even near the coast) standing 1,000 feet or more above sea level. No large areas of low plains exist on the continent, as the entire mass has been rising slowly from the sea. The Congo River and a few of its tributaries are navigable for short distances, sometimes interrupted by falls and rapids, and the Nile River is navigable through Egypt and in the southern part of the Sudan. Otherwise, only a few rivers reaching the coast are navigable, and then only for short distances inland. Lack of penetration of the continent by navigable rivers was a major factor retarding the exploration of Africa in contrast to the lengthy penetration of navigable streams into North and South America.

The Soviet Union has a number of large rivers which are navigable during part of the year, but they freeze over during the winter. The Volga, the Donets, and several other rivers in the European portion of the country are extensively used for transportation, along with the Caspian Sea. In non-Soviet Asia a few rivers, such as the Ganges of India, the Yangtze of China, and the Mekong of Vietnam and Cambodia, are navigable for considerable distances.

Ocean Transportation

The most heavily traveled oceanic trade route is in the North Atlantic between the United States and western Europe. A great variety of manufactured goods, raw materials, and other products are traded along this routeway. A second highly significant routeway extends from the Persian Gulf and eastern Mediterranean to northern and southern Europe and is used primarily for the movement of oil. Oil shipments are also relatively heavy along routeways that extend from the Persian Gulf around southern Asia to Japan and around the southern tip of Africa to Europe and North America. Other heavily used trade routes involve shipments of oil and iron ore from Venezuela to the United States and Europe, shipment of agricultural commodities from Argentina and Brazil to Europe, and a diverse trade between the west and east coasts of the United States through the Panama Canal.

URBAN TRANSPORTATION

Ironically, the vast improvements in transportation which have made it possible for people and goods to move over great distances at low cost and at great speed have created enormous problems for urban areas. The automobile has encouraged development of urban centers which sprawl over hundreds of square miles. Residential, commercial, and industrial areas are often spread so thinly over the landscape that the provision of profitable mass transit systems has become nearly impossible. Problems such as pollution from automobile exhausts, congestion, the high cost of building new highways, the large quantities of land absorbed by highway construction, the threat of energy shortages, and the migration of employment from central cities to suburban areas have combined to focus a great deal of attention upon urban transportation during recent years.

Prior to the automobile, most cities were built rather compactly. Sources of employment were found primarily in central city areas and workers lived near their jobs or near mass transit routeways which gave them access to central city jobs. Even today, in parts of the world where automobiles are not affordable or available to most families, this pattern of urban development remains. In the United States, however, which possesses approximately 41 percent of the world's motor vehicles, automobiles have provided extraordinary mobility to individuals. Widespread automobile ownership has liberated workers from the necessity of living near their jobs or near public transit lines, making possible the rapid growth of low density suburban residential areas. Since World War II, some two-thirds of all new single-family homes have been built in suburbs. More than half of the nation's metropolitan population now lives in suburban areas and during the last two decades sources of employment have joined the migration to the suburbs. In the meantime, public mass transit systems have deteriorated because commuters and shoppers prefer the greater freedom and flexibility of movement provided by automobiles (Fig. 6-5).

Suburbanization of residences and jobs has produced major changes in travel patterns within cities. In the past, most trips were inbound to the central city in the morning and outbound in the afternoon and evening. Today's flows are more widely diffused, however, with a large percentage of trips originating and ending within the surburbs. Low population densities and the availability of automobiles within the suburbs have made it unprofitable to extend urban mass transit systems into suburban areas. As a consequence, relatively low income or disabled central city residents who do not own or who do not drive automobiles find it difficult or impossible to reach jobs when places of employment move to the suburbs.

Efforts to relieve congestion and to provide access routes for metropolitan area residents by building more and larger highways have often created more problems than they have solved. Urban land has been swallowed up by roads and parking lots, most street and highway facilities have proved obsolete by the time they were completed and have rarely led to improvements in travel efficiency, and new high-speed highways have often caused an increase in congestion on older connecting streets by pouring onto them far greater volumes of traffic than they were designed to handle.

Strategies for handling traffic have recently shifted from the construction of new highways toward better management of traffic, encouragement of multiple occupancy of vehicles, and improving mass transit. The management strategies employed include promotion of car pooling, van pooling, minibus systems, express buses, and better planning for and extension of services of traditional mass transit systems. Some cities have reserved certain traffic lanes for automobiles involved in car pooling and for transit buses. Employers and employee unions are being urged to establish van pool systems whereby vans capable of seating 8 to 12 persons are used to transport persons to jobs. Express buses collect workers living in specific suburban areas for speedy and inexpensive trips to or near to their places of employment. Some cities are banning automobiles from their downtown areas and others are providing heavy subsidies to mass transit systems so as to reduce fares and make transit riding more economically attractive than before.

Several types of mass transit systems are in use in the world's cities. Most small cities possess only a system of motor buses if they have a system at all. The largest cities may utilize motor buses, streetcars, subways, and some form of surface rail transit. Motor bus systems have the advantage of routeway flexibility and relatively low cost, for they do not require construction of system-specific roadbeds, tracks, or subsurface facilities. Light rail transit (primarily streetcar and trolley cars) was in its heyday during the early 1900s prior to the coming of the automobile. Streetcars and trolleys are now almost nonexistent in the United States (a few remain in San Francisco and Pittsburgh), although they are still in use in many European cities. The advantage of light rail systems is that they can operate in conjunction with automobiles, buses, and trucks, running on rails embedded in city streets. In Europe light rail transit is frequently employed in the larger cities to provide feeder service to rapid rail transit. Several cities in the United States and Canada now have light rail transit systems in planning or construction stages.

Rapid rail transit (commuter trains) has the advantages of speed and large passenger capacity and it is used primarily in densely populated corridors of large cities. Because rapid rail systems operate at high speed, stations for boarding and departing the system are relatively long distances apart, which hampers the collection and distribution of passengers. The Bay Area Rapid Transit System (BART) in the San Francisco area is one of the newest rapid rail systems in the world. Older systems in the United States, however, are less attractive than those operating in Europe. The primary disadvantage of rapid rail systems is high cost of construction. They also have fixed routeways, which focus upon the downtown areas of cities when trends are toward more lateral than radial movements.

A subway is an underground railway which has the capability of moving passengers quickly over relatively long distances within large, densely populated metropolitan areas. The cost of subway construction is high, generally running several million dollars per mile. Thus subways are found only in the world's largest cities such as London, New York, Moscow, Tokyo, Paris, Chicago, Buenos Aires, and Boston. The world's first subway system was opened in London in 1863. Boston built the first American subway system, opening about 1½ miles of line in 1897. New York has the largest system in the world; and Moscow, the cleanest and most attractive. A new subway system opened in Washington, D.C., in 1977. The subway trains travel as fast as 75 mph, and average 35 mph, compared to an average speed for automobiles during rush hours of 8 mph [1]. Other cities with subway systems include Madrid, Sydney, Philadelphia, Mexico City, and Toronto.

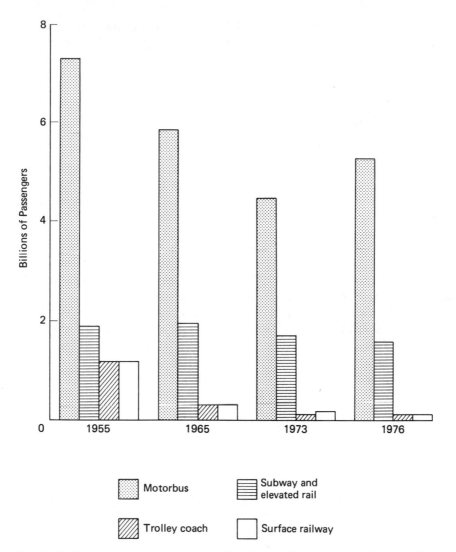

Fig. 6-5. Number of passengers carried by public transportation in the United States: 1955 to 1976. (Courtesy, Washington D.C.: Bureau of the Census, American Public Transit Association.)

Demand Responsive Transit (DRT)) systems include taxicabs, dial-a-ride services, and subscription bus service. Taxicabs may be the most used of all inner city forms of transportation, although data to support this conclusion are not available. Dial-a-ride systems generally use vans or small buses which operate over flexible routeways according to schedules which adjust to demands for the service. Subscription bus service depends for success on rather large groups having common origins and destinations. The most expensive of the DRT systems is taxi service, with costs of other systems falling some-where between taxis and the more traditional modes of public transit.

Numerous cities, especially in Europe, have partially or completely ban-ned use of private automobiles within downtown urban areas. A major motive for such "auto-restraint" policies is the large portion of downtown areas that must otherwise be devoted to moving, parking, and servicing automobiles. As much as 50 percent of the downtown areas of some cities consist of roads, parking lots, and other auto service facilities. Thus the elimination of private vehicles enables a more compact and efficient develop-ment of land within downtown business districts; reduces congestion, pollu-tion, and noise; and allows for more carefree and convenient shopping.

Most public transportation facilities in the United States serve primarily poor, elderly, and handicapped persons who do not have access to private automobiles. An exception is rapid rail transit systems whose customers are primarily residents of affluent suburbs who work in central city areas.

Mass transportation systems have the potential for effecting substantial savings to consumers by reducing the need for new highway construction. Mass transit also reduces the amount of land required for transportation routeways, saves energy, lessens pollution, and eliminates the frustration of driving and searching for parking space in congested areas. The disadvantages of mass transit include decreased flexibility in home-to-work trips, more time is often required in the commuting process than when traveling by private auto, schedules are sometimes inconvenient, and some vehicles are less comfortable than automobiles. When properly operated, however, most of the discomfort, extra time required for the work trip, and scheduling inconveniences can be eliminated.

CONCLUSIONS

Improved transportation has made possible the growth of great cities and the availability of vast numbers and quantities of goods and services at rela-tively low cost, and it has extended travel and educational horizons. At the same time, many new problems have arisen because of modern transporta-tion, with the leading culprit being the private automobile. Although modern transportation places many burdens upon society, the alternative of an-tiquated and poorly developed transportation systems is an even greater handicap to achievement of the economic and social goals of most of the world's peoples.

REFERENCES

[1] *Metro '77 Owner's Manual* (Washington, D.C.: Washington Metropolitan Area Transit Authority, 1977), p. 4.

CHAPTER SEVEN

economic disparities and human spatial behavior

INTRODUCTION

One of the most interesting developments of modern human geography is the recent concern with the way in which people structure the world within their own heads. These "mental maps" differ among individuals and have been shown to be a function of cultural background, socioeconomic status, environmental experiences, and numerous other factors [1]. Studies of human behavior have yielded many useful generalizations about human spatial decision making and patterned responses that affect our interaction with others and with our environment [2]. The emphasis of this chapter will be upon worldwide variations in ways of thinking and structuring reality. Research in the economic consequences of human decision-making processes is in an incipient stage of development within geography. Because of the scant research on this important subject, many of the conclusions reached in this chapter are conjectural and subject to debate.

OPTIMISM VERSUS FATALISM

One of the most important distinctions between the majority of the peoples of the developing world and those of the developed nations is their outlook toward the future. With little formal education and little exposure to modern ideas and life-styles, many of the millions of peoples living in the isolated rural villages of developing nations have adopted a fatalistic attitude toward life. Although many psychologists would argue that attitudes are not particularly good predictors of behavior, attitudes nonetheless color the decisions that individuals make. Attitudes are difficult to change once they are formed [3]. Millions of rural dwellers who rely directly upon the land for their survival have adopted a fatalistic attitude toward their environment. During years of sufficient rainfall when the growing season is of adequate length, the environment is viewed as a benevolent force. Catastrophic weather events are, however, looked upon as "acts of God," dispensed as punishment for human wrongdoing. Many of the animistic tribal religions prevalent in portions of equatorial Africa and southeastern Asia hold to such fatalistic viewpoints. If natural events are viewed as capricious acts of unappeased gods, then humans can do nothing to prevent or minimize the damage wrought by such events.

A person with an optimistic viewpoint might react in a wholly different manner to the same natural forces. Realizing that damage from catastrophic natural events can often be eliminated or reduced by human modification, precautionary measures would be taken. In an agricultural setting the farmer might build levees, terrace the land, channel irrigation waters, or dig wells to tap groundwater sources in order to minimize the environmental harm of flood or drought.

Evidence that such differences in attitudes have perceptible economic consequences was provided by a recent study of tornadoes in Illinois and Alabama [4]. Although the frequency and intensity of tornado activity is approximately the same in the two states, the death rate caused by tornadoes is nearly twice as great in Alabama as it is in Illinois. Discounting factors such as differences in housing construction and housing quality, it was concluded that the significant difference in the tornado-related death rate was caused primarily by differences in the degree to which residents of the two states hold fatalistic viewpoints about natural events. Illinois residents were portrayed as more willing than Alabamians to take precautions that would minimize the danger of personal and property damage. Alabama residents, who heard the same type of media broadcast reports of tornado watches and warnings as did Illinoians, were more resigned to their "fate" and less willing to take preventative measures which might have saved lives. Part of the difference in the degree of fatalism was attributed to the higher proportion of Alabama residents who were affiliated with fundamentalist Protestant religious sects. Some evangelistic and pentecostal religions emphasize that the outcomes of events are part of God's will and His Divine Plan. The study has been criticized for failing to consider that Alabama has a much greater percentage of intense tornadoes which occur at night than does Illinois. Such tornadoes are likely to catch residents unprepared [5]. Although many other factors could be used to explain the difference in death rates, the optimism-fatalism continuum provides a provocative hypothesis for further testing.

PERCEPTION OF NATURAL HAZARDS

The degree to which precautions are taken to counteract the impact of catastrophic natural events is a function of the event's frequency. People seem to have short memories. If the probability of a flood is low, little is normally done to protect against potential flood damage. Even in a well-watered region such as east Tennessee, where flooding of some small streams usually occurs about once in 5 years, only 25 percent of those endangered by flooding take protective measures [6]. Individuals who have resided in an area a long time and those who are high achievers tend to be better prepared for such disasters than their newer or lower achieving counterparts [7].

The consequences of differing hazard perception on the economic geography of a region is only vaguely understood. More than 50 percent of the world's population, for example, lives on the fertile floodplains of major rivers. Because floodplains have the level land so desirable for commercial, industrial, residential, and agricultural uses, they become magnets for development. The potential for loss of life and property on floodplains is enormous. More than 300,000 lives were lost during flooding in the wake of strong winds that struck coastal Bangladesh in 1970 and again in 1971 [8]. Even in the United States where such natural events are not generally viewed as "acts of God," the potential exists for disastrous economic repercussions. Earthworks, levees, and other preventative flood control measures often lull people into a false sense of security concerning hazards. The collapse of dams in Idaho and Georgia during 1976 and 1977 tragically illustrates the problem. Recent federal policy has addressed the unwillingness of individuals to protect themselves from potential flood disaster. Until recently the emphasis of federal policy was placed upon protection from floods. When protection failed, monetary assistance was offered in the aftermath of such events. New federal regulations now require local governments to assure that the design of buildings on floodplains incorporates flood-resistent features. Otherwise owners of floodplain structures cannot purchase government flood insurance. Without such insurance, no bank would be permitted to make a construction loan or grant a mortgage on the property. Further, no property owner in a community that is not part of the program will be eligible for disaster relief [9]. The United States Government thus recognizes that psychologically most people tend to minimize the probability of catastrophe and are loathe to take precautionary measures. The new federal regulations should result in less property damage attributable to flooding.

In many of the poorer nations of the world limited funds force most

One form of behavior is despair. This farmer observes his field, which has received no rain for more than six months. (Reprinted from *War on Hunger*, a publication of the Agency for International Development.)

government efforts to be reactive in nature. Disaster relief may be provided in the aftermath of such events, but little is done to educate the people about the potential dangers of floodplain occupance before a disaster happens.

LEVELS OF ECONOMIC RISK

The natural hazard research discussed in the previous section illustrates *coping mechanisms* that individuals and governments have developed to deal with uncertainty. Individuals tend to downplay, or to eliminate from their thinking, the uncertainty associated with hazards [10]. Individuals may deny or downgrade the existence of the hazard ("We have no floods here, only high water.") or the recurrence of such a catastrophic event ("Lightning never strikes twice in the same place."). Other individuals attempt to eliminate the uncertainty by either assuming that such situations are determinate ("Floods come every 5 years.") or transfering their uncertainty to a higher power ("It's in the hands of God."). Individuals vary in the sense of efficacy they possess. *Efficacy* can be defined as the extent to which an individual feels capable of affecting the world. We have hypothesized that this sense is more strongly felt by individuals in advanced societies than those in developing nations.

It is difficult to generalize about entire culture groups, but even if we assume that people facing the same conditions would make similar choices, worldwide differences in behavior would be observed because of the variable circumstances in which people find themselves. Factors which affect decision making include income, educational attainment, age, religion, cultural background, occupation, and organizational roles. Experts on food production have often been frustrated by the slow rate of adoption in third world nations of new "miracle" varieties of staple foodstuffs such as rice, millet, and wheat. The immensity of the task of communicating information on the properties of high yielding varieties of grain to the thousands of agricultural villages which could benefit by their adoption is a major barrier to adoption.

Communication channels are further confounded by resistance of the farming population to new varieties of grain. Resistance to change may be economically justified in agricultural regions typified by the lack of fertilizer, machines, marketing mechanisms, storage, and an incentive to drive prices downward.

Small landholders may be unwilling to change their agricultural practices because they can't afford the fertilizer and machines necessary to grow the new varieties. Only the relatively large landholder can afford the luxury of experimentation. Adopting new innovations involves a degree of risk that the farmer who is literally staking his family's life on inefficient but time-tested methods may be unwilling to take. Reticence of the small landholder may be attributed to a conservative attitude (i.e., an aversion) toward risk taking.

Some reasons for not adopting "beneficial" innovations may seem odd to Western mentalities. A particularly prolific strain of rice developed as an outcome of the "green revolution" was not readily adopted by farmers in Thailand because the gluten content of the kernels did not produce the sticky rice cherished in the Thai diet. Even though the yield was almost double that of the traditionally grown varieties, the new hybrid "tasted funny" and was only slowly adopted in that cultural milieu.

Not only do individuals vary in their economic ability to take risks, but they also vary in their predisposition to taking risks. Some people are gamblers; others will attempt to minimize potential losses whether or not such a strategy results in lower than maximum monetary (or other) gain. Three different decision-making strategies may be illustrated graphically (Fig. 7-1). Strategy 1, which includes the greatest risk factor, would be pursued by individuals ("gamblers") who are so overwhelmed by the poten-

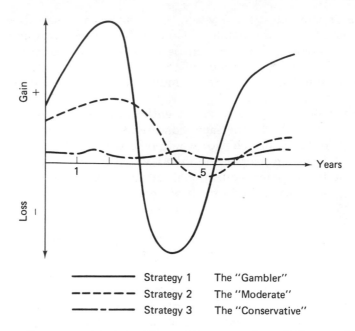

Fig. 7-1. Three individual decision-making strategies which vary in their degree of risk.

tial gain to be reaped during good times that they almost ignore the equally disasterous losses they might accrue during bad times. In a Western capitalist economy such individuals might invest solely in "long shots" (e.g., new companies, speculative ventures, unproved technologies). As the amount of discretionary income one has to invest increases, the propensity to invest in such risky, but potentially lucrative, ventures should also increase.

Strategy 2, which involves only a moderate degree of risk, is pursued by a majority of individuals in developed societies, as it avoids the vicissitudes of the higher risk ventures and yet returns more gain in the long run than the conservative strategy (Strategy 3). Examples of pursuing such a strategy would include individuals who diversify their investments by purchasing stocks with high growth potential as well as "blue chip" stocks and bonds which are steady gainers. Farmers who diversify their crop and livestock mix may also be engaging in such a "moderate" decision-making strategy. If, however, environmental conditions are so uniform that a single crop would yield a high return with relatively low risk, crop diversification would then be a highly conservative strategy.

Strategy 3, the lowest risk-taking alternative, is employed by individuals who wish to minimize the risk associated with a bad investment. Individuals who might pursue such a strategy are those who have everything to lose by even a small loss and who possess no discretionary income.

GAME THEORETICAL APPROACHES
TO DECISION MAKING

In the previous section decision making was viewed as a function of both the characteristics of the individual and the environment within which decisions are made. One method of formalizing these two important elements of decision making is to use game theory [11]. The figures obtained by this mathematical procedure offer the decision maker an objective method to choose among several alternatives. Through game theory one may calculate the probability of various outcomes and determine optimal procedural strategies under different initial conditions.

For purposes of illustration, let us assume that there are two players in a game — the decision maker and the environment. We are not assuming that the environment is an active agent capable of making choices but rather that the environment presents different regimes against which the decision maker must react.

In our game theory example, agriculturalists live in a region of rather low natural rainfall but near a large river which periodically floods. To keep the illustration simple we shall assume that the choices available to the farmer are to grow either wheat or rice; the river may or may not flood during a given year. If the river floods, the waters may be used to advantage; the fertile silt can boost the yield on a crop such as rice, which needs lots of water during the early growth stage. Wheat, on the other hand, could be irreparably damaged by floodwaters. The decision as to which crop to grow involves economic risk. If, for example, a farmer decided to grow wheat and the fields became flooded, the farmer would lose the entire crop and would have to dip into savings in order to buy new seed for the succeeding crop.

Given the states that the environment can assume (flood or no flood) and the crops that the farmers may grow (wheat or rice), the amount of monetary return under the four possible combinations of individual choices and environmental conditions may be determined and expressed in the form of a *payoff matrix* [Fig. 7-2(a)]. The figures within the cells of the matrix represent the expected return from a particular environmental condition and farming choice expressed in monetary units. A farmer who decided to grow rice in a flood year would stand to gain 60 monetary units (e.g., American dollars, British pounds) per unit of land under cultivation (in our example). The negative number in the lower left-hand cell (wheat, flood) indicates a net loss of money per land unit because not only is the crop lost by flooding but also new seed needs to be purchased from savings to obtain a crop the following year.

What crop should a farmer plant in order to maximize the return on his or her investment? The answer to that question depends on the probability of having adequate moisture in a given year. Let us assume that three farmers

(A, B, and C) own land at differing elevations from the river. The probability of flooding declines with increasing distance from, and elevation above, the river's bank [Fig. 7-2(b)]. Let us assume that the probability of having a spring flood is 60 percent on the floodplain, 30 percent at an intermediate distance from the river, and 0 percent at higher elevations far from the river. For farmer C tending a plot on the high ground, the question of which is the best decision strategy is simple. That farmer is in the privileged position of facing a no-risk situation. Over a 10-year period, farmer C would make 800 income units per land area if he grew wheat:

$$10 \text{ years} \times 80 \text{ units/land area} = 800 \text{ units/land area/10 years}$$

and only 200 units if he planted rice:

$$10 \text{ years} \times 20 \text{ units/land area} = 200 \text{ units/land area/10 years}$$

The answer to the question of optimal decision strategy is not quite so obvious for farmers B and A. Farmer B, occupying an intermediate elevation, must calculate the payoff of each strategy as follows:

Rice:

$$3 \text{ years} \times 60 \text{ units/land area and 7 years} \times 20 \text{ units/land area}$$
$$= 320 \text{ units/land area/10 years}$$

Wheat:

$$3 \text{ years} \times -40 \text{ units/land area and 7 years} \times 80 \text{ units/land area}$$
$$= 440 \text{ units/land area/10 years}$$

Only 3 of every 10 years have sufficient moisture (30 percent) to grow rice with a high yield and, given these long-run conditions, farmer B would be wise to grow wheat.

Farmer C would calculate the economic returns, given the two alternatives strategies, in a similar manner:

Rice:

$$6 \text{ years} \times 60 \text{ units/land area and 4 years} \times 20 \text{ units/land area}$$
$$= 480 \text{ units/land area/10 years}$$

Wheat:

$$6 \text{ years} \times -40 \text{ units/land area and 4 years} \times 80 \text{ units/land area}$$
$$= 120 \text{ units/land area/10 years}$$

Farmer C would thus be advised not to grow wheat in an environment where flood years occur 60 percent of the time. It should be emphasized that the goal of the farmer is assumed to be *long-run* profit maximization. Marginal subsistence farmers may not be willing to take any risk which could result in negative short-run returns to their investments. Such subsistence farmers

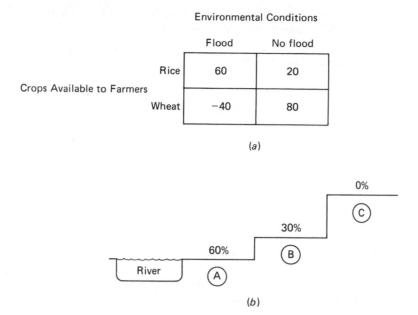

Fig. 7-2. (*a*) A hypothetical payoff matrix. Cells of the matrix are calibrated in monetary units per unit of land area per year. (*b*) Probability of flooding as a function of land elevation.

would never grow wheat except on the highest ground in our example because one flood might wipe out their life savings.

SATISFICING BEHAVIOR

In our previous game theory example we assumed that the primary decision-making motive was profit maximization. The use of profit maximization as a norm or goal pervades most of the capitalistic location theory literature. Not only is it fallacious to assume profit maximization a goal in centrally planned economies, it is also naive to assume that profit maximization is the only goal of economic decision making in the capitalist economies.

To what extent is the modeled ideal of profit maximization actually achieved in daily economic transactions? Are there identifiable geographical patterns of the degree to which actual decisions depart from the optimum? Both of these important questions have been addressed in an article dealing with farming decisions in central Sweden [12]. A determination was made, within the limits of the land's productivity, of the yield that could poten-

*Cells of the matrix are calibrated in monetary units per unit of land area per year.

tially be obtained by an optimum combination of inputs (including fertilizer) and sound farm practices. Nowhere within the study area did any farmer's earnings equal the ideal amount. The larger farm operators and those located near agricultural experiment stations, the source of much technological information on improved farm practices, came closer to the ideal productivity than their smaller and more distant counterparts.

Personal and geographical factors would, therefore, be invoked to explain the pattern of departures from potential yield. Interviews with farmers in the area indicated that the people were, in general, content with their lot in life and felt they were doing the best they could. These farmers were not simply rationalizing the suboptimal decisions they had made; they were unaware of the full economic potential of their farm parcels. In addition to ignorance of the range of farming options available, motives other than profit maximization influenced their decisions. Farming decisions may be influenced by past experience, subjective evaluations of market prices, desire for personal freedom from farm chores, and a host of other noneconomic goals, some of which are in conflict with the profit maximization principle. Decision makers may often be satisfied with a decision that returns some profit to the investment (*satisficing behavior*) even if that decision is less than the profit maximizing solution (*optimizing behavior*). Such a decision-making framework has been labeled *bounded rationality* [13]. It was suggested that these farmers exhibited *satisficing behavior* because they were satisfied with suboptimal returns to their labors.

THE BEHAVIORAL MATRIX

The economic consequences of suboptimal behavior were systematically examined by Pred [14]. Pred was dissatisfied with the profit maximizing assumptions of most of the economic location theory literature. Humans do not function as automatons, who have perfect knowledge and perfect ability to synthesize and integrate that knowledge to solve complex locational problems. In much of the theoretical literature of economics, however, this is exactly how humans are assumed to behave. Economists introduced the term *economic man* to describe such optimal human decision-making behavior. Knowledge, and the ability to use it, may be viewed as two independent dimensions of human decision-making ability (Fig. 7-3). The two dimensions may be used to form a matrix in which the optimal decisions of economic man would be located in the upper right-hand corner (indicated by *x* in Fig. 7-3). Economic man is only a goal or an ideal that decision makers may strive for but never achieve. The reasons why real-world economic decisions are far from perfect may be attributed to a myriad of factors but may be generalized into aspects of human fallibility and the imprecision of the communication process. Some, such as Mr. A represented

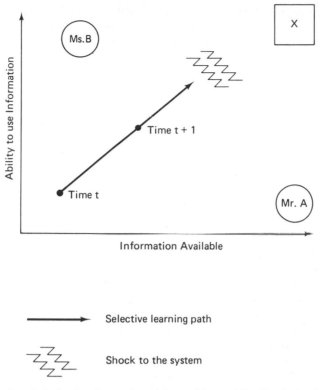

Fig. 7-3. Pred's behavioral matrix. (Adapted from Allen Pred, "Behavior and Location, Part I. Lund Studies in Geography," Series B, No. 27, 1967.)

in the lower right-hand corner of the behavior matrix (Fig. 7-3), have much information available to them but are unable to integrate the information successfully into a comprehensible whole. As an example, Mr. A might have located a gasoline service station at the intersection of the busiest streets in town, but the business still fails because he is an inept manager of his resources. On the other hand, Ms. B, located in the upper left-hand area of the matrix, is a shrewd individual who is perceptive enough to make a successful location decision without much information upon which to base the decision. The degree to which such decisions represent a conscious choice process as opposed to being lucky is considered in the next section.

Successful manufacturers during the industrial revolution, for example, resemble the relative location of Ms. B within the behavioral matrix. These manufacturing pioneers were experimenting with new materials, new equipment, and new processes. The most efficient and cost effective methods of production, such as the use of interchangeable parts developed by Eli Whitney for the firearms industry, were soon adopted by other manufacturers in the same industry and were adapted by industries manufacturing other products.

A selective learning path would normally be followed as time progresses (represented by the diagonal movement of the directed line in Fig. 7–3). Even though quality of locational decisions may proceed toward the upper right-hand corner of the behavioral matrix, barriers in the learning process make economic man (x in the upper right-hand corner) unattainable in the real world. Channels of communications are far from perfect. The failure rates of businesses offer evidence that entrepreneurs often do not learn from the mistakes of others. In a highly competitive business atmosphere new technologies, decision strategies, and tricks of the trade are often kept secret lest the competitor gain an advantage; hence the reasons for a business failure may be only imperfectly known by others in the same product lines. How often have you observed continual business failures at the same location in your own hometown? The corner gasoline station fails and is replaced by a used-car lot which in turn in converted into a short-order restaurant only to be taken over by a muffler shop. Marginal small-scale enterprises probably have the weakest communication channels of all. Like the myth of the Phoenix rising from the ashes of dispair, optimism seems engrained into the business acumen of our Western culture. It is common for a small businessperson to blame poor management of predecessors for failure of the business at a particular location. That same person has confidence, however, that with diligence and hard work he or she will succeed at that same location. Failure statistics for selected business categories do not bear out such optimism. Fully one-half of all businesses fail within 2 years of operation. Most of the failures are accounted for by a few retail categories, most notably eating and drinking establishments and gasoline service stations. The economic loss from bankruptcy of such marginal enterprises is staggering.

Other factors which thwart the learning path of decision-making improvement within the behavioral matrix are termed *shocks to the system*. An example of such a shock would be a change in technology. In the early iron and steel industry, for example, it took as much as 8 tons of coal to produce a ton of finished steel. Because coal was bulky and low in value per unit of weight, it could not be transported over long distances. Thus foundries which located near sources of abundant coal grew to predominance. Newer technologies have considerably changed the nature of today's iron and steel industry. With these newer technologies high-quality steel can be made in smaller batches using lesser quantities of bulky raw materials (iron ore, coal) in a shorter time than with the older methods. Locations closer to markets have grown rapidly, whereas steel centers located near raw materials have declined. New steelmaking processes represent shocks to the system which may force the entrepreneurs back to an earlier and less knowledgeable stage of decision making. Although not explicitly considered by Pred in his behavior matrix model, one could imagine shocks to the system which have the salutary effect of expediting the learning process. The formation of a bargaining cartel in steel might, for example, allow an exchange of technical information on production processes that previously would have been impossible. Such a new forum for idea exchange might lead to improved decision making.

A familiar example of a shock to the system has recently occurred in the electronics industry. Introduction of solid-state circuitry, microprocessors, and silicon chips have revolutionized the industry. Electronic calculators are one of the few recent consumer products that we have observed decreasing in price as new technologies become standardized. Many new companies have been formed to meet the demand for such electronics products. Santa Clara County, California, has already gained a reputation as "Silicon Valley," the focus of the high-growth sector of the electronics industry [15]. Other products are rendered obsolete by such technological shocks. For example, Keuffel and Esser Company, once the world's largest producer of slide rules, stopped manufacturing them in 1972 because slide rules could not compete with the faster, more accurate, and less expensive pocket calculator [16].

ADAPTIVE VERSUS ADOPTIVE BEHAVIOR

Doubts have been raised about the capability of economic decision makers to make optimal choices. Confounding the problem is the question of the relevant time frame. Decisions which are made to optimize short-term goals may not be ideal in the long run. The economic environment within which decisions are made is not static. Changing tastes and preferences of consumers, changing resource imputs, and changing technologies may all interact to make a valid decision at one time invalid at another. Because we cannot predict the future with certainty, it is impossible to identify the best long-run choices.

It is possible that some activities are successful simply by fortuitous circumstance. An entrepreneur operating in an area of relative ignorance (the left-hand side of the behavioral matrix in Fig. 7–3) may choose a location for a variety of reasons other than economic criteria. Personal factors such as a community's cultural attractions and living environment may play an important role in the final location decision. Fear of the unknown may, for example, influence an entrepreneur to choose a business location in his or her hometown. The hometown location might also have been encouraged by availability of loans from local banks, knowledge of existing local markets, and knowledge of local distribution channels. Whether such a local enterprise ever expands and matures is a function of many factors, including the relative accessibility to the potential market for the company's products, strength of competing firms in the same product line, demand for the product, and the value of the product relative to its weight. As the economic environment changes, firms that are well-located, whether as the result of a conscious decision-making process or simply a lucky locational choice, are more likely to survive than those with poor locations. An analogy might be made to the theory of the survival of the fittest [17]. Nature can be viewed as an active agent which selects those traits, mutations, and adaptations within species that are essential for the survival of the species. In like evolutionary manner, the economic environment might be viewed as adopting those locational strategies, locations, and technical processes which are essential for the economic survival of an industry [18]. Business locations, chosen with less-than-perfect knowledge, may survive as the economic environment itself changes.

The concept of economic adoption may be related to the geographic concept of the *spatial margins to profitability* (Fig. 7-4). Spatial margins to profitability may be defined as the geographic limit beyond which a product can no longer generate a viable economic return to the entrepreneur's investment. In our hypothetical example, firm B is much closer to the optimum point during the initial time period (t) than is firm A. As the economic environment changes through time (time period $t + 1$), however, firm A's marginal location has improved dramatically until it is presently very close to the optimum. On the other hand, the previously more advantageously located firm B is no longer within the spatial margins to profitability and would drop out of the economic system by time $t + 1$. Without knowing the rationale for choices made, we do not know whether firm A chose its location through a rational process of accounting for the factors that might affect its viability (e.g., transportation, labor, capital availability, raw material procurement, land and building costs, taxes) or whether the choice

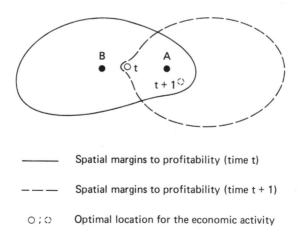

———   Spatial margins to profitability (time t)

— — —   Spatial margins to profitability (time t + 1)

O ; ○   Optimal location for the economic activity

Fig. 7-4. The dynamics of adoptive behavior in the economic environment. [From David M. Smith, *Industrial Location*, (New York: John Wiley & Sons, 1971), p. 272.]

was based on noneconomic criteria (e.g. familiarity, amenities, cultural environment, personal factors). Whether firm A consciously adapted to the changing economic environment or the environment's changes simply adopted A's fortuitous location, the results are the same.

Present locational patterns of economic activities are a legacy of past decisions and environmental changes and opportunities. It is sometimes difficult to sort out any specific factor that would account for a particular geographical distribution. Why is the southern Michigan region near Detroit the premiere automotive center in the United States? That automotive pioneers such as Ransom Olds, the Duryea brothers, and Henry Ford lived and worked in the Detroit area was important, and yet Detroit was only one of several hundred manufacturing locations during the early years of the automotive era. Detroit had the following important prerequisites for rapid development: (1) labor force requirements (e.g., tool-and-die makers, skilled craftsmen), (2) closely related industries (marine engine manufacturing, carriage construction), (3) bankers willing to risk capital on the internal combustion engine which became the means of locomotion eventually accepted by the vast majority of the consuming public. Couple this early start with the introduction of efficient production techniques that kept the cost low (e.g., the assembly line, and interchangeable parts) and the southern Michigan region soon rose to predominance in the industry. The economic environment kept changing, however, and during the 1920s and 1930s forces of decentralization led to a relative decline in the importance of southern Michigan as an automotive center. Labor volatility, standardization of the manufacturing process, management decisions, and the nature of transportation costs on assembled automobiles led to an increasing separation of component parts production and final automobile assembly.

An assembly plant near Atlanta, Georgia, would not have been economically viable in 1930, but as the spatial margins to profitability shifted and the economic environment changed, such a regional assembly function became desirable. The General Motors assembly plant in Doraville and the Ford Motor Company's plant in Hapeville (both Atlanta suburbs) bear witness to this locational shift.

Another example of the change in the economic environment and, therefore, in the spatial margins to profitability is the decline of Chicago as a meat-packing center. The decline may be largely attributed to changes in freezing technology, a shock to the economic system. Change in technology allowed the meat-packing industry to move closer to the cattle-rearing areas of the Great Plains and western corn belt states and thereby reduce the amount of weight the cattle lost when being shipped from the cattle-rearing areas in the West to the feed lots and slaughtering houses of Chicago. Moving the industry closer to the raw material supply allowed the animals to be slaughtered and then immediately chilled. Frozen animal carcasses could be shipped to eastern markets, thereby reducing the amount of weight loss and increasing profits to the packers.

COGNITIVE DISSONANCE

Humans have a remarkable ability to deceive themselves. People like to feel they have made the correct choice even when contrary evidence may be presented. We do not particularly enjoy making decisions involving choices between alternatives, especially if some cost is attached to making such choices. A common strategy humans employ to reduce the stress (*dissonance*) associated with a conscious (or cognitive) choice among several alternatives is to choose the same alternative continually [19]. Much of our behavior is, therefore, routinized or habitual in nature in order to reduce the cognitive dissonance associated with innumerable choice decisions. Habitual behavior is predictable, an important benefit for the social scientist attempting to explain human decision making. We change our behavior patterns only when presented with evidence that the original choice has been a bad one, and even then the change will probably be made reluctantly.

Take, for example, the choice of a route for the journey to work [20]. When a person first moves into a new neighborhood, he or she may engage in an initial search process, trying several routes to get between workplace and residence. After the initial search behavior, the individual will select the route perceived to be the best. Choice of route from this point on is habitual, lowering the stress level associated with conscious choice processes. If the worker receives negative information about the route choice (e.g., a fellow worker claims to know a much better route), the stress level again increases and the person must decide whether to continue the previous behavior pattern or alter the route in light of the new information. The alternative route must be *perceived* as being clearly superior to the former choice. When a conscious decision to switch routes has been made, the decision is often rationalized in order to minimize any misgivings or regret associated with the decision. In a marketing context, such rationalized behavior has been labeled *postpurchase rationalization* [21]. For example, a consumer might reason that he or she purchased an automobile from a particular dealer because that dealer offered the auto at the lowest price. Often only a few dealers were even examined and the consumer had little basis for price comparison. Rather, the choice was rationalized after the purchase had been made.

COGNITIVE IMAGES

Habitual behavior of the type described above may be another manifestation of risk minimization. Behavior is a reaction to objective reality as it is filtered through the human brain. It is often our image of reality and not reality itself upon which we base our decisions [22]. Because we cannot cope with the complexity of all the perceived world's elements and their confounding interactions, we attempt to classify similar objects into categories. Classification is a form of simplification in which meaningful generalizations might be developed. Simplification of complex environments is necessary for humans to function. Sometimes our simplifications of reality are distorted and biased. Stereotypes we hold about other countries or ethnic groups may not square with reality, but our attitudes and actions are nonetheless colored by such stereotypes. An almost universal stereotype is that a country's leaders view their enemies as more hostile and aggressive toward them than they are toward the enemy. The arms race, an escalation of preparedness against perceived aggressiveness, is a manifestation of this lack of equality in images held by the Western and Soviet blocs. Aggregate images of the peoples of a nation are often composites of small groups of powerful leaders, and the image of the mass of ordinary citizens who are affected by the decisions of the elite but take little part in making them. Though not important at the individual level, the influence of the images of ordinary people in the aggregate is great. The image of the elite should not diverge too greatly from that of the masses or else the political regime could be in jeopardy unless the society is held together by coercion of the masses. Images can, however, be manipulated. If the leaders of a country wish to achieve certain goals without resorting to coercive practices, they must convince the people that those goals are consistent with the commonly shared ideals of the country.

The manner in which such a common heritage is inculcated to the masses is a subject of research by social scientists [23]. The rapid diffusion of the transistor radio has been important in the growth of national consciousness among the peoples of many developing nations. The presence of a transistor radio in the tiniest of rural villages has made the majority of the developing nations' citizens aware of the modernization efforts of their central governments. The governments of such nations usually edit or carefully monitor the news content of broadcasts, and important changes in governmental policy can be rapidly transmitted throughout the country.

Awareness leads to a growth of empathy, a major determinant of progress toward modern nationhood. The more conscious a people is of its history, the stronger the national image is likely to be. The consciousness of great shared events and experiences is of utmost importance in building empathy and a desire for progress.

COGNITIVE MAPPING

Way-finding ability varies between individuals and cultures. The Puluwatans of Micronesia, a seafaring people, are able to find their way accurately in outrigger canoes between islands hundreds of miles apart [24]. They have no navigational charts and only recently have used compasses.

Their navigational system exists within the mind of each navigator. Having committed to memory a sequence of stars and constellations, they have learned how to hold their course precisely. Following the stars can be reinforced by studying the sun's path during the day as well as by studying conditions of the oceans (e.g., the height and type of swells) and the presence of animal life (e.g., the homing ranges of various land-based birds). Long-distance seafaring is a way of life for the Puluwatans and their mental or cognitive map of the South Pacific is incredibly accurate. In developed societies the need for precise mental maps of complex urban environments has diminished, as road signs and other cues serve as our guideposts. Some researchers have argued that as the need for precision in mental maps has diminished, so too have the skills for creating precise mental maps [25]. Enough similarities between modern urban areas exist, however, so that the ability to orient ourselves in one urban environment may be transferred to another. We have come to expect that the central business district is a bustling commercial, office, and financial core and that an inner city area near factories and warehouses will be the residences of the poor in the American city. We anticipate that the suburbs of American cities will be populated by middle-class families. The homogeneity of the outer city stands in sharp contrast to the diversity of the inner city. These images are, of course, stereotypes and do not apply to all American cities; nor are they held by all urban residents. They certainly do not fit the morphology of cities in developing countries. The persistence and reinforcement of these images does, however, enable most newly arrived city residents who have some familiarity with urban areas to make sense out of the confusing array of streets and buildings. Other features that help people orient themselves in most American cities are the grid pattern layout of streets, radial highways along which commercial enterprises appear in profusion, the height of downtown buildings, and the familiar sight of a branch of some chain store we have come to know elsewhere. Franchised enterprises have been much maligned as examples of how "plastic" our society has become, and yet the "Golden Arches" and other examples of this genre often serve as familiar and reassuring places for the traveler and recent city migrants as well. Acclimatization to a new environment can be a painful transitional process. Familiar landmarks may help to speed up the adjustment period.

Planners have developed some insight into the manner in which urban residents structure their environments. Five major elements that make cities "imageable" and "legible" have been identified:

1. Paths—routes of frequent travel shared by many residents (e.g., freeways, corridors).
2. Edges—boundaries between different areas (e.g., rivers, rail yards, bridges).

3. Nodes — strategic points of urban interest (e.g., civic buildings, statues, major intersections).
4. Districts — areas having some perceived common identity (e.g., residential areas, university campuses).
5. Landmarks — objects that stand out because of their height, color, or construction (e.g., modern skyscrapers, suspension bridges).

Cities vary in their imageability, as measured by the ability of residents to draw quick sketch maps of their communities [26]. Some cities, such as Boston, are very imageable, as they have numerous points, or landmarks, with which residents or visitors can identify. Other cities, such as Jersey City, have poor imageability. The few commonly held images made a composite impression of Jersey City difficult to formulate.

The image of the city is also partly a function of the activity space of the individual. Individuals who are constrained in their daily activities to a small section of the city tend to have poorly formed images of the city's overall spatial structure. Poorer Hispanic and black residents of the inner city areas of Los Angeles (Boyle Heights and Watts, respectively) have images which are almost exclusively limited to their neighborhoods; only the most cursory image of the ocean and general orientation of the Los Angeles Basin is held by these residents [27]. On the other hand, middle-class suburbanites in the San Fernando Valley area of Los Angeles (Northridge and Westwood) have a much more comprehensive image of the entire city because of their greater mobility. They could sketch with considerable detail their own residential area and elements of the city. Much of the poorer inner city of Los Angeles was, however, not differentiated in the minds of these suburbanites. They knew well only the paths which connected their residences to downtown work locations.

What are the economic consequences and aesthetic implications of cognitive mapping? Just as the Puluwatans memorized a complex series of star positions in order to guide their way, modern urban residents rely upon elements of the environment, past experience, and stereotypes to orient themselves. Being lost implies more than temporary dislocation; it may cause feelings of despair and anxiety [28]. Imageable cities may provide a higher quality of life, a heightened sense of satisfaction, and feelings of sentimental loyalty not felt in their less imageable counterparts. Planners should pause before razing a blighted ethnic neighborhood to which the residents attach much symbolism and sentiment [29]. The disruption of a community caused by the relocation of residences in an urban renewal project is difficult to reinstitute. Architects should broaden their concern about the psychological impact of the buildings they design. Architectural designs which provide functional, utilitarian space at lowest cost may optimize only shortsighted goals. More expensive buildings which provide stimulation of the senses and which excite the imagination may be a better investment in the long run. The proved drawing power of exciting architecture has led to the construction of downtown hotel–apartment–office–shopping complexes such as Peachtree Center in Atlanta and dramatic monuments such as Gateway Arch in St. Louis [30]. If residents and businesses can be attracted, or at least retained, in these downtown environments, the central city may remain a viable entity. Middle- and upper-income residents and businesses would contribute a large share to the maintenance of essential urban services by their property tax payments. Perceptions of such centers as the nuclei of vital expanding core areas will, it is hoped, attract new investment. The psychology which spawned the new urban architecture has diffused to the suburbs as well. Suburban activity centers such as those found in Orange County, California, and Fairfield County, Connecticut, and corridor developments such as the Metropolitan Complex growing up around the new Dallas–Ft. Worth Airport are but a few examples of the suburban attempt to retain old business and to attract new business from central city areas.

ECONOMIC CONSEQUENCES OF IMAGES AND STEREOTYPES

In addition to enabling us to orient ourselves, stereotypes can also be divisive forces, impeding progress toware security and cooperation. *Xenophobia* (the fear of foreigners or strangers) and *ethnocentrism* (the ego-centered preference for one's own group) are both manifestations of stereotypes which affect attitudes, behavioral motivations, and overt behavior. Because it is the image of people, events, and places that leads to particular behavior patterns, it is important that the informational networks by which we receive and form such images are as unbiased and complete in content as possible. The means through which images are shaped and by which values and beliefs are inculcated are complex processes. Two influences affecting economic behavior will be singled out for closer examination — religion and colonialism. Each influence will be considered in turn.

Religion. Religious differences have been cited as one of the major centrifugal forces (forces of disunity) impeding development of viable nation states [31]. The violent confrontations between Protestants and Catholics in Northern Ireland bear witness to the animosity that religious differences can cause. If religious differences are confounded by ethnic and linguistic diversity, the probability of such a culturally pluralistic society remaining a sovereign nation is greatly diminished. The present turmoil in Canada over the Quebec Separatist movement is but one example of deeply troubled pluralistic societies [32].

The geography of meat avoidance is one of the more easily recognized economic consequences of religious differences [33]. Hindus, Moslems, and Jews shun eating the flesh of certain animals because of religious precepts. The reasons for the meat avoidance may involve perceived cleanliness of certain animals (e.g., Jewish and Moslem refusal to eat pork) or a philosophical abhorrence to eating animals which are believed to contain the spirits of individuals who possessed human form in another life (e.g., Hindu vegetarian practices). The economic effects of meat avoidance are clearly felt in India. Although a pluralistic society with more than 300 major spoken languages, India's economic structure is most affected by Hindu religious practices. Cattle are allowed to roam the countryside and cities, devouring valuable crops while foraging. India has the largest number of cattle of any nation on earth, but the cattle are of limited economic benefit. The dung produced by these animals does provide a major source of cooking fuel in the rural villages, and milk by-products (especially butter) are produced which partially supplement the food supply. The burdens created by the almost insatiable appetites of these inefficient energy converters is, however, overwhelming. It takes from 7 to 14 pounds of vegetable matter to produce 1 pound of animal protein. It may seem unthinkable to carnivorous Westerners that Indians starve during periodic famines while the cattle are allowed to live. Attitudes are, of course, a function of socialization. We are often intolerant of a value and belief system that is foreign to our own.

A second aspect of religious practice that has obvious economic consequences is variation in attitude toward birth control, although a myriad of other factors influence the birthrate of a country as well. Where the Roman Catholic church is a predominant force in developing societies (e.g., Latin America), rates of natural increase are generally high. Rates of natural increase are even higher in portions of Asia and Africa where the Roman Catholic church has practically no influence. The amount of world population increase accounted for by Roman Catholic views on abortion and birth control is, therefore, difficult to assess.

In the developed world only slight differences in birthrates may be attributed to Roman Catholicism. France, a heavily Roman Catholic nation, has a somewhat higher birthrate than some of its industrially advanced neighbors, but a larger percentage of the population of France resides in the rural countryside than in many neighboring countries. Differences in birthrate might as easily be attributed to the generally higher rate of birth among rural women as to the influence of the Roman Catholic church. In the centrally planned economies of Czechoslovakia and Hungary, the number of abortions actually exceeds the number of live births. The declining birthrate worries the architects of economic policy for these satellite nations of eastern Europe. Plans call for rapid industrialization and in order to accomplish those goals a much higher birthrate coupled with improved agricultural efficiency must be achieved than is presently the case. Labor needed to work in the planned new factories will become increasingly scarce. The governments of these countries are, therefore, offering monetary incentives for wives to bear more children. Poland does not face the same problem of population decline as do some of the other Soviet satellite nations of eastern Europe. At least part of the difference in Poland's case may be attributed to the still important influence of the Polish Catholic church in this otherwise Communist state.

On a more philosophical level, differences in religion may lead to different outlooks and attitudes toward economic life. The prevailing philosophy of western Christendom in the Middle Ages did not allow Christians to lend money or engage in mercantile enterprises for a profit (usury). Jews, on the other hand, had no such religious constraints against the profit motivation. Jews were allowed to extend credit and charge interest to Jew and Christian alike but were not allowed to reside within the walls of western European cities. Because Jews practiced what the majority Christian population felt to be usury, Jews were forced to live in segregated residential areas, called *ghettos*, outside the walls of the city. The inertia of an early start in commercial enterprise partially accounts for Jewish predominance in many trading endeavors throughout the Renaissance. Changed attitudes on what constituted usurous practices finally allowed Christians in western Europe to engage in mercantilistic ventures fully and eased the tensions between Christian and Jew.

A more striking philosophical distinction can be noted between Western religions which view humans as dominant over nature and Eastern religions which stress human harmony with nature [34]. In the West, there is a desire to impose order upon the landscape in keeping with the Biblical edicts for dominion over the land. Regularity of landscapes in the grid pattern systems of many Western cities and the patchwork settlement fabric laid out by the rectangular township and range survey system in the American Middlewest are but two examples of an attempt to define a Western view of order on the land [35]. The same philosophical difference can be seen when the imposed regular order of the classical English formal garden is compared to the oriental garden. The Oriental *feng-shui* garden, defined so eloquently as "the art of adapting the residences of the living and the dead so as to cooperate and harmonize with the local currents of the cosmic breath," [36] leads to an Eastern preference for curvilinear pathways and naturally sculpted gardens which are viewed as an extension of the home. Too much can be made of such differences in philosophical attitude. Irrespective of religious differences, both Western and Oriental societies have managed to desecrate the natural environment. The discrepancy between the harmonic ideal and reality has been documented from the time of the earliest Chinese dynasties. Parts of China have, however, been continuously cultivated and densely settled for over 6000 years, whereas Westerners have managed to devastate portions of their environment in a much shorter time with considerably lower population densities. Overgrazing, strip-mining on steep slopes, and poor conservation practices may be economically expedient only in the short run. A new land ethic, close to the Eastern ideal of reverence for nature and the ecological balance, appears to be prevalent in the United States. This new land ethic is probably more firmly rooted in the *economic realities* of nonrenewable resources than in *religious attitudes.* Awareness by Americans of the finite nature of many of the important resources needed to maintain their present life-style may finally begin to close the gap between expressed attitudes toward the environment and their economic management of it.

Colonialism. Religious fervor during the Age of Exploration had many spin-offs, not the least of which was the desire of many western European powers to spread Christianity among the peoples of Africa, Asia, and the Americas. Colonialism existed for a variety of reasons, the more important of which were religious piety, monetary greed, strategic location of the colony, and nationalistic ego of the colonial power.

The collective psyche of some western European nations has never recovered from the end of the colonial era. The Netherlands was a powerful nation in the seventeenth century, with colonies stretching from the Americas (Surinam) to Asia (Dutch East Indies). When these colonies were lost, the great commercial seafaring nation received a blow to its collective ego that was difficult to accept. The phrase "the sun never sets on the British Empire" was at the turn of this century literally as well as figuratively true. Britain controlled a larger empire than any other colonial power. Loss of most of that empire has been a traumatic experience for the British.

The legacy of colonialism lives on. The leading trading partner of most of the former colonies of Africa and Asia are their former colonial masters. Trade alliances form a type of "economic colonialism" in which the former colonies are still very dependent on their former masters for finished products and, in turn, are dependent on markets in the former mother country to purchase the products of their mines, forests, and fields.

Colonialism affected and still affects the outlook of former colonies. The colonial power would often force the colony to accept its language, religion, and customs. For example, France had a colonial policy known as "assimilation" in which the native peoples were taught French and converted to Roman Catholicism. Failing to spread the French cultural heritage to *all* peoples within their colonies, France embraced a policy of "association" in which the elite of the colony would be taught the rudiments of French culture. American soldiers involved in the Vietnam War may have been surprised to hear French being spoken by native Vietnamese in the major cities of the country, formerly part of French Indochina.

Many of the organizational problems faced by the newly emerged nations are a legacy of colonialism as well. The mother country often rigidly administered the colonies and did not train a local administrative elite capable of effectively organizing the country when colonial rule ended. Failure to protect the right of individuals, historic tribal factionalism, and premature independence led to disastrous results even in some of the more effectively administered colonies.

Once the colony became independent, it was often a difficult matter to engender a spirit of nationalism. Shared cultural backgrounds make the job of nation-building easier. Nationalism requires allegiance of all parts of the country to the legitimate central government. Judging from the degree of insurgency within the borders of some of the newly emerged nations, the necessary empathy with the goals of the central government discussed earlier is still a long way off. The government in authority can speed the process of national integration by creating a shared cultural heritage. Flags, national anthems, ceremonies, and holidays are important elements of shared culture. As sentiment and attachment to these symbols (or icons) are formed, the bonds holding the state together are strengthened.

CONCLUSIONS

It is difficult to generalize about the influence of human behavior on the economic geography of the world. Behavioral influences are so pervasive that they often defy description; they are so much a part of all of us that they are often second nature. We all *form mental images* and react to the world *as we perceive it* even when our perceptions do not square with reality. It is the function of the human brain to simplify, organize, and structure the complexity of the world so that we may be able to use our cognitive abilities in a meaningful way. Mental disorders can result if the brain cannot sort out the important signals from the background noise of our complex environment. Stereotyping of people and places is not necessarily bad; it is viewed in this chapter as an essential part of the brain's integrating function. The avoidance of cognitive decision making by following routinized behavior patterns is as important to our understanding of human behavior as decisions that are consciously made. The degree to which human behavior is repetitive and explainable by socioeconomic and cultural determinants makes the scientific study of economic geography possible.

REFERENCES

[1] Peter Gould, "On Mental Maps," *Michigan Inter-University Community of Mathematical Geographers*, No. 9, 1966.
    Peter Gould and Rodney White, *Mental Maps* (New York: Pelican Books, 1974).

[2] David Stea and Roger M. Downs, *Image and Environment* (Chicago: Aldine Press, 1973).

J. Douglas Porteous, *Environment and Behavior* (Reading, Mass.: Addison-Wesley, 1977).

Paul Ward English and Robert C. Mayfield (eds.), *Man, Space, and Environment* (New York: Oxford University Press, 1972).

Thomas F. Saarinen, *Environmental Planning: Perception and Behavior* (Boston: Houghton-Mifflin, 1976).

[3] M. Fishbein (ed.), *Readings in Attitude Theory and Measurement* (New York: John Wiley & Sons, 1967).

[4] John H. Sims and Duane D. Bauman, "The Tornado Threat: Coping Styles of the North and South," *Science*, **176**, June 30, 1972, pp. 1386-1392.

[5] R. Davies-Jones, *et al.*, "Psychological Response to Tornadoes," *Science*, **180**, No. 4086, May 11, 1973, p. 544.

[6] Robert W. Kates, *Hazard and Choice Perception in Flood Plain Management*, Department of Geography Research Paper No. 78, University of Chicago, Chicago, 1972.

[7] Ian Burton and Robert W. Kates, "The Perception of Natural Hazards in Resource Management," *Natural Resources Journal*, 3, No. 412, 1964, pp. 412-441.

[8] Kenneth Hewitt and Ian Burton, *The Hazardousness of a Place: A Regional Ecology of Damaging Events*, Department of Geography Research Publication No. 6, University of Toronto, Toronto, 1971.

[9] Edward F. Bergman, *Modern Political Geography* (Dubuque, Iowa: W. C. Brown, 1975), pp. 125-126.

[10] Burton and Kates, *op. cit.*, Table 5.

[11] Peter R. Gould, "Man Against His Environment: A Game Theoretic Framework," *Annals of the Association of American Geographers*, 53, 1963, pp. 290-297.

[12] Julian Wolpert, "The Decision Process in Spatial Context," *Annals of the Association of American Geographers*, 54, 1964, pp. 537-558.

[13] Herbert A. Simon, *Models of Man* (New York: John Wiley & Sons, 1957).

[14] Alan R. Pred, "Behavior and Location, Parts I and II", *Lund Studies in Geography*, Series B, No. 27 and 29, 1967.

[15] "The Computer Society," *Time*, February 28, 1978, p. 54.

[16] *Ibid.*, p. 54.

[17] Charles Darwin, *On the Origin of the Species* (Philadelphia: University of Pennsylvania Press, 1959).

[18] A. A. Alchian, "Uncertainty, Evolution, and Economic Theory," *Journal of Political Economy*, 58, 1950, pp. 211-221.

Charles M. Tiebout, "Location Theory, Empirical Evidence and Economic Evolution," *Papers, Regional Science Association*, 3, 1957, pp. 74–86.

[19] Leon Festinger, *A Theory of Cognitive Dissonance* (Palo Alto, Calif., Stanford University Press, 1947).

[20] Anthony Downs, "The Law of Peak-Hour Expressway Congestion," *Traffic Quarterly*, 16, 1962, pp. 393–409.

[21] Leon Festinger, et al., *Social Pressures in Informal Groups* (New York: Harper Row, 1950).

[22] Kenneth E. Boulding, *The Image* (Ann Arbor, Mich., University of Michigan Press, 1965).

[23] David Lerner, *The Passing of Traditional Society*, (Glencoe, Ill: The Free Press, 1958).

[24] I. Lewis, *We, the Navigators* (Honolulu: University Press of Hawaii, 1972).

[25] Roger M. Downs and David Stea, *Maps in Minds* (New York: Harper & Row, 1977).

[26] Kevin Lynch, *The Image of the City* (Cambridge, Mass.: MIT Press, 1960).

[27] Peter Orleans, "Differential Cognition of Urban Residents: Effects of Social Scale on Mapping," In R. M. Downs and D. Stea (ed.), *Image and Environment* (Chicago: Aldine Press, 1973), pp. 115-130.

[28] R. M. Downs and D. Stea, *op. cit.*, 1977.

[29] Herbert Gans, *The Urban Villagers* (Glencoe, Ill.: The Free Press, 1962).
Marc Fried and Peggy Gleicher, "Some Sources of Residential Satisfaction in an Urban Slum," *Journal of the American Institute of Planners*, 29, 1961, pp. 179-198.

[30] "Downtown is Looking Up," *Time*, July 5, 1976, pp. 54-62.

[31] Richard Hartshorne, "The Functional Approach in Political Geography," *Annals of the Association of American Geographers.* **40** 1950, pp. 95-130.

[32] "Secession v. Survival," *Time*, February 13, 1978, pp. 32-43.

[33] Frederick Simoons, *Eat Not This Flesh* (Madison, Wis.: University of Wisconsin Press, 1959).

[34] Lynn White Jr., "The Historical Roots of our Ecologic Crises," *Science*, 155, 1967, p. 1203-1207.

[35] Hildegard Binder Johnson, *Order on the Land* (New York: Oxford University Press, 1976).

[36] Yi-Fu Fuan, "Discrepancies Between Environmental Attitude and Behavior: Examples from Europe and China," *Canadian Geographer*, 12, 1968, pp. 176-191.

CHAPTER EIGHT

strategies of economic development

INTRODUCTION

The major goal of any nation should be to make the most efficient use of scarce resources so that the people obtain maximum benefits from them. Even though such a goal might be generally agreed upon, vastly different approaches are used in efforts to achieve it. Which resources should be developed, and how and where should they be utilized? What opportunities are lost by investing resources in a particular way or by diverting resources from one investment category or geographic area to another? Are benefits really maximized if the citizens of a particular region are hurt by an investment strategy which may improve the overall development of the country? How can the benefits (and disadvantages) of development be measured? The problem of which development strategy is best has no simple answer. The answer is contingent upon the monetary and human resources that can be effectively brought to bear on the development problems, the economic resource base of the country in question, the resourcefulness and dedication of the citizenry to achieve particular objectives, and the stated goals and underlying philosophies of the development process.

Resources available for development programs should be viewed as discretionary funds, above and beyond those needed for system maintenance. Many countries have great difficulty in making any development headway because barely enough capital resources can be mustered to maintain the economic system at current levels. Such countries might progress, however, if their resources were better managed. Bureaucratic waste and inefficiency in allocating resources to meet basic needs is a major stumbling block to development.

FORCES OF DISEQUILIBRIUM

Gunnar Myrdal, the famous development economist, pointed out a fundamental paradox in the development policies of countries that he terms "soft states"—those states which lack the bureaucratic apparatus to properly administer central planning [1]. Solely from the standpoint of economic efficiency many countries would be best managed using the bureaucratic structure employed in the socialist nations. Developing nations, however, suffer from a chronic shortage of a trained indigenous population needed to administer developmental programs.

Ideally, administration of development should be as decentralized as possible. Benefits of development should be disseminated quickly to all the people; rural poverty is commonly an important development problem in developing countries. Lack of trained administrators limits the options available, however, often resulting in highly centralized programs in which the benefits are slow to diffuse to backward rural areas.

A study of disparities in economic development patterns challenges a commonly held belief in the existence of mechanisms of equilibrium which will reduce the gap between rich and poor countries and between rich and poor regions within a given country. Rather than convergence toward some international or regional parity, the gap between the developed and developing nations and between rich and poor regions often widens as a result of developmental efforts. An equilibrium view of economic development assumes that if a poor area has high unemployment (a large labor surplus) and relatively low wages, then industry will be attracted to the region by the savings it could attain by such a move. Myrdal points out that disequilibrium is, however, more common. Development is often a vicious circle in which inequities are amplified rather than mitigated. Such a disequilibrating process was labeled "circular and cumulative causation" [2]. Myrdal was dubious about the role of trade as a means to counteract inequities. At the international scale, trade between the developed and the developing nations has promoted the patterns of economic inequities seen in the world today. Primary products (e.g., agricultural commodities, minerals), which are the export mainstay of most developing countries, may be extracted with unskilled labor. Low skill levels, in turn, exacerbate the problems of economic development. Without intervention in the trade patterns (e.g., tariffs, quotas, embargos), therefore, the forces of economic stagnation may be strengthened by trade instead of leading nations toward a more equitable exchange base.

GROWTH POLE THEORY

Other economic theorists have pointed out that the detrimental effects of regional and international developmental disparities can be broken by controlled economic development. These theorists believe that the disequilibrating forces of circular and cumulative causation can be used to advantage in development planning. Unequal growth is viewed as essential and potentially useful in development [3]. In time unequal growth may lead to improved efficiency in the use of resources because of the dynamics of the growth process. Growth in one sector of a nation or of an economy may stimulate growth in other related areas or sectors. Initially lagging sectors of the economy may not have been able to generate enough demand for their products in order to generate needed capital for expansion, but growth stimulated by another interrelated dynamic sector may bring idle people and equipment back into useful production. The growth pole strategy involves taking advantage of the developmental potential of economic sectors and geographic areas which have the greatest comparative advantage for economic growth.

A spatial strategy for economic investment called *growth pole theory* derives from this positive view of uneven growth [4]. A *growth pole* is usually a large city or regional capital located within a lagging region. Rather than spreading scarce development funds evenly through such a region, resources are concentrated within the growth pole and in relatively few economic sectors. Ideally investment funds would be concentrated on a particular *propulsive industry* which would have both forward and backward linkages with other economic sectors. *Forward* linkages are a form of economic interrelationship in which the products of one industry form the raw materials for other industries. *Backward* linkages are the interconnections between an industry and its suppliers of raw materials. The propulsive industry is usually a *basic* or city-forming economic activity in which most of the output is distributed to markets outside the growth pole and even outside the lagging region. Exports generate external capital needed to develop the region further and cause economic multiplier effects to occur. Thus, growth in a propulsive industry breeds growth in interrelated (both forwardly and backwardly linked) industries, which in turn creates an enhanced economic environment for new investment.

The enhanced investment environment afforded by the location of a propulsive industry and related ancillary activities increase local entrepreneurial market opportunities. New jobs are created in the *nonbasic* sector of the economy; products and services are provided for the consumption of workers employed in the basic sector. Grocery stores, gasoline stations, and a barber's services would be examples of such nonbasic activity. These mutually reinforcing benefits may eventually be felt throughout a lagging region.

Development experts who favor the growth pole strategy are quick to point out some initial drawbacks. At first there are negative impacts (called *backwash* or *polarization effects*) upon the hinterland region. Rural-to-urban migration, already an acute problem in many developing nations, is aggravated by uneven investment. The brightest and the best of the rural villagers flock to the growth pole in search of better job opportunities. This selective migration contributes to an increased income polarization between the relatively wealthy core (growth pole) and the poorer peripheral areas. Normally, a substantial period may elapse before the positive impacts of the growth pole spread to the surrounding hinterland. An analogy might be made to a rock thrown into a pond. The rock represents the propulsive industry and the concentric ripples created by the rock's impact are analogous to the spread effects of the growth pole strategy. Just as the ripples diminish in height and intensity as distance from the rock's impact point increases, so also the spatial distribution of the *spread effect* diminishes with distance from the growth pole (Fig. 8-1). Before the investment in a propulsive industry such as an iron and steel mill, the prospective growth pole had a higher

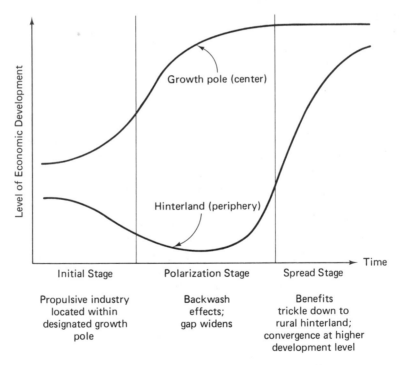

Fig. 8-1. Graphic portrayal of the impact of a growth pole strategy upon a lagging region. Initial stage: Propulsive industrial located within designated growth pole. Polarization stage: Backwash effects; gap widens. Spread stage: Benefits trickle down to rural hinterland; convergence at higher development level.

relative development level than its surrounding rural hinterland. After investment, these developmental differences are exacerbated and the gap between center and periphery widens. As the spread effect finally overwhelms the polarization effect, both urban and rural areas progress toward higher developmental levels than previously possible and the gap between them narrows. Although proposed as a theory of development for both the developed and the developing nations of the world, evidence of the growth pole theory's application in the developing world is scant. Limited evidence that growth pole theory works as the regional economists who proposed it said it would may be found in France. The French government has been able to stimulate the economic growth of some lagging regions and slow the continual concentration of economic production in the Paris Basin although it may be argued that free market forces might have created the same development pattern without the interventionist policy of the government [5]. It is often difficult to trace the pattern of economic development back to a particular policy decision because of the complex nature of the development process.

POLITICAL IMPLICATIONS OF A GROWTH STRATEGY

Can such a growth pole strategy be implemented? Can developing nations afford to wait the length of time necessary for the economic benefits generated by the propulsive industry to trickle down to the surrounding rural hinterland? The increasing integration of center and periphery made possible by such a growth pole strategy leads to rising expectations on the part of the residents of rural areas. These rural people are likely to be unwilling to accept great disparities between their living levels and those of urban residents. Growth pole strategies, if successful, would enhance job opportunities in the city and attract migrants from the rural hinterland to the urban areas. If the perceived relative deprivation between living standards of the center and periphery becomes intolerable, a politically sensitive situation is created that sometimes leads to confrontations with government. Successful insurgency movements which have overthrown central authorities in developing nations often gain momentum in poverty stricken rural regions after initial urban terrorist activity and after the urban–rural disparities in living levels are comprehended [6]. Citizens of those rural areas are no longer willing to accept the lower living standards associated with the rural periphery. When militarily organized, such rural residents have, at times, taken drastic measures to achieve a share of regional equity.

We can speculate upon the manner in which level of economic development and political and unrest are related (Fig. 8-2). During the stage where economic development is at a low level (Stage I), political unrest is also a minor problem. If disturbances against the central government occur, they are likely to be localized. Low development retards the spread of insurgent

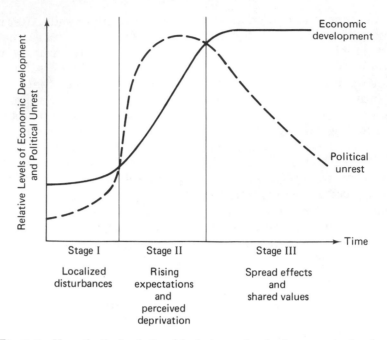

Fig. 8-2. Hypothetical relationship between level of economic development and political unrest. Stage I: Localized disturbances. Stage II: Rising expectations and perceived deprivation. Stage III: Spread effects and shared values.

movements because channels of communication and transportation are not well-developed. If the economic structure of the country is not well-integrated, local insurrections are relatively easy to contain. As the level of development increases, however (Stage II), "islands" of development become better integrated into a national economy and hopes for development spread to the majority of the populace. A crisis of rising expectations is sometimes created. Anger and violence may erupt if the central government fails to deliver a better life for its citizens. If the government can weather this "crisis of confidence," the political unrest attributable to the level of development should subside (Stage III). At this final stage the benefits of the development process have filtered down to the rural countryside and an in-filling process takes place in which optimism for development becomes widespread. Potential unrest in a particular region of low development is dissipated because the ambitious elements within the population migrate to other regions offering superior economic opportunities. Instead of isolated pockets or islands of development strung together by major transportation arteries, the developing nation at Stage III is tapping all the nation's space for raw materials needed to maintain the system at the higher development level. Impacts of the shift from a "space-bridging" economy to a "space-filling" economy are widely felt [7].

Growth pole concepts have most often been applied in economically advanced nations which suffer from one or more lagging regions within their boundaries (e.g., Appalachia in the United States, Brittany in France, the Mezzogiorno of southern Italy). The French regional economists have established a series of eight regional metropoles outside the congested Paris Basin which might serve as growth poles for future French development (Fig. 8-3). The regions tributary to these 8 metropoles are supposed to act as counter-magnets to continued industrial and urban development in the already over-crowded Paris Basin. Their purpose is to entice industries away from Paris

Fig. 8-3. French growth poles designed as alternatives to industrial concentration in the Paris Basin. [From J.R. Boudeville, *Problems of Regional Economic Planning* (Edinburgh: Edinburgh University Press, 1966), p. 166.]

and into the outlying provinces. The French attempt to spread industrial development more evenly throughout the country is exacerbated by the overwhelming centrality of Paris in their national transportation system. Virtually all rail lines converge on Paris and it is often impossible to ship goods from one lagging region to another without the shipment first passing through the Paris region.

Concerned about the continual concentration of population in the larger urban areas of the United States during the 1960s, a Presidential committee under the direction of John D. Rockefeller, III, was asked to recommend policies which would lead to population decentralization. The Rockefeller Commission suggested the establishment of a series of medium-sized growth centers outside the established influence of large metropolitan centers in the United States which were intended to fulfill a purpose similar to the French regional development plan [8]. The medium-sized growth centers were intended to provide an alternative for rural people to continued migration in to the large urban areas. The recommendations of the Rockefeller Commission on population redistribution were never implemented because the commission took politically sensitive and controversial stands on other population-related issues such as birth control and sex education.

Doubts have been raised about the efficacy of growth pole strategies. Much of the strategy relies upon "trickle down" effects through a hierarchical system of urban centers. Because "the mechanism by which economic growth is transmitted from core to periphery is uncertain, the planner can never be sure that encouraging a particular urban hierarchy represents the optimal allocation of resources" [9].

RURAL INTENSIFICATION STRATEGIES

Many development economists feel that only by investing in the rural areas of developing nations can successful development proceed. Because a rural intensification strategy is almost diametrically opposed to the growth pole strategy, we must seek to understand the reasoning behind it. The rationale for rural development is that, by increasing the productivity of the agricultural sector, excess labor can be released from agriculture for application to nonagricultural pursuits. Increased agricultural production should raise the quantity and quality of food consumption which, in turn, would raise the health standards of the general population. Food exports would also increase, thus generating much needed foreign capital to expand development in nonagricultural sectors.

Rural development strategies hold certain dangers that must be avoided if development is to progress. Because rural areas so often suffer the lowest development levels, the ingredients necessary (e.g., adequate transportation,

Increased food production in developing countries depends in good measure upon improving varieties of cereal foods. (Reprinted from *War on Hunger*, a publication of the Agency for International Development.)

important industrial sectors) for spreading the effects of increased invest-ment will likely be lacking. A "worst-first" rural intensification strategy, in which investment capital is first poured into the rural region with the highest level of poverty, will probably not be able to generate the multiplier effects necessary to sustain the initial investment.

The problem in most developing nations is an excess of underemployed labor in rural areas. Projects to improve agricultural production should there-fore be *labor intensive* so that employment levels increase. The building of farm-to-market roads, drainage canals, irrigation works, land contouring, and terracing are examples of labor-intensive projects which would fulfill the dual objectives of providing employment for rural people and improving the agricultural productivity of the land. If advances in agricultural technology and dissemination of technical knowledge result in substitution of capital for labor, development could be counterproductive in the long run. Increasing mechanization and higher yielding varieties of crops often force rural people off farms and into cities faster than the urban nonagricultural sector can absorb them.

A further barrier to rural intensification strategies is the system of land-holding that exists within developing nations. The system of landholding is often a legacy of the colonial era (e.g., large private commercial holdings).

The state, church, or wealthy aristocrats may hold vast parcels of land out of production, thus slowing modernization and commercialization of agriculture [10]. Many of the largest landholdings in Latin American, for example, came from grants to the Roman Catholic church and private landlords during the early period of colonial development.

A further impediment to a rural intensification development strategy is that is often results in large landholders absorbing small farms, as has been the case in the early stages of the "green revolution." Such entrepreneurial landholders may misuse funds earmarked for rural development by introducing labor saving techniques and scale economies, thereby eliminating many subsistence farmers. The potential dangers of a rural intensification strategy emphasize the role of the central government in monitoring and regulating public works projects, crop prices, and farm acreages and in promoting marketing channels and land conservation techniques.

ECONOMIC VERSUS SOCIAL OVERHEAD CAPITAL

Choices over use of scarce funds for economic development often involve a dichotomy between those who favor investment in "things" (economic overhead capital, including highways and public works projects) and those who favor investment in "people" (social overhead capital, such as schools, medical care, and job training). Most development economists agree that the benefits of investments in things are more quickly felt that those in people. A modern highway system can, for example, connect formerly isolated regions and bring about much needed political and economic integration. If, however, the skill levels of the people are not sufficient to organize an effective administrative structure, interconnection counts for little. The impacts of investment in rural health care delivery (e.g., primary care centers) and paramedical personnel, for example, may improve the health and even the mental capacities of the population, for malnutrition is a major cause of irreversible brain damage among infants. The fruits of such an investment strategy may not, however, be felt immediately. It is not so easy to measure the benefits which accrue from investment in people as it is to measure the more tangible benefits of investments in things. More than 20 years may elapse before benefits from investment in a comprehensive compulsory educational system are realized, whereas a road linkage improvement may produce more immediate results. The simultaneous application of economic and social overhead capital is necessary to fulfill developmental goals. Economic overhead investment is needed to create the initial impetus for growth, and investment in human resources is needed to sustain the growth once it has begun.

IMPORTANCE OF TRANSPORTATION
INFRASTRUCTURE IN DEVELOPMENT

For any country to become developed, all regions need to be accessible to each other. The inaccessibility of semiautonomous (often rebellious) regions from the core area of the central state has hampered governmental efforts to consolidate authority in many nations. Situations do occur, however, in which initial inaccessibility of potentially incompatible groups have actually been a boon to economic development and political integration. Isolating potentially hostile groups until nationalistic feelings of loyalty develop toward the country may be a viable development strategy in portions of Africa and Asia [11]. When Africa was divided among the colonial powers of Europe, for example, boundaries were often drawn without the advice or consent of the tribal groups affected. The result was that many hostile tribal groups were brought together within the boundaries of the same colony, causing difficulties in effecting a smooth transition from colonial status to nationhood.

Once common goals are shared by the people of a developing nation, transportation holds the key to a series of mutually reinforcing processes that will speed development. The level of a country's economic progress is closely related to the stage of development of its transportation system. The more technologically complex road and rail networks are associated with high levels of individual well-being [12].

Transportation systems in most developing nations are a legacy from the infrastructural development of a colonial period. There is enough generality in the way colonial powers developed the infrastructure of their colonies that a stage model has been suggested [13]. Although developed specifically for the cases of Ghana and Nigeria in West Africa, the model may be generally applied to most colonial situations in Africa, Asia, and Latin America (Fig. 8-4). The first stage in the development sequence is called the *stage of scattered ports*. When the British first established their Gold Coast colony (now Ghana) in West Africa, there were many scattered "surf ports" at which ships could load and unload cargo (e.g., Winneba, Cape Coast, Accra, Secondi). The lack of natural harbors required natives to paddle outrigger canoes to meet the larger ships beyond the treacherous shallow waters near shore. The agricultural and mineral products of the Gold Coast were thus transferred from coastline to waiting ships bound for England and British imports were brought to shore. Such roads as existed seved only as local farm-to-ports roads. There were few interconnections among the port cities and practically no penetration into the country's interior region where the rich cocoa plantations and gold and coal mining activities were later to take place.

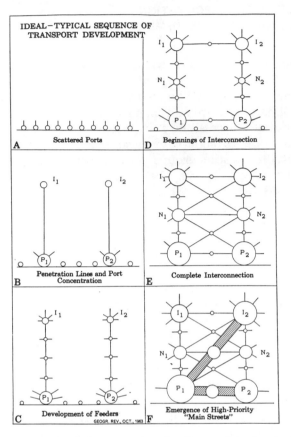

Fig. 8-4. Stage model of transportation development in developing nations. (Reproduced by permission from Edward J. Taaffe, Richard L. Morrill, and Peter R. Gould, "Transport Expansion in Underdeveloped Countries: A Comparative Analysis," *Geographical Review*, 53, No. 4, 1963, Figure 1, p. 504.)

The second stage of transportation development might be called the *stage of port concentration*. In a spatially competitive process of development, some port cities languished (e.g., Cape Coast, Winneba) at the expense of more successful competitors (e.g., Secondi-Takoradi, Accra-Tema) (Fig. 8-5). The major factor affecting the viability of these port cities was the development of transportation lines which penetrated into the Gold Coast's rich interior. The choice of route locations might have been a political decision, but the choice set in motion a series of circular and cumulative development processes. The reasons for the development of penetration lines were varied — to connect coastal colonial centers to the interior area in order to extend political control, to reach areas of mineral exploitation, to reach areas of potential export agricultural production, and to establish military control.

During the third stage, *feeder roads* developed which led away from the lines of penetration, allowing even larger rural hinterland areas to be tapped. It was also during the feeder stage that some lateral interconnection developed, bridging together major cities throughout the nation. During the lateral interconnection stage the important mining and agricultural center of Kumasi became linked with the port city of Secondi and the capital, Accra, to form a roughly triangular axis of development (Fig. 8-5). Urban centers located at major rail heads and along major transportation arteries began to grow during this interconnection stage and a second tier of the urban hierarchy evolved to serve as wholesale centers. Secondary urban centers served as bulking and distribution points for agricultural, mining, and forest products bound for world markets. Small loads of goods from the rural hin-

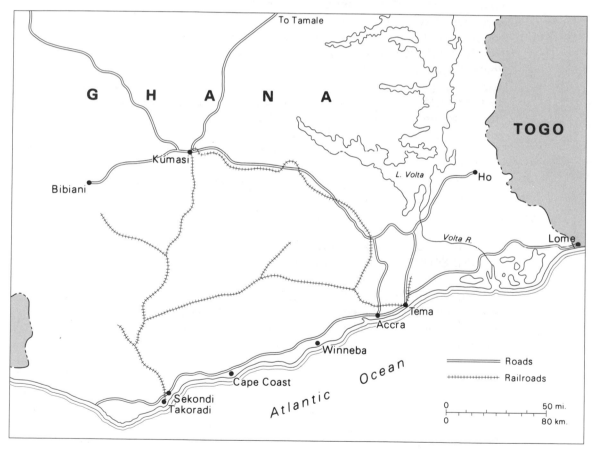

Fig. 8-5. Location map of Southern Ghana. [From A. T. Grove, *Africa, 3rd ed.* (New York: Oxford University Press, 1978), p. 172, Fig. 55.]

terlands were gathered into larger shipments at accessible locations along the transportation arteries and forwarded to the major port cities.

The final stage of transportation development was the advent of *differentiated high-priority routes.* The earlier axis of development was reinforced by the differential development of certain high-priority linkages.

The case for transportation investment as a means to achieve higher levels of economic development is a strong one. When transportation facilities are poor, regions are likely to maintain a limited subsistence with little potential for an exchange economy to develop. Movement of goods over transportation networks allows for regional specialization. Without exchange, the comparative areal advantage of particular regions could not develop. As transportation develops, regions within a country begin to specialize and to become more dependent on each other. Interdependence fosters more exchange and the entire development level of the country advances. Even if transportation services cost more to construct than the revenues they generate, the investment may still accrue significant external economies of scale because of the multiplier effect of increased accessibility.

Once infrastructural development has been agreed upon as an investment goal, the question of proper allocation of funds remains. Should the transportation system be designed to provide the greatest service to the user or to cost the least to the builder? Given the limited budgets of most developing nations, builder criteria usually prevail. Minimal sufficient connections between places is the usual rule and such countries are typified by a relatively low density of roads and railways per unit of area. Careful central planning is needed to assure that the transport networks access is designed to provide the maximum amount of accessibility possible, given the budget constraints under which the planning occurs.

THE EVOLUTION OF INDUSTRIAL STRUCTURE
AND ECONOMIC DEVELOPMENT

The importance of the manufacturing sector in generating multiplier effects throughout the economic system has been discussed previously. What mix of industries should the developing nations attempt to foster? Relatively heavy emphasis in the developing nations is placed upon food processing and the textile and apparel industries. Most development economists agree that such industries are well-suited to developing countries, but they disagree about why such industries seem to seek out such locations. Multinational corporations (MNC's), for example, consciously attempt to choose locations for various phases of a particular industry which are best suited to the technological skill levels of the labor force at those locations. The high technology research and development phase of the industry might be located in an advanced industrial nation because of the expertise available, whereas the production assembly line might be located in a developing nation because the skill requirements are not high and the labor force in these nations will accept a lower wage scale than labor in the advanced industrial areas.

At each stage in the life cycle of an industry the costs of various aspects of production and marketing differ [14]. The comparative advantage of a paticular region as the location of a given industry is a function of the technological stage of the industry. When an industry first develops, production runs are low and costs are high. If the product represents a technological advance over existing market choices, or has no substitutes, the product will be in great demand. The inputs needed in the greatest relative amounts during the incipient stage of industrial development are a highly skilled scientific and engineering labor force and sufficient capital to establish the industry. As the industry matures, it enters a period of rapid growth typified by mass production and mass distribution. Production runs are lengthened, special machinery is developed in order to reduce unit costs, the industry becomes more capital intensive, and the number of firms in the industry increases to take advantage of an expanding market. As there are many suppliers to choose from, successful firms must offer a full complement of customer services. Marketing assumes a crucial role during this growth stage.

The industry may continue to expand, but the rate of growth will eventually level off. At that time the industry may be said to have entered a mature stage. As an industry makes the transition between the growth phase and maturity, individual firms are eliminated by intense competition so that the number of firms decreases. Those remaining are larger than their counterparts during the industry's growth phase.

Production techniques at the mature stage are well-developed and the technology of production may be easily transferred to other locations. At this stage the labor force is likely to be highly organized and manufacturers substitute machines for labor. The percentage of unskilled and semiskilled workers increases during the mature phase and demand for the product becomes more sensitive to price competition.

Industries in their mature phase seem to hold the most promise for developing nations even though that stage is typified by heavy capital investment. The impetus and capital for industrialization is often generated external to the developing nation; capital for industry in developing areas was formerly funished by colonial powers and more recently it has been supplied largely by multinational corporations and government loans. It is unlikely that developing nations will have many high technology industries, as these industries are more appropriately located in developed industrial nations. According to one development economist, the small developed countries (e.g., Switzerland, Israel, Sweden) should have a competitive advantage over their larger developed counterparts for highly technical industries because the requisite scientific personnel would work for lower wages and are equally well-trained and productive [15]. The sophisticated distribution systems in larger developed nations (e.g., United States, West Germany, Japan) give them a comparative advantage in industries entering the growth phase. The larger developed nations possess large local consumptive markets and associated business services are widely available, allowing external economies of scale to accrue.

NONMONETARY CONSTRAINTS TO DEVELOPMENT

Although lack of investment capital is a major stumbling block to economic advancement, other problems retard developing nations as well. Population pressures in some countries are so great that even relatively large rates of economic growth are offset by increased demands of a rapidly growing population. Reducing the rate of population growth should aid the advancement of such nations in most instances.

Lack of adequate educational facilities within the developing nations forces many of these countries to send their most promising students overseas to universities in the developed world for training. Many of the best students never return to their homeland because of the job opportunities available to them in advanced nations. Likewise, scientific personnel from the developing areas continue to immigrate to the developed nations. The magnitude of this "brain drain" is serious enough to reduce the ability of the developing nations to close the gap between the rich and poor nations.

In some instances the developing nations compete against each other for world markets, thus retarding their economic advancement. In parts of equatorial Africa, for example, the climatic regime and the colonial histories of the nations are so similar that essentially the same products are being produced for export to world markets. Such countries are subject to fluctuations in world prices for these products unless some supranational trade arrangement is formed. Though desirable from the viewpoint of the developing nations, the overwhelming bargaining power of the economically advanced nations, neocolonial ambitions, petty jealousies, and severe internal development problems have hampered the formation of such trading and bargaining organizations.

Trade ties between former colonies and their colonial powers are strong, but they favor the colonial powers. Members of the European Economic Community (the "Common Market" nations) have, for example, given their former colonies privileged access to western European markets [16]. The developing nations are, however, much more dependent on their former rulers than the colonial powers are on their former colonies. The degree of dependence of the African nations on western Europe appears to be decreasing, but a distinct pattern of dominance remains (Table 8-1). Little basis exists for inter-African trade because many of the nations produce the same products or because they lack the purchasing power necessary to buy

TABLE 8-1. Trade Partnerships Between Africa and Western Europe[a]

| | PERCENTAGE OF IMPORTS | | | | | PERCENTAGE OF EXPORTS | | | |
| | Year | | | | | Year | | | |
Area	1958	1963	1971	1975	Area	1958	1963	1971	1975
By Africa (from Western Europe)	65.5	59.3	52.9	50.6	By Africa (to Western Europe)	69.5	69.2	69.6	60.5
By Western Europe (from Africa)	7.4	6.2	5.8	6.1	By Western Europe (to Africa)	9.3	6.3	4.6	6.3
Inter-African	5.4	5.6	5.3	3.7	Inter-African	6.7	6.1	5.4	4.4

[a]SOURCE: Table 147, World Exports by Provenance and Destination, *United Nations Statistical Yearbook 1972* (New York: United Nations, 1973); and Table 150, World Trade by Commodity Classes and Region, *United Nations Statistical Yearbook 1976* (New York: United Nations, 1977).

products produced in other parts of the continent. As these countries begin to diversify their exports, a larger basis for trade may develop. Complementarity is a necessary condition for exchange to take place, but it is insufficient alone to overcome inertial forces of tribal factionalism and linguistic, religious, and cultural differences. Traditional trading alliances between former colony and mother country are reinforced by preferential trade agreements and tariff arrangements such as those described above.

THE ROLE OF THE PRIVATE SECTOR IN DEVELOPMENT

We have seen that many options for development investment exist. Thus far we have examined alternative investment strategies that developing areas may choose from to reach their developmental ambitions. The question of what entity should be doing the investing remains. Specifically, what should the role of private industry be in the development process? The job creation potential of private industry, whether national or multinational in scope, is great. The threat of exploitation, however, is also real. During colonial times when economic exploitation in trading and banking existed, manufacturing conglomerates operating in the developing nations often created demand for the products of the developing world in the mother country. The Dutch East India Company, for example, operated a virtual monopoly over many exports from the Dutch East Indies (now Indonesia). Such private sector investment was not necessarily detrimental to the development plans of the developing nations. Private agricultural and industrial holdings often provided the impetus for initial economic development, and the capital for these holdings was often external in origin.

Flagrant exploitation of developing countries' resources has often been harshly dealt with by the leaders of newly emerging nations. Expropriation of foreign holdings and nationalization of foreign-owned industries are among the more drastic measures used to counteract the excesses of some private developers.

With the realization that the resource bases of developing nations are finite, the demand for control over use of resources grows. Perceived scarcity often mobilizes governmental action. The tendency has been, and will in all likelihood continue to be, to turn the decision on planning strategies over to central authorities. Enlightened development policy in many cases would be to use the private corporations to advantage to increase the welfare of all citizens. Japan's amalgam of private corporations and governmental guidance, for example, has achieved high levels of economic development [17]. Checks can be placed upon possible excesses of private businesses by requiring the company to manufacture its products locally or requiring manufacturers to use local raw materials and to serve local markets.

CONCLUSIONS: THE DEVELOPMENT RACE

Several spatial investment strategies have been either discussed or alluded to in the chapter. Choosing the best strategy is a complex problem. Each country must inventory its own resources, set its own development goals, and establish policy to achieve the goals within the constraints of available resources. To illustrate different spatial investment strategies, assume that you were the ruler of the hypothetical developing nation depicted in Fig. 8-6. If you opted to invest in physical resources [Fig. 8-6(a)], you would allocate most of the development capital in the northeastern quadrant. Your hope would be that the initial impetus given by development of an abundant resource would stimulate other sectors of the economy until the whole economy was moving toward maturity [18]. A problem in using this strategy would be that the great distances separating local markets from the resource would require large expenditures for an adequate transport system.

Another strategy would be to spread the scarce investment capital evenly throughout the country so as not to favor any particular region or industry [Fig. 8-6(b)]. By dispersing the funds no particular industry or region may be able to achieve a "critical mass" needed to grow and to generate external economies of scale which would stimulate the growth of interrelated activities.

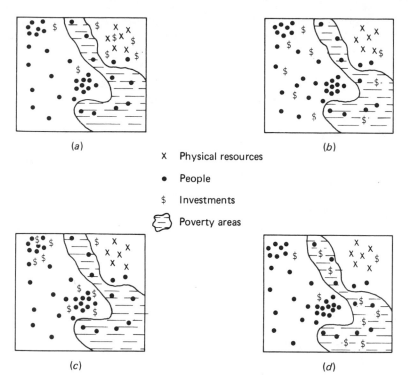

X   Physical resources

●   People

$ Investments

   Poverty areas

Fig. 8-6. Four spatial investment strategies. (*a*) Investment in resources; (*b*) even distribution of investments; (*c*) investment in growth poles; (*d*) investment in poorest area.

Following the recommendation of the French school of regional economists, you might concentrate investment at the major population agglomerations (growth poles) in hopes that the money would lead to spread effects throughout the country [Fig. 8-6(c)]. A policy of encouraging a rapid diffusion of economic benefits from growth poles into surrounding rural regions might avert a political crisis caused by rising expectations and rural–urban development disparities.

Finally, you might attempt a form of "worst-first" policy by concentrating development funds in the poorest areas of the country in hopes of raising those regions to parity with the rest of the country [Fig. 8-6(d)]. If no significant resources are found in the poor regions, few spread effects will be generated by investing in such a resource-poor area. Enlightened leadership should realize that unless population pressures can be checked and the requisite skill levels needed for economic development can be mustered, the development potential of some areas will be limited. Perhaps out-migration from such a poor region should be encouraged and the areas be allowed to "decline gracefully," as the Rockefeller Commission proposed for many overpopulated rural regions in the United States [19]. Intermediate-size growth centers near such overpopulated rural regions should provide viable job alternatives to the migration of the rural residents to distant cities. Out-migration from certain rural areas to intermediate-size cities nearby could be encouraged, making agricultural pursuits more viable for those who chose to remain in the rural areas. A high degree of risk is associated with whatever development strategy is employed. What appears to be the correct prescriptive tool often produces a result that is diametrically opposed to expectations. The strategies used to achieve desired goals must allow flexibility to account for the complexity of the international economic system. Without flexibility, the development plan may not be able to respond quickly enough to changes in the wants and needs of the world's population to be an effective policy tool.

REFERENCES

[1] Gunnar Mydral, *The Challenge of World Poverty* (New York: Vintage Books, 1970), Chapter 7.

[2] Gunnar Mydral, *The Economic Theory and Underdeveloped Regions* (London: Duckworth Press, 1957).

[3] Albert O. Hirschman, *The Strategy of Economic Development* (New Haven, Conn.: Yale University Press, 1957).

[4] Francois Perroux, "Economic Space, Theory and Application," *Quarterly Journal of Economics*, **64**, 1950, pp. 80–104.

[5] J.-R. Boudeville, *Problems of Regional Economic Planning* (Edinburgh: Edinburgh University Press, 1966).

[6] Robert McColl, "The Insurgent State: Territorial Bases of Revolution," *Annals of the Association of American Geographers*, **59**, 1969, pp. 613-631.

[7] Edward W. Soja, *The Geography of Modernization in Kenya* (Syracuse, N.Y.: Syracuse University Press, 1968).

[8] John D. Rockefeller, III, Chairman, *Presidential Commission on Population and the American Future.*

[9] David M. Smith, *Industrial Location* (New York: John Wiley & Sons, 1971) p. 456.

[10] Edward F. Bergman, *Modern Political Geography* (Dubuque, Iowa: W. C. Brown, 1976), p. 240.

[11] Amitai Etzioni, *Political Unification: A Comparative Study of Leaders and Forces* (New York: Holt, Rinehart and Winston, Inc., 1965), Chapter 2.

[12] K. J. Kansky, *Structure of Transportation Networks*, Department of Geography, Research Paper No. 84, Chicago, University of Chicago, 1963.

[13] Edward J. Taaffe, Richard L. Morrill, and Peter R. Gould, "Transport Expansion in Underdeveloped Countries: A Comparative Analysis," *Geographical Review*, **53**, 1963, pp. 503-529.

[14] Seev Hirsch, *Industrial Location and International Competitiveness* (Oxford: Clarendon Press, 1967).

[15] *Ibid.*, Chapter 2.

[16] Bergman, *op. cit.*, pp. 363–366.

[17] Robert B. Hall, Jr., *Japan: Industrial Power of Asia*, 2nd ed., New Searchlight Series (New York: D. Van Nostrand Co., 1976).

[18] W. W. Rostow, *The Stages of Economic Growth: A Non-Communist Manifesto* (Cambridge: Cambridge University Press, 1960).

[19] Rockefeller, *op. cit.*

PART THREE
FOOD

CHAPTER NINE

disparities in food production and consumption

INTRODUCTION

If the success or failure of agriculture is measured by whether or not the nutritional needs of the world's people are being met, we must conclude that agriculture is now, and nearly always has been, a failure. Throughout history most of the world's people have suffered from a variety of food-related health problems ranging from malnutrition, disease, and mental retardation to death from starvation. Whereas the worldwide picture appears menacing, however, some portions of the earth have enjoyed such rapid increases in output during recent decades that in localized situations overnourishment has been a greater problem than undernourishment. The classic example of overproductivity for domestic needs is the United States, although nations such as Australia, Canada, New Zealand, Uruguay, and Argentina are also major food exporters. Nations which traditionally have experienced short-ages of food from domestic agriculture include those in southern and eastern Asia and portions of Europe, Latin America, and Africa.

Until the nineteenth century, agricultural systems around the world were limited to imputs of solar, human, and animal energies in the production of crops. Differences in the efficiency of labor were minimal, and the only feasible method for a rapid increase in agricultural production was through adding new lands to the cultivated area. Because farmers were able to pro-duce little more food than that required to feed their own families, however, adequate supplies of labor to open up new lands were usually limited. Most undeveloped land was far-removed from major population concentrations and transportation was slow and often prohibitively expensive.

During the nineteenth century, revolutionary changes were initiated in European and Anglo-American agriculture as machines began to replace human and animal labor, new and more productive plant varieties emerged from agricultural laboratories, and chemical plant foods came into use. Productivity per worker and per unit area increased enormously, and as the amount of land which one worker could cultivate accelerated, farms began to increase in size to accommodate the efficiency requirements of larger machines. Work animals gradually disappeared from farms, and millions of acres that had once been used to grow their feed were liberated for human food or for fiber production. Inanimate energy became the basic support for agricultural productivity through its use to produce chemicals and machines, propel machines, process agricultural commodities, and transport those commodities to market.

Although the revolutionary developments in use of energy, machines, and chemicals came to affect nearly all agricultural output in the advanced nations by the 1960s, the bulk of the world's farms and croplands have been only marginally affected. Agriculture within most portions of southern and eastern Asia, in Africa, and in much of Latin America has experienced little change during modern times. Energy to cultivate and harvest crops is still supplied primarily by human and animal labor, agricultural chemicals are used sparingly if at all, human and animal manure are the major sources of supplementary soil nutrients, farms are small, output per worker is relatively low, and the local community is the primary market. Under these circumstances it is virtually impossible to cause an appreciable increase in food productivity within a short period of time. When rapid population growth occurs, there is little choice in the short run but to accept heightened malnutrition or starvation or to import food from areas of surplus production.

FACTORS AFFECTING DISPARITIES IN PRODUCTION

Differences in adequacy of world agricultural output may be attributed to combinations of locational differences with respect to (1) the natural environment, (2) population density, and (3) the manner in which the natural environment is managed. Type and effectiveness of a system of management depends on the cultural, economic, and political circumstances prevailing within a given area.

The physical environment sets broad limits upon the kinds of crops planted and the systems of cultivation employed. Within these broad limits choices are made based upon tradition and upon institutional and other constraints imposed by the cultural characteristics of the particular areas and peoples involved. Additional limitations upon what and how much is pro-

Agricultural village in the Netherlands. (Courtesy, Embassy of the Netherlands.)

duced are imposed by such economic factors as availability of capital to purchase equipment and materials and upon the adequacy of marketing, transportation, and processing facilities. Political factors which affect types and quantities of crops produced include the degree of governmental support for agricultural research, subsidies paid to farmers to encourage or to discourage output of particular crops, trade arrangements with other areas, and government involvement in the provision of services to farmers. In most instances farmers in any area attempt to operate within the limits imposed upon them by various forces so as to minimize risks to their personal and economic survival.

LOCATIONAL FACTORS

Factors which affect the types and quantities of crops produced in any area are subject to change through time. Changes in the location of production and of the characteristics of agriculture are more frequent occurrences in developed than in developing areas. These changes represent responses to such influences as mechanization, improved transportation, rapid urbanization, rising real incomes, and new trends in marketing. The Ganges Plain of

India, for example, has been much less penetrated by cultural, technological, and economic innovations and its agricultural characteristics have experienced greater stability than those of the American Midwest.

Problems in agricultural location usually differ substantially from those characteristic of other industries. Agricultural activities are normally spread over a larger area than manufacturing or service industries. Agriculture has less resiliency in responding to changes in supply and demand and is more sensitive to variations in physical conditions such as weather and climate. Whereas manufacturing and service industry locations are often dealt with from the standpoint of a single firm, agricultural location is considered in light of output from a multiplicity of farms.

Location Theory

Whatever kind of locational problem is being addressed, the factors which influence locational decisions are varied and highly complex. The complexity of such problems has led to efforts by many persons in a variety of fields (including geography and economics) to sort out those locational variables which are of paramount importance in the selection of optimum location and to incorporate them into theories and models. A location theory which could be applied to *all* agricultural products *everywhere* would need to comprehend the totality of physical, economic, and cultural forces which influence production. Such a theory, if successfully developed, could probably be used to explain the location of any kind of economic activity, for all economic pursuits are mutually interrelated in one way or another. Agricultural and manufactural activities relate to each other and to other economic functions such as wholesale and retail businesses. Although many theories are worthy of consideration, the following discussion will be limited primarily to the contributions of Johann Heinrich von Thünen and Robert Sinclair.

Von Thünen.   Johann Heinrich von Thünen managed an estate in Germany during the first half of the nineteenth century. From his observations of the agricultural activities in his area and from studying the farm accounts under his management, he developed a theory of location which pioneered the concepts of *economic rent* and the *dimension of distance* as factors in location [1].

Of basic importance to studies in agricultural location is an understanding of economic rent — or *the net return from an agricultural activity minus all costs of production and marketing.* It is sometimes useful to base economic rent upon land units, such as acres, sections, or hectares. The following formula is an expression of economic rent per unit of land producing a single commodity at a certain distance from the commodity's marketplace: R (economic rent per land unit) equals E (yield per land unit) multiplied by p (market price per unit of the commodity being produced) minus a (production cost per unit of commodity) minus E (yield per land unit) multiplied by f (transport cost per unit of distance per commodity) multiplied by k (distance from area of production to the market) [2].

$$R = E(p - a) - Efk$$

Assume, for example, that the commodity being produced is corn, at a distance of 10 miles from the market. Production amounts to 50 bushels per acre at a cost of $0.20 per bushel. Transport costs amount to $0.01 per bushel per mile, and the market price is $1.00 per bushel. Using the formula above, the economic rent per acre is derived as follows:

$$R = 50(\$1.00 - 0.20) - 50 \times 0.01 \times 0.10$$

$$R = \$35.00$$

Under the assumption that transportation costs increase with increasing distance from market and that production costs are constant, a farmer could in theory determine which of several crops would yield highest returns on the farm by calculating the economic rent for each crop. Although by moving production of any crop closer to the market economic rent could be increased, such a solution is unrealistic because farms are fixed in place. The question, then, is to determine which of several possible crops will yield highest returns, given the location of the farm relative to the market. Figure 9-1 shows the relationships between economic rent and distance from market for one crop. Figure 9-2 shows which crops, from a choice of four, would yield the greatest economic rent (profit) at varying distances from the market.

Realistically, of course, fluctuations in prices, production costs, skills of farmers, physical conditions, and other variables limit the usefulness of such methods of crop selection. The concept of economic rent as a function of distance from the market, however, is a basic tool for more sophisticated studies (using more variables) of the location of agricultural production. Moreover, a rule of thumb that has general application is that the higher the value of a commodity per unit weight, the greater is the distance that the product can be economically transported.

Von Thünen's theory postulated a featureless plain with a single market city in its center and with transportation limited to horse-drawn wagons. He further assumed that transport costs were proportionate to distance. Under these rigid assumptions agricultural production would occur within a series of concentric circles, or belts, around the market city (Fig. 9-3). Commodities produced within each belt would be those yielding the greatest economic rent at that distance from the market. Perishable and low-value bulky goods have a high priority for location nearest the market because of the danger of

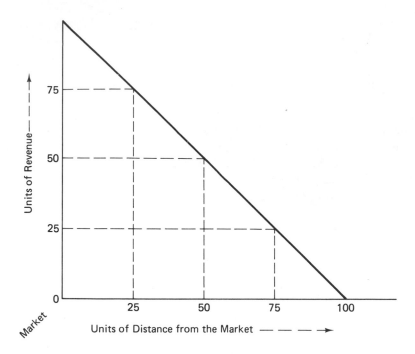

Fig. 9-1. A single-commodity expression of economic rent as a function of distance from the market. Production costs and the market price are assumed to remain constant, no matter what the distance from the market. At 25 units of distance from the market the net return less all costs is 75 units of revenue, etc., until at 100 units of distance from the market the net return less all costs is 0 units of revenue.

spoilage or because of high transport costs per unit weight relative to value. Furthermore, because land nearest the market represents the best possible location for all commodities, *land-use intensity* would be highest near the market and would decrease proportionately with increased distance from the market.

It is unlikely that any area meets all the arbitrary physical and economic qualifications established by Von Thünen for his isolated state. A few areas in some of the more sparsely populated and underdeveloped lands where clusters of settlements occur in near isolation from other settlements come closest to meeting the conditions specified in Von Thünen's model. One should remember, however, that a theory is an abstraction, often containing generalizations that apply to all or to many areas in a general way but to no area in particular. Whereas featureless plains, completely isolated settlements, and areas limited to only one method of transport are rare occurrences, Von Thünen's model remains of value in explaining distributions of spatial phenomena as they relate to market centers.

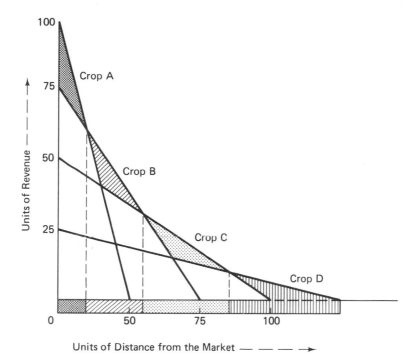

Fig. 9-2. A four-commodity expression of economic rent as a function of distance from the market. The shaded, triangular-shaped segments on the graph indicate distances (transferred to the distance line at bottom of graph) at which each of the farm crops will yield more economic rent (net revenue) than any of the other three crops.

Sinclair's Theory. One of the major economic and social developments since Von Thünen published *The Isolated State* in 1826 is the rapid urbanization which has occurred in the developed nations. By comparison, urbanization in Von Thünen's time was so slow that city size was almost as static as the Rock of Gibraltar.

It seems logical that expansion of urban areas would affect nearby agricultural patterns. Rapid changes in land use near major urban areas — as influenced by transportation systems and suburban residential, business, and industrial developments — led Robert Sinclair to offer a modern theory which explains how present land-use types and patterns contrast with those during Von Thünen's time [3]. Sinclair added the pressures of urbanization as a competitive bidder, along with agriculture, for use of land near cities. He also applied the concept of relative value of land for agricultural and urban use to the idea of a belted arrangement of agricultural land use near urban centers.

According to Sinclair, Von Thünen's theory was consistent with reality

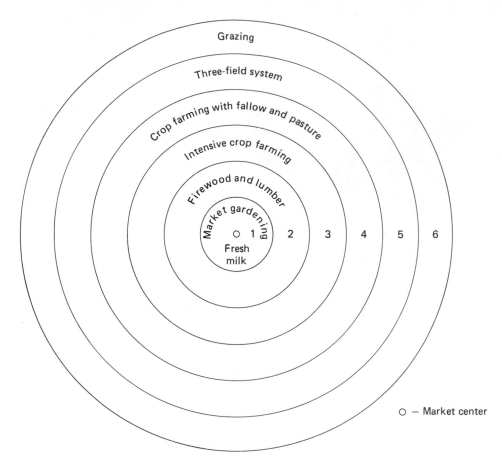

Fig. 9-3. Agricultural zones in an isolated state, as hypothesized by von Thünen.

until vast changes in technology, living habits, and human organization began to occur. (Where industrialization and its related changes have not taken place, Von Thünen's theory remains relevant.) Transportation is vastly more efficient than in Von Thünen's time, with transport costs having declined more than virtually any other major cost factor in the production and marketing of agricultural commodities. Moreover, refrigeration now allows perishables to be hauled long distances and transport costs per commodity unit per unit of distance tend to decline with increasing length of shipment (Fig. 9-4). Whereas transport costs may be $0.10 per ton-mile for a load of grain being shipped to the market from a farm 10 miles away, costs may drop to $0.09 per ton-mile from a farm 100 miles from market or to $0.07 per ton-mile from farms 1,000 miles away. Sinclair also points out

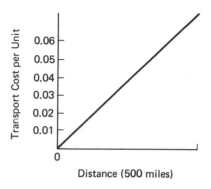 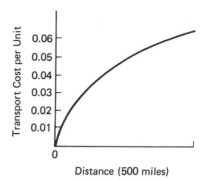

Fig. 9-4. Relationship between distance and transport cost. The left diagram represents transport costs which are proportional to distance. The diagram on the right is more representative of modern transportation cost structures, where costs are less than proportional to distance.

that modern agriculture favors large-scale farming and specialization of production for nationwide instead of local markets.

Von Thünen's theory of economic rent is retained by Sinclair. That land use which yields the greatest return makes the highest bid for the land and displaces other land uses. In modern industrialized areas, land which is suitable for urban and agricultural use will normally become urbanized because urban functions can offer the highest rent for the land [4].

As in Von Thünen's theory, economic rent declines with increasing distance from market, but near the market city much of the economic rent is derived from urban rather than agricultural land values. As land becomes more valuable for urban use, its relative value for agriculture declines. Contrast the concentric circle and graphic indications of land uses at varying distances from the city as shown in Sinclair's model (Fig. 9-5) with those in Von Thünen's model (Figure 9-3). Farmers living in a soon-to-be-urbanized area may be affected by one or more of the following practices and problems:

1. Property taxes may be based upon actual land values rather than on land use, and the income from agricultural use may not be adequate to cover production expenses and taxes.
2. In anticipation of urbanization no long-term investments are made in the land. No barns are built, fences are not replaced, and costly conservation practices are ignored.
3. Nuisances of urbanization such as increased traffic and noise, efforts by speculators and developers to purchase the land, pollution of air and water, zoning regulations, and taxes may make continued farming difficult or impossible.
4. Some farmers may sell their land to speculators and leave, causing local farm supply stores and other farm-related businesses to close.

5. Wages for farm laborers must be made competitive with wages in the city if hired labor is to be obtained.

When pressures of urbanization become too heavy, farmers are likely to sell to land speculators or to developers, and each urban expansion increases the pressures of urbanization upon outlying farming areas.

Sinclair's theory, in contrast to Von Thünen's theory, states that agricultural land-use intensity increases with *increasing* distance from the market city. Sinclair recognizes that his theory has limited application. He points

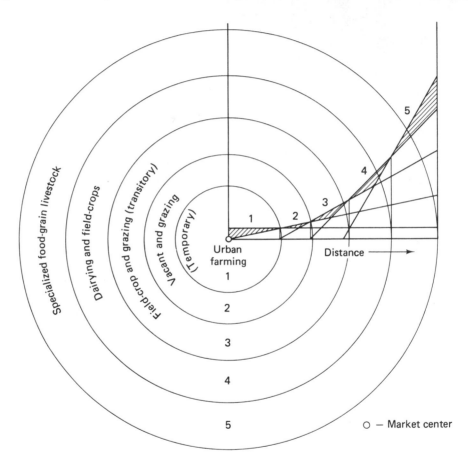

Fig. 9-5. Robert Sinclair's hypothesis of land-use zones extending outward from a modern city. Note that the intensity of land use increases as distance from the city increases and that this is the opposite of the von Thünen hypothesis. Also note the differences in graphic expressions of economic rent in the two hypotheses. (From R. Sinclair, "Von Thünen and Urban Sprawl," *Annals of the Association of American Geographers*, XLVII, March, 1967, p. 80.)

out, for example, that a marked zonation does not appear near some cities
which are located in highly specialized agricultural areas. He describes his
model as a "theoretical construct" rather than a "pure economic model" [5].
On the whole, however, the theory is a useful aid to understanding agricultural land use in urban fringe areas of developed nations.

The Natural Environment

Conditions of the natural environment interact in endless combinations over
the earth's surface to form a highly varied base for agricultural activities.
Only about 30 percent of the earth's land surface has a suitable combination
of temperature conditions, moisture supply, soil quality, and slope for agricultural development, and only about one-third to one-half of this is *arable*,
or suitable for raising cultivated crops (Fig. 9–6). The remainder is too cold,
dry, hot, wet, steeply sloping, or high in elevation for successful agriculture.
Although the effects of some elements of the natural environment have been
locally modified through human ingenuity, the modifications often provide
only temporary advantages and do not alter fundamental limitations placed
upon agriculture by the natural elements.

   The natural processes themselves often function perversely relative to

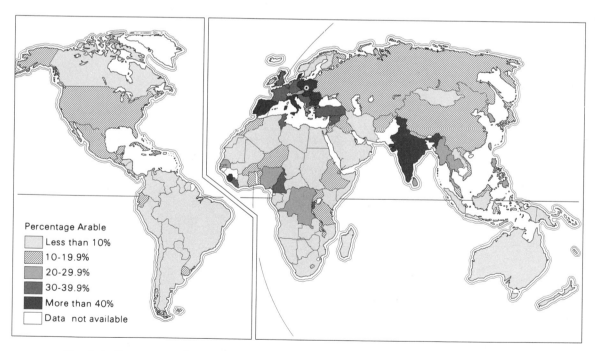

Fig. 9–6. Percentage of land which is arable. (From *FAO Yearbook.*)

agricultural development. Soils with high natural fertility are formed almost exclusively where precipitation is inadequate for high levels of agricultural productivity. Where precipitation is abundant, on the other hand, natural soil fertility is normally poor because essential soil ingredients are washed or leached out of the soil. In some areas precipitation occurs primarily during the coldest months. In other instances temperatures are suitable for year-round agriculture, but inadequate moisture during one or all seasons limits use of the land. In still other areas slopes are too steep for agriculture even though temperature and moisture conditions are satisfactory.

Problems of Managing the Natural Environment. Successful management of the natural environment requires recognition that the environment operates as a system. The more complex the system, or the more precarious its ability to function consistently, the greater is the likelihood that manipulating the environment will result in reactions which may substantially alter some intrinsic part of the system.

Here we shall concentrate upon the physical strengths and weaknesses of large segments of the earth as they apply to use of land for agriculture. The strengths and weaknesses are descriptively evaluated according to temperature conditions, moisture availability, soil quality, and slope. In so doing, the earth's land surface is divided into four highly generalized zones, as follows (Fig. 9-7):

Zone A — Nonagricultural.

Zone B — Suitable for grazing and/or marginal cultivation.

Zone C — Moderately favorable for agriculture.

Zone D — Most favorable for agriculture.

The boundaries of these zones are readily debatable, and anyone knowledgeable of the earth's physical characteristics and basic requirements for agriculture may arrive at regional boundaries and descriptions which differ substantially from those offered here.

Most evaluations of the suitability of the natural environment for agriculture are based upon crops, tastes, and techniques of cultivation which are common in middle-latitude northern hemisphere regions. Such crops and techniques are often inappropriate in environments exotic to the middle latitudes. If techniques of cultivation are developed especially for those exotic environments, or if plants indigenous to those areas become acceptable foods for middle-latitude populations, the amount of land considered suitable for cultivation may be somewhat enlarged.

Zone A — Nonagricultural Land. Zone A contains lands where any form of sustained agriculture is virtually impossible because of extreme cold, short

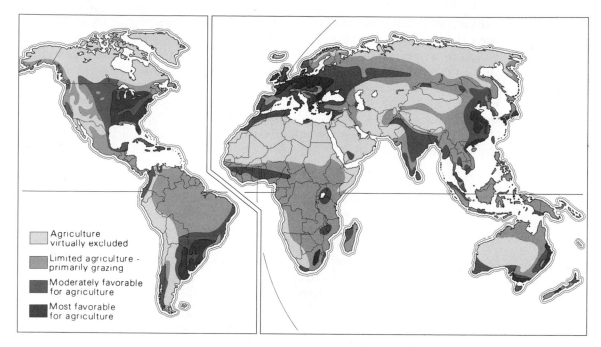

Fig. 9-7. Suitability of the natural environment for agriculture.

growing seasons, extreme drought, high elevations, or steep slopes. These
regions contain a few cultivated areas within mountain valleys and along
exotic streams which cross deserts with enough water volume to maintain a
year-round flow. The Nile Valley in Egypt is the largest of such desert oases,
supporting a population in excess of 38 million. Other dry areas which have
been made suitable for agriculture through use of irrigation water obtained
from humid regions include the Back Slopes (the gently sloping western
sides) of the Eastern Highlands of Australia and some of the irrigated valleys
of central and southern California. Few permanent streams cross deserts, and
in many cases irrigation water is obtained from subsurface reservoirs or it is
pumped or gravity-fed into dry regions suitable for cultivation through
man-made channels from man-made reservoirs.

Within those parts of Zone A which are excluded from agricultural development because of cold temperatures, the frost-free season is normally less
than 90 days. The subsoil is permanently frozen and vegetation is restricted
to small, fast-maturing plants. The soil is waterlogged, for although precipitation rarely exceeds 10 to 15 inches per year, the evaporation rate is minimal
because of low temperatures. Low temperatures also retard the action of
microorganisms in the soil and make for immature soils with little organic
content.

In deserts drought imposes many of the same limitations upon agriculture
as cold in the polar regions. Because desert surfaces consist primarily of

pebbles, bare bedrock, and sand, only small areas are suitable for agriculture even if irrigation is employed. Soils that do exist are poorly developed. Agriculture is further discouraged by daily temperature ranges of as much as 28 to 39 degrees Centigrade and by hot, excessively dry winds and dust storms.

Besides the extremely cold and extremely dry areas, Zone A contains the earth's highest and roughest mountain regions where elevations are so high, temperatures so cold, and slopes so steep that agriculture is virtually impossible. Two of the largest mountain regions where such conditions exist are the Himalayan-Tibetan system in Asia and the Andes of South America.

Zone B — Suitable for Grazing and (or) Marginal Cultivation. Zone B contains lands which are too dry, too wet, or too cold for sustained cultivation or for the most productive grazing activities. The dry areas are best described as semiarid, but the precipitation is sufficient for crops whose moisture needs are minimal, and dry farming is practiced in small portions of the zone. *Dry farming* consists of various practices designed to store moisture within the soil for 2 or 3 years in order to have a sufficient supply for one crop. Conservation practices include cultivating the land after a rain to break up soil capillaries, through which moisture moves to the surface and is evaporated, and the spreading of straw over fields, also to reduce evaporation. Grazing animals are limited primarily to sheep and goats.

In the wetter portion of the tropics, rainfall is so heavy and temperatures are so high that soil fertility is quickly exhausted under modern methods of large-scale mechanized cultivation of cleanly tilled fields. Sustained use of land is possible only with extremely heavy applications of commercial fertilizers and the high cost of such operations make them prohibitive in most areas. Native methods include cultivation of partially cleared plots for 2 or 3 years, after which cultivation is shifted to another partially cleared plot. Abandoned plots are allowed to return to forest and are again suitable for agricultural use after a few years. Some forms of wetland agriculture such as rice cultivation may be sustainable for long periods, but population densities are sparse except in portions of Indonesia and southeast Asia.

The utility of thousands of square miles of land in Zone B, and in other zones, is limited primarily to grazing. Animal production in these areas, therefore, need not deplete the world's food supply by consuming grains upon which so many of the world's poor peoples depend for life. Rather, animals furnish the only feasible means through which a large part of the earth's surface can be made productive.

Zone C — Moderately Favorable for Agriculture. Lands in Zone C are handicapped by seasonal drought, by terrain irregularities, and in some areas by soils of low natural fertility. Agriculture is possible and is practiced within most parts of the zone, and some areas such as southeastern China are among the most intensively cultivated lands on earth. Although much of the land is

Stages of development. (Courtesy, Agency for International Development.)

too hilly for modern methods of large-scale machine agriculture, it can be intensively utilized under the system of hand-tilled subsistence farming which is prevalent in China. In the same vein, much of Appalachia in the United States was once capable of supporting a relatively dense population at levels of living not appreciably different from those of farm families in other parts of the country. When large-scale machine agriculture became the order of the day, however, Appalachian farmers found that their small hill-country farms and small field sizes were not so easily adaptable to mechanization as the larger farms located on the huge expanses of level land in the Middle West, on the Great Plains, and along the Atlantic and Gulf coastal plains.

Zone D — Most Favorable for Agriculture. Lands in Zone D have no major natural handicaps to agricultural production. The land is level, soils are relatively fertile, summer precipitation is adequate, droughts are rare, and the growing season is long enough for most crops. Most of the land is in cultivated crops, and output per acre and per worker are exceptionally high and dependable. With a few notable exceptions people who live within Zone D are among the most prosperous and well-nourished on earth and they have substantial quantities of surplus foods to export to peoples in less productive areas.

Nonphysical Management Factors

Culture. Although the natural environment largely determines which portions of the earth *can* be used for agricultural development, cultural factors are responsible for influencing *how* the land will be used. Crops produced, methods of cultivation, work characteristics of the population, practices of land ownership or control, and methods of food preparation are primarily cultural decisions. The distinguishing characteristics of cultures, such as religion, language, concepts of work and entertainment, and related institutional structures, are rooted in history.

Variations in cultures are reflected in world agriculture largely through different types of farming and cropping systems. Most of these systems have evolved through lengthy periods of trial and error experimentation to determine which crops and which farming practices offered adequate supplies of essential commodities with lowest risk of failure. It is also essential, especially in nontropical and seasonally dry areas, that the staple food crops have adequate keeping qualities so that they can be stored during cold or dry seasons.

Availability of Capital and Technology and Scale of Farm Operations. Whereas the advanced nations have liberally substituted mechanical energy for animal and human energy in agriculture, the poor nations are constrained against the adoption of modern technology by lack of capital, ignorance, small farm and field sizes and by strong cultural resistance to mechanization. Such simple things to most Americans as maintenance of proper oil levels and tire pressures for their vehicles involve the introduction of an entirely new and foreign set of concepts which cannot ordinarily be learned quickly or easily by illiterate peoples accustomed to simple tools and simple methods.

Because of the lack of modern technology, lands often lie idle that might be made productive and lands which might give large yields produce low to modest amounts of food and fiber. Although nearly 85 percent of the land capable of crop production is being utilized for that purpose in Asia, only about 26 percent is being used in Latin America [6]. In neither area is adequate capital available for purchase of machines to facilitate preparation of hard to cultivate soils and to develop extensive agricultural areas. In much of Asia, however, a vastly larger labor force than in Latin America has been employed over a much longer period of time to develop most of the land which is capable of cultivation. In Latin America only the most accessible and the most naturally fertile, productive, and readily cultivated areas have been utilized with intensity. Where human and animal manure are the sole nutrients available for supplementing heavily used soils, only the best quality soils which are least susceptible to erosion or floodplain soils that are naturally fertilized by annual floods can be utilized for extended periods. Other soils which have low natural fertility or which are subject to moderate to heavy rates of nutrient loss can be used only for short or irregular intervals. If commercial fertilizers, machines, and modern plant varieties were available, much of this land could be made productive for indefinite periods.

Where capital and technology are abundantly available, where population densities are relatively low, and where a large percentage of the population lives in urban areas, farms are likely to emphasize maximization of profits and of output per worker. Such farms attempt to realize the economies which are obtainable through large-scale operations (Fig. 9-8). Individual farms often contain several hundred acres of cropland or pasture. Capital investments ranging from $100,000 to more than $1 million are not uncommon. Supplies are purchased in large quantities at favorable prices, the largest and most efficient equipment is obtained and utilized to maximum effectiveness, and output per man hour is high. Labor is usually scarce and costly, and savings are possible in most instances where machines can be substituted for people or where a machine can be used to bring about a major increase in labor productivity. Areas where agricultural holdings are largest are the primary sources of agricultural commodities entering international trade.

In undeveloped areas where populations are dense, capital is scarce, and

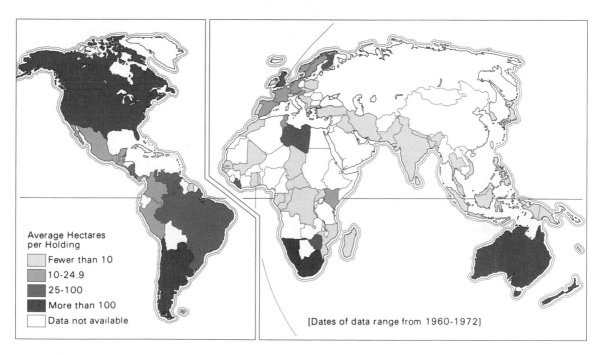

Fig. 9-8. Average size of agricultural holdings. [From *Production Yearbook: 1973,* **27** (Rome: Food and Agriculture Organization of the United Nations, 1974), p. 8.]

most people depend on agriculture for a livelihood, farm units are small, labor productivity is low, and machines are uncommon. The amount of land that can be cultivated per worker is small, and large farm units are not practical as only a few acres can be cultivated by an average family.

Uses of commercial fertilizers, pesitcides, fungicides, farm equipment, and more productive varieties of plants are increasing within the developing areas, but acceptance of these spin-offs from the modern world is often slow and not without incidence of failure. Fertilizer output is limited and farmers who are fortunate enough to receive government-provided supplies or who can afford to purchase their own may use it improperly with disastrous results. An additional problem with extensive mechanization of agriculture in developing areas is that it may displace farm workers more rapidly than nonfarm employment can be created to absorb them.

Field Losses, Spoilage, Contamination, and Waste. A particularly serious problem for agriculture in developing areas is the amount of food lost as a result of spoilage, plant diseases, preharvest damage, and postharvest contamination by insects and rodents and through inefficient removal of weeds from fields. These factors reduce the amount of food actually available to consumers by at least 50 to 75 percent. Insects and rodents destroy at least half of the harvest in the poorest countries, and the Food and Agriculture Organization has estimated that preharvest damage by insects and weeds rob the world of at least 23 percent of its annual production of all crops [7]. Marketing systems in most undeveloped areas are so poorly developed that movements of commodities over distances as short as 20 to 50 miles is often economically or physically impossible. Intense shortages may exist only a few miles from areas where there are surpluses. When foods are imported during times of shortages, they may spoil at the docks either for lack of an adequate marketing system or for lack of facilities for transporting the goods to needy customers. Without a system for marketing surplus production, farmers are discouraged from attempting to increase output and the "green revolution," which seems to offer considerable hope for increasing the food supply to needy areas, will not be able to achieve its considerable potential. Marketing systems designed to facilitate inland distribution of imported foods from port cities may be incapable of handling surpluses produced at interior domestic locations [8].

Seen in this light, the food supply problem in many parts of the world is more a product of inefficient methods of harvesting, storage, preservation, and marketing than the result of underproduction. It may be possible that the time and cost required to solve these problems would be far less than that involved in increasing food output either by adding new lands to the cultivated area or through increasing the intensity of production on lands already in crops.

Energy Inputs. Although the sun is the primary source of energy for agricultural production in all parts of the earth, relative dependence on inanimate energy sources varies enormously. The primary inanimate energy source used in agriculture in nearly all areas is petroleum, which provides the fuel for farm machinery, the manufacture of fertilizers and pesticides, transporting and processing agricultural commodities, and refrigerating and cooking foods consumed in homes and restaurants.

The availability of energy to farmers depends largely on its price and upon the purchasing power of potential consumers. When energy is reduced in availability because of an increase in price, decreased output, decreased purchasing power, or trade embargoes, the negative effects of the reduced supply are greatest in the most highly developed nations and in portions of the developing nations which have gone farthest in adopting modern technologies. The impact of energy shortages also varies according to the kinds of crops produced. Yields of crops such as corn and wheat, which are highly responsive to applications of fertilizers, may be substantially reduced if high energy costs result in reduced utilization of fertilizer. Yields of crops such as soybeans and the traditional varieties of rice grown in southern and eastern Asia, on the other hand, are relatively unaffected by fertilizer applications.

In most modern agricultural systems the amount of energy used to produce crops is several times greater than the food energy the crops contain. Crop yields generally increase with higher applications of fertilizer but at a diminishing rate. As energy costs rise relative to prices received for crops, therefore, farmers may find it profitable to reduce fertilizer use to the point where each input yields higher returns.

In the United States approximately 3 percent of the total energy consumed is used in production of food crops, and another 9 percent is required in their transportation, processing, and home preparation. Fertilizer accounts for about 36 percent of the energy used in producing food; another 43 percent is used in the manufacturing, operation, and maintenance of farm machinery; 11 percent, for electricity; and about 1 percent for crop pesticides.

Opportunities for increased agricultural output within the developing nations depends in large part on the availability of a relative abundance of low-cost energy. The new high yield crops such as those introduced through the green revolution require fertilization and some degree of mechanization. Besides fertilizers and machines the developing nations need modern systems of transportation and processing — all of which require significant inputs of energy.

More than any other factor, differing degrees of energy availability and differing levels of energy inputs are keyed to variations in agricultural output. When energy prices increase significantly faster than prices received by farmers for their crops in areas of high energy usage, output per acre almost inevitably declines and pressures to bring previously unused lands into production may rise correspondingly. It is also likely that substantial increases in land productivity within developing areas is a direct function of energy availability.

Economic and Political Systems. The types of economic and political systems under which agriculture operates exert an especially strong influence upon what goods are produced and where and how they are produced and marketed. Most economic and political systems operate according to either a democratic "free market" principle or a totalitarian "command" principle. Where the free market principle is employed, the types and quantities of goods produced and the places or areas where they are produced depend primarily on demand from the marketplace. In a command economy, on the other hand, the types and quantities of goods produced and the areas where they are produced are determined by centralized planning authorities. In reality, most nations employ a mix of the free market and command principles. The United States, for example, attempts to control production and prices of some crops but not others. In the Soviet Union, where the command principle predominates, central authorities have in recent years become increasingly cognizant of market demand in planning for production and in the pricing of agricultural commodities.

Most national governments employ acreage controls, production quotas, price controls, subsidies, direct grants, and commands to stimulate or to reduce output of specific commodities. Governmental authorities are also responsible for negotiating international trade agreements which, in themselves, can be used to stimulate or to discourage domestic production of particular goods. At times governmental decisions are influenced largely by internal political considerations, whereas in other instances decisions are prompted primarily by external factors related by international maneuverings for military or political influence.

Health. Low productivity per worker in many of the poor countries can be attributed in part to the existence of debilitating diseases. Most of these diseases either have been brought under control in or they are absent from the richer nations. Malnourishment leads to retarded mental and physical development and is directly responsible for such chronic ailments as pellagra, scurvy, and beriberi. It also increases susceptibility to bacterial and parasitic infections and leaves its victims in a weakened state which leads to poor work performance and an apparent lack of ambition or concern for their own welfare. These results have sometimes been interpreted by unknowing but healthy and well-fed observers as representative of slovenliness in character.

Two measures of variations in the availability of health care to the peoples of the world are infant mortality rates and expectation of life at birth. Infant deaths during the first year of life vary from between 10 and 20

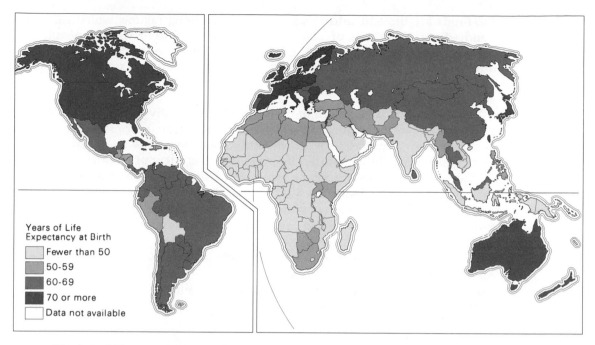

Fig. 9-9. Life expectancy at birth (years). (Courtesy, Washington, D.C.: Population Reference Bureau, Inc., 1976.)

per 1,000 in most European countries to more than 200 in parts of Africa and Asia (see Fig. 4-5). Life expectancy tends to be lowest in Africa, where it seldom exceeds 50 years, and highest in northern Europe and Anglo-America (Fig. 9-9). Almost invariably, countries with high infant mortality rates are those with least exposure to modern science and technology. Their birthrates are high, per capita gross national product and productivity per worker are low, and 30 percent or more of the population is under 15 years of age. The labor force is overwhelmingly employed in agriculture, and a high percentage of the population suffers from infectious and parasitic and nutritional diseases.

DISPARITIES IN FOOD PRODUCTION AND CONSUMPTION

Disparities in Food Consumption

Most people living within affluent nations (those with per capita gross national products exceeding the world average) enjoy relatively high-quality diets of considerable diversity in types of foods consumed. The quantities and qualities of foods consumed are not dependent on local production, for foods are brought into these areas from farming regions which often lie hundreds or thousands of miles away. Because of their wealth, peoples in such nations can outbid those of poor societies for available food supplies during times of shortages, and through their purchases from distant producing regions a wide variety of foods are normally available to consumers at all times during the year.

Within the relatively poor nations diets are normally of lower quality and less diversity than within affluent areas. They may become monotonous during cold or dry seasons when the only foods available are those that can be produced locally and stored in crude facilities without benefit of modern methods of food preservation or protection from damage by the elements or from insects and rodents. Lack of capital, lack of transportation and marketing facilities, and lack of familiarity with exotic crops are among the several factors which inhibit availability of commodities produced in distant areas.

Per capita food consumption in most affluent areas exceeds that which is required to furnish an adequate supply of body energy and sufficient protein (Fig. 9-10 and 9-11). Areas with most pronounced deficiencies in food energy consumption are located in Africa, in the western part of tropical

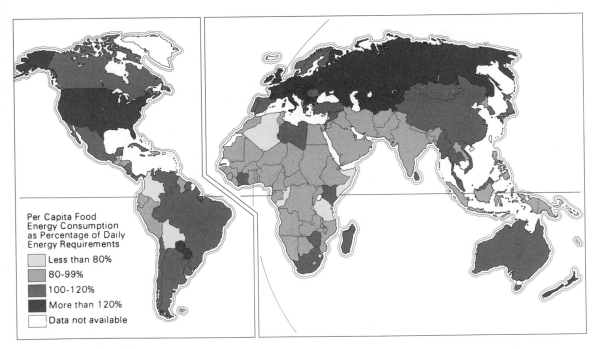

Per Capita Food Energy Consumption as Percentage of Daily Energy Requirements

Less than 80%

80-99%

100-120%

More than 120%

Data not available

Fig. 9-10. Relative sufficiency of food intake, 1970. (From *The State of Food and Agriculture, 1974* (Rome: Food and Agriculture Organization of the United Nations, 1975), Table 3-C.

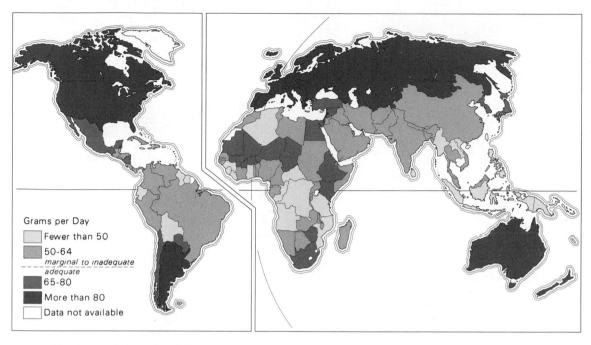

Fig. 9-11. Per capita daily protein consumption: 1970. (From *The State of Food and Agriculture, 1974, op. cit.,* Table 3-C.)

South America, and middle, south, and southwestern Asia. Protein deficiencies are found in most of these same areas and also in all tropical South America and in eastern and southeastern Asia.

With several notable exceptions these same areas are experiencing a more rapid rate of increase in demand for food than in food production (Fig. 9-12). Among these nations only Canada and Argentina produce large surpluses of food crops for export and are in no immediate danger of severe food shortages. In most of western Europe, on the other hand, food production is increasing more rapidly than demand. That imports of foodstuffs also continue to increase annually indicates that the quality of western European diets is improving. Particularly large increases have occurred in consumption of animal products. Some of the feeds used to fatten American and European cattle are imported in the forms of grains or fish products from developing areas which suffer from chronic malnutrition. Because animals are poor converters of grain energy into meat energy, this often means that amounts of food available to peoples in poor nations are reduced in favor of foreign exchange obtainable through exports. Exported foods fatten animals for the diets of the affluent in other nations, and foreign exchange is often used to purchase luxury goods for wealthy domestic groups.

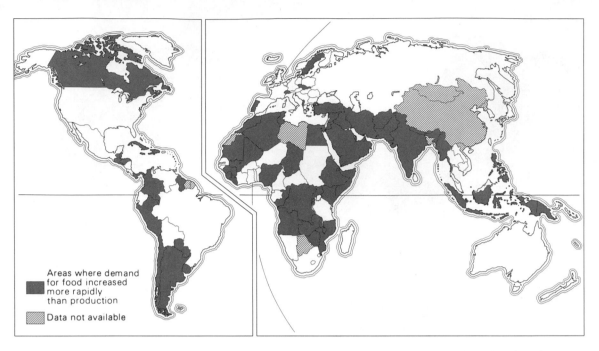

Fig. 9-12. Areas experiencing a more rapid increase in demand for than in production of food: 1952-1972. (From *The State of Food and Agriculture, 1974, op. Cit.*, Table 3-A.)

By comparing areas of protein and food energy deficiencies with those where demand for food is increasing more rapidly than food production, nations with the most critical present and potential food supply problems can be identified (Fig. 9-13). These areas include much of southeastern Asia, nearly all of south central and southwestern Asia, the three more or less contiguous northeast–southwest trending tiers of nations in Africa stretching from Tunisia to Liberia, Egypt to Nigeria, and Ethiopia to Angola; Guatemala and Honduras in Central America; and northwestern South America. With the exception of the oil-rich nations bordering the Persian Gulf, these areas have meager financial resources with which to introduce rapid improvements in agriculture or to compete in the world market for surplus foods produced elsewhere. Additional nations which have significant petroleum resources under development are Indonesia, Algeria, and Nigeria. Altogether nations with the most serious current and potential food supply problems contain more than 35 percent of the world's population.

Disparities in Production and the Aversion of Risk

A primary objective of farmers, whether in affluent or in developing areas, is aversion of risk. In affluent areas this is achieved through specialized produc-

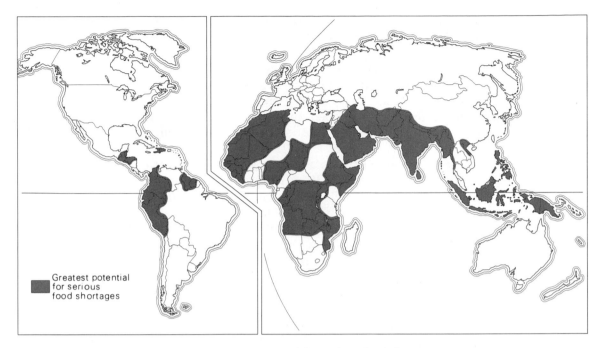

Fig. 9-13. Areas with greatest potential for serious food shortages.

tion techniques and lavish employment of external inputs such as machines, energy, and agricultural chemicals. In developing areas risk aversion is achieved through crop diversification and through development of cropping and cultivation systems whose demands for soil nutrients, moisture, and solar energy balance those available from natural sources. Lack of external inputs and external markets discourages production of surpluses, for the surpluses will normally spoil or serve to drive down local prices or both.

Cropping systems within the affluent regions are for the most part highly specialized, with most farms producing from one to three commodities for sale. The crop or crops around which particular farmers center their efforts are those with relatively low susceptibility to weather adversities and those for which each farmer's education and experience provide expertise in producing. Most farmers in affluent areas make heavy use of machines in cultivating and harvesting operations, but a single piece of harvesting equipment is normally capable of harvesting only one or two types of crops. Such equipment is also expensive, and a particular farmer is rarely able to afford the purchase of numerous machines to harvest numerous crops.

Large inputs of technology in affluent areas also aid in reducing the risk of crop failure. Through plant breeding and use of chemical fertilizers and pesticides many common environmental threats are reduced in severity. Machines enable the rapid planting and harvesting of crops, thereby reducing threats caused by shorter than normal growing seasons or by other weather adversities. Pesticides reduce threats of loss from insects, and chemical fertilizers are used to overcome or to diminish natural or man-caused soil deficiencies.

Agriculture within the developing parts of the world operates primarily as a closed system. Because few, if any, inputs of external origin such as fertilizers and fuels are available, the extraction of nutrients from the soil must be matched by equivalent inputs that occur naturally or as the result of strictly local farming practices. The most critical and normally the most difficult to manage of necessary plant nutrients is nitrogen. Certain quantities of nitrogen are added to the soil each year through natural phenomena such as lightening and rainfall. Nitrogen levels may also be enhanced by adding organic matter to the soil and by careful selection of the kinds of crops raised. Most varieties of peas and beans take nitrogen from the air and add it to the soil by action of nitrogen-fixation bacteria living in nodules on the roots of the plants. In any event the absence of externally obtained inputs of soil nutrients places rigid limits upon the kinds of crops that can be raised and upon the amount which can be produced per acre if agriculture is to be sustained over long periods of time. Achievement of a balance between nutrients added to the soil and those extracted has resulted from a long process of trial and error experimentation, with the generations of experi-menters having little knowledge of the scientific rationale for what was taking place. Any significant change in the system of agriculture, the kinds of crops produced, or output per unit area could upset the nutrient balance with strikingly negative consequences to the local populations.

Farmers within the labor-intensive subsistence farming regions such as southern and eastern Asia use crop diversification to maintain a balance between nutrients taken from and those added to the soil. Diversification also helps to distribute labor requirements throughout the growing season and to reduce the risk of crop failure when adverse weather or insect damage takes a particularly heavy toll of one crop. At the same time, the risk that one or more of the crops will be lost or damaged is increased because each crop is likely to have somewhat different requirements for moisture, temperature, and length of growing season. Those requirements may not be met for all crops during any single season. Because planting and harvesting are extremely time-consuming when accomplished by hand, absence of machines reduces the ability of farmers to make rapid adjustments in planting and harvesting dates. Lack of agricultural chemicals, including commercial fertilizers, also hampers farmers in expanding productivity to meet surges in demand.

One of the better measures for comparing the relative success or failure of farmers in different areas in avoiding risks is the degree of stability in crop production (Fig. 9–14). In some areas farm output varies enormously from year to year, whereas in other areas fluctuations in output seldom exceed 1 or 2 percent. Although no specific relationship exists between output

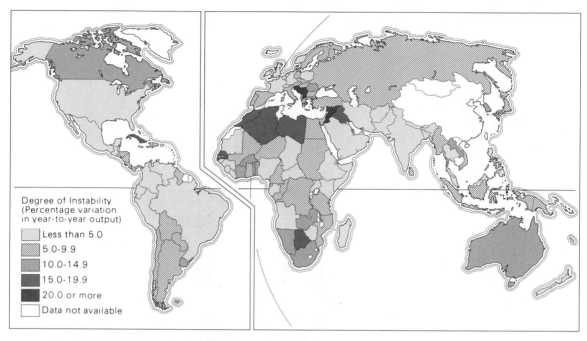

Fig. 9-14. Instability in food and cereal production: 1952–1972. (From *The State of Food and Agriculture, 1974, op cit.,* Table 3-B.)

stability and either affluence or diet quality, those parts of the world which depend almost entirely on locally produced goods which barely meet or fail to meet demand are far more vulnerable to even minor variations in food output than areas which normally produce large surpluses. Whereas a harvest which is 2 or 3 percent below normal could lead to widespread hunger in India, for example, the same relative drop in harvests in the United States would have little or no effect upon the amount or the quality of per capita food consumption. Areas which produce surpluses are also more likely than deficit food-producing areas to maintain stocks (reserves of foods that can be used to blunt the negative effects of lean crop years).

An additional indicator of disparities in production is crop yield per acre. Among the major regions of the world, areas with highest yields produced more than three times as much wheat, rice, and maize per acre during 1971–1973 as areas obtaining lowest yields (Fig. 9-15). Africa, Asia, and South America are consistent in that they produce lower per acre yields of all three crops than the more modern agricultural systems of North America and Europe. Highest yields of rice and wheat are obtained in Europe and of maize, in North America. When considered nation by nation, those with smallest yields per acre of these commodities produced only one-eighth to one-fifteenth as much per acre as nations with highest yields per acre.

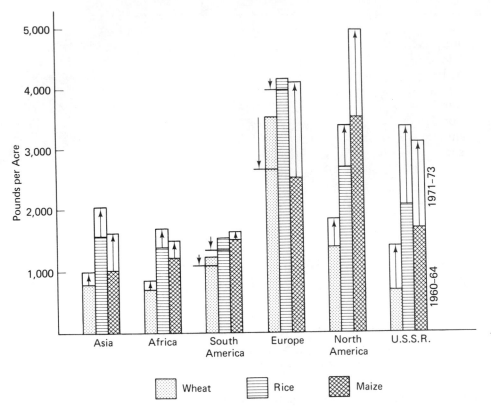

Fig. 9-15. Yields per acre of wheat, rice, and maize: 1960–1964 and 1971–1973. (Courtesy, Washington D.C.: U.S. Department of Agriculture.)

Between 1960–1964 and 1971–1973, per acre yields of the major grains increased most rapidly in the Soviet Union and North America. Yields also increased in Asia and Africa, although in smaller amounts per unit area. In Europe and South America per acre yields of wheat and rice dropped, but yields of maize increased.

One of the major factors explaining the wide differences in yield per acre between the developed and developing parts of the world is the large investment made in agricultural research and in the training of farmers and agricultural scientists in the advanced nations. Better education of their farmers, alone, is estimated to account for at least 30 percent of the superiority in per acre yields achieved in the advanced, compared to the developing, nations. Advanced areas are also able to direct enormous amounts of highly trained talent and huge sums of money toward agricultural problems as they arise, and well-staffed and well-funded research efforts are constantly being made to develop new and higher yielding varieties of crops and to improve methods, chemicals, and machines used in crop cultivation. Although

positive spin-offs from research in advanced nations have substantially bene-
fitted developing areas, most of the research has been directed toward crops,
environmental conditions, and farming systems which are not easily transferred to the developing nations. During recent years, however, developed
nations have channeled significant quantities of research funds and scientific
talent into programs intended to benefit developing areas. The new high-
yield varieties of wheat and rice and a high protein maize have been the major
crops powering the green revolution. Even these efforts, however, are dependent for success on a marriage between traditional agriculture and the
large-scale chemical- and machine-oriented techniques used in the advanced
areas.

The Green Revolution

The "green revolution" refers to several major breakthroughs in plant
breeding which have occurred primarily since World War II. Several new
varieties of cereal grains have been developed which can produce yields
double or more than those of previously used strains. Greatest successes have
been achieved thus far with new varieties of rice and wheat. Promising results
have also been obtained from a high protein maize (corn) and new grain
called *triticale.* In most areas where the new varieties of grains have been
adopted, considerable increases have occurred in production per cultivated
unit and in output per farm worker. Introduction of a new dwarf wheat in
Mexico was instrumental in raising yields from 750 kilograms per hectare
in 1940 to 3,200 kilograms in 1970 [9]. Similar results have been obtained
from introduction of new strains of rice and wheat in India, Japan, the
Philippines, Colombia, and elsewhere. In Colombia, for example, rice yields
rose from less than 3 metric tons per hectare in 1968 to 5.4 tons in
1974 [10]. Research in development of plant varieties with improved production capabilities is occurring in a number of areas with respect to crops
such as peas, beans, potatoes, cassava, grasses, and cotton.

Early successes of the new strains of crops led to much speculation that
the green revolution provided, if not a solution to world hunger, at least
some breathing room during which the problems of rapid population growth
and increasing demands upon food supplies might be resolved. Successes
with the new crops were also cited as evidence of the power of technology to
solve major world problems. It soon became apparent, however, that increased
production of food does not necessarily reduce hunger among the poor. The
new strains of plants being introduced into the agricultural systems of the
developing lands require large capital expenditures for such things as irrigation, machines, fertilizers, fuel, and pesticides and for the creation of
marketing, transportation, and communication systems. Only the larger,
wealthier farmers can afford to purchase the machines, irrigation equipment,

fuels, and fertilizers required by the new crops, have the knowledge to use them properly, and have access to marketing and transportation facilities through which large increases in output can be sold. Institutional establishments, also, are better designed to provide informational, technical, and economic services to large enterprises than to small producers and to those located in remote areas [11]. Increased output has had the effect in many instances of depressing prices. Large farmers may find production of the new grains profitable even at lower prices because of increased yields. Poor farmers who cannot afford the capital requirements associated with adoption of the new grains, however, have experienced increasing impoverishment because of the depressed prices for any small surpluses they might produce.

An additional effect of increased productivity and lower prices for grains has been a sharp rise in the quantities of grain fed to meat animals. Because the meat animals are consumed primarily by affluent persons and because 7 to 15 pounds of grain must ordinarily be fed to an animal to produce 1 pound of meat, much of the potential benefit from larger yields is being lavished upon the rich rather than to improve nutrition among the poor.

If the green revolution is to be judged on the basis of its contribution to improved nutritional standards for the poor, its successes to date are limited. It represents an intrusion of modern capital-intensive, high-energy technology into traditional agricultural areas and its benefits have gone primarily to those who are already relatively well-off. The intrusion of modern agricultural methods into traditional areas poses certain risks, for to the degree that the intrusion continues food production in traditional areas will become increasingly vulnerable to natural and human-originated circumstances which might stop, interrupt, or reduce domestic or international flows of machines, chemicals, and especially energy. When resource shortages occur, agricultural output may drop precipitously because the wealthier nations can outbid less wealthy nations for available supplies. On the other hand, if output is increased sufficiently through adoption of green revolution methods so that large reserves of surplus grains can be stored against temporary shortages of resources and occasional calamities of weather, overall living standards and dietary qualities might be improved. Even the maldistribution of benefits may be reduced if the adoption of green revolution techniques by the wealthy is only a necessary first step in their later diffusion to smaller, poorer farms and farmers.

CONCLUSIONS

From examining the major factors which result in the differential characteristics of agriculture in different areas, it is clear that methods which are most suitable to agricultural needs of one area are unlikely to find beneficial applications in all other areas. Large modern machinery, for example, may be less suitable to the skills possessed by farmers in developing areas, to the kinds of soils they must cultivate, and to the sizes of their farms, than an improved hoe or hand operated seed planter. In numerous such areas a system of cultivation has evolved, largely through trial and error, which provides an acceptable balance between nutrients being removed from the land and those being restored by natural processes. To introduce a new technology, which the people are unable to understand or to use in a rational manner, may have enormously negative long term results. The use of modern energy intensive systems of cultivation are almost wholly alien to the self-sufficing systems employed in most of the world's poor regions. Such modern systems tend to increase the vulnerability of poor areas to economic and political fluctuations within the rest of the world. Whereas such fluctuations may affect the welfare of affluent peoples only to a minor degree, they can be devastating to those in poor regions.

An additional threat to the agricultural stability of many poor regions is their rapidly growing populations. Population growth leads to pressure upon the agricultural system to obtain higher yields from lands already under cultivation, thus threatening to disturb the balance between inputs and outputs of soil nutrients. It also stimulates efforts to add new lands to production and encourages shorter periods of fallow. Shorter periods of fallow often lead to soil exhaustion and erosion. Alternatives to such practices include allowing the population to suffer increasing malnutrition, or to adopt some aspects of modern energy intensive agriculture with all of its dangers to long term stability.

Perhaps the overriding notion, here, is that the world's food problems are enormously complex. In efforts made to improve the food supply, especially to poor regions, therefore, it is highly important that those making decisions first gain an understanding of the physical and cultural environments they are tampering with and of the impacts their decisions are likely to have upon those environments.

REFERENCES

[1] J. H. von Thünen, *Der Isolierte Staat in Beziehung auf Landwirtschaft und Na-tionalokonomie* (Hamburg: Perthes, 1926).

[2] E. S. Dunn, *The Location of Agricultural Production* (Gainesville, Fla.: University of Florida Press, 1954), p. 7.

[3] Robert Sinclair, "Von Thünen and Urban Sprawl," *Annals of the Association of American Geographers*, XLVII, March, 1967, pp. 72-87.

[4] *Ibid.*, p. 82.

[5] *Ibid.*, p. 82.

[6] *The World Food Situation and Prospects to 1985* (Foreign Agricultural Economic Report No. 98, Economic Research Service, U.S. Department of Agriculture, Washington, D.C., 1974).

[7] Ned Greenwood and J. M. B. Edwards, *Human Environments and Natural Systems* (North Scituate, Mass.: Duxbury Press, 1973).

[8] Lester R. Brown and Gail W. Finsterbush, *Man and HIs Environment: Food* (New York: Harper & Row, 1972), pp. 137–138.

[9] Peter R. Jennings, "The Amplification of Agricultural Production," *Food and Agriculture* (San Francisco: W. H. Freeman, 1976), p. 128.

[10] *Ibid.*, p. 133.

[11] Edwin Cohn and John Eriksson, "Employment and Income Distribution," *War on Hunger*, VII, No. 7, July, 1973, p. 15.

CHAPTER TEN
farming characteristics: types and commodities

INTRODUCTION

The commodities that farmers produce and farming practices vary greatly from one part of the world to another in response to cultural, economic, political, and physical forces. The crops produced and the practices used are subject to relatively rapid change in the more advanced parts of the world, but changes are more difficult to accomplish in the developing nations. Changes occurring within advanced areas have normally involved more rapid increases in the use of energy to produce crops than in the energy content of the crops being raised. Such practices may make good economic sense when energy is abundant and energy prices are declining. They become questinable, however, if energy supplies become scarce or when energy prices are rising more rapidly that the prices of agricultural commodities. In developing areas the land management practices used by farmers are capable of sustained yields over indefinite periods of time because they involve few, if any, energy inputs of external origin. A balance has often been achieved between the amount of energy (plant nutrients, etc.) extracted from the soil and that which is restored by natural processes. Such systems of agriculture, however, find it extremely difficult or impossible to adjust output to rapid increases in demand. Somewhat paradoxically, it is in the areas where agricultural systems are slowest to adjust to increased demands that populations are growing at the most rapid rates and in the greatest absolute numbers. In these same areas systems of farming are coming under mounting pressures to adopt modern capital-intensive, high-energy methods in order to furnish food for grow-ing numbers of inhabitants. This is occurring despite the countervailing influences of mushrooming energy prices and serious shortages of capital.

The commodities produced by the world's farmers currently emphasize plants with a high yield of food energy rather than protein [1]. Again, some-what paradoxically, parts of the world which suffer most from protein defi-ciencies are those with greatest emphasis upon low-protein, high-energy plants. Where the demand for food is abnormally large, considering the pro-duction capability of the agricultural systems, the advantage almost always rests with high-energy rather than high-protein crops because low-protein plants produce larger amounts of food energy than high-protein plants. Low-protein plants make more efficient use of natural solar energy, water, and soil nutrients than high-protein plants.

Because cereal crops are the most efficient converters of solar energy and soil nutrients into food energy, they have become the most important crops in world agriculture. Cereals have further advantages in that they are rela-tively easy to cultivate, store, and transport; they are adaptable to a wide variety of climates; and they are able to tolerate substantial extremes and variations in weather conditions. Thus cereals account for some 75 percent of the total energy and protein content of human diets.

Actual selection of the crops to be produced is the product of human culture, for most physical environments are suitable for raising a large variety of plants. Present farming systems have evolved over long periods of time and after a great deal of experimentation with different farming techniques and with growing and eating a variety of crops. Surviving crops and tech-niques are those that a particular culture group has perceived to meet its taste and nutritional requirements and to produce harvests which are de-pendable enough to provide for the continuation of the culture. Whether or not traditional processes of adjustment in agricultural systems will prove ade-quate to meet accelerating demand, especially within the less developed parts of the world where population is rapidly increasing, is a major concern within the world community.

Heavy use of machines and chemicals is characteristic of relatively afflu-ent farming regions. Such inputs are possible only where all or some portion of the crops are produced for sale; otherwise, farmers have no income to purchase machines and chemicals. Land cultivated per worker is relatively large, output per unit area is comparatively high, and crops are more likely to be raised for feeding to meat or dairy animals or for mechanical process-ing than in poor regions. Farmers within affluent areas also tend to be good entrepreneurs. They are well-educated and highly skilled specialists who are anxious to find and to use new and improved plant varieties and methods of cultivation. Within the developing nations, on the other hand, entrepre-neurship among farmers is a rare occurrence. Changes in plant varieties or in methods of cultivation normally come as the result of stimulation provided

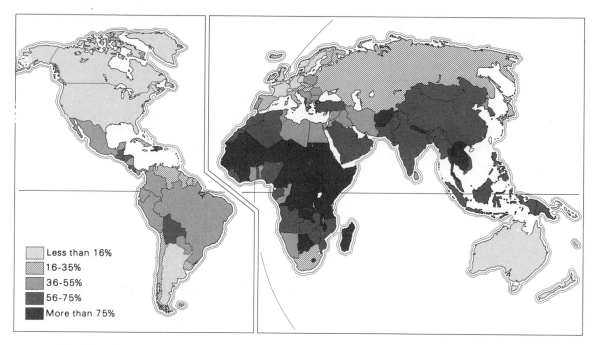

Fig. 10-1. Percentage of economically active population employed in agriculture, 1970. [From *Production Yearbook, 1973* (Rome, Italy: Food and Agriculture Organization of the United Nations, 1974), pp. 17-21.]

Legend:
- Less than 16%
- 16-35%
- 36-55%
- 56-75%
- More than 75%

from more affluent areas. In advanced economic areas the labor force employed in agriculture seldom exceeds 20 percent, whereas in less developed regions agricultural workers may represent 80 percent of the total work force (Fig. 10-1).

Types of Farms

In most parts of the world several types of farms are likely to exist in the same area, although one or two types are usually dominant. The predominant type of farm in any given area is that which has been found workable under the constraints of that region's peculiar physical, economic, social, and political circumstances. The types of farms selected for brief description are as follows:

1. Subsistence farms
2. Commercial family farms
3. Corporate farms and plantations
4. Factory farms
5. Collective farms

6. State farms
7. Part-time farms

Subsistence Farms. Subsistence farms are characterized by use of relatively unsophisticated tools and techniques to produce goods intended primarily or entirely for home consumption. Where population densities are high, such as in southern and eastern Asia, land is used intensively in an effort to obtain maximum yields from each acre under cultivation. In sparsely populated areas where pressures upon the land are minimal, the cultivated area is frequently *shifted* or moved every few years. This is especially true within hot and rainy climates where soil fertility is quickly lost as a result of leaching and erosion.

Crops associated with subsistence farms vary from paddy rice, yams, sorghum and vegetables in the crowded areas of Asia to maize, upland rice, cassava, and vegetables in less crowded areas such as Brazil. The amount of land under cultivation by each family is normally small, ranging from about 1 to 20 acres. Yields suffer from use of antiquated methods, poor seed, and lack of commercial fertilizer and other chemicals. Livestock are of minor importance.

Nomadic herding is also a form of subsistence farming, but it differs markedly from sedentary operations. Nomads make few modifications in the physical environment. Their time is consumed in domesticating and caring for livestock, and their principal habitats are in the dry and cold regions of the world. Whereas most subsistence farmers live primarily upon cereals and vegetables and rarely eat meat, nomadic herdsmen subsist on a diet consisting chiefly of milk and meat. Movement of the herds is in response to the availability of forage. The length of time a tribe spends in any one area is directly related to the availability of water and local forage.

Commercial Family Farms. Commercial family farms are similar to subsistence farms in that they are operated primarily by labor from the immediate farm family. They may, however, employ hired labor during times of peak activity such as planting and harvesting, and they produce crops primarily for sale rather than for home consumption. Most commercial family farms are found in relatively affluent middle-latitude nations where private land ownership is encouraged by governments.

Where commercial family farms are highly mechanized, such as in nearly all parts of the United States, each farm worker is capable of cultivating an area up to and often exceeding 100 acres. Output per worker and per farm is frequently 50 or more times that of subsistence farmers and farms. Because of increasing mechanization, improved cultivation techniques, and other factors, the size of fields and farms required for efficient production units has constantly increased (Table 10–1). In many instances farmers rent, lease, or sharecrop lands belonging to other farmers in order to make efficient use

TABLE 10-1. Farms in the United States: 1850–1977

Year	Number of Farms (Thousands)	Total Acreage in Farms (Thousands)	Average Farm Size (Acres)
1850	1,449	294,561	203
1870	2,660	407,735	153
1890	4,565	612,219	137
1910	6,362	878,789	138
1930	6,546	986,771	151
1940	6,350	1,060,852	167
1950	5,648	1,202,000	213
1960	3,963	1,176,000	297
1970	2,954	1,103,000	373
1977[a]	2,752	1,081,000	393

[a]Preliminary

SOURCE: *Statistical Abstract of the United States, 1977* (Washington, D.C.: U.S. Government Printing Office, 1978), p. 674.

of machinery. Such farms, when they are in noncontiguous units, are often called *fragmented* farms.

Commercial family farms are found primarily in Anglo-America, Europe, Australia, and South Africa. In the United States family farms have been decreasing in number and their share of the nation's agricultural output has been declining. Economically efficient farm operation requires large investments in machinery and in sizable land holdings which individual farmers find difficult to afford. The tendency, therefore, is for family farms to give way to corporate farms, which have greater capacity for raising the quantity of capital required for purchasing machines and land.

Corporate Farms and Plantations. Corporate farms and plantations, although different in some respects, are similar in basic operational characteristics. Both types of farms use large amounts of land, operate under a centralized management, concentrate upon production of one to three crops for sale on national or world markets, emphasize high volume output at relatively low unit production costs, and represent large investments.

Plantations differ from corporate farms in that they are normally associated with tropical or subtropical locations and are less highly mechanized. Plantations more often produce crops for international markets, their labor supply is more firmly tied to the land, and their labor costs per hour or per day are lower. Land prices per unit area are generally lower on plantations, and they are more likely than corporate farms to be owned by foreign investors. Both farm types strive for efficient management, but the emphasis on plantations is upon management of land and labor, whereas corporations emphasize management of capital. Most of the world's plantations are located in Central and South America, Africa, and portions of southeast Asia, whereas the United States probably has most of the world's corporate farms. Where land prices are relatively low, the principal products are likely to be cattle, wool, or crops such as wheat that produce well under extensive farming methods. Relatively high land prices, on the other hand, normally encourage more intensive farming methods such as those used to produce horticultural commodities.

Factory Farms. Factory farms meet many of the criteria used to describe factories. Factories occupy relatively small surface areas and have regular inputs of raw materials and regular outputs of processed goods. Farming, on the other hand, usually occupies large surface areas with minimum raw material inputs and a highly seasonal output. More and more, however, agricultural activities are acquiring factory characteristics. Scientifically developed and efficient "chicken factories" cover small acreages, they have a regular input of feed and other raw materials that are often produced hundreds of miles away, and they produce a regular output of "finished" (market-ready) chickens. The same type of operation is performed with beef cattle, where thousands of animals are "finished" for market in feedlots of only a few acres in size. Feed is the primary raw material input and fattened animals comprise the regular output. Even waste disposal and pollution are problems in these factory-type farms. The excrement produced by 30,000 cattle in a feedlot, for example, is about equal to that produced by a city of approximately 500,000 people.

The factory-farm principle is also being employed in production of crops such as lettuce and tomatoes. Specialized techniques and machines similar to those used in manufacturing are being applied with such success that in several instances the value of agricultural output per unit of area is approaching that of a number of manufacturing industries [2]. The trends toward specialization, mechanization, improved scientific management of production, and the raising of crops in man-made soils and chemicals are almost certain to stimulate the growth of factory-farm agriculture in the future.

Factory farms are presently found only in the more advanced countries, especially the United States and some nations in western Europe. They may be privately or corporately owned and managed but differ from other farming activities in their high intensification of land use and in the quantity of inputs and outputs per unit of land used.

Collective Farms. Collective farms are identified primarily with the Soviet Union and China, where they involve a pooling of land, labor, and tools by a number of farmers who work the land cooperatively and who, in theory at least, share in the proceeds of the farm in accordance with the amount of work they contribute. Collective farms provide many of the same economic advantages offered by corporate farms. In both instances numerous small farms are consolidated into a few large units where machinery and other large-scale production techniques can be employed to achieve production efficiencies. Whereas corporate farms are private ventures, however, collective farms in the Soviet Union and China were created through state coercion.

Soviet collectives have continually increased in size as larger farm machines have become available and as farm workers have left the collectives for urban jobs. Each household on the collectives is normally given a small garden plot, the products from which may be consumed at home or sold in the free market at whatever price the seller can obtain. The private plots have never received the enthusiastic support of the central government, but they account for a major portion of Soviet meat, milk, and vegetable output.

Chinese collectives are relatively small by Soviet standards, use of machines is uncommon, and production is primarily for subsistence purposes. Following collectivization, however, Chinese agricultural output increased significantly and China has achieved near self-sufficiency in food production.

State Farms. State farms are also associated primarily with Soviet and Chinese agriculture. They are owned and managed directly by the State, and employees are paid regular wages in the same manner as factory workers. Collective farms generally occupy the most favorable agricultural lands in the more densely settled areas, whereas state farms frequently serve as experimental units in areas of hazardous climate or poor soils where population is sparse and farming is a high risk venture. State farms are larger than collectives and have been favored over collectives in most recently initiated farming operations.

Part-time Farms. Part-time farming has increased substantially during recent decades, especially near large cities. The part-time farmer usually owns too little land to make efficient use of most agricultural machinery and lacks capital for purchasing farm units of sufficient size to make farming highly profitable. Even with limited mechanization the farm may be too small to command the farmer's full attention or to supply a satisfactory income. Many such farmers commute to urban jobs from the farm home, carrying on farm work in spare time and on weekends. Although hired labor is used only sporadically, part-time farmers may employ their own children during after-school hours, on weekends, and during summer vacations. In addition to deficiencies in land, capital, and income, farmers may change from full- to part-time farming because of ill health, because of encroaching urbanization, or for other personal reasons.

More than one-third of all farms in the United States are now operated on a part-time basis. Where industrialization, high population density, and large cities have existed for several generations, so has the practice of part-time farming. Southern New England and the Middle Atlantic states were the first areas where part-time farming became popular, but more recently it has

Tractors cultivating a large farm in India. (Courtesy, Information Service of India.)

become prevalent near almost every major city in the United States. The practice is also popular near most European cities. In the Soviet Union many urban residents spend weekends and vacations cultivating vegetable plots on the outskirts of the cities.

General Farming

General farming occurs in areas that either do not possess or have not discovered a clear-cut advantage over other areas in production of a particular crop or combination of crops. On the other hand, general farming areas have physical and economic characteristics that permit profitable production of a variety of commercially significant crops. General farming is also practiced in relatively primitive economies that engage in subsistence agriculture.

As a rule, general farming is on the decline. Specialized farm operations usually attain levels of production efficiency against which general farming cannot compete. Prior to the mechanization of agriculture the tendency was normally to produce a variety of crops with different planting and harvesting dates so as to spread labor requirements as evenly as possible throughout the growing season. As industrial jobs attracted workers away from farms into urban areas, however, farmers turned to mechanical planters and cultivators. Cultivating machines made it possible for one worker to care for a much larger acreage of crops than formerly, and they caused no major restrictions on the variety of crops that could be planted. The cultivators could not normally be used to harvest crops, however, and harvesting problems became the major bottleneck limiting the amount of land that could be worked by one farmer. This led to development of harvesting machinery, but because each crop has its own peculiar harvesting requirements, the machines for gathering crops are usually oriented toward a single crop. Their sophisticated design and construction normally make them more expensive than cultivating machines. Corn pickers cannot harvest lettuce. Cotton pickers cannot pluck corn. Because of the high cost of purchasing harvesting equipment for several crops, farmers normally find it more profitable to raise a large acreage of one crop.

MAJOR FARM COMMODITIES

Grain Farming

Grains occupy more than 70 percent of the world's croplands. The three major grains, wheat, rice, and maize (corn), account for about two-thirds of the world's grain supply. Other grains, such as rye, oats, barley, and sorghum, tend to be outstanding only where physical conditions are unfavorable for producing wheat, maize, or rice. Wheat is the most widely produced grain, claiming nearly 25 percent of the world's cropland area. The four leading nations in wheat production (USSR, United States, China, and India) contain about one-third of the world's inhabited land area and approximately 50 percent of the population; they raise about one-half of the wheat (Table 10-2). Wheat is the staple food in 43 countries containing more than one-third of the world's population.

Rice and maize production is more spatially concentrated than production of wheat (Table 10-2). Southern and eastern Asia account for about 85 percent of the world's rice, and it is the primary staple in some 13 countries. These countries, however, contain more than half of the world's people. Although wheat occupies almost twice as much cropland area, rice supplies a slightly larger proportion of the total food energy consumed in the world and is a more critical commodity in meeting the food requirements of the people who depend on it as their food staple than is the case with wheat.

Nearly one-half of the world's maize is produced in the United States, primarily in the corn belt. Whereas nearly all rice and most wheat are consumed directly as human food, most of the maize output is used as animal feed except in developing areas. Wheat and maize are the principal grains moving into international trade, and the United States is the leading exporter of both crops. Approximately 25 percent of the world's wheat output moves into international trade compared to only 2 to 3 percent of world rice production.

TABLE 10-2. Production of Wheat, Rice, and Maize, Selected
Countries, 1973 and 1976 (Thousands of Metric Tons)

WHEAT

Country	Production		Percentage of World Total	
	1973	1976	1973	1976
U.S.S.R.	109,784	96,900	29.1	23.2
United States	46,561	58,307	12.4	13.9
China	36,001	43,001	9.6	10.3
India	24,735	28,846	6.6	6.9
France	17,850	16,150	4.7	3.9
Canada	16,159	23,587	4.3	5.6
Australia	11,987	11,713	3.2	2.8
WORLD TOTAL	376,675	418,383	—	—

MAIZE

Country	Production		Percentage of World Total	
	1973	1976	1973	1976
United States	144,042	159,173	46.2	47.6
China	30,084	33,114	9.6	9.6
Brazil	14,109	17,845	4.5	5.3
USSR	13,216	10,138	4.2	3.0
South Africa	4,360	7,312	1.4	2.2
France	10,692	5,544	3.4	1.7
Argentina	9,700	5,855	3.1	1.8
Mexico	8,609	8,393	2.8	2.5
WORLD TOTAL	311,861	334,276	—	—

RICE

Country	Production		Percentage of World Total	
	1973	1976	1973	1976
China	120,954	129,054	36.4	36.8
India	66,077	64,363	19.9	18.4
Indonesia	21,490	23,300	6.5	6.7
Bangladesh	17,863	17,627	5.4	5.0
Japan	15,778	15,292	4.7	4.4
Thailand	14,898	15,800	4.5	4.5
Burma	8,602	9,307	2.6	2.7
WORLD TOTAL	332,188	350,260	—	—

SOURCE: Harry Jiler (ed.), *Commodity Year Book: 1978* (New York: Commodity
Research Bureau, Inc., 1978).

The high yielding varieties of wheat and rice and the new high protein maize are giving added significance to these three grains in world agriculture. India's widespread adoption of the new dwarf wheat and the speedy diffusion of high yielding varieties of rice offer the densely populated areas of south Asia and elsewhere an opportunity to feed themselves while they come to grips with the problems of rapid population growth. The new high protein maize should help to produce a healthier and more vigorous population in places such as Mexico where diets include a great deal of maize and where protein deficiencies have caused major health problems.

During the last two decades grain production has risen at a faster rate than population, but more grains are being used for animal feed, which reduces the supply otherwise available for direct human consumption. Coarse grains such as maize and barley have risen rapidly in world trade, whereas wheat enjoyed a smaller rise until the vagaries of nature during 1971–1973 resulted in short crops in such areas as the Soviet Union, India, and China. Since 1971 exports of wheat have gone up sharply and China has become a major importer of agricultural foodstuffs.

Wheat. Wheat production occurs primarily in the marginally wet areas of the continents where annual precipitation varies from 10 to 20 inches and where the growing season exceeds 90 days (Fig. 10-2). The two major varieties of wheat are *winter wheat* and *spring wheat*. Winter wheat is planted in the fall, lies largely dormant during the winter, resumes growing in the spring, and is normally harvested in late spring or early summer. Spring wheat is produced where winter wheat cannot survive severe winter temperatures. It is planted in the spring and harvested during late summer or early fall. Winter wheat is the dominant variety and accounts for the bulk of the world's crop, for its yields are more dependable and normally larger than those of spring wheat. Wheat varieties may also be classifed as *hard* or *soft*. Soft wheats are raised primarily in the more humid wheat growing areas and they provide larger and more dependable yields per acre than the hard wheats which are produced in drier and colder regions.

In the Soviet Union wheat is produced on approximately one-third of the total sown acreage, although its relative importance is declining as Soviet agriculture becomes more modern and its output more diversified. The declining relative importance of wheat also reflects Soviet dietary changes toward more meats and vegetables and away from cereals and potatoes. Increased consumption of meat has created a rapidly rising demand for feed grains.

The triangular-shaped area extending from Leningrad and the Black Sea to Lake Baikal produces nearly all Soviet wheat and the majority of other agricultural commodities. Spring wheat is the dominant variety, although winter wheat is grown in the Ukraine near the Black Sea. The Ukraine is frequently referred to as the "bread basket" of the Soviet Union. The rela-

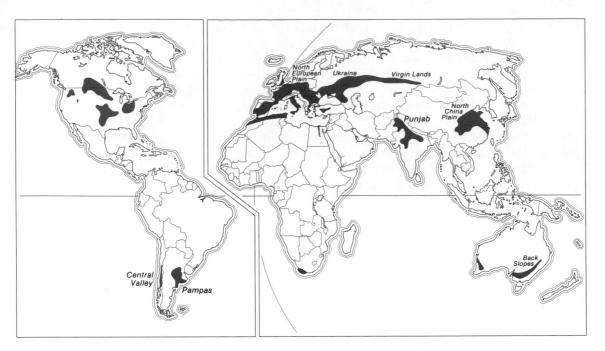

Fig. 10-2. Major areas of wheat production.

tively moderate climate of the region encourages dependable yields and a high output per acre. The Ukraine is also located near the major population centers of the Soviet Union.

Extending eastward from the Ukraine the growing season and amounts of precipitation decline, and yields become less and less dependable. Wheat is produced on soils which rank among the world's best in natural fertility, but lack of moisture and the short growing season create risky conditions for crops and result in wide annual variations in output.

During 1954–1956 Soviet leaders initiated the Virgin Lands Project, a grandiose scheme for adding some 100 million acres to the cultivated area of the country. Hopes were high that the scheme would solve the nation's periodic grain shortages. Wheat was to be the primary crop, and the area selected for the project was in the semiarid zone of northern Kazakhstan and the southern portion of the Russian Soviet Federated Socialist Republic to the east of the Urals. The new wheat lands represented a risk-operating venture, for rarely had disastrous droughts occurred simultaneously in the Virgin Lands region and in the Ukraine. During 1955, for example, the Ukraine produced a bumper wheat crop, whereas unusually dry weather caused a poor crop in the Virgin Lands. In 1956 harvests in the Ukraine were below normal, but the Virgin Lands produced a record crop.

Agricultural problems in the Virgin Lands are common to other parts of the Soviet Union, but in the Virgin Lands they are more severe. Almost all the agricultural areas in the country suffer from a short growing season and from meager and unreliable precipitation. Precipitation in northern Kazakhstan averages only 8-14 inches annually, and amounts vary from 1 or 2 inches during some years to 15 or 20 inches during other years. Nearly half of the nation is underlain by permanently frozen subsoil and few areas receive more than 20 inches of precipitation annually. Maximum precipitation occurs during July and August at ripening and harvest times when dry weather is desirable. May and June, critical months in the germination and early growth of wheat plants, receive small and variable amounts of moisture. Crops planted late enough in the spring or summer to receive adequate moisture for seed germination and early growth are likely to freeze in the fields in the fall before they can be harvested. Despite the numerous natural handicaps, however, total yields from the region were reasonably good until 1963 when droughts and other adverse weather conditions occurred simultaneously in the Ukraine and in the Virgin Lands. Wheat output fell by more than one-fourth from the previous year, and the Soviets were forced to import large amounts of wheat to avert widespread food shortages. Relatively small harvests were also obtained in 1965-1966, 1969-1970, and 1972-1973. Much of the driest portion of the Virgin Lands area was taken out of production during the late 1960s, but in the northern wettest parts of the region production has been maintained.

Wheat production is also widely practiced in the United States and Canada, where the chief producing areas are the Great Plains and the corn belt. Winter varieties account for approximately 60 percent of the United States' wheat crop. The leading winter wheat-producing state is Kansas, followed by Washington, Oklahoma, and Nebraska. North Dakota accounts for about two-thirds of United States' spring wheat production, followed by Minnesota, Montana, and South Dakota. Washington raises winter and spring varieties although winter wheat is dominant.

In the corn belt of the Middle West wheat is often used in a rotational scheme with maize, soybeans, and hay. Although corn belt farmers obtain higher per acre wheat yields than farmers in the wheat belt, maize and animal agriculture is normally a more profitable alternative. In the wheat belt, on the other hand, wheat is usually the more profitable of the crops which can be raised.

Wheat production has also been expanding in the Mississippi Valley and other portions of the South where it is used in a multiple cropping system with soybeans or other grains. *Multiple cropping* involves the harvesting of two or more crops from the same acreage during one growing season.

As in other major producing nations, wheat occupies the drier agricultural areas of India and China. In India the northwestern part of the country and the interior of the peninsula account for most of the wheat output. Chinese production occurs primarily in the northeastern quarter of the country. India's perpetual food shortages were partially relieved with the widespread adoption beginning in the late 1960s of a new dwarf wheat developed in Mexico. When natural adversities during the early 1970s were combined with rapidly rising prices for fuel, fertilizer, pesticides, and other farming inputs, India's output temporarily declined. As the high yielding varieties are more widely introduced, however, it is anticipated that India will be able to achieve near self-sufficiency in wheat production during the next two or three decades even if population growth rates are not significantly reduced.

In Europe wheat is of substantial importance in parts of the North European Plain and in the south. France, Italy, and Spain are the leading producers, with France and Spain exporting large quantities to such countries as the United Arab Republic, the United Kingdom, West Germany, The Netherlands, and Switzerland.

In the southern hemisphere, Australia and Argentina are the only producers of a significant wheat surplus. Australian wheat moves primarily to Japan, the United Kingdom, and India, with the remainder going to Europe. The bulk of Argentina's exports are sold in Brazil and Peru.

Wheat Stocks. Since World War II world wheat reserves have been held mainly by the United States, Canada, and Australia. These reserves have been a valuable source of food during periods when natural or economic adversities have resulted in reduced wheat crops, especially in areas where food production is marginal even during good production years. The farm support measures which led to accumulations of huge wheat surpluses in the United States were reduced radically during 1974, following a temporary period of adverse weather and low yields in much of the world. Grain was in heavy demand on world markets, prices were high, and the formerly large reserve stockpiles were depleted. Because of the high cost of maintaining large reserves, the United States, Canada, and Australia signaled their intent to minimize stocks in the future. Later in the decade, however, favorable weather conditions resulted in bumper crops in most major wheat-producing areas, leading to a new round of support prices and stockpiling.

Without the large wheat reserves which have become normal to United States', Canadian, and Australian agriculture, major wheat-consuming nations would be forced to rely upon annual production to meet annual needs, and the vulnerability of the more marginal food-producing areas to periods of severe malnutrition and famine would increase. This has led to a widespread interest in development of a world food bank under the auspices of the United Nations.

Rice. More human lives depend on rice than upon any other crop. It is the staple diet of about 60 percent of the world's people. As one of the world's most dependable crops, rice is associated primarily with subsistence agriculture in the densely populated and technically retarded countries of

Farms in the Northeast Polder area of the Netherlands. (Courtesy, Embassy of the Netherlands.)

southern and eastern Asia. In most instances its cultivation is highly intensive, and it is used almost entirely for direct human consumption.

Rice is raised primarily between the equator and 35° north or south latitude. The principal varieties require substantial quantities of moisture, with humid tropical and subtropical climates generally having the most favorable temperature and moisture conditions for its growth. When irrigation water is readily available, however, rice can be raised successfully even in desert climates.

Level land for irrigation of the paddies is required for most varieties of rice. Sloping land must be terraced. Rice will grow in a variety of soil types, but best results are obtained where a layer of fine clay lies a few inches below the surface to prevent the downward percolation of irrigation water.

Approximately 85 percent of the world's rice is produced in southern and eastern Asia (Table 10-2 and Fig. 10-3). During the 20 years prior to 1973-1974, world rice acreage increased by approximately one-third and output rose by 90 percent. Introduction of the new high yielding varieties have accounted for about 20 percent of the increase in output during recent years. Despite the large increase in output, however, production in the developing countries of southern and eastern Asia and Africa has barely kept pace with population growth. Per capita production of paddy rice in southeast Asia was 320 pounds in 1973-1974 compared to 325 pounds in 1961. Dur-

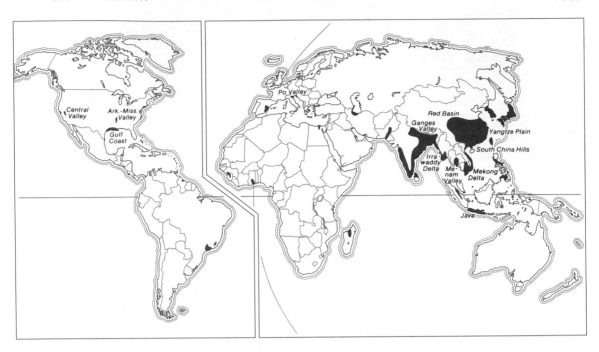

Fig. 10-3. Major areas of rice production.

ing the poor crop season of 1972 production was only 290 pounds per capita.

China and India account for slightly more than half of the world's rice, with China alone producing about one-third. Most of China's production comes from the southeastern one-fourth of the country where rainfall is relatively abundant and growing seasons are long. Too little moisture and too short growing seasons prohibit rice cultivation in much of northern and interior China.

Most of India's rice is grown in the northeastern portion of the country and in the narrow coastal plains along the Indian peninsula. The eastern part of the Ganges Plain and the Ganges–Brahmaputra Delta in India and Bangladesh (formerly East Pakistan) receive 60 or more inches of precipitation annually, largely from the summer monsoon, and are the main sources of rice in southern Asia. Rice output in India and Bangladesh could be substantially increased with larger applications of commercial fertilizers or with effective control over insects. Experiments conducted in the Philippines, for example, indicate that effective insect control can increase rice yields by about 80 percent. Religious beliefs in the sacredness of all life prohibit the use of insecticides in India, and poverty and ignorance retard the adoption of modern agricultural methods in India and Bangladesh.

Burma, Thailand, and Indochina (Laos, Cambodia, and Vietnam) have traditionally exported rice to India, Japan, China, and elsewhere. Exports from Burma dropped by nearly 50 percent between 1960 and 1970, however, and the Vietnam War turned Indochina into a rice-importing area. Only Thailand remains a major exporter in southeastern Asia, and during recent years the United States has been one of the world's chief rice-exporting nations. Rice is not among the major items in world trade, however, as less than 3 percent of total production crosses international boundaries.

Brazil produces most of the South American crop, whereas the United Arab Republic and the Malagasy Republic account for nearly 60 percent of Africa's rice. European production originates in Italy, Spain, Portugal, and France, in that order, although total European output (excluding the Soviet Union) amounts to only about one-ninetieth of the amount produced in Asia. Nearly all the rice grown in the United States is produced by extensive methods in Texas, Louisiana, Arkansas, and California.

Maize. Maize (commonly referred to as corn in the United States) can be grown under a greater variety of climatic conditions than either wheat or rice and in almost any kind of soil. Commercial production extends from equatorial regions to 50° north and south latitudes. One or more of the numerous varieties of the grain can be raised where rainfall varies from 15 to more than 100 inches (Fig. 10-4).

Despite its wide range of growth, maize production is heavily concen-

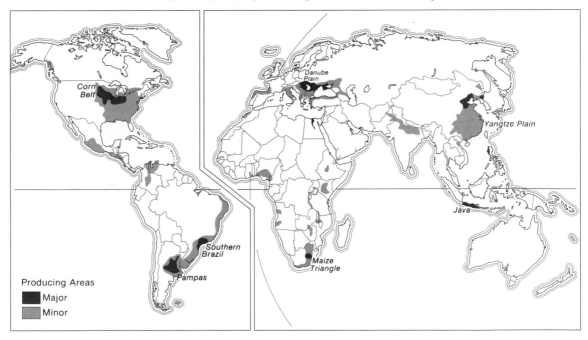

Fig. 10-4. Major areas of maize production.

trated. About one-half of the world's output is raised in the corn belt region in the United States. Approximately 90 percent of the maize used in the United States is fed to livestock. About 15 percent of the total crop is normally exported. Although destinations of maize exports vary significantly from year to year, Japan, The Netherlands, Italy, the United Kingdom, West Germany, Spain, and Canada are among the leading markets.

The corn belt of the United States is one of the outstanding agricultural regions in the world. Soils are naturally fertile, the surface is level to gently rolling, precipitation ranges from about 40 inches along its eastern boundary in central Ohio to about 20 inches along its western margin in central Nebraska, and the growing season averages about 140 to 180 days. Farming operations are highly mechanized and efficient, and productivity per acre and per man-hour are high. Approximately 70 percent of the land is in crops in a given season and most of the land in crops is in maize. Iowa normally accounts for more than 20 percent of the maize produced in the United States, followed by Illinois, with about 18 or 19 percent. Other leading maize-producing states are Indiana, Nebraska, Minnesota, Ohio, Missouri, and Wisconsin. Although most of the maize is used as feed for livestock, especially hogs, during the 1970s high maize prices and relatively low prices for meat animals led to an increase in cash sales. In the late 1970s, however, meat prices soared, reaching all-time highs.

Maize is also an important crop in the southeastern United States, where traditionally it has been an important part of the human diet in the form of grits and cornbread. Current production is fed primarily to animals. High yielding hybrid varieties found widespread acceptance in the South following World War II, and as yields per acre increased, total acreage in the crop declined in favor of greater production of soybeans.

Maize is of major importance for human food in Mexico and several other Latin American countries. In southern Brazil it is produced largely as feed for hogs. Other major maize-producing regions are the Danube Valley and Hungarian Plain in Europe, the southern Ukraine of the USSR, northern India, northeastern China, the maize triangle of South Africa, and the area north and south of Buenos Aires in Argentina.

Other Grains. Other grains important to world agriculture include sorghum, oats, rye, barley, and flaxseed. These crops are normally raised where climate or soil is not well-suited to wheat, rice, or corn. In the advanced nations they are produced primarily as feed grains for livestock, whereas in the poorer countries they are important as human food.

Grain sorghums are planted on about one-fourth as much acreage as wheat in the United States, but total yields in bushels amount to nearly 60 percent of wheat output. The main sorghum-producing states are Texas, Kansas, and Nebraska. In China, India, and Africa sorghums are major food items and occupy lands which are too dry for successful production of the more favored grains.

Barley is a very hardy grain with a short growing season. Major producers are the Soviet Union, western Europe, and the United States. Flaxseed is primarily a North American crop, and the Soviet Union and the United States account for about half of the world's oats. The Soviet Union and Poland produce about two-thirds of the world's rye.

Other Commodities

Although grains occupy a premier position in world agriculture because of the huge amounts of land devoted to their cultivation, they are often less important in the human food supply than other crops such as meats, potatoes, and vegetables (Compare Fig. 10-5, 10-6, and 10-7). Per acre yields of potatoes and vegetables are substantially higher than for wheat and rice, and two or three crops of vegetables can often be harvested from the same land during one growing season. Many of the meat animals raised in the United States and Europe (swine, fowl, and some cattle) are heavily grain-fed. Indirectly they represent substantial cereal consumption. In Australia, much

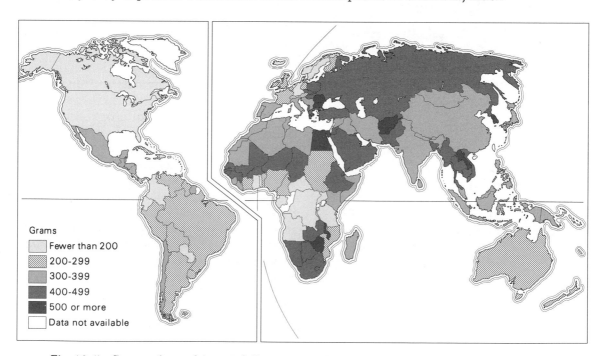

Grams
Fewer than 200
200-299
300-399
400-499
500 or more
Data not available

Fig. 10-5. Grams of cereal in net daily per capita food intake. (From *United Nations Statistical Yearbook, 1972*.)

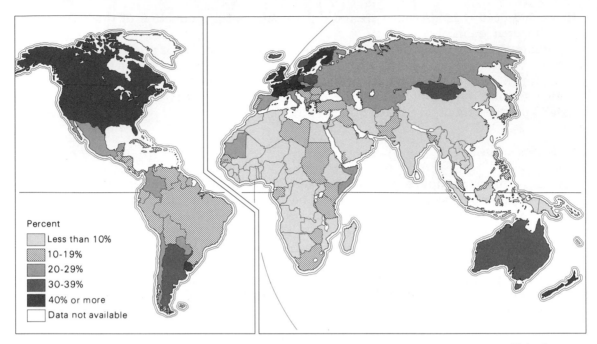

Fig. 10-6. Percentage of caloric intake of animal origin. (From *United Nations Statistical Yearbook, 1972.*)

of Latin America, and Africa, however, most meat animals are fed almost entirely on grasses. In nearly all nations that produce meat animals much of the area used for grazing is not suited for the cultivation of crops. Almost all sheep are grass-fed and lamb and mutton comprise a major portion of the meat products consumed in the United Kingdom, Australia, and New Zealand. In the United States grasses comprise the predominant foods for raising cattle, although the animals are usually fattened on grain prior to marketing.

Heaviest direct dependence on cereals occurs in Asia, eastern Europe, northern and southern Africa, and Central America (Fig. 10-5). Potatoes and other starchy tubers such as cassava and manioc are most important in the diets of persons in Central Africa and South America (Fig. 10-7). Meat products are of foremost significance to food supplies in Canada, the United States, western Europe, Australia, New Zealand, and southern South America (Fig. 10-6). Areas where these items are of greatest dietary importance do not necessarily coincide with the principal areas of commercial production, and some major differences in levels of consumption are obscured by the broad ranges of data used for classification purposes on the maps. For example, the average Soviet, German, or east European citizen consumes about twice as many potatoes as the average person in the United States. It is also worth noting that manioc and cassava are the principal tuberous foods

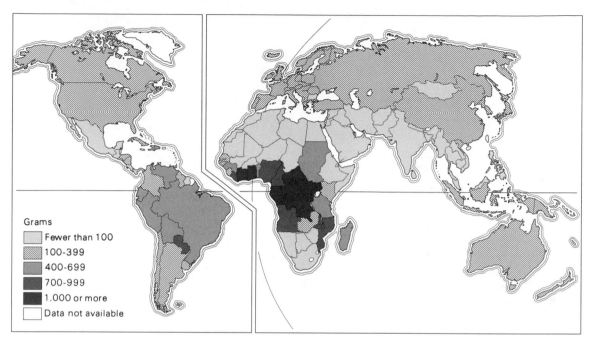

Fig. 10-7. Grams of starchy tubers in the net daily per capita food intake. (From *United Nations Statistical Yearbook, 1972.*)

consumed in most of tropical Africa and South America and that sweet potatoes (rather than Irish, or white, potatoes) are the major tubers in China and portions of southern Asia. The relatively low intake of cereals in China and India can be accounted for in part by the lower than average total caloric intake of peoples in those countries compared with peoples in much of the rest of the world.

Root Crops. Among the principal root crops are white (Irish) potatoes, sweet potatoes, sugar beets, taro root, and cassava. White potatoes and sugar beets are produced primarily in the cooler portions of the middle latitudes, sweet potatoes are grown in the subtropics and tropics, and taro root and cassava are tropical products.

White potatoes grow wild on the plateaus of Middle and South America, but their production has reached greatest importance in the Soviet Union and northwestern Europe. For greatest success in production, potatoes need a loose, sandy soil and cool weather. These conditions are ideally met in parts of the North European Plain and the Soviet Union (Fig. 10-8 and Table 10-3). In the United States white potatoes are most important in a few sandy river valleys such as the Aroostook Valley of Maine, the Red River Valley in Minnesota and North Dakota, and the Snake River Valley of Idaho.

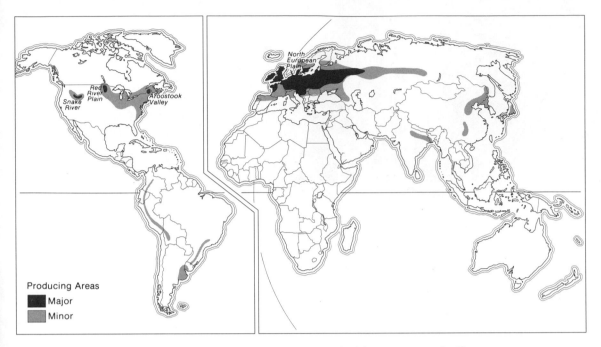

Fig. 10-8. Major areas of white potato production.

China is the principal producer of sweet potatoes, accounting for about 40 percent of the world's crop. In the United States they are grown along the Atlantic and Gulf Coasts from New Jersey to Texas. Taro is a major food crop for the people of many Pacific islands and is an exceedingly nutritious plant. In the middle latitudes taro is used as an ornamental plant known as "elephant ears." Cassava (manioc) is confined almost entirely to the tropics. Neither taro nor cassava enters world trade in quantity.

Sugar beets have attained greatest importance in roughly the same areas where white potatoes are produced. The Soviet Union, again, is the world's outstanding producer. Most of the Soviet beet output occurs as an eastward extension of the beet-producing region which stretches across the North European Plain from northwestern France to the Ural Mountains (Fig. 10-9 and Table 10-4).

In the United States beet production occurs primarily in irrigated valleys in the western and Great Lake states. Loose, porous soils in dry climates where water is available for irrigation appear to provide optimum conditions for maximum output.

Beets compete with sugarcane for the world's sugar markets. Beets are a cool summer, mid-latitude crop, whereas cane is produced chiefly in the tropics. Because of the relatively low cost of tropical labor, sugar can be pro-

TABLE 10-3. White Potato Production in Selected Countries: 1970 and 1977 (Thousands of Metric Tons)

Country	1970	1977
WORLD	258,707	239,123
USSR	96,783	83,400
Poland	50,301	42,000
West Germany	16,250	11,350
United States	14,776	15,895
East Germany	13,054	9,000
France	8,868	8,190
United Kingdom	7,482	6,350
Spain	5,419	5,680
The Netherlands	5,648	5,480
Czechoslovakia	4,793	4,200
Japan	3,611	3,193
Italy	3,668	3,250

SOURCE: Harry Jiler (ed.), *Commodity Year Book: 1978* (New York: Commodity Research Bureau, Inc., 1978), p. 276.

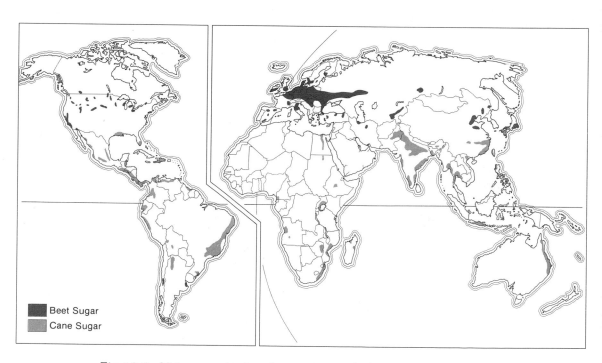

Beet Sugar
Cane Sugar

Fig. 10-9. Major sugar beet- and sugarcane-producing areas.

TABLE 10–4. Sugar Production, Selected Countries: 1977–1978 (Thousands of Metric Tons)

Country	Cane Sugar	Beet Sugar
WORLD TOTAL (All)	90,656	
USSR		9,300
Brazil	8,600	
United States	1,400	3,000
Cuba	6,000	
India	6,000	
France		3,913
Australia	3,400	
Mexico	2,880	
Philippines	2,300	
Poland		2,200
West Germany		2,740

SOURCE: Harry Jiler (ed.), *Commodity Year Book: 1978* (New York: Commodity Research Bureau, Inc., 1978), p. 325.

duced at lower cost from cane than from beets. Millions of acres of tropical lands are suitable for cane production should markets become available. Several mid-latitude nations produce beet sugar in an effort to achieve as much self-sufficiency as possible and because of the economic and political difficulties of phasing out a crop once production has become well-established.

Most of the beet-producing nations have normally imported cane sugar on a quota system, although quotas have declined as a basis for sugar trade during recent years. The amount purchased from a particular area may vary substantially from year to year, as the sugar industry is highly sensitive to international political conditions. For example, the United States once purchased most of Cuba's sugar exports. After Fidel Castro came to power, he developed a close alliance between Cuba and the Soviet Union and expropriated properties of Americans; the United States then canceled Cuban sugar imports, increased domestic production, and raised the import quotas of more friendly nations such as Brazil and Mexico.

Soybeans

The soybean is one of the world's most versatile crops. Besides its use as a high-protein animal food, it is a major source of cooking oil and margarine and is used to make paint, varnish, resins, and plastics. The soybean is a relatively recent addition to agriculture in the United States, although it has long been an important source of human food in China. Areas with a high percentage of sunshine are best for soybean production as soybeans are not so efficient in utilizing solar energy as many other major crops. Because the

TABLE 10-5. Soybean Production in Selected Countries: 1967 and 1977 (Thousands of Metric Tons)

Country	1967	1977
WORLD	36,543	73,354
United States	25,269	45,796
China	6,800	10,000
Brazil	716	11,500
USSR	543	700
Argentina	20	1,700

SOURCE: Harry Jiler (ed.), *Commodity Year Book: 1978* (New York: Commodity Research Bureau, Inc., 1978), p. 318.

soybean plant is self-pollinating, geneticists have been unable to develop high yielding hybrids. Promising results, however, have come from new dwarf varieties which allow maximum penetration of available sunshine to all parts of the plant and which concentrate the plant's strength into the production of beans rather than stalk and leaves.

Cultivation of soybeans spread through the Middle West of the United States following World War I, but China led in world production until the early to middle 1940s. Production increased rapidly in the United States after World War II as farmers began substituting soybeans for hay in animal feed. During the 1960s production more than doubled and several southeastern states became major producers. By 1977 United States' farmers were accounting for more than 60 percent of the world's output (Table 10-5). Major producing areas include the corn belt states, the Mississippi Valley, and the South Atlantic Coast. The Mississippi Valley is a principal source of exported beans, which go mainly to western Europe.

The most spectacular relative increase in soybean production during recent years has occurred in Brazil. Brazilian soybean output increased by more than 16 times between 1967 and 1977, allowing Brazil to become the world's second largest exporter. The potential for further expansion of the Brazilian crop is excellent, for Brazil may have the largest area of undeveloped land which is suitable for soybean cultivation of any country in the world. It is unlikely, however, that the dominant position of the United States in soybean production and exports can be surpassed by Brazil or any other country during this century.

Horticultural Crops

Fruits and vegetables are among the most widely grown food crops. In the world as a whole enough vegetables and melons are grown to supply the average person with some 300 pounds annually. Not all vegetables are produced for direct human consumption, for some are used in the manufacture of products such as starch and alcohol and some are fed to livestock. Nearly all parts of the world can produce a variety of vegetables during one season or another. Some varieties, such as yams, are tropical crops but can be produced in temperate regions. Others, such as cabbage, yield best in cool climates but are also grown extensively in the tropics.

Vegetables. The growing season for most vegetables is relatively short. Harvest times can be varied somewhat, although early harvests may reduce yields substantially. Cabbage, for example, may be cut at 2 pounds, 4 pounds, or more; cucumbers can be harvested at 2 inches, 6 inches, or more; beans may be plucked at various stages of growth; and carrots may be pulled over a relatively wide range of time after planting.

Most vegetables are produced under intensive methods of cultivation and a relatively small acreage can supply a large number of people. One acre of tomatoes, for example, can supply 700 or 800 persons with one medium-sized tomato each day for a year [3]. In dry lands vegetables produce well under irrigation and in humid areas supplemental irrigation normally results in increased yields. Near large cities vegetables are often produced in greenhouses, especially during winter months. Because of improvements in transportation efficiency and in the quality of vegetables produced in such warm winter areas as south Florida, however, the range of vegetables that can be produced competitively in greenhouses has been declining.

Most vegetables have relatively poor keeping qualities and must be consumed or processed within a few days after harvest. By canning, freezing, or dehydration, however, they can be kept for indefinite periods. Some vegetables, such as onions, cabbage, carrots, and beets, can be safely stored for a few months without refrigeration.

Farm and nonfarm families in nearly all parts of the earth set aside small plots for production of the family's vegetables and in a few areas farmers produce substantial quantities for sale. In most of the poor nations, where modern systems of transportation, communication, and marketing have not yet developed, commercial vegetable production is limited to farms that are in proximity to urban markets. In the advanced nations, on the other hand, production is primarily from areas where a large percentage of the farmers specialize in growing vegetables. Individual farmers may cultivate hundreds of acres for markets that are hundreds of miles away.

Areas that specialize in vegetable production usually supply particular markets during particular seasons. South Florida, for example, has near optimal conditions for supplying the fresh market of the eastern United States during the late fall, winter, and early spring, whereas portions of New Jersey, eastern Pennsylvania, southern New England, and New York supply the huge nearby markets and processing plants during the summer and early fall. Smaller producing areas in Georgia and South Carolina supply northern markets during the interim between the demise of large-scale production in Florida and the commencing of harvests in the Middle Atlantic region.

Field being prepared for paddy rice in India. (Courtesy, Information Service of India.)

California vegetables are especially prominent during spring and fall, although some are marketed during all seasons. Vegetables produced in California, Oregon, and Washington have excellent qualities for freezing and canning. The freezing industry has grown rapidly since World War II, and frozen foods from the West Coast (the primary vegetable freezing area) are marketed in all parts of the United States and Canada. Texas and Arizona produce substantial quantities of winter vegetables, and Michigan, Wisconsin, Illinois, and other states engage in large-scale summer production for fresh market and processing. During recent years Mexico has become increasingly important in supplying fresh winter vegetables to the United States. Low labor costs and absence of frost are Mexico's major advantages. Newly constructed or improved rail and highway facilities allow Mexican produce to reach markets in the United States and Canada. Because of the severity of its winters, Canada produces vegetables only during the summer.

Countries of southern Europe and northern Africa supply fresh vegetables to northern Europe during the cold seasons. Glasshouse (greenhouse) vegetables supplement northern European imports from the Mediterranean area. The Netherlands has the most intensive horticultural industry, with 25 percent of the world's glasshouse area. Tomatoes, cucumbers, and lettuce are the major crops.

Most European vegetables are sold on the fresh market, although processing of tomatoes is an important industry in Portugal, Italy, Spain, and France. Cabbage, broccoli, cauliflower, and brussels sprouts are grown in all

European countries, and carrots, parsnips, beets, and rutabagas are also widely produced. The Paris Basin supplies fresh and canned mushrooms to most of western Europe, the Nile Valley is the chief source of spring onions, and Poland exports its fall crop of yellow onions to markets on both sides of the Iron Curtain.

In the Soviet Union most vegetables come from the private plots of collective farm members and from urban fringe gardens where vegetables are cultivated for private use or for sale by urban residents. Fresh vegetables are normally in short supply during the winter.

Because of poor transportation, lack of refrigeration, and the perishability of fresh vegetables, most commercial production in the Far East, Africa south of the Sahara, and South America occurs near the larger cities.

With improved transportation and technical knowledge, vegetable production could be vastly increased in many parts of the world. Yields per acre are high, but until modern methods of transporting, storing, preserving, processing, fertilizing, and cultivating vegetables are introduced, significant additions to per capita output from underdeveloped areas is unlikely.

Fruits. Fruit growing is almost as widespread as production of vegetables (Fig. 10-10 and 10-11). Fruit growing in the advanced nations has become

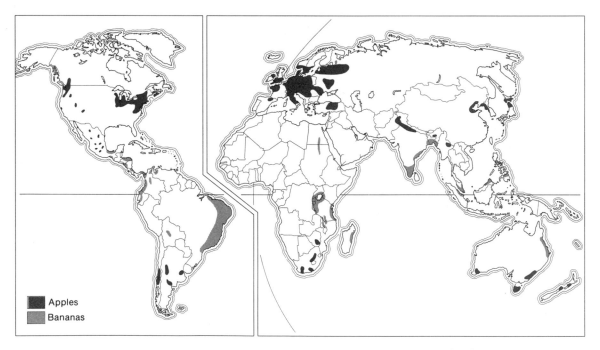

Apples
Bananas

Fig. 10-10. Major areas of apple and banana production.

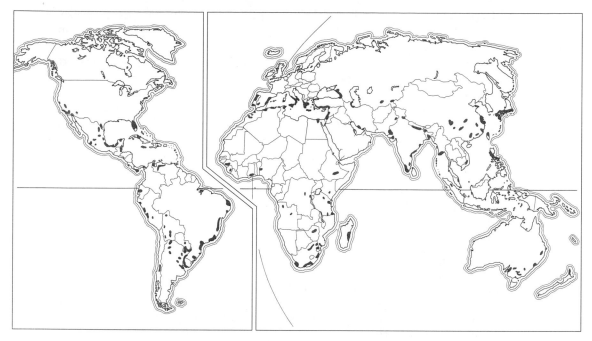

Fig. 10-11. Major areas of citrus fruit production.

increasingly concentrated in areas possessing optimal or near optimal conditions for fruit production. Whereas apple production was widely distributed over the United States in 1900, for example, it had become concentrated into some five or six specialized regions by 1940.

Fruit is of much greater importance than vegetables in international trade. Northern Europe and the United States account for the bulk of fruit imports, whereas exports are furnished by the nations of southern Europe, the United States, the Republic of South Africa, Australia, Ecuador, and others. As a result of foreign exchange shortages and the desire to protect domestic producers, however, most nations have placed rigid limitations upon fruit imports.

California dominates fruit production in the United States, leading all other states in output of peaches, grapes, plums, prunes, apricots, and lemons. Florida is the major producer of oranges, grapefruit, and limes, and Washington leads in apple output. Other important fruit-producing regions include the southern and eastern shores of the Great Lakes, the northern Blue Ridge, and the Piedmont of South Carolina and Georgia.

Southern Europe produces and exports large quantities of oranges, lemons, grapes, olives, pears, peaches, and apples. Israel has recently become a major exporter of oranges and grapefruit, and northern Africa and the

Cape Region of the Republic of South Africa produce and export citrus fruits and grapes.

Bananas grow nearly everwhere in the tropics, but they have reached large-scale commercial importance primarily in Ecuador, Honduras, Costa Rica, Panama, Brazil, Colombia, Guatemala, and the Canary Islands. Ecuador accounts for approximately one-fourth of the world's exports.

Pineapples are produced commercially in Hawaii, Brazil, Mexico, Malaya, Taiwan, the Philippines, Cuba, South Africa, and Australia. Pineapple enters international trade primarily in canned form, with Hawaii accounting for more than half of the world's pack.

Several additional fruit-producing areas are worthy of note. Japan and Brazil, for example, are outstanding exporters of oranges, Australia ships large quantities of apples to Europe, and eastern and central Europe produce most of the world's plums.

Beverage Crops

Among the many beverages used daily around the world are coffee, tea, cocoa, and wine (Fig. 10–12 and 10–13). Major producing areas for the raw products of each of the four beverages differ markedly, as do the prinicpal areas of consumption.

Coffee. Coffee could be afforded only by the well-to-do in most parts of the world prior to the twentieth century. It became popular in the United States after the British imposed a tax upon tea during the colonial period. The major rise in coffee consumption in the United States, however, occurred after Brazil became the world's major producer during the late 1800s. Although the United States formerly purchased nearly half of all coffee entering international trade, its share of imports during recent years has fallen to approximately 35 percent, whereas European imports have increased to about 50 percent. Paradoxically, high coffee prices during 1977 caused by relatively small harvests in South America and Angola during 1975 and 1976, and the withholding of coffee from world markets by the major producers, stimulated consumer boycotts of coffee in the United States. Consumers were urged by government agencies and by large grocery chains such as A & P Stores to switch from coffee to tea — a move reminiscent of consumer opposition to the British tax on tea some 200 years earlier.

Brazil normally accounts for about 30 percent of the coffee that enters world trade, more than twice that of Colombia, which ranks second. The bulk of Brazil's coffee is produced on large plantations located in the plateau region of São Paulo State at elevations of 1,500 to 2,500 feet. Almost all the coffee is of the Arabica variety, although considerable variations in taste and quality occur in Arabica coffees produced in different places.

In Colombia, coffee is grown at elevations of 4,000 feet or above on

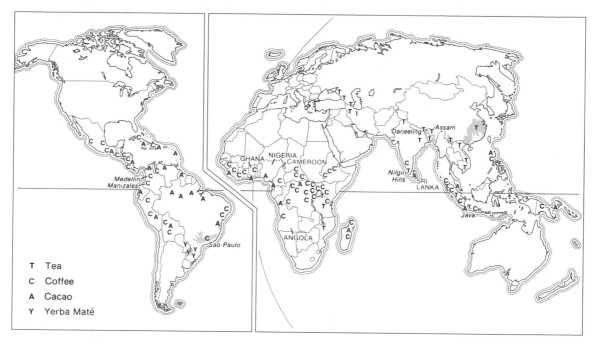

Fig. 10-12. Major areas of coffee, tea, and cacao production.

small hillside farms. Colombian coffee is milder and more aromatic than Brazilian coffee and sells for higher prices. Coffee is also a major product in El Salvador, Guatemala, Costa Rica, and Mexico.

African coffee production has more than tripled since 1950, and combined exports from all African countries are only slightly under those from Brazil. Although some 25 African nations raise coffee commercially, the leading producers are the Ivory Coast, Angola, Uganda, Ethiopia, Cameroon, and the Malagasy Republic. Most African coffee is of the Robusta variety, which can be produced at lower elevations and under heavier rainfall than the Arabica coffees of South America.

Nearly all grinding, roasting, and blending is carried out in the coffee-consuming countries. Latin American Arabica varieties go primarily into the preparation of coffees that are to be perked, and African Robusta coffees are used mainly in making instant (or soluble) coffee. Instant coffee normally costs less per cup than perked coffee, because by eliminating much of the bulk and weight of the raw coffee during processing the cost of transporting and marketing instant coffee is minimized.

Tea. Tea has been a major beverage much longer than coffee. It was first used in Asia, which remains the major consuming area. Outside of Asia tea is most heavily used in the United Kingdom and the Commonwealth countries, although it is used to some degree in nearly every country in the world.

Tea is grown in the tropics and subtropics at elevations up to 6,000 feet (Fig. 10–12). Bushes are pruned to 3 to 5 feet in height, and leaves are usually picked every 7 to 15 days during the harvest season.

Asia produces more than 90 percent of the world's tea and Africa accounts for most of the rest. India and Sri Lanka (Ceylon) each provide more than one-fourth of all tea that enters international trade. In Africa the chief exporters are Kenya, Malawi, Mozambique, and Tanzania. In South America, Argentina expanded production rapidly during the 1960s and now accounts for about 3 percent of the world's export crop.

The United Kingdom is the leading importer of tea, although British per capita comsumption declined by more than 15 percent between 1960 and 1973. The United States ranks second in total imports, followed by The Netherlands, West Germany, and France. The major sources of tea consumed in the United States are Sri Lanka, Indonesia, Kenya, and India.

Cocoa. Cocoa is relatively new among the food and beverage crops, having gained widespread importance primarily since 1900. Cocoa beans are seeds of the *cacao* tree and grow in pods along the trunk and older branches. Cocoa is produced in commercial quantities only in the rainy tropics where strong winds are almost entirely absent (Fig. 10–12). Cocoa trees are frequently grown under the shade of larger trees for protection against excessive sunlight and strong winds.

Ghana accounts for approximately one-third of the world's output and is followed in production by Nigeria, the Bahia Coast of Brazil, the Ivory Coast, Cameroon, Ecuador, and the Dominican Republic. Most of the cocoa that enters world trade is consumed in the United States and western Europe.

Wine. Italy, France, and Spain are the world's leading producers of grapes and in all three countries the chief use of grapes is in wine making (Fig. 10–13). In the United States, on the other hand, grapes are produced primarily for fresh use and for raisins. Only about one-fifth of the grapes are of the wine type, although some raisin varieties are also used for wine. California accounts for more than 90 percent of the grape output in the United States, with New York, Pennsylvania, and Michigan producing most of the rest.

Nearly all areas possessing Mediterranean climates have large vineyard and wine industries and wine is a major table beverage, often being consumed two or three times daily. Areas such as the Cape Region of South Africa, the Central Valley of Chile, and the regions near Perth and Adelaide, in Australia produce and consume significant amounts of grapes and wine. The Mediterranean border of North Africa also produces wine in large quantities, but domestic comsumption is low because the predominant

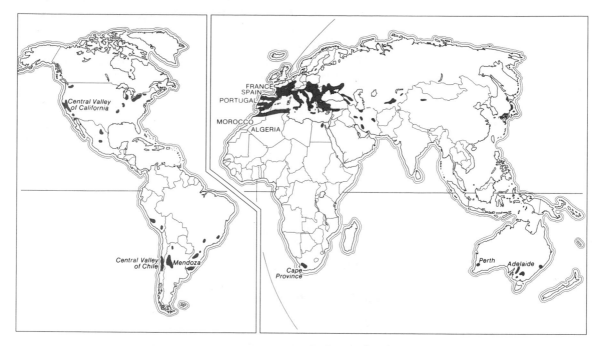

Fig. 10-13. Major areas of grape and wine production.

Moslem religion forbids its followers to use alcoholic beverages. Algeria is the world's leading exporter of wine, most of which goes to France. Spain, Portugal, France, Italy, and Morocco follow Algeria in exports. France exports its best quality wines, which are replaced on the domestic market by cheaper wines from Algeria. West Germany follows France as an importer and the United States is seventh.

The Animal Industries

Animals are normally raised for their meat, milk, skins, hair, or some combination of these products. With the exceptions of swine and fowl, much of the world's meat and animal fiber are produced in areas which, because of their climatic or terrain characteristics, are not suited for raising cultivated crops. The exceptions are primarily in large areas of surplus grain production, such as the American corn belt, where grain is marketed primarily in the form of meat. Demand for livestock products normally increases with increasing economic affluence, although meat and milk consumption are relatively high among poor people in some of the more sparsely populated parts of the world where animal industries are a major source of livelihood. Cows produce 90 to 95 percent of the world's milk and about half of the world's meat. Hogs contribute another 40 percent of the world's meat, with the remainder coming primarily from sheep, goats, and horses.

Because the quality of animals and the efficiency with which they are fed and cared for varies so greatly from one part of the world to another, one can rarely equate number of animals with output of meat, milk, or fiber. With slightly under 10 percent of the world's cattle, for example, the United States produces approximately 30 percent of the world's beef. Beef output per meat animal in Europe is about seven times higher than in Africa, and although India possesses more cattle than any other nation on earth, meat consumption there is negligible because of religious practices that forbid the taking of life and the eating of meat.

The United States normally produces more than 25 percent of the world's meat supply, followed by the Soviet Union with nearly 15 percent. Mainland China, West Germany, France, Argentina, Brazil, the United Kingdom, Australia, Poland, and Italy account for most of the rest.

Milk and other dairy products are produced primarily in Europe and North America, with the Soviet Union, the United States, the United Kingdom, West Germany, France, The Netherlands, Denmark, and Italy the major producers. Dairy products enter international trade largely in the form of butter, cheese, dried milk, and canned milk. The major sources of exports are New Zealand, The Netherlands, and Denmark. The United Kingdom, Italy, and West Germany are the major importers of butter. These same countries, plus the United States, are the principal markets for cheese. Most of the trade in canned milk is between The Netherlands and the Far East, whereas the United States, New Zealand, and Australia ship dried milk to the United Kingdom and numerous other European, Far Eastern, and Latin American countries.

Animal fibers include wool, mohair, feathers, fur, and silk. Japan is the major producer and exporter of silk and the United States is the largest importer. Australia is the world's leading producer and exporter of wool.

Wool. The sheep is the principal producer of animal fiber. The world's more than 1 billion sheep are spread over some 80 countries, but Australia and the Soviet Union, each with approximately 140 million animals, raise about 30 percent of the total (Fig. 10-14). Because Australia's animals are of better quality, output of wool per sheep is higher there than in the USSR (approximately 11 lb in Australia compared to about 7 lb in the USSR). Approximately 70 percent of the wool entering international trade originates in Australia and New Zealand, and the major importers are the European nations and the United States.

Sheep raising for wool is confined largely to sparsely populated and relatively dry regions where rough terrain or excessive moisture limits alternative land uses. Many of these areas have suffered a decline in output during recent years because synthetic fibers are competing effectively with wool.

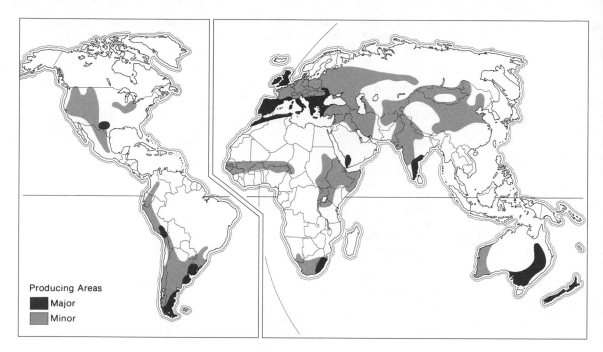

Fig. 10-14. Areas of sheep production.

Commercial Beef-Producing Areas. Commercial production of beef cattle occurs primarily in parts of the middle latitudes which are economically advanced, or thinly populated, or both (Fig. 10-15). Beef production is relatively small in the hottest and wettest portions of the tropics, in the coldest and driest portions of the earth, and in mountainous areas. Most cattle feed primarily upon grasses, although they are often heavily grain-fed for a period prior to slaughter.

Although beef is produced in nearly all sections of the United States, commercial production occurs primarily in the central portion of the country from the Dakotas and Minnesota southward into Texas where population densities are relatively low, land values are moderate, and large acreages of rangeland and pasture are available for use as grazing land (Fig. 10-15 and Tables 10-6 and 10-7). Texas produces about twice as many cattle as the other leading beef-producing states, most of which are in the western and drier portion of the corn belt region. Large numbers of cattle are raised in all parts of the corn belt, as well as in the South and the far West, and the corn belt has traditionally served as a fattening area for cattle raised in the Great Plains.

In South America the major beef-producing areas include the rich grasslands of the Pampas in Argentina and Uruguay and of southern Brazil.

TABLE 10-6. Number of Cattle and Buffalo in Selected Countries:
1961 and 1977 (Millions of Head)

Country	1961	1977
United States	97.7	122.1
USSR	75.8	110.3
China	90.0[a]	92.9[b]
Brazil	74.0	96.0
Argentina	43.2	58.4
Australia	17.3	32.5
Mexico	21.1	28.6
France	19.4	23.5
Colombia	15.4	23.9
Turkey	13.0[a]	15.0[a]
West Germany	12.9	14.5
United Kingdom	11.7	13.3
South Africa	12.0	13.1
Canada	10.9	13.2

[a]Estimate.
[b]1974

SOURCES: Foreign Agricultural Service, U.S.D.A.: Harry Jiler (ed.), *Commodity Year Book: 1978* (New York: Commodity Research Bureau, Inc., 1978), p. 91.

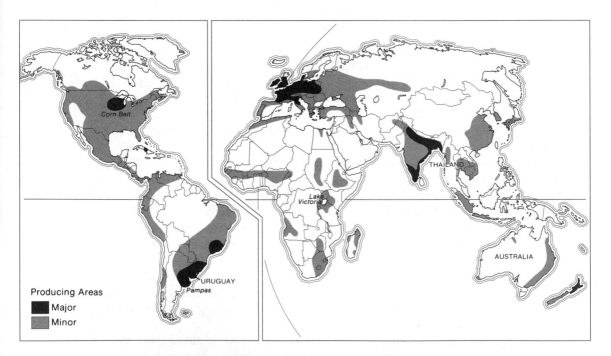

Fig. 10-15. Distribution of cattle (including dairy cattle).

TABLE 10-7. Cattle and Calves on Farms and on Feed, Leading
States in the United States: 1961 and 1977 (Thousands of Head)

STATE	ON FARMS		ON FEED[b]	
	1961	*1977*[a]	*1961*	*1977*[a]
Texas	9,379	15,800	254	1,710
Iowa	6,460	7,650	1,540	1,520
Nebraska	5,134	6,450	699	1,580
Kansas	4,562	6,400	337	1,315
Missouri	4,099	6,400	318	255
Oklahoma	3,513	5,650	—	—
California	4,207	4,750	715	801
South Dakota	3,327	3,650	294	3,650
Wisconsin	4,296	4,275	121	176
Minnesota	4,094	4,000	478	340
Colorado	2,282	3,030	414	915
Illinois	3,901	3,200	729	620
Mississippi	2,149	2,670	—	—
Ohio	3,513	2,205	236	325

[a]Preliminary.
[b]Cattle and calves being fattened for slaughter on grain and other concentrates.
SOURCE: Crop Reporting Board, U.S.D.A.

In Europe the leading beef-producing area stretches from northern France to the Ural Mountains. The Republic of South Africa, the area adjacent to Lake Victoria in Central Africa, central Ethiopia, eastern China, Thailand, and eastern Australia also raise significant numbers of beef cattle.

Commercial Pork-Producing Areas. Swine are dependent on crops or some form of concentrated food such as garbage and are not suited to pasturing. Hogs are good scavengers, however, as reflected by their diet of garbage in China, milk and potatoes in Europe, and maize in the United States. Although they are more efficient than cattle in converting grain into meat, they are more dependent than cattle on food crops which are suitable for direct human consumption.

Most of the world's hogs are raised within a few relatively small areas, but these areas are also those which are environmentally best suited to production of cultivated crops, especially maize and potatoes. China accounts for about one-third of the world's hogs, most of them being raised in the southeastern portion of the country which also produces the majority of the nation's rice. Another major pork-producing region is the North European Plain, which stretches from France into the Soviet Union and which is one of the more productive agricultural areas in the world. The United States follows China and the Soviet Union in hog production, with most hogs being raised in the corn belt where their diet consists largely of maize and soybeans. Brazil, which ranks fourth in hog production, raises the animals primarily in association with the maize industry in the southeastern portion of the nation.

International Trade in Meat. Meat exports originate primarily in Australia, New Zealand, and Argentina, in the southern hemisphere, and in Denmark, the Netherlands, and Ireland in northern Europe (Table 10-8). Ireland is less densely settled than most European countries and has few resources other than a climate which is conducive to animal production, whereas Denmark and the Netherlands engage in a highly intensive animal agriculture with per acre yields that are high enough to be classified as "factory farming."

The major meat-importing nations are the United Kingdom, the United States, and several countries in western Europe. The proximity of the leading importer, the United Kingdom, to three of the major exporters — Denmark, the Netherlands, and Ireland — is fortunate in that transport costs are minimized. Although meats exported from Argentina, Australia, and New Zealand must move long distances to reach their European and North American markets, they have the advantage of lower production costs than producers in northern Europe. The United States purchases approximately one-third of its meat imports from Australia and another 15 percent from New Zealand. Other major sources of meat for the United States are Denmark, the Netherlands, Canada, and Argentina.

The relationship between affluence and meat eating is clearly demon-

TABLE 10-8. Leading Meat Importing and Exporting Nations: 1974 (Thousands of Metric Tons)

IMPORTING NATIONS		EXPORTING NATIONS	
Nation	*Quantity*	*Nation*	*Quantity*
United Kingdom	1,134	Australia	645.6
United States	973	New Zealand	655.5
Italy	543	Denmark	629.4
West Germany	422	The Netherlands	601.1
France	324	Argentina	354.9
Japan	312	Ireland	298.5
USSR	134	France	336.8
Greece	124	Poland	238.7
Canada	122	Brazil	134.7
Belgium and Luxembourg	83	Uruguay	111.3
The Netherlands	76	Canada	82.0
Czechoslovakia	65	USSR	157.0
East Germany	57	United States	109.0
Switzerland	54	Mexico	26.5

SOURCE: Foreign Agricultural Service, U.S.D.A.

TABLE 10-9. Per Capita Meat Consumption, Selected Nations: 1964 and 1974 (Pounds)

NATION	CONSUMPTION		NATION	CONSUMPTION	
	1964	*1974*		*1964*	*1974*
New Zealand	211	207	France	128	143
Argentina	169	203	United Kingdom	143	132
Australia	218	209	Denmark	129	154
Uruguay	238	146	Austria	121	146
United States	175	187	Switzerland	118	135
Canada	148	161	Ireland	110	146
West Germany	120	148	Paraguay	127	57
			USSR	59	104

SOURCE: Foreign Agricultural Service, U.S.D.A.

strated in that nearly all the leading nations in meat production, consumption, imports, and exports rank among those having the highest per capita incomes (Tables 10-6 through 10-10). These areas include the United States, Canada, Western Europe, the Soviet Union, Australia, and New Zealand. Japan is the only non-Western country among the leading importing nations, and no Asian or African country is among the leading exporters. This emphasizes the extent to which African and Asian peoples depend on direct consumption of grains and starchy tubers in their diets.

Dairying

Dairying, like most animal industries, is associated primarily with advanced nations in North America and Europe and with Australia and New Zealand (Table 10-11). Dairy farming is one of the most intensive forms of land use involving animals and it is a demanding activity because of the regularity of

TABLE 10-10. Meat Production, Selected Nations: 1969 and 1976 (Millions of Metric Tons)

NATION	PRODUCTION		NATION	PRODUCTION	
	1969	*1976*		*1969*	*1976*
United States	16.0	18.0	Argentina	3.4	3.2
USSR	9.0	9.8	Australia	1.9	2.6
West Germany	3.4	3.9	United Kingdom	2.0	2.2
France	2.9	3.5	Poland	1.5	2.4
Brazil	2.5	3.1	Canada	1.4	1.7

SOURCE: Foreign Agricultural Service, U.S.D.A.

TABLE 10–11. Production of Milk, Butter, and Cheese, in Selected Countries

MILK			BUTTER			CHEESE		
	1972	1977		1972	1977		1972	1976
	(Million			*(Thousand*			*(Million*	
Country	*Metric Tons)*		*Country*	*Metric Tons)*		*Country*	*Metric Tons)*	
USSR	83.2	92.4	USSR	1,081	1,400	United States	1,181	1,505
United States	54.3	55.6	France	540	545	France	871	967
France	29.9	32.2	West Germany	497	536	West Germany	545	655
India	22.7	24.5	United States	500	496	Italy	424	550
West Germany	21.5	22.4	New Zealand	246	277	USSR	483	538
Poland	15.9	17.1	The Netherlands	163	178	The Netherlands	322	379
United Kingdom	13.4	14.5	Denmark	136	131	Argentina	205	245
Brazil	7.5	11.2	Australia	195	119	United Kingdom	184	205
The Netherlands	9.0	10.6	United Kingdom	95	115	Denmark	131	151
Canada	8.0	7.6	Canada	132	111	Canada	163	128
New Zealand	6.2	6.4	Ireland	77	99	Australia	81	112
Australia	7.3	5.9	Italy	61	70	Switzerland	96	110

SOURCE: Harry Jiler (ed.), *Commodity Year Book: 1978* (New York: Commodity Research Bureau, Inc., 1978), pp. 87, 99, and 227.

milking schedules and the special care that must be taken with highly bred and sensitive animals.

In the United States the most concentrated dairying activity is in the northeastern region from southern New England and the Middle Atlantic states westward into Minnesota. Most of the milk produced in the area from the Atlantic Ocean westward to the Great Lakes is sold as fresh milk in the large metropolises of the northeastern seaboard. Each city has its own "milkshed" area or region from which it draws its milk supply.

In Michigan and farther west, much of the milk is manufactured into cheese and butter, with butter reaching its greatest importance in the westernmost part of the region. Butter production has declined significantly as most people have found that less costly oleomargarine is an acceptable substitute. The demand for cheese has increased substantially, however, and a major shift has occurred from butter to cheese manufacturing in most of the major dairy states. The amount of milk used in butter manufacturing has declined by more than one-third since 1965, whereas the amount used in cheese manufacturing has increased by about 40 percent. Wisconsin leads all other states in production of milk and cheese, and Minnesota is the major butter-producing state.

Most of the milk produced in Europe is consumed fresh, although the Netherlands, Denmark, and Switzerland make a great deal of cheese and butter. High population densities in Europe place heavy demands upon the continent's dairy industry, with considerable quantities of cheese and butter being imported, especially by the United Kingdom. New Zealand, which specializes in cheese and butter production, and Australia are major sources of British imports.

During the early 1970s the European Common Market began offering large subsidies to dairy farmers for producing butter. The farmers responded so magnificently that a huge surplus developed. Europeans, like Americans, found that they could substitute oleomargarine for butter. The Soviet Union finally relieved the Common Market of its butter surplus, but at bargain prices which were well below those paid by citizens in the Common Market countries.

The Soviet Union has expanded its own dairy industry significantly since World War II and leads all other nations in number of dairy cattle and in butter output. Most Soviet dairy cows are found in the European part of the country between the Black Sea and Moscow.

Vegetable Fibers

As a whole, vegetable fibers are produced and consumed in greater volume than animal, mineral, and man-made fibers. Cotton is the leading fiber, but jute, kapok, flax, hemp, ramie, sisal, henequen, and abaca are also important. Except for flax and hemp, vegetable fibers are produced primarily in the tropics and subtropics.

Cotton. Although known for at least 5,000 years, cotton has been of worldwide commercial importance only during the last 200 years. Prior to the 1800s, cotton cloth was so expensive that only the wealthy could afford its use. Invention of the cotton gin in 1783 and of spinning and weaving machinery shortly thereafter, along with other technical and economic improvements associated with the industrial revolution, encouraged a rapid expansion in cotton production beginning in the late eighteenth century.

Cotton requires a growing season of 180 to 200 days and the equivalent of 40 to 60 inches of rainfall. The plant produces well under irrigation, and relatively dry regions have fewer problems with insects and diseases than wet areas (Fig. 10–16).

The United States, the Soviet Union, and China are the world's premier producers of cotton (Table 10–12). The Soviet Union and China have expanded output rapidly during recent years, whereas acreage and production in the United States have declined since the record crop of nearly 18 million bales in 1926. Average output was about 14,795,000 bales during 1960–1964, 11,300,000 bales during 1970–1974, and 14,500,000 bales during 1977–1978. Soviet output has exceeded that of the United States during most recent years and has been more stable than production in the United States, where year-to-year output is strongly affected by legislation and subsidy levels as well as by variations in the weather.

TABLE 10–12. Cotton Production in Selected Countries, 1962–1963 and 1977–1978 (Thousands of Bales)

| COUNTRY | PRODUCTION | | COUNTRY | PRODUCTION | |
	1962–63	1977–78		1962–63	1977–78
USSR	6,850	12,750	Turkey	1,130	2,260
United States	14,920	14,500	Egypt	2,109	1,850
China	4,300	10,900	Mexico	2,400	1,600
India	4,950	5,400	Sudan	750	750
Pakistan	1,702	2,400	Iran	425	800
Brazil	2,250	2,350	Peru	635	275
			Colombia	305	700

SOURCES: Harry Jiler (ed.), *Commodity Year Book: 1974* (New York: Commodity Research Bureau, 1974).

Ibid., 1978.

The old cotton belt, which encompassed the southeastern states from Virginia into Mississippi and Texas, has undergone drastic changes. Cotton has almost disappeared from the agriculture of Virginia and from many parts of the Carolinas and Georgia. The industry has remained strong in Texas and Mississippi, and production has expanded in California, New Mexico, and Arizona. Generally, therefore, the cotton belt has moved westward where farms, allotments, and field sizes are more suitable to modern mechanized cotton cultivation and harvesting than the small farms of the Southeast (Table 10–13).

Recent federal, state, and county decisions allowing the transfer of cotton allotments within and across county lines have resulted in the concentration of the bulk of the industry into a few specialized producing areas. The shift is primarily toward areas of level land where farms are large and

TABLE 10–13. Lint Cotton Production in Selected States: 1961 and 1972 (Thousands of 480 lb. Bales)

| STATE | PRODUCTION | | STATE | PRODUCTION | |
	1961	1977		1961	1977
Texas	4,786	5,550	Alabama	617	280
Mississippi	1,625	1,650	Tennessee	554	255
California	1,689	2,880	Missouri	377	235
Arkansas	1,456	1,050	Georgia	512	80
Louisiana	479	660	Oklahoma	369	440
Arizona	828	1,050	South Carolina	412	110
			U.S. TOTAL	14,318	14,496

SOURCE: Crop Reporting Board, U.S.D.A., and Harry Jiler (ed.), *Commodity Year Book: 1978* (New York: Commodity Research Bureau, Inc., 1978).

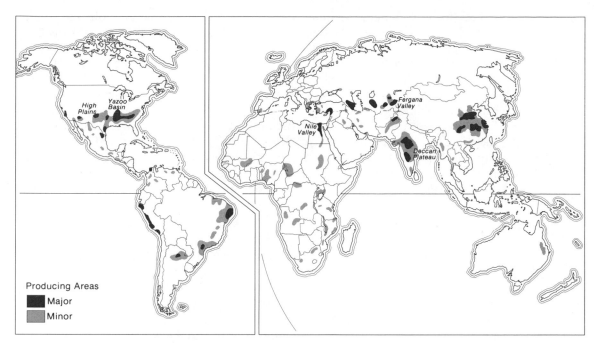

Fig. 10-16. Major areas of cotton production.

where the crop is produced under irrigation [4]. The High Plains Cotton District around Lubbock, Texas, is the largest producer of cotton in the United States and is the recipient of a large percentage of the allotment transfers within Texas. The future of the industry in the High Plains District is limited, however, in that much of the area depends on irrigation water from underground sources which are not being replenished.

Most Soviet cotton is grown in the south-central portion of the country in the Kirghiz, Uzbek, and Tadzhik Republics where natural rainfall is scarce and irrigation of the crop is essential. Most of the Chinese crop is raised in the east-central part of the country where it supports a large textile industry that has become increasingly competitive on world markets during recent years. In India production is concentrated in the northern and western portions of the Deccan Plateau. India also has a large textile industry which consumes domestic output of cotton as well as some imports.

Egypt is noted for the exceptional quality of its cotton, which is grown in the Nile Valley where it competes for land and irrigation water with food crops. Sale of cotton abroad accounts for a large share of Egypt's trade and foreign exchange.

Other Vegetable Fibers. Several vegetable fibers are near monopolies of particular regions. About 95 percent of the world's jute, for example, is raised in the Ganges–Brahmaputra Delta region of Bangladesh and India. Jute is a coarse vegetable fiber used in making "burlap" bags, as a backing material for carpets, and as a baling twine. Synthetic fibers have made substantial inroads into the market for jute, but producers hope that higher prices of synthetics (caused by shortages and high prices of the fossil fuels, from which most synthetics are made) will have a positive effect upon demand for jute.

Abaca is used in making high-quality cordage, specialty paper, and handicrafts. The Philippines produce more than 90 percent of the world's supply. Henequen, a relatively coarse cordage fiber, is associated chiefly with the Yucatan Peninsula of Mexico, which accounts for about 90 percent of the world's output. Sisal, which is used in making ropes, twines, bags, and upholstery paddings, is grown in many parts of the tropics, but Brazil and Tanzania together account for more than 60 percent of world output.

Kapok, or tree cotton, is known for its buoyancy and resilience. Used primarily as a cushion, upholstery, and life preserver padding or filling, kapok grows on trees that reach up to 100 feet in height. Thailand is the source of about 90 percent of the world's commercial kapok production, although the tree produces well in nearly all tropical areas.

Linen is obtained from flax, a temperate land crop. It is one of the oldest known fibers, but it began to decline in importance after cotton and other cheaper fibers became widely available. The Soviet Union is the largest producer, with lesser amounts being raised in Poland, Belgium, The Netherlands, and France. Belgium has been known for the exceptional quality of its linen for a thousand years.

Fibers are obtained from a wide variety of products such as coconuts, okra, redwood bark, Spanish moss, bunchgrass, and browncorn. Some have worldwide uses, whereas others are important only locally.

CONCLUSIONS

Agricultural industries in most parts of the world are in various stages of transition relative to management, methods of cultivation, and types of crops produced. Change occurs most rapidly in advanced nations such as the United States which are able to react quickly to the benefits of modern science and technology. In many of the developing nations, on the other hand, the same agricultural methods are being used to grow the same crops, in the same places, as hundreds of years ago. In other instances agricultural developments are being financed in relatively primitive areas by businesses or governmental agencies from affluent nations. Inputs of foreign capital have often disrupted traditional self-sufficient agriculture by the introduction of commercial crops, and the results are not uniformly beneficial.

Because most people still make their living through agriculture, it remains the dominant problem in world social and economic affairs. Whether or not agriculture will be able to supply future needs for food, fiber, and other materials depends largely on how effectively humankind can control population size; conquer problems of erosion, pollution, and waste; improve per acre yields; and develop adequate facilities for storing, processing, and transporting the crops that are produced.

REFERENCES

[1] Robert S. Loomis, "Agricultural Systems," in *Food and Agriculture* (San Francisco: W. H. Freeman, 1976), pp. 69–76.

[2] Richard Fussell, "Food Factory: Farms of the Future (Imperial Valley Model)." Unpublished paper presented during November, 1968, before the Southeastern Division of the Association of American Geographers in a meeting in Gainesville, Florida.

[3] A. Clinton Cook, "Growing and Using Vegetables," in Alfred Stefferus (ed.) *Farmer's World: The Yearbook of Agriculture, 1964* (Washington, D.C.: U.S. Governmental Printing Office), p. 139.

[4] William H. Bailey, "Government Policy and the Location of Cotton Production," *Southeastern Geographer*, 18, No. 2, November, 1978, pp. 93–103.

PART FOUR
MINERALS

CHAPTER ELEVEN

disparities in energy production and consumption

INTRODUCTION

The basic source of all movement, change, pollution, income, food, technology, minerals, life, death, politics, people, and everything else is energy. Without energy nothing happens. Unless energy availability can be increased or its use made more efficient, there can be no real growth in creature comforts, food production, industrial output, home construction, or income. Without increases in the per capita availability of energy or in the efficiency with which it is used, the developing nations cannot be developed, and the developed nations cannot continue to develop.

The forms of energy used by humankind, the methods for using energy, the levels of dependence on particular energy forms, and the results obtained from energy use are extremely varied and complex. Most inhabitants of the developed world think of energy as gasoline, coal, natural gas, electricity, and nuclear power. Inhabitants of the developing nations are more likely to think of energy in the form of wood, animals, dung, falling water, and wind.

Energy and Entropy

Although the first law of thermodynamics (often referred to as the *law of the conservation of energy*) teaches us that the total supply of energy in the universe can neither be increased nor decreased, only changed from one form to another, the second law of thermodynamics states that energy tends to decrease in quality, or in availability. Deterioration occurs naturally, but during recent times humankind has caused an acceleration of the process by conversion of *stored energy* (in the form of coal, oil, gas, or wood) into *work energy*. Thus in converting energy in the form of coal or petroleum into work energy to drive machines or for heating and cooling buildings and propelling vehicles, a certain amount of energy is lost in availability. The energy is not lost to the universe, but it has been converted to a more highly dispersed form from which it cannot be recovered to make additional work energy. The principle is that of *entropy*, which tells us that the larger the amount of energy converted into work energy, the larger the amount made unavailable for work. Although many forms of energy exist within the universe, the form most utilized by humans is chemical, or heat, energy. This is particularly important in understanding the role played in the entropy process, for although other forms of energy may be converted into heat energy without entropy, heat energy cannot be converted into work energy without a loss of usable energy.

Entropy and Survival

As high temperature energy (such as that in a nuclear reactor) is reduced in temperature through its application to work tasks (such as lighting a home or a classroom), the degree of entropy increases because low temperature energy has less potential for conversion into work energy than high temperature energy. Stated differently, the concentrated high temperature energy generated within the confines of a nuclear reactor can be utilized to produce work energy. As the energy contained within the nuclear reactor is dispersed throughout the area served by a nuclear power plant, however, the temperature is lowered through dispersion and its recoverability for use as work energy declines. As energy is converted from concentrated into dispersed form, therefore, entropy increases and the amount of potential work energy decreases. As entropy increases, so does the degree of disorder associated with the energy.

The relationships among temperature, energy consumption, entropy, and disorder may be applied to an analysis of human societies. Regions with highest amounts of per capita energy consumption may be classed as *high temperature* areas because they convert enormous amounts of energy from concentrated into dispersed forms through changing stored energy (coal, oil, natural gas, uranium) into high temperature work energy (generating plants to produce electricity, automobile engines, steel mills, etc.). Thus the rate at which entropy occurs and the potential for disorder are high (Fig. 11-1). Regions with lowest amounts of per capita energy consumption may be classed as *low temperature* societies because of the relatively small amounts of stored energy they convert into high temperature work energy. Low

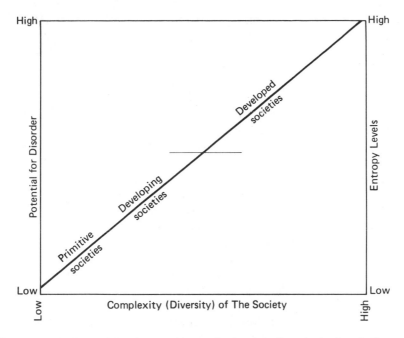

Fig. 11-1. Relationships between complexity (or diversity) of societies and entropy levels and their potentials for disorder.

temperature societies depend primarily on conversion of solar energy (sunlight) into plant energy and upon plant energy to sustain human life and societal functions. In such societies the use of electrical energy, automobiles, and factory-made products is minimal, and the potential for disorder is low (Fig. 11-1).

In a general sense the higher the degree of affluence associated with a society, the greater is the diversity within that society. The greater the diversity, the more highly organized the society must be in order to maintain itself. The higher the degree of organization and diversity, the more energy that is required to keep the society functioning. Because most of the energy used by humans is heat energy, the more complex, diverse, affluent, and highly organized a society becomes, the greater is the degree of energy entropy and the higher is the probability of disorder (Fig. 11-1).

Among the more advanced nations, such as the United States, diversity, organization, and levels of energy consumption have reached such an elevated state of development that entropy and the potential for disorder are high. Vast quantities of energy are required to produce, process, transport, and dispose of the enormous variety of goods consumed by such societies. The organizational framework required to administer the production and processing of the right types and amounts of goods and to transport them to the right places in the right quantities at the right times is extremely complex.

Thus increasing amounts of energy are required for the operation of computers and other machines which compile and analyze information about performances in output, where goods are being produced in what quantities, what facilities are needed for moving the goods, and the locations and sizes of various levels of demand for those goods. Additional inputs of energy are needed to administer a mounting list of nonmaterial services in demand by these societies. As individuals and regions reach greater degrees of functional specialization, their capacities for self-sufficiency decline.

Under such circumstances the amount of energy required to maintain the system increases exponentially, even when the population is stable. Entropy and the potential for disorder which is associated with entropy are also increasing exponentially. Consider, for example, what would happen in the United States if energy supplies for transportation were suddenly made unavailable. During a strike of approximately one-fourth of the nation's truckers in the early 1970s, grocery store shelves began to empty within a week. Had the strike involved most of the nation's truckers and had it lasted for several weeks, the likelihood for chaos would have been strong as food supplies dwindled, disease-carrying garbage piled up in city streets, and consumers began to go hungry or to become ill. Consider also the traumas that might occur if the nation's electrical power were shut off or if energy could not be supplied for the operation of the thousands of computers which control commodity movements, keep track of bank accounts, and write paychecks. Imagine what would happen to food prices if a major drought destroyed all crops in the corn belt states.

Contrast these alarming potentials for disorder and choas with the operation of a relatively primitive society, where energy consumption remains primarily of the low temperature variety, the bulk of the energy inputs are from human and animal labor, and there is a high degree of family and local self-sufficiency. Such areas contain few or no high temperature energy systems, and the entropy rate is relatively low.

Although high temperature, high energy societies are threatened with disorder and chaos from many directions, these societies also have an enormous capacity for rapid innovation and adjustment when disorder threatens. Because they are high energy societies and because energy is the primary agent of change, they have strong survival capabilities. They can often control the direction and the rate of change, and they have the ability to devise and implement a variety of backup systems which can be brought quickly into operation when some basic element within the system threatens to cease functioning. Low temperature, low energy societies, on the other hand, find that change is difficult to achieve, that innovations are rare, and that increases in productivity are virtually impossible unless levels of energy consumption can be raised. Whereas high temperature societies face risks of extremely high magnitude but low levels of frequency, low temperature areas face risks of low magnitude and high frequency. Most persons living within high temperature societies, moreover, are willing to trade away a certain degree of security in order to enjoy the benefits of high levels of living. High energy, high temperature societies depend for their survival on innovation and positive change — or on the so-called "brain industries." Low temperature, low energy societies are more inclined toward following tradition rather than the creation of new things, methods, and processes.

TYPES OF ENERGY

Although the most abundant form of energy in the universe is gravitational energy, humans have been able to harness it to meet only a small percentage of human energy requirements. Other forms of energy include chemical, kinetic, and nuclear energy, but the form which powers most present-day human activities is chemical energy.

Fossil Fuels

During recent times the bulk of the inanimate energy utilized by humans has come from the fossil fuels: coal, petroleum, oil shale, and natural gas.

Underground coal mine in Kentucky. (Courtesy, Tennessee Valley Authority.)

The fossil fuels are forms of stored solar energy. Their origins consist of biological materials, primarily plants and marine animals, that grew in abundance under warm, moist climates and in warm seas some millions of years ago. These materials were buried in the ground underneath sedimentary formations which were deposited primarily on the bottoms of ancient seas and oceans. There they were protected from oxidation, compressed or squeezed into their present locales, and preserved as an energy bank to be drawn upon by humankind primarily during the last hundred years. (More information on the fossil fuels is given later in the chapter.)

Nuclear Energy

Because deposits of fossil fuels are limited in size, humans must eventually turn to other energy sources. Nuclear energy is already being produced in a number of countries, but as yet it provides a relatively small portion of total energy requirements. Nuclear energy as a practical source of power and as a possible replacement for some of the fossil fuels was a spin-off of World War II. Its development since that time has been delayed because of fear of its dangers to humans and because energy from the fossil fuels has been available at low cost.

Although all matter is made up of atoms, the only material which has thus far proved economically suitable for use in nuclear power generation is uranium. The only type of uranium which is readily fissionable is U^{235}, which must be processed into plutonium for use in nuclear power plants. Thorium (Th^{232}) can be used in breeder reactors and it is extremely abundant in nature. At this writing, however, the breeder remains in a largely experimental stage of development and is not expected to become a significant source of energy until the middle or late 1980s or 1990s. Breeders are already operating in France and the Soviet Union, but they have been given a low priority in recent energy programs in the United States because of uncertainties over their safety and because the plutonium they generate can be used in making nuclear weapons.

Considerable research is also being conducted on the fusion reactor, but economic and technical problems make its commercial use unlikely before well into the next century, if then. Fusion reactors would have few of the undesirable side effects of fission reactors, they would be highly efficient, and the principal fuel for the fusion process, deuterium, is available in ocean water in adequate quantities to equal some 50 million times the earth's total initial stock of fossil fuels.

Nuclear power remains a highly controversial source of energy, even after more than three decades of development, application, and experimentation. Estimates of the world's usable uranium reserves vary widely, as do estimates of the potential hazards to human populations from nuclear fuel and power

Nuclear power plant under construction at Bellefonte, Alabama. (Courtesy, Tennessee Valley Authority.)

production, disposal of nuclear wastes, international proliferation of nuclear weapons, and theft of fissionable materials for criminal purposes. The potential benefits from nuclear power are also large. Its production appears to offer relatively minor threats to air and water quality, costs of transportation are comparatively low per unit of power produced, and energy resources are potentially available for supplying world needs for many generations. Costs of transferring a major share of energy dependence from fossil fuels to nuclear power are huge, however, and they are affordable only as a part of long-term strategies for energy development.

The question of reactor safety has revolved primarily around the potential for power plant accidents, which would release deadly radiation into the atmosphere with quick death to those found in the vicinity of the plants and an increase in cancer-related deaths over a wide area. Advocates of nuclear power point to the extremely low risk of such an accident and to the excellent safety record of nuclear plants to date. Deaths related to uranium mining and milling; fuel processing, reprocessing and transportation; reactor design, manufacture, and operation; and waste disposal were estimated in

1976 to total about one for each 2 years of operation of a 1,000-megawatt nuclear unit [1]. The number of fatalities attributed to mining, transporting, and burning coal was much higher, especially when deaths from respiratory ailments caused by plant emissions and by black lung disease (a disease of coal miners caused by breathing coal dust) are included [2]. Adherrence to air quality standards set by the United States Environmental Protection Agency in 1975 would reduce deaths from coal burning to about the same risk level as that associated with nuclear plants.

The problem of disposal of nuclear wastes, especially spent fuel from nuclear reactors, is caused by the length of time the wastes remain toxic (as long as several million years). All methods devised for disposal or storage of such wastes have proved environmentally unsound or popularly or politically unacceptable at the time of this writing. Proposals for storing the wastes in abandoned salt mines or other underground areas have received strong objections from nearby residents. Earlier efforts to dispose of them in the ocean deeps, where they were supposed to rest harmlessly through their toxic stages, proved not so harmless as had been anticipated. Recently developed methods for processing nuclear wastes unto usable fuel, leaving the remaining material with a toxicity of about 700 years duration, have met with disfavor because the reprocessed materials are potentially usable for making nuclear weapons. This problem has led to cancellation of proposed sales of reprocessing plants by the United States and efforts to discourage sales of such plants by other nations. Because of the proliferation which has already occurred in nuclear fuels, power plants, and fuel reprocessing facilities, however, efforts to control their further spread may be futile.

Nuclear power plants operating in the United States are widely scattered, but their distribution is roughly proportional to the distribution of the nation's population. To alleviate partially public fear of large scale loss of human life in the event of a power plant accident, nuclear scientists and engineers have proposed that future nuclear plants should be clustered into "nuclear parks," removed to a safe distance from population concentrations [3]. Others have suggested that nuclear plants be built underground or that they be placed in offshore clusters that are separated from human habitation by several tens of miles of ocean water. Whereas offshore locations may reduce potential hazards from atmospheric contamination, however, they would increase potential hazards from radioactive contamination of ocean waters — and most of the world's largest population concentrations are along coastlines.

Although nuclear scientists have often pointed to the good safety record of nuclear power plants, and although the probability of major losses of life from failures of dams and from increased burning of coal may be much higher than those from reactor accidents, public awareness of the horrifying results of the atomic bombs dropped on Japan during World War II remains strong. The newness of the radioactive hazard, the sheer numbers of lives which could be taken as the result of a single major accident, and the enormous length of time required for recovery from radioactive contamination, are mind-boggling to most people.

A major accident at the Three Mile Island nuclear plant near Harrisburg, Pennsylvania, during March, 1979, resulted in the escape of substantial amounts of radioactive gases, fears of a meltdown of the reactor core, and partial evacuation of nearby areas. Several days were required before the dangers of an explosion, leaking radioactive gasses, and a possible meltdown could be brought under effective control. The conflicting reports issued by power plants officials, members of the Nuclear Regulatory Commission, and other scientists, did little to allay public apprehension. The incident occurred shortly after release of a movie, "The China Syndrome," whose plot depicted a similar accident and a near meltdown of a reactor in California. The title of the movie referred to a situation in which because of some sort of accident the heat being generated in the reactor core cannot be controlled and the core melts through its containment vessel into the ground below. In such an event some thousands of square miles of territory could become contaminated with radioactivity and rendered uninhabitable for many years. The combination of the accident at Three Mile Island and the coincidental release of the movie resulted in a substantial elevation of public fear of the dangers of nuclear power, more stringent attention to power plant safety, and a slowdown in nuclear energy development. This followed a period during which nuclear power developments had already suffered serious setbacks because of the length of time required to obtain approval of design and site specifications for power plant construction, delays caused by legal challenges from environmentalists and other groups, costs involved in meeting increasing safety requirements, harrassment from protestors, and rapidly inflating fuel and materials prices.

In contrast to the widely held fear of nuclear energy, the public has come largely to accept as essential to the pursuit of comfort and convenience the several thousands of deaths from electrocution each year, the occasional heavy losses of life from dam disasters, the regular maiming and killing of thousands of motorists, and even the large losses of life from spectacular aircraft mishaps. An additional factor in the opposition to nuclear power is the reluctance of people to accept risks over which they feel they have no personal control [4]. Thus a person may willingly and enthusiastically observe or participate in a sporting event which carries high risk of personal injury or death but stand resolutely against construction of a nuclear power plant near his or her hometown. Should the public face a choice between severe changes in life-style because of reduced energy availability or acceptance of the risks of nuclear power, however, it is likely that resistance to nuclear power will diminish.

Uranium ore is widely found and produced. Largest output comes from the Colorado Plateau and Rocky Mountain areas of the United States, the

Brown's Ferry nuclear power plant in Tennessee. (Courtesy, Tennessee Valley Authority.)

Beaverlodge and Quirke Lake areas in Canada, the Transvaal region in South Africa, and several mining areas stretching from Brest to Montpellier in France. Producing areas are also found from southern East Germany into southern Yugoslavia. In the Soviet Union uranium is mined near the Black and Aral Seas and within the Altai Mountains. In China uranium is mined near Canton; in Japan, near Kobe. Australia produces uranium in Arnhem Land in northwestern Queensland and from Radium Hill in the Flanders Range. Gabon and the Central African Republic are producers in Africa, and Gabon is the site of a deposit which was so rich approximately 2 billion years ago that it "went critical" and operated as a nuclear reactor for several hundred thousand years [5]. South American uranium production occurs primarily in northwestern Argentina, although promising finds have been made in Brazil, Uruguay, and Chile.

If commercial breeder reactors find acceptance as a practical energy source in the United States and elsewhere, the potential supply of nuclear fuels will be virtually unlimited. Low-grade fuels usable in breeders, such as thorium, are found in abundance in numerous areas. The amount of uranium available for use in conventional fission reactors depends largely on the price of the fuel and on mining and processing technology. As prices increase or technology improves, it becomes possible economically to exploit deposits of lower grade than those previously used. Much of the debate concerning the size of uranium reserves stems from assumptions of different prices for the processed fuel and greater or lesser expectations of advances in production technology.

About three-fourths of the world's approximately 100 operating and planned nuclear power plants are in the United States. The Soviet Union possesses most of the remaining 25 percent. Most non-Soviet plants depend on the United States for supplies of fuel and for much of the technical know-how needed to construct and maintain reactors. The nuclear reach of the United States, therefore, goes considerably beyond the nation's boundaries.

Water Power

Hydroelectric power (power from falling water) "is the most efficient and the cleanest major source of power yet developed by man" [6]. Water power in one form or another has been used for more than 2,000 years, and until development of the steam engine in 1769 it was the major source of inanimate energy for manufacturing. The technology to transmit electrical

Hydroelectric facility at Fontana, North Carolina. (Courtesy, Tennessee Valley Authority.)

energy was not developed until about 100 years after invention of the steam engine, however, and the mobility of steam engines gave them an advantage over more locationally restricted water power sites. Modern hydroelectric plants did not appear until early in the present century. Many hydroelectric developments have multiple purposes, where the dams and reservoirs constructed to produce power are also parts of large-scale projects to provide for navigation, irrigation, water storage, flood control, recreation, and wildlife management.

Although hydroelectric power produces virtually no air or water pollution, requires no input of mined fuels, and gives off little waste heat, its locational restrictions remain a major handicap. The best sites for hydroelectric developments are along streams which have steep gradients and a large and regular flow of water. These conditions are most frequently met in areas of relatively high elevation and (or) steep slopes where precipitation is abundant the year-around. Regions possessing such characteristics are often sparsely populated and they are located long distances from the world's major markets for electrical energy.

Water power developments have the further disadvantage of requiring construction of large reservoirs which destroy the scenic value of wild rivers and occupy considerable areas of land which are often excellent for agriculture. Because power generation in hydroelectric plants can be started and stopped quickly, they are increasingly used to supply peak power demands. The intermittent operation of the plants causes wide fluctuations in stream flow, however, as water is irregularly released and held back. An additional disadvantage of water power is that reservoirs eventually become filled with silt.

Geothermal Energy

Geothermal energy is generated within the earth by decay of radioactive elements, by gravitational and rotational energy, and by other forces such as the changes which occur in rock structures as a result of increases in heat and pressure from the surface into the interior. Interior heat flows continuously toward the surface, from which it is radiated into space. The earth's rocks are poor conductors of heat, however, and rocks near the surface are hot enough for commercial utilization as an energy source only where geological disturbances are relatively common, such as in areas of earthquake or volcanic activity. In these regions, such as the "ring of fire" (the belt of volcanoes and earthquake activity bordering the Pacific Ocean), superheated rocks have moved from deep in the earth's interior toward the surface, or they have been heated by some other process such as friction. Nearby reservoirs of underground water, and some groundwater supplies, are heated by these rocks. Sometimes the water is converted into huge subterranean deposits of steam. Such chambers can be tapped with drilling techniques similar to those used in seeking petroleum. The steam or hot water which is brought to the surface can be used to generate electricity.

Besides the limited areas where geothermal energy can be developed, other disadvantages are associated with this energy source. Geothermal plants release several times as much waste heat as conventional coal-fired steam plants of similar generating capacity. Noxious gasses, chemicals, and large concentrations of salt are often contained in the steam or hot water, and removal of large amounts of water or steam from subsurface areas may cause the land surface to sink. Major problems are often encountered, therefore, in preventing pollution of the atmosphere and of surface water supplies and in preventing subsidence.

Potential development of geothermal energy in the United States is greatest in the western states, in Hawaii, in Alaska, along the Gulf Coast, and in the Appalachians and the Ozarks, somewhat in that order. Additional areas of potentially large developments include the Andean system of South America and the mountainous area along the western Pacific from northeastern Siberia to New Zealand. Soviet geothermal potential is primarily in the eastern and southern mountains, and in Europe the greatest potential appears to be in the Mediterranean region.

Solar Energy

Solar energy obtained directly from the sun's radiation may be the ultimate form of energy for use by humans. The amount of solar energy reaching the earth's atmosphere each year is approximately 35,000 times the amount of energy used by humankind [7]. Only a fraction of this energy is intercepted by the earth's surface, but the amount received is hundreds of times greater than current world consumption of fossil and nuclear fuels.

Although the total amount of solar energy reaching the earth is more than adequate to meet all projected human needs, problems arise because of its diffusion over the earth's surface and because the amounts received by particular areas vary so widely from season to season, with different atmospheric conditions, and from daylight to darkness. Whereas solar energy is highly diffused and variable, the energy needs of modern industrial societies are spatially concentrated and consistent. The major barriers to use of solar energy, therefore, involve its collection and storage in sufficient amounts, at low enough costs, to meet spatially concentrated demands. Solar energy has been used for thousands of years for drying foods and for evaporating water from brines to obtain salt. It has also been used in dry regions to distill drinking water from saltwater. Economical applications of solar energy are limited at present primarily to small-scale and widely diffused demands. Its use in supplying at least part of the needs for heating and cooling individual homes is rapidly becoming feasible in affluent areas, and a solar cooker has met with some success in developing areas where other fuel sources are scarce.

Among the numerous processes being studied for their feasibility in collecting large amounts of solar energy for concentrated use are orbiting satellite power stations, flat plate surface collectors, and systems of lenses or mirrors designed to focus solar energy onto smaller collectors. Satellites have the advantage of continuously receiving sunlight, but disadvantages include problems of transmitting the energy to surface receiving stations and their enormous cost per unit of energy generated. Flat plate collectors might be located in deserts where the huge surface areas they occupy would offer little interference with human activities, but maximum obtainable temperatures are low, leading to low efficiency and large amounts of waste heat. Reflecting mirrors or focusing lenses are complex and costly and would occupy large surface areas. All such surface collectors have the additional problem of storage of energy to supply needs during darkness or on cloudy days. One solution to this problem may be to use solar energy collected at offshore locations to produce hydrogen gas from seawater, with the hydrogen being transported by pipeline to storage areas and consumers occupying nearby land areas. An additional disadvantage of small-scale use of solar energy (as a partial source of energy for individual structures) is that it increases an already serious problem caused by the differential between peak and minimum demands for power from commercial utility companies. Without costly and bulky storage facilities, solar systems would be in operation only during daylight hours of sunny days. Commercial utilities would still need a large enough capacity to furnish all power needs at times, but because the capacity would go unused for much of the time the cost of commercial energy would rise.

Hydrogen Gas

Hydrogen gas is potentially available in almost unlimited quantities, for it can be extracted from seawater and when it is burned, the only pollutant is water. Although hydrogen has a lower thermal rating than natural gas, it could be transported through existing natural gas pipelines, stored in existing storage facilities, and used with only minor modifications in existing furnaces, stoves, and heaters. A major problem in use of hydrogen energy is public fear caused by its widely recognized combustability. Another problem is the low efficiency obtained through conversion of other sources of energy, such as solar or nuclear energy, into electrical energy, which in turn is used to produce hydrogen gas.

Synfuels: Liquid Fuels From Coal, Oil Shale, and Tar Sands.

The production of liquid fuels from coal and from oil shale has been carried out on a limited scale in a few areas since prior to World War II. Germany obtained a portion of its liquid fuels from coal during World War II, and the Republic of South Africa does so today. Small quantities of oil have been produced from shale in the Soviet Union, Australia, Scotland, China, Germany, and Brazil. Largest deposits of tar sands are in Canada, Colombia, and the Soviet Union. Until recently the cost of producing liquid fuels from these sources was substantially greater than that of crude petroleum. Escalating energy prices and the desire to decrease dependence upon imported oil has yielded a sharpening interest in synfuels, however, since 1973. Nations with immense coal reserves, such as the United States, are exploring the possibilities of large scale distillation of liquid fuels from coal. The most cost-competitive processes for the short run, however, appears to rest with extraction of fuels from oil shale and tar sands.

The Athabaska tar sands in Canada contain an estimated 710 billion barrels of oil, of which more than 300 billion barrels are potentially recoverable. Whereas the fuel in oil shale is actually an insoluble organic material called kerogen, tar sands contain soluble organic materials which are about 90 percent recoverable from deposits now being mined. Canadian production remains small because of the experimental nature of the operation. Minor quantities of oil from tar sands are also being produced in the Soviet Union, Albania, and Romania.

Large reserves of oil shale are found in the United States, the Soviet Union, China, and Brazil, with much smaller reserves in several European countries. Reserves in the United States are estimated to contain at least 2 trillion barrels of oil, nearly 3 times the known quantity of crude oil reserves in the entire world. The best quality shale (that capable of yielding about 25 gallons of oil per ton of rock) is found in the Green River area of Wyoming. Lower quality deposits are in Colorado, Utah, and in a large part of the eastern United States ranging from Michigan to western Pennsylvania and southward into Mississippi.

Because the Green River shale is of highest quality and can be developed at the lowest cost per barrel of oil recovered, most plans for shale oil extraction are focused upon Wyoming. Two basic techniques are available for removing oil from shale; both involve heating the rock to liberate the oil. In one technique the shale is mined, crushed, and moved to processing plants. In the other the shale is crushed and heated in place (*in situ* processing), and the oil is pumped out of the ground. Both techniques require huge amounts of water in an area which already suffers from severe water shortages. The Colorado River and its tributary, the Green River, will have to furnish the bulk of the water and Colorado River water is already overallocated. Thus the energy industries will be competing for water with farmers and urban and industrial users. A partial solution to the water problem may be for the energy industries to purchase supplies from low return agricultural users such as those raising hay and other animal feed crops under irrigation. Environmental problems are also expected to be severe because of the vast quantities of rock which must be removed or crushed in place and because of the immense quantities of waste rock left after the oil has been recovered. Some of the waste can be returned to the extraction sites, but crushed rock has substantially greater volume than when solid. Damage to vegetation and wildlife, and groundwater problems, are among other major environmental hazards posed by the shale oil processes. Thus when environmental costs are added to those for extracting the oil from the shale, what might first appear as an energy bonanza becomes another difficult, complex, and perplexing economic puzzle.

Other Sources of Energy

Small amounts of energy may be obtained from several additional sources during the next few decades. Among these are biomass (vegetation), wind, tides, and various organic materials. Biomass (wood) was the largest source of fuel for space heating until about 100 years ago. As wood became scarce in areas of heavy population concentrations and industrial development, it was replaced by coal and coke. Wood contains less energy per unit weight and is a less efficient fuel than coal. Given a choice of transporting either coal or wood to a distant market, therefore, the most economical alternative is coal. Wood is in high demand as a fuel today only in low energy, poorly developed societies where fossil fuels are too costly for use by the average family for cooking and space heating. Within many of the low energy societies, wood has declined in use because of forest depletion. In advanced societies, on the other hand, biomass is being considered as a direct source of fuel or more likely as a source of alcohol which might be used as a substitute for gasoline. Through use of large-scale harvesting, marketing, and processing techniques and improved technology (including new engine designs), alcohol may become competitive with gasoline. Engines designed for gasoline consumption cannot operate efficiently with more than a small mix of alcohol with gasoline.

In a number of areas, such as India and China, and in arid areas, where trees cannot grow and where forests have been depleted, animal and vegetable wastes are major sources of fuel. High energy societies such as the United States normally consider these products as waste disposal and pollution problems rather than as sources of energy. Recently, however, several cities have installed facilities to extract energy from organic wastes through using them to generate methane gas or by burning them to produce electricity. The process is expensive when the only consideration is cost per unit of energy produced, but such projects become more financially acceptable when costs of other means for disposing of the wastes as well as environmental costs of disposal are deducted from the price of such projects. Organic materials (including agricultural products such as grains and potatoes and the tall grasses of the savanna lands) may be used for production of alcohol — as demonstrated by brewery production of whiskey and beer.

Nearly 4,000 years ago the Egyptians were building sailing ships. Wind powered the voyages of conquest and trade which established ties between Europe and the Orient and which opened the Americas to European settlement. Wind also furnished the power, until recently, which pumped seawater from behind man-made dikes in the Netherlands and opened the *polder* lands (land reclaimed from the sea) for agriculture and other developments.

Because winds blow with greater consistency over the relatively smooth oceans than over irregular land surfaces and because other sources of energy have formally been available on land, wind power has historically found its greatest application on the sea. Land applications of wind energy have been restricted primarily to windmills for pumping water and in a few instances for grinding grain and generating electricity. Steam engines, and then diesel- and gasoline-powered engines, rapidly displaced most sailing vessels after 1850, and windmills have almost disappeared as sources or energy on land areas in the high energy societies. A few windmills have been preserved in The Netherlands because they attract tourists, but even the Dutch have turned to oil-based fuels and natural gas for pumping water from their polder lands.

Recent research in the use of wind energy has involved experimentation with huge windmills as well as with clusters of small windmills. Irregularity and variable velocity of wind and consequent problems of storage of wind energy for use during periods of calm continue to plague efforts to develop dependable supplies at competitive costs.

Tidal power depends on the damning of tidal basins which have wide openings to the sea and which narrow toward the head of the basin. Tidal ranges (differences between water levels at high and at low tides) vary with the configuration of individual basins or embayments, but the greater the range, the greater is the potential energy-generating capacity of the tidal facility. Because of the high cost and relatively low energy output of tidal power projects, they are not expected to become significant sources of energy. Even if all available tidal power sites in the world were to be developed, the energy produced would supply only a small fraction of the world's needs.

ENERGY-RICH AND ENERGY-POOR NATIONS

Most of the world's nations may be classed as energy rich or energy poor. Per capita production of energy in more than 90 percent of the world's nations is either more than double or less than half the world average (Fig. 11-2 and 11-3). Nations with a per capita output more than twice the world average contain less than 20 percent of the world's population, whereas those where per capita production is less than half the world average contain more than 70 percent of the world's people (Fig. 11-2). Nations where per capita output is less than the world average are primarily in Latin America, Africa, and southern and eastern Asia. Several European nations are also among the energy poor with respect to production of energy, for their domestic energy resources are meager.

The bipolarization of the world's nations into those which are energy rich and those which are energy poor is equally as pronounced in consumption as in production of energy (Fig. 11-2 and 11-3). No nation in Latin America or in Africa is among the energy rich in consumption, and only the small nations of Kuwait, Qatar, the United Arab Emirates, and Brunei are energy rich consumers in non-Soviet Asia (Fig. 11-3). In consumption as

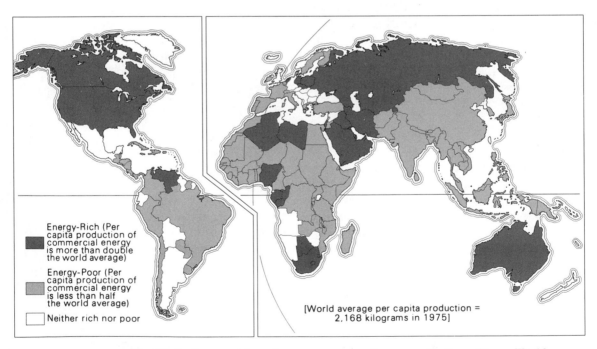

Energy-Rich (Per capita production of commercial energy is more than double the world average)

Energy-Poor (Per capita production of commercial energy is less than half the world average)

Neither rich nor poor

[World average per capita production = 2,168 kilograms in 1975]

Fig. 11-2. Energy-rich and energy-poor nations: production. (From *World Energy Supplies: 1971-1975*, United Nations, Series J, No. 30, 1977, Table 2.)

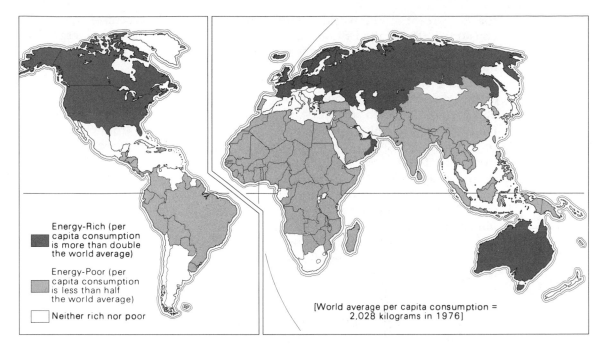

Fig. 11-3. Energy-rich and energy poor nations: consumption. (From *World Energy Supplies: 1971-1975, op, cit.,* Table 2.)

well as in production, approximately 20 percent of the world's people live in energy-rich nations; and 70 percent, in energy-poor nations.

Among the major petroleum-exporting nations only Kuwait, Qatar, and the United Arab Emirates are among the energy rich in per capita consumption, with Saudi Arabia, Iraq, Libya, Algeria, and Nigeria among those classed as energy poor. Venezuela, Iran, and Mexico, among the oil-exporting nations, are in the middle range of consumers.

Nations with highest per capita incomes are also the energy-rich nations. They include the United States, Canada, the northern European nations, the Soviet Union, and Australia. France, Sweden, and Finland are energy rich in consumption, although they are among the energy poor in production of energy. The United Kingdom, Norway, and West and East Germany are also among the energy-rich consumers, whereas they are of intermediate rank in per capita production of energy.

Only 11 nations (United States, Canada, The Netherlands, East Germany, Poland, the Soviet Union, Kuwait, Qatar, the United Arab Emirates, Brunei, and Australia) are energy rich in production and consumption. These nations contain fewer than 15 percent of the world's people, but they produced and consumed approximately 55 percent of the world's commercial energy during 1974. Together, the United States and the Soviet Union accounted for 42 percent of the world's energy produced and 47 percent of the energy consumed. The United States consumed about 16 percent more energy than it produced, whereas the Soviet Union produced approximately 14 percent more than it consumed.

Using the same criteria for 1950 as for 1974 to distinguish between energy-rich and energy-poor nations in energy consumption, it appears that considerable upward mobility occurred during the period. Five nations (Cuba, Iran, Mongolia, Greece, and Yugoslavia) advanced from energy poor to the middle category between rich and poor, two energy-poor areas (Bulgaria and the United Arab Emirates) advanced to energy-rich status, and seven nations (Kuwait, Qatar, France, The Netherlands, Finland, Norway, and the USSR) advanced from the middle category to energy-rich status. Only New Zealand dropped to a lower status, from energy rich to the middle category. In most instances the advance in rank was associated, at least in part, with development of domestic energy resources, especially oil and natural gas. This was especially true in the Persian Gulf nations, The Netherlands, and the USSR.

PATTERNS AND TRENDS IN WORLD PRODUCTION
AND CONSUMPTION OF ENERGY

World production and consumption of energy has increased steadily during recent history, although the rise has been most rapid since the beginning of the industrial revolution (1769) and especially since World War II. Between 1950 and 1976 world production and consumption of energy more than tripled, and significant shifts occurred in the regional distribution of output and use. Most of the developed nations, such as the United States and those in western Europe, declined substantially in energy self-sufficiency, whereas surplus energy production increased enormously in some of the developing areas (Table 11-1 and Fig. 11-4 and 11-5). Most nations with centrally planned economies (USSR, eastern Europe, China, Mongolia, Vietnam, and North Korea), on the other hand, maintained near self-sufficiency in energy supplies. The decline in self-sufficiency among the advanced nations did not occur because of decreased production but because of a rapid rise in consumption (compare Fig. 11-4 and 11-5). Indeed, although production within the developed market economies rose by 180 percent during the 25 years from 1950 through 1974, consumption increased by 257 percent.

The most spectacular increase in energy production between 1950 and 1976 occurred in the Middle East, where energy output rose by more than 1300 percent. Other major areas of surplus production during the period were in Algeria, Libya, Nigeria, Indonesia, and Venezuela. The Middle East

TABLE 11-1. Production and Consumption of Commercial
Energy: Selected Areas

AREA	PRODUCTION (Million Metric Tons of Coal Equivalents)		PERCENTAGE OF WORLD OUTPUT		CONSUMPTION (Million Metric Tons of Coal Equivalents)		PERCENTAGE OF WORLD TOTAL	
	1950	1976	1950	1976	1950	1976	1950	1976
WORLD	2,664	8,951	100.0	100.0	2,493	8,318	100.0	100.0
United States	1,165	2,050	43.7	22.9	1,114	2,485	44.7	29.9
Canada	31	259	1.2	2.9	73	230	2.9	2.8
Western Europe	507	680	19.0	7.6	574	1,573	23.0	18.9
USSR	285	1,674	10.7	18.7	287	1,350	11.5	16.2
Eastern Europe	186	488	7.0	5.5	160	573	6.4	6.9
Middle East	129	1,688	4.8	18.9	9	144	0.4	1.7
Africa	34	537	1.3	6.0	41	164	1.6	2.0
Latin America	162	429	6.1	5.0	62	342	2.5	4.8
Australia	19	120	0.7	1.3	25	91	1.0	1.1
Japan	44	38	1.7	0.4	46	415	1.8	5.0
China	43	615	1.6	6.9	43	590	1.7	7.1
India	34	121	1.3	1.4	35	133	1.4	1.6

AREA	CONSUMPTION AS PERCENTAGE OF PRODUCTION		ABSOLUTE CHANGE, 1950 TO 1976 (Million Metric Tons of Coal Equivalents)		RELATIVE CHANGE, 1950 TO 1976 (Percentage)	
	1950	1976	Production	Consumption	Production	Consumption
WORLD			6,287	5,825	336.0	333.7
United States	95.6	121.2	895	1,371	176.0	223.1
Canada	235.5	88.8	228	157	835.5	315.1
Western Europe	113.2	231.3	173	999	134.1	274.0
USSR	100.7	80.6	1,389	1,063	587.4	470.4
Eastern Europe	86.0	117.4	302	413	262.4	358.1
Middle East	7.0	8.5	1,559	135	1,308.5	1,600.0
Africa	120.6	30.5	503	123	1,579.4	400.0
Latin America	38.3	79.7	267	280	264.8	551.6
Australia	131.6	75.8	101	66	631.6	364.0
Japan	104.5	1092.1	− 6	369	86.4	902.2
China	100.0	95.9	572	447	1,430.2	1,372.1
India	102.9	109.9	87	98	355.9	380.0

SOURCES: *World Energy Supplies: 1950–1974* (New York: United Nations, 1976), Series J, No. 19,
Tables 1 and 2; and *Statistical Yearbook, 1977* (New York: United Nations, 1978), Table 142.

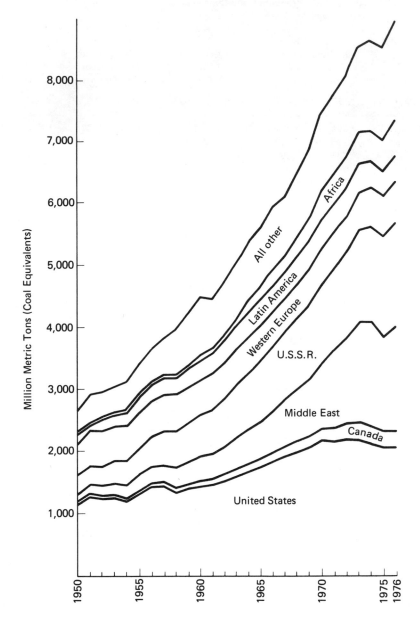

Fig. 11-4. Production of commercial energy: selected areas, 1950-1976. (From *World Energy Supplies: 1950-1974,* United Nations, Series J, No. 19, 1976, Tables 1 and 2; and *Statistical Yearbook, 1977* (New York: United Nations, 1978), Table 142.]

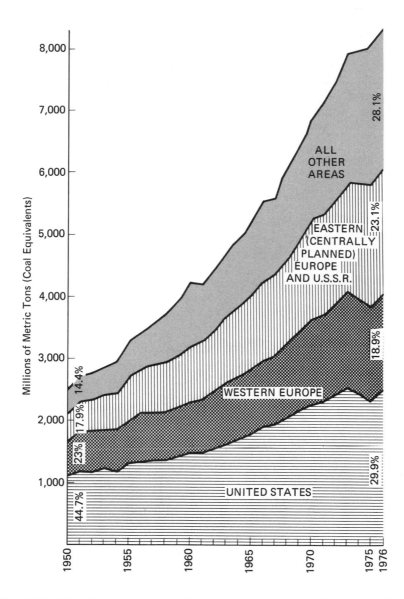

Fig. 11-5. World consumption of commercial energy, 1950–1976. (From *World Energy Supplies: 1950–1974, op. cit.,* Tables 1 and 2; *World Energy Supplies: 1971–1975, op. cit.,* Tables 1 and 2; and *Statistical Yearbook,* 1977, *op. cit.,* Table 142.)

was by far the largest exporter, however, and western Europe, the largest importer (Fig. 11-6).

Among the advanced nations Japan occupies the potentially most dangerous position. Japanese reserves and production of fossil fuels are small, and production actually declined between 1950 and 1976 (Table 11-1). At the same time, Japan's fuel consumption increased more than 900 percent. Japan imports energy from several areas (including coal from the

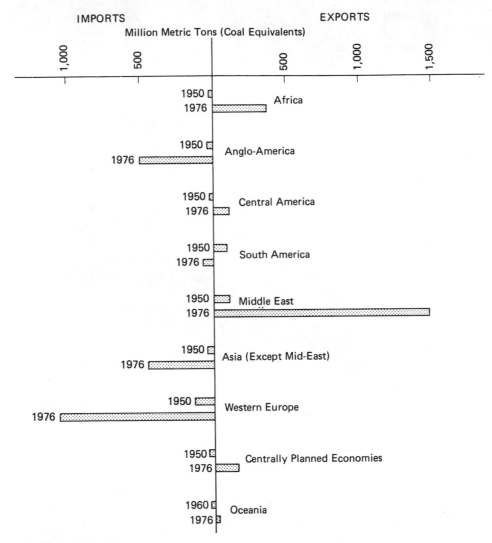

Fig. 11-6. Net imports (exports) of commercial energy, 1950 and 1976. Note the relatively small volume of imports (exports) during 1950, compared with 1976. (From *World Energy Supplies: 1950-1974, op. cit.,* Table 1; and *Statistical Yearbook, 1977, op. cit.,* Table 12.)

United States), but most of her energy needs are met by petroleum from the Middle East.

Production and consumption of energy among the developing nations of Africa, Latin America, and Asia also increased rapidly during the period. The rate of increase in African production was higher than that within any other major world region (Table 11-1). In Africa, Latin America, and Asia as well as in the Middle East and northern Africa most of the increased output during the period was exported to western Europe, the United States, and Japan.

In the world as a whole, per capita energy consumption increased by 106 percent (1,065 kilograms) between 1950 and 1976, compared with about 90 percent (2900 kilograms) in the developed market economies, 220 percent (280 kilograms) within the developing market economies, and 245 percent (1500 kilograms) within the centrally planned economies (Table 11-2 and Fig. 11-7). The rate of increase among developing market economies and centrally planned economies was more than double that within the devel-

TABLE 11-2. Per Capita Consumption of Commercial Energy: Selected Areas (Includes Coal, Petroleum, Natural Gas, Hydro-electricity, and Nuclear)

AREA	PER CAPITA CONSUMPTION (Kilograms)		AREA	PER CAPITA CONSUMPTION (Kilograms)	
	1950	*1976*		*1950*	*1976*
WORLD	1,004	2,069	India	99	218
United States	7,316	11,554	Indonesia	54	218
Canada	5,334	9,950	Bangladesh	–	32
Belgium	3,354	6,049	Thailand	22	308
Denmark	2,032	5,320	Iran	75	1,490
France	1,912	4,380	Iraq	141	725
West Germany	2,490	5,922	Saudi Arabia	164	1,901
Italy	417	3,284	Kuwait	1,332	9,198
Luxembourg	9,461	15,788	Mexico	567	1,227
The Netherlands	1,948	6,224	Cuba	480	1,225
United Kingdom	4,358	5,268	Argentina	787	1,804
Portugal	264	1,050	Bolivia	86	318
Sweden	2,061	6,046	Brazil	198	731
Bulgaria	469	4,710	Venezuela	901	2,838
Czechoslovakia	2,979	7,397	Algeria	172	729
East Germany	2,832	6,789	Libya	69	1,589
Poland	2,087	5,253	Egypt	251	473
USSR	1,593	5,259	Nigeria	26	94
Australia	3,098	6,657	Mali	–	27
Japan	554	3,670	Zaire	55	62
China	81	706	Kenya	71	152

SOURCES: *World Energy Supplies: 1950–1974,* United Nations, Series J, No. 19, 1976, Table 2; and *World Energy Supplies: 1971–1975,* United Nations, Series J, No. 20, Table 2.

oped market economies, but the absolute increase in the developed market economies was several times that among the other two groups of nations (Fig. 11-7). The developed nations, however, were consuming much more energy, per capita, in the base year of 1950 than either the developing nations or the centrally planned economies. Per capita energy consumption dropped by about 6 percent between 1973 and 1975 in the developed market economies following the 1973 oil embargo and a quadrupling of oil prices, whereas consumption increased by 6 and 8 percent, respectively, in

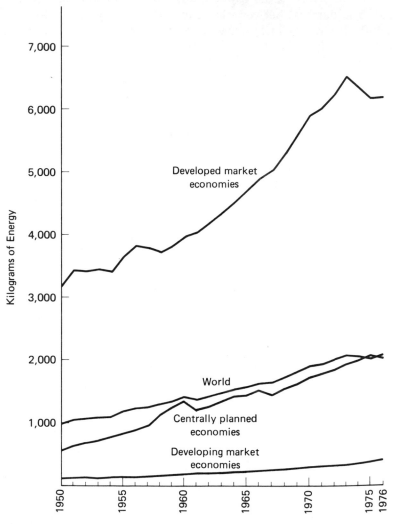

Fig. 11-7. Per capita energy consumption, 1950-1976. (From *World Energy Supplies, 1950-1974,* United Nations, *op. cit.,* Table 1: *World Energy Supplies, 1971-1975, op. cit.,* Table 1; and *Statistical Yearbook, 1977, op. cit.,* Table 142.)

the developing market and centrally planned economies. Following 1975, however, consumption in the developed market economies resumed its upward course.

PATTERNS AND TRENDS IN FORMS OF ENERGY PRODUCED AND CONSUMED

Changes Prior to 1950

During modern history several major changes have occurred in the forms of energy utilized in the world. Wood was the major source of energy for most of the world's people through the 1700s, but during the 1800s coal began to replace wood in nations undergoing the industrial revolution. Substitution of petroleum for coal began in the late 1800s, and more recently natural gas has captured a major share of the market formerly served by coal and petroleum. The world is currently in the initial stage of transferring from the fossil fuels to some other form, or forms, of energy, such as nuclear, solar, geothermal, wind, and tidal energy. The earlier transfers were prompted primarily by greater convenience of use, greater efficiency, or lower environmental costs of the new as compared to the previous energy form. As transfers were made from wood to coal to oil to natural gas, each successive form reflected improved efficiency in producing, processing, transporting, storing, and using energy. The world became accustomed to regular reductions in relative costs of energy. As each transfer was made, however, it was to an increasingly exhaustible form of energy. At the same time, world energy consumption was escalating. There was less concern for a long-term supply of energy than for an immediate abundance of low-cost energy. Current efforts to transfer energy dependence from oil and natural gas to other forms such as coal, nuclear, and solar energy represent a reversal in the long-term trends toward cheaper energy, for the transfers are being made largely out of necessity rather than for economy or efficiency.

Continued heavy dependence on the fossil fuels entails increasing vulnerability, especially among advanced nations which already import a large share of the energy they use, to economically and socially damaging fuel shortages. Additional problems include rapidly rising energy prices, decreased energy self-sufficiency, increased balance of payments problems, and perhaps less flexibility in matters of foreign policy.

Changes Since 1950. In 1950 coal accounted for 59.3 percent of the world's commercial energy; oil, 29.8 percent; and natural gas, 9.3 percent (Fig. 11–8). Petroleum first surpassed coal as a source of energy in 1965, and by 1976 it supplied nearly 49 percent of the world's energy compared with 30 percent from coal and about 19 percent from natural gas. Hydroelectric

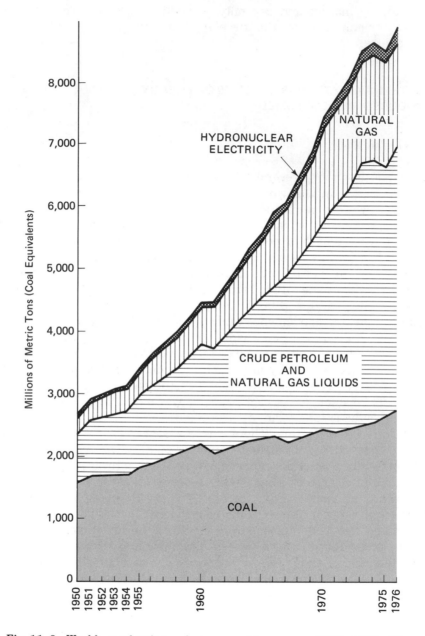

Fig. 11-8. World production of commercial energy, 1950–1976. (From *World Energy Supplies: 1950-1974*, United Nations, Series J, No. 19, 1976, Table 2; and *World Energy Supplies: 1971-1975*, United Nations, Series J, No. 20, 1977, Table 2.)

power supplied about 1.6 percent of the world's energy in 1950 and, together with nuclear power, about 2.5 percent in 1976.

The most persistent trend in energy consumption during 1950–1976 was
the shift from coal to petroleum as the primary energy source among the
world's nations (Fig. 11-9 and Table 11-3). In 1950 nearly all the "high
energy" nations as well as a few "low energy" nations in Africa and Asia de-

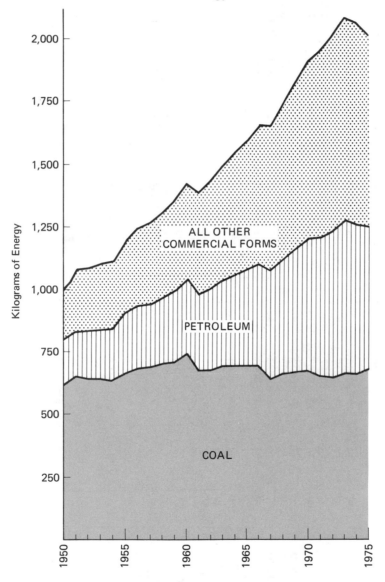

Fig. 11-9. Per capita world consumption of commercial energy, 1950–1975,
by type of energy. (From *World Energy Supplies: 1950–1974, op. cit.,* Table
1; and *World Energy Supplies: 1971–1975, op. cit.,* Table 1.)

TABLE 11-3. Production and per Capita Consumption of Fossil Fuels: Selected Areas

AREA	COAL Production[a] 1950	1970	1974	COAL Per Capita[b] Consumption 1950	1975	PETROLEUM Production[a] 1950	1970	1974	PETROLEUM Per Capita[b] Consumption 1950	1975	NATURAL GAS Production[a] 1950	1970	1974	NATURAL GAS Per Capita[b] Consumption 1950	1974
World	1980	2420	2513	618	665	795	3461	4248	175	579	247	1385	1675	74	324
United States	506	552	544	2932	2449	421	792	729	1829	3111	225	793	781	1094	2875
Canada	16	13	19	2918	1099	6	103	139	1143	3164	2	76	98	139	2052
Belgium	27	11	8	2978	1350	–	–	–	236	1859	Neg.	Neg.	Neg.	8	1131
France	52	39	25	1527	764	Neg.	4	3	214	1652	Neg.	9	10	5	334
West Germany	160	144	133	2387	1713	2	11	9	49	1741	Neg.	17	27	2	690
East Germany	44	79	75	2814	4961	–	Neg.	Neg.	10	826	–	2	10	–	613
United Kingdom	219	146	110	3958	2225	Neg.	Neg.	1	254	1349	–	15	46	–	632
The Netherlands	12	4	1	1622	248	1	3	2	210	1210	Neg.	42	111	1	2966
Poland	79	150	174	2049	4170	Neg.	1	1	15	338	Neg.	7	8	9	233
Romania	2	11	14	150	880	8	20	22	120	552	4	33	40	199	1427
USSR	220	450	494	1265	1918	56	519	675	180	1325	8	264	347	32	1025
Australia	19	53	67	2338	2970	–	13	30	472	1873	–	2	6	–	351
China	43	383	445	81	570	Neg.	30	96	–	73	–	2	4	–	4
India	33	75	85	85	161	Neg.	10	11	8	33	–	1	1	–	1
Saudi Arabia	–	–	–	NA	NA	39	280	627	106	589	–	3	4	–	367
Kuwait	–	–	–	NA	NA	25	224	191	879	1110	–	5	7	–	5675
Iran	Neg.	1	1	12	35	47	282	445	41	518	–	16	29	–	406
Iraq	–	–	–	0	0	10	112	143	91	336	–	1	2	–	121
Libya	–	–	–	5	–	–	235	110	41	643	–	Neg.	4	–	–
Algeria	Neg.	Neg.	Neg.	63	12	Neg.	71	74	69	175	–	4	7	–	171
Nigeria	1	Neg.	Neg.	19	4	–	80	164	4	47	–	Neg.	1	–	11
Gabon	–	–	–	–	–	–	8	15	–	593	–	Neg.	Neg.	–	89
Venezuela	Neg.	Neg.	Neg.	0	22	115	288	234	398	770	1	12	15	210	1000
Mexico	1	3	5	37	95	15	35	48	288	504	1	16	19	59	246
Argentina	Neg.	1	1	89	61	5	30	32	455	801	–	8	10	–	351
Indonesia	1	Neg.	Neg.	10	2	10	62	100	21	73	1	4	8	8	45

[a]Million metric tons: coal equivalent
[b]Kilograms
[c]Cubic meters

SOURCES: *World Energy Supplies: 1950-1974* (New York: United Nations, 1976), Series J, No. 19, Tables 2, 3, 6, and 15, and *World Energy Supplies: 1971-1975* (New York: United Nations, 1977), Series J, No. 20, Table 2.

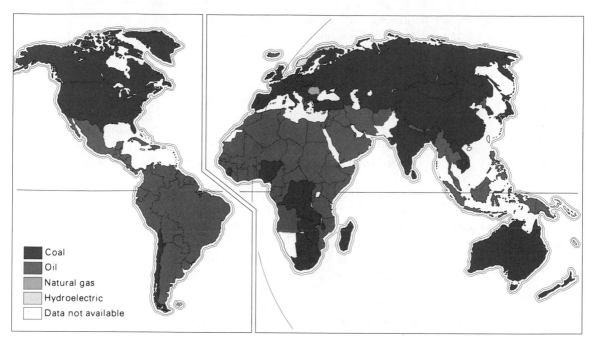

Fig. 11-10. Major types of energy consumed, 1950. (From *World Energy Supplies: 1971–1975, op. cit.*, Table 2.)

pended primarily on coal as their major source of energy (Fig. 11–10). Primary dependence on petroleum was virtually synonymous with relatively low levels of economic and technical development. By 1974, however, petroleum had surpassed coal as the first source of energy in developed as well as developing nations in nearly all the world (Fig. 11–11). Among the few nations with primary dependence on coal in 1974, Australia and South Korea had derived more energy from petroleum than from coal in 1973, and petroleum consumption was rising more rapidly than that of coal. In Yugoslavia, Hungary, and Bulgaria, as well, use of petroleum was nearly equal to that of coal and its consumption was rising more rapidly. Based upon 1950–1974 trends, the only nations obtaining most of their energy from coal by the 1980s would be South Africa, India, China, Mongolia, North Korea, Poland, Czechoslavakia, and East Germany. It is not that coal has declined in absolute production and consumption but that the bulk of the world's increased demand for energy since 1950 has been met by petroleum and natural gas (Fig. 11–8 and 11–9 and Table 11–3).

Among the factors which have resulted in the shift from coal to petroleum and natural gas are the following:

1. Increasing costs of mining coal, relative to costs of producing oil and gas.
2. Decreasing relative costs of transporting petroleum and natural gas.

3. Fewer problems with pollution and waste disposal from burning oil and, especially, natural gas relative to those encountered with use of coal.
4. Rapid growth in use of gasoline-powered engines (especially for use in automobiles and motor trucks).
5. Growth in economic and political power of multinational energy companies (during recent years the oil and gas companies have expanded their interests into coal and nuclear energy production).
6. Development of a wide range of new technology which depends on petroleum or natural gas as a fuel or raw material.
7. The greater convenience and economy of handling oil and gas.

Among the fossil fuels the greatest relative growth in production between 1950 and 1976 was in natural gas, whose output increased by 672 percent compared with a 548 percent increase for oil and 138 percent for coal. Natural gas burns cleanly, it leaves no residual waste, it burns in inexpensive furnaces that are almost free of maintenance, and it requires no storage facilities at the site of its use. For most purposes natural gas is an ideal fuel.

Prior to the 1920s natural gas was considered largely a nuisance by oil producers, and most of it was allowed to escape into the atmosphere or it

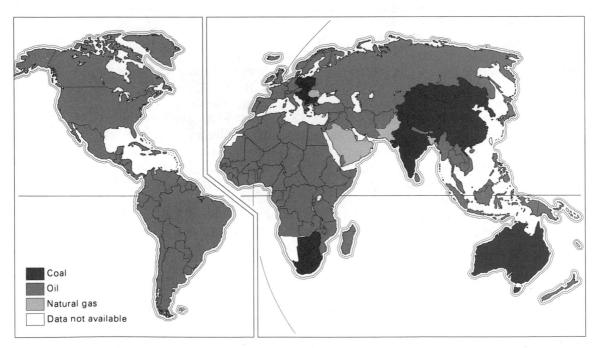

Coal
Oil
Natural gas
Data not available

Fig. 11-11. Major types of energy consumed, 1974. (From *World Energy Supplies: 1971-1975, op. cit.,* Table 2.)

was "flared off" (burned) at the oil well site. Advances in pipeline construction during the 1920s made it possible to transport natural gas at relatively low cost, but its use was not widespread until the 1940s. Supplies, however, had increased steadily along with growth in production of oil. Because it was available in such large surplus, it was offered at extremely low prices in order to encourage use, and its price remained artificially low into the late 1970s.

Even today in many oil-producing areas of Africa and the Middle East much gas produced in conjunction with oil is wasted. Relatively little natural gas has been involved in international trade. The problem is basically one of transportation, for it has not been possible to lay gas pipelines across broad oceans and its movement in a gaseous state by ship was not profitable until recently. Facilities for liquifying natural gas have been in operation since the 1940s, and specially designed tanker ships for transporting the gas have been in limited use since the 1960s [8].

COAL

Types

Three basic types of coal are produced. *Lignite* has the lowest energy content, and its uses are limited largely to space heating and the production of electricity. Although *bituminous* coal varies a great deal in quality, it has a higher energy content than lignite and is the most commonly used coal for space heating, in manufacturing, and for electric power generation. *Anthracite* coal has the highest carbon content; it burns longer and produces less smoke and solid residue than bituminous coal. Disadvantages of anthracite include its relative scarcity and higher mining costs.

Mining

Coal mining is accomplished by stripping, augering, or deep mining. *Strip mining* occurs where the coal lies near enough to the surface so that overlying materials (usually less than 200 feet thick) can be economically removed (Fig. 11-12). The advantages of strip mining are that all the coal in the exposed seam can be extracted, costs of mining are lower than by deep-mining methods, and there is less danger to miners from such deep mine hazards as gas explosions, cave-ins, flooding, and exposure to coal dust (black lung disease is a common ailment of deep miners). Also strip mines can begin producing coal within as little as 2 to 3 months after work on the mine begins, compared with 18 to 24 months for deep mines. The primary disadvantages of strip mining involve landscape disturbances, surface and groundwater pollution from mine acids and other wastes, and dangers resulting from erosion

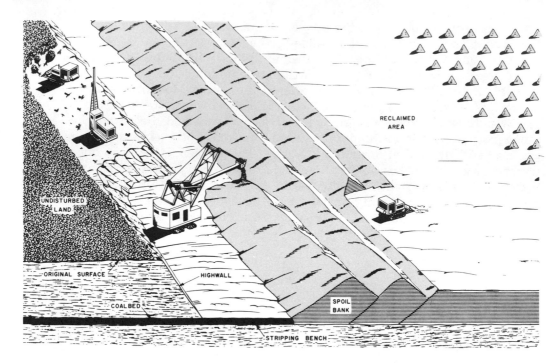

UNDISTURBED LAND

RECLAIMED AREA

ORIGINAL SURFACE   HIGHWALL

COALBED   SPOIL BANK

STRIPPING BENCH

Fig. 11-12. Area stripping mine with concurrent reclamation. (Courtesy, U.S. Department of the Interior.)

or sliding of *spoil banks* (mounds of loose materials removed from atop the coal seam). Recent legislation in the United States requires that strip-mined lands be restored to original surface conditions and that other precautions be taken against environmental hazards associated with the mining technique.

Auger mining normally follows strip mining. It involves the boring of large holes into that part of the coal seam above which overlying materials could not be economically removed (Fig. 11-13). After a notch has been cut in a hillside and the exposed coal removed, giant auger machines bore holes into that part of the seam which remains buried. Augering can extract only a portion of the coal, for the maximum distance holes can be bored into the seam is about 150 feet and the holes must be spaced far enough apart to prevent collapse of the overlying materials.

Deep mining occurs where the coal is too deeply buried for economic extraction by other methods. In most instances a shaft is sunk from the surface into the coal seam (Fig. 11-14). The coal is then removed, frequently by use of the *room-and-pillar* method, and lifted or hauled to the surface (Fig. 11-15). Because of the large amounts of coal left in the ground by the room-and-pillar method, other methods, such as longwall mining where the roof is allowed to break and fall following extraction of the coal, are gaining in popularity.

Fig. 11-13. Auger mining. (Courtesy, U.S. Department of the Interior, Bureau of Mines.)

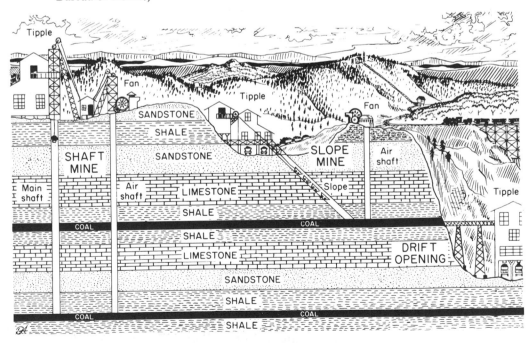

Fig. 11-14. The three types of underground coal mines. (From Bureau of Mines Diagram.)

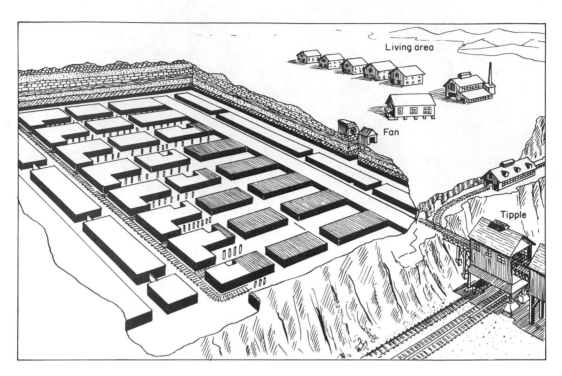

Fig. 11-15. Room-and-pillar system of mining a typical coal bed. (From Bureau of Mines Diagram.)

Transportation

One of the more significant factors in the shift from coal to oil and gas during recent decades is the relatively higher cost of transporting coal. Coal contains less energy and has a lower value per unit weight than oil, and as a solid it is more difficult and expensive to move by pipeline than oil or gas. Furthermore, most of the world's major energy-consuming areas are located within or near to regions that mine coal. Thus coal is more likely than oil or gas to be used within a radius of 200 to 500 miles of its place of production. Moreover, whereas less than 10 percent of the world's coal output enters international trade, the comparable figure for petroleum is more than 50 percent. Use of unit trains during recent years has extended the distance over which coal can be transported, but land movements of more than 500 miles remain the exception.

Major Producing Regions

Approximately 90 percent of the world's fossil fuel resources consist of coal. The bulk of the world's coal reserves and output occur within the mid-

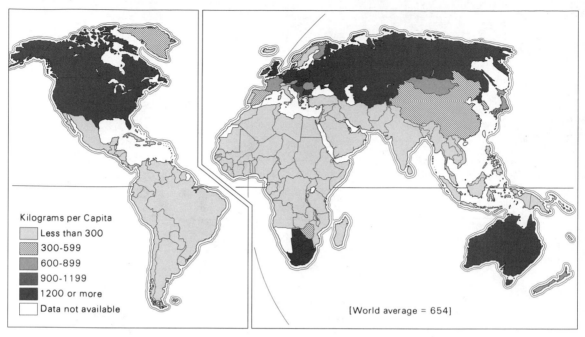

Fig. 11-16. Per capita consumption of coal, 1974. (From *World Energy Supplies: 1950-1974, op. cit.,* Table 3.)

dle latitudes of the northern hemisphere (Fig. 11-16 and 11-17). The Soviet Union and the United States together possess about 75 percent of the world's known bituminous and lignite reserves; and China, nearly 10 percent. Canada and western Europe contain most of the remainder, with Africa, Oceania, and Latin America together possessing only about 2.5 percent of world reserves. Availability of large coal reserves is one of the more important factors involved in the development and growth of industrial output within the middle latitude areas of the northern hemisphere, and it enabled those areas to outdistance most of the rest of the world significantly in such economic indicators as per capita gross national product, level of consumption, and life expectancy. The Soviet Union leads all other nations in tonnage of coal produced, but based upon energy content the United States is the world's leader in coal production. This is because the Soviet Union produces much larger amounts of lignite and low-grade bituminous coal than the United States.

United States. In no other nation are physical conditions so favorable for the mining of coal as in the major coal fields of the United States. The Appalachian bituminous field, stretching from New York southward into Alabama, contains enormous reserves of high-grade bituminous coal lying

Fig. 11-17. Major coal fields of the world.

Scotland
Midlands   North-
S. Wales   umberland   Tula
Sambre Meuse Ruhr   Silesia   Pechora
                              Donets

Karaganda

Kuznets   Central
           Siberian   Irkutsk

                       Fushun
Shensi·Basin
                       Tatung
Szechwan   Huainan
Damodar

Wankie

Pretoria
Natal

Rockhampton
Newcastle

near the surface in relatively thick, undisturbed seams. In many places the coal is near enough to the surface to be strip-mined. The rapid increase in stripping has resulted in Kentucky, where most of the coal is strip-mined, replacing West Virginia, where most of the coal is extracted from underground mines, as the leading producing state in the nation. In 1969, for example, Kentucky produced 109 million tons of coal and West Virginia, 141 million tons. In 1977 Kentucky produced 142.9 million tons and West Virginia, 95.4 million tons. An additional problem handicapping the coal industry of much of the northeastern United States is the deterioration of the region's railroads. Roadbeds in much of the eastern United States are in such poor condition that trains using them are forced to travel at low speeds.

Because of favorable geological conditions within the Appalachian field,

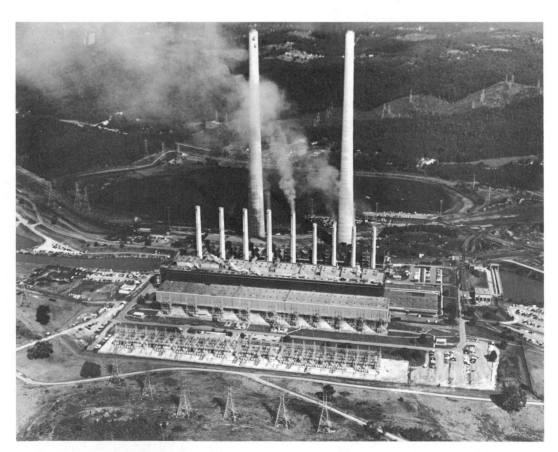

Coal-fired steam electric plant at Kingston, Tennessee. (Courtesy, Tennessee Valley Authority.)

it has been possible to mechanize the mines heavily. Mechanization, along with the high percentage of coal produced by low-cost strip mining, gives the United States the highest output of coal per worker per day of any nation in the world. The Appalachian field accounts for about 75 percent of the nation's coal.

The eastern interior coal field, stretching from northern Illinois through southern Indiana and eastern Kentucky, is the nation's second largest producing field. Here, and in most of the Appalachian field, however, the coal is relatively high in sulfur content. When burned it emits large quantities of sulfur dioxide (SO_2), which is potentially damaging to human health. Congressional legislation and court-supported regulations of the Environmental Protection Agency have placed strict limitations upon the amount of SO_2 that can be released into the atmosphere by industries or by coal-fired electricity-generating plants. These plants and industries have been forced either to install expensive devices to remove the SO_2 from emissions or to burn relatively high-cost, low-sulfur coal. Low-sulfur coal is available in quantity only from deep mines in the East and from western states such as Wyoming. Unit trains haul western low-sulfur coal to eastern markets, where it sells for premium prices. A new *fluidized-bed* process, in which coal is burned in a mixture of pulverized limestone, may greatly reduce sulfur emissions and permit wider use of Appalachian and other eastern United States coals.

Additional coal mining regions in the United States include the western interior field, which stretches from Iowa southward into Arkansas and Oklahoma, the huge lignite deposits of the Dakotas and Montana, and various other fields in the several western states. With the exception of cases such as Wyoming, however, where thick seams of low-sulfur coal can be exploited at relatively low cost, deposits located to the west of the Mississippi River are too far from major markets or they are too low in quality to justify large-scale exploitation.

Soviet Union. The major problem in the coal industry of the Soviet Union is that nearly all minable deposits are located long distances from major markets. About 90 percent of Soviet coal is located to the east of the Urals, *whereas* the bulk of the population lives to the west of the Urals. The Donets Basin coal field, near the Black Sea, is the most heavily mined field in the country, although it contains less than 3 percent of the nation's reserves. It has the best market location of any major deposit in the nation, however, and the coal is of coking quality.

The Kuznets Basin, located in south–central Siberia, is the nation's second most productive field. It contains huge reserves of high-quality coal, some of which can be strip-mined. Much of the coal produced in this region is hauled westward to the southern Ural Mountains, a distance of more than 1,200 miles. During the 1930s and 1940s when steam locomotives were used

Strip mining of coal near Paradise Steam Plant in Kentucky. (Courtesy, Tennessee Valley Authority.)

to move the coal, approximately one-fourth of the amount leaving the Kuznets was burned as fuel in reaching the industrial areas of the southern Urals.

Additional areas producing significant amounts of coal include the Moscow, Pechora, and Karaganda basins, the Ural region, and a number of sites scattered along the Transiberian Railway between the Kuznets Basin and Vladivostok on the Pacific Coast (Fig. 11-17). With the exception of the Pechora and Karaganda basins, and a few locations to the east of Kuznets, most of the coal is of low quality. Huge reserves of low-grade coal also underlie the Central Siberian Plateau, but severe climate and remoteness have retarded development of mining activities.

China. The bulk of China's coal output occurs in the northeastern portion of the nation, although mining is widely distributed over the most populous areas. Some of the more significant producing areas are the Fushun, Shensi Basin, Szechwan Basin, and Hainan areas. Unlike coal production in most highly developed nations such as the United States, much of China's output comes from relatively small mining operations that serve local agricultural communities and industries. Small mines, widely scattered through the country, help to compensate for lack of adequate transportation facilities and to promote the dispersion of industrial facilities and power plants [9].

United Kingdom. Coal was a commonly used manufacturing fuel in Great Britain as early as the thirteenth century, but its large-scale production began after 1709 when methods were discovered for using it in the production of iron. Development of the steam engine in 1769 and of steamships and locomotives a short time later not only added new markets for coal but provided means for transporting the fuel over greatly increased distances at much lower costs than previously. British production and consumption of coal grew markedly, as the nation led the world into the industrial revolution. British coal supplied not only domestic markets but until after World War I it was a major export commodity. Location of coal deposits along the coast, combined with ownership of the world's largest fleet and political and financial control of a far-flung empire, gave Britain a preeminent position among the world's nations. Following World War I, British coal exports declined sharply. Petroleum was beginning to compete effectively with coal as a fuel, and mining costs in Britain were rising because of the increasing depth of mines, high labor costs, and difficulties in extracting coal from thin, faulted seams. The major producing areas are in Scotland, the Northumberland and Durham fields in northeastern England, the Midlands, central England, and south Wales.

Europe. In Europe the Westphalian, Silesian, and Sambre Meuse are the most important coal fields. The Ruhr Valley is the most famous producing area within the Westphalian field, and West Germany led all other European nations in production until the early 1970s when Poland became the preeminent European producer.

The Sambre Meuse field extends through northern France, southern Belgium, Luxembourg, and into the southernmost tip of the Netherlands. All of these nations are deficient in coal output. Mining is difficult and expensive, for the coal is deeply buried. Seams are broken and often dip steeply away from the surface.

The Silesian field supplies coal to Poland, Czechoslovakia, and East Germany. Mining conditions in Silesia are the best in Europe, with seams which are shallower, thicker, and more conducive to mechanized mining techniques than other large fields.

Other Areas. Additional coal fields of particular significance include the fields in the Damodar area, near Calcutta, India. Australia exports nearly half of its coal output, which comes primarily from fields near the east coast in southern Queensland and around Newcastle. Japan is Australia's major customer. In South Africa coal is produced near Pretoria and Natal, and the Wankie field accounts for most of Rhodesia's output. Latin American production comes primarily from the Coahuila field in Mexico, the Belencito field in Colombia, the Santa Catarina field in southern Brazil, and the Arauco field near Concepción in Chile.

Trade

In international coal movements there are two major importing areas — western Europe and Japan — and three major exporting areas — the United States, eastern Europe, and Australia. Whereas most petroleum exports move from developing to developed areas, most coal movements are from one part of the developed world to another (Fig. 11–18 and Table 11–4). Because the developed nations contain most of the world's coal reserves, it is unlikely that this general pattern of movement will change.

Coal is a bulky material, and the cost of transporting a given amount of energy in the form of coal is more expensive than moving an equivalent amount in the form of petroleum. The major exporting nations are those which can mine the fuel with exceptional efficiency near coastal areas or where export markets may be reached after a short overland haul. Coal which is imported by ocean ship (shipments from the United States to western Europe) is usually consumed in or near to the importing ports.

The United States is the major coal-exporting nation, accounting for approximately 25 percent of all coal entering international trade. Japan received nearly 45 percent of United States' exports in 1974, followed by

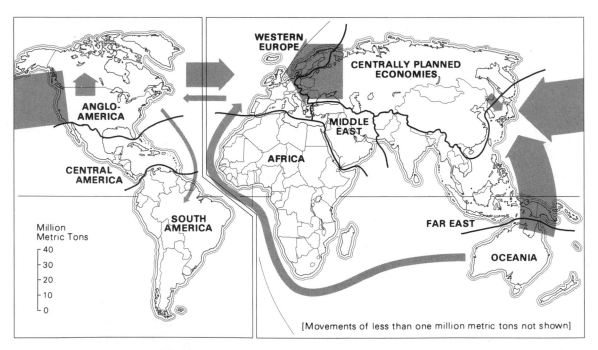

Fig. 11-18. Major international coal movements, 1974. (From *World Energy Supplies: 1950-1974, op. cit.,* Table 4.)

TABLE 11–4. Major Exporters and Importers of Coal

| EXPORTERS | THOUSANDS OF METRIC TONS | | IMPORTERS | THOUSANDS OF METRIC TONS | | PERCENTAGE OF WORLD TOTAL |
	1971	*1974*		*1971*	*1974*	*1974*
United States	53,280	56,145	Japan	46,505	63,930	28.70
Poland	33,525	43,985	France	16,415	19,960	08.96
USSR	29,050	30,435	Canada	16,815	13,465	16.04
West Germany	22,995	29,130	Belgium	9,615	13,435	06.03
Australia	20,275	29,570	Italy	11,960	12,930	05.80
			East Germany	11,035	11,105	04.98
WORLD TOTAL	188,495	222,780	USSR	9,125	10,185	04.57
			TOTALS	121,470	145,010	65.09

Source: *World Energy Supplies: 1950–1974,* United Nations, Series J, No. 19, 1976, Table 4.

western Europe, which received 26.2 percent, and Canada, which received about 24 percent (Fig. 11–18). Poland accounted for 20 percent of world exports, nearly 52 percent of which went to western Europe. About 60 percent of the Soviet Union's exports went to satellite nations in eastern Europe and 27 percent to western Europe. Japan received more than 78 percent of Australia's exports and western Europe, most of the remainder.

PETROLEUM AND NATURAL GAS

Petroleum and natural gas are often found together. Gas, the lighter element, rests atop the oil. The oil and gas industries have traditionally been high risk industries, for despite the advances which have been made in exploration technology the only method for proving the existence of an oil or gas deposit is by drilling. The industry has been characterized by the acquisition and loss of great fortunes and during recent decades by the rising dominance of a few huge multinational corporations which control oil and gas from the producing wells to the final consumer. These corporations are now more appropriately labeled "energy companies," for they have diversified their interests into natural gas, coal, uranium and nuclear power plants, shale oil, and even solar energy. The huge financial and technical resources of such corporations provide them with protection against the high risks associated with oil and gas exploration.

Until recently the only source of information available concerning oil and gas reserves of the United States was from the companies themselves. Because of increasing governmental involvement in energy problems since the oil embargo of the early 1970s, however, the federal government is now attempting to make its own estimates of reserves.

Approximately two-thirds of all the wells drilled in the world in search of petroleum have been drilled in the United States, although the United States contains only about 10 percent of the area considered favorable for petroleum [10]. The United States and Canada also contain more than 70 percent of the oil and gas fields discovered in the world [11]. Most recently discovered fields and wells in the United States are relatively small, however, reflecting the advanced state of oil and gas development on the North American continent [12]. It is likely that almost all major discoveries in the future will be made outside the United States and Canada.

The actual sizes of remaining reserves of oil and gas in the world are little more than educated guesses. As with most other minerals, reserve estimates are often based upon how much is known to be obtainable at a certain cost or which can be profitably sold at a particular price. By increasing the price, recoverable reserves can frequently be multiplied. It does appear certain, however, that the energy content of the world's oil and gas reserves is substantially less than that of the world's coal. Because of the value of petroleum products in lubrication and as a raw material in the production of a wide variety of products such as plastics, fibers, soaps, and medical supplies, it is sometimes suggested that its use as a fuel should be terminated. Because of their versatility, convenience, and widespread use, however, a significant decline in consumption of oil and gas is unlikely without rigid governmental controls over their use or unless their prices become substantially higher than those of competing fuels.

Major Producing Areas

Enormous changes have occurred in the location of oil production since 1950, but the major areas of consumption remain relatively the same. The quantities of petroleum entering international commerce have increased vastly year by year. Most of it moves in huge supertankers, each carrying millions of gallons. The shift in areas of production is unprecedented in world history, as has been the immensity of the transfer in control over world financial resources. Tens of billions of dollars are exchanged annually between importing nations such as the United States, Japan, and those of western Europe and exporting nations in the Middle East, Africa, and Indonesia. Many recipients of these petro-dollars are only shortly removed from, or remain in, states of intense poverty. Much of the new-found income is squandered by wealthy sheiks and princes on military arms and personal extravagances. Much is also reinvested in the economically advanced oil-consuming nations.

The most outstanding area of oil production at present, and probably during the next two or three decades, is the region immediately adjacent to the Persian Gulf (Fig. 11-19). This region possesses approximately 60 percent of the world's known reserves. Tiny Kuwait, which is about the same size as the combined areas of Connecticut and Rhode Island, contains more than double the proved reserves reported for the United States. Saudi Arabia has the largest reserves (with the possible exception of Mexico) and is the largest producer, followed by Iran, Kuwait, and Iraq. Although much of the natural gas produced in the Middle East is wasted, domestic consumption is rising rapidly and exports of liquified gas have begun. Gas is produced in conjunction with oil and costs of producing both fuels are low. Production costs per barrel of oil in 1974 were only about $0.12 to 0.14, as the oil is relatively easy to find, it is near the surface, and the pools are huge.

Almost directly north of the Persian Gulf is the Caspian Sea, near to and within which the Soviet Union has long produced large amounts of oil and gas. Known gas reserves in the Soviet Union are the largest in the world, and known oil reserves are larger than those of the United States. Large-scale oil production began around Baku, on the Caspian Sea, but the major producing region at present is the Volga–Ural field, about 1,250 miles north of Baku and 400 miles north of the Caspian. Oil output is also expanding rapidly in the West Siberian field, which centers on the city of Tyumen. Gas is produced in all the major oil-producing areas, as well as in a relatively new gas field near Salekhard, on the Arctic Circle near the Ob River embayment. Large gas reserves are also known to exist in the Lena River area near Zhigansk, but little development has taken place to date.

Extensive pipeline systems have been built to move oil and gas to major population centers in the Soviet Union, with oil being piped as far west as Berlin. A huge pipeline extends westward from the gas fields near Salekhard, with a branch line running to the port of Murmansk on the Kola Peninsula. The Soviets expect to export liquified natural gas from the port, with some of it moving to the United States.

Westward from the Persian Gulf, in northern Africa, major oil and gas fields are found in Libya and Algeria. Libya is the larger producer, and most exports from both nations go to western Europe. Small supplies of liquified natural gas have started moving between Libya and Algeria to western Europe and the United States.

To the south of the Sahara, oil fields are being developed in Nigeria, Gabon, and Angola. Nigerian reserves are primarily in the southeastern portion of the country in Biafra. The desire of Nigeria to maintain possession of the economic benefits of the oil in that region was an important factor in the civil war which developed as the result of Biafra's abortive attempt to secede from Nigeria during 1966. Nigeria supplied oil to the United States during the Arab nation embargo in 1973, and afterward Nigeria became the leading source of oil imported into the United States.

Gabon, the Republic of the Congo, and Angola have also been sites of rapidly expanding oil output during recent years. These producing areas, along with those in Nigeria, have been developed almost entirely since 1960.

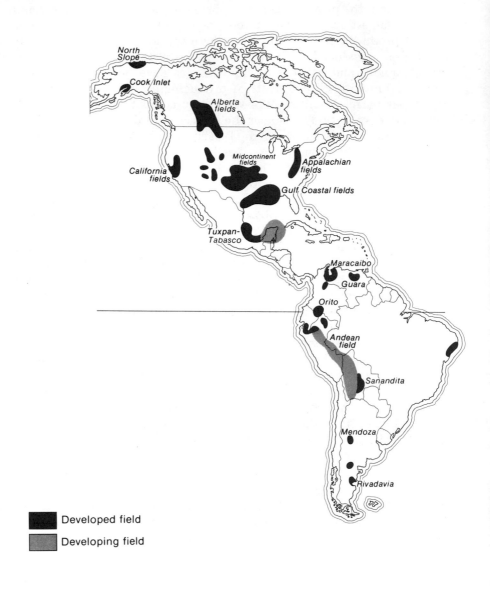

Fig. 11-19. Principal oil fields of the world.

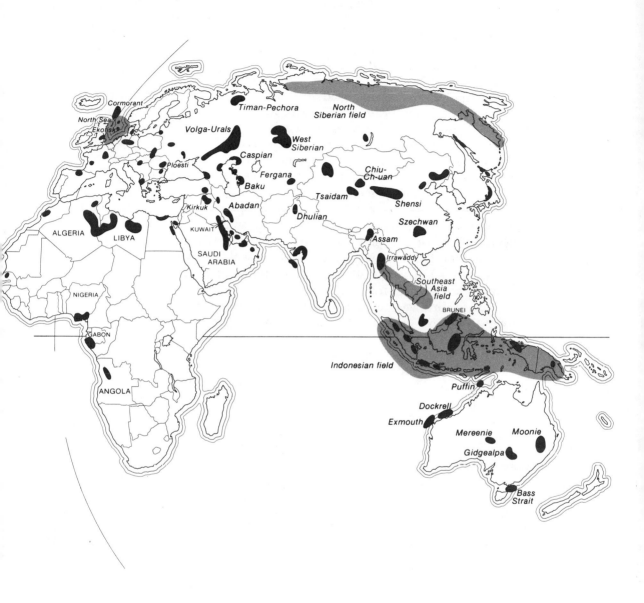

Cormorant

Timan-Pechora

North Siberian field

North Sea

Ekofisk

Volga-Urals

West Siberian

Ploesti

Caspian

Fergana

Chiu-Ch'uan

Baku

Tsaidam

Shensi

ALGERIA

LIBYA

Kirkuk

Abadan

Dhulian

Szechwan

KUWAIT

Assam

SAUDI ARABIA

Irrawaddy

Southeast Asia field

BRUNEI

NIGERIA

GABON

Indonesian field

Puffin

ANGOLA

Dockrell

Exmouth

Mereenie

Moonie

Gidgealpa

Bass Strait

They have provided Africa, south of the Sahara, with its first significant fossil fuel production other than the coal produced in the heretofore white dominated territories of South Africa and Rhodesia. In addition to oil, Nigeria and Gabon are now marketing appreciable amounts of natural gas.

In southern and eastern Asia the chief oil-producing areas are in western China and Indonesia, whereas natural gas has become a major fuel in Afghanistan, Pakistan, Bangladesh, and Indonesia. China has recently become a small exporter of oil, and Indonesia is the site of one of the world's largest oil and gas exploration and development programs — primarily in offshore locations. Japan is an eager observer of Indonesian developments, for Indonesia could provide a feasible alternative to the nation's near complete dependence for oil upon Middle Eastern suppliers.

Australia is another recent entrant into the business of producing oil and gas. Proved reserves are not large, but developments since the middle 1960s have been sufficient so that national fuel consumption is now almost equally balanced between oil and coal. Most of the petroleum is produced from offshore deposits in the southeast, in the Bass Strait, whereas gas reserves are being exploited in the strait and in the interior fields at Gidgealpa. Although prospects seem good for additional production from the offshore field at Exmouth (northwest coast), recent discoveries have not kept pace with growing demand and the Australian government is sadly anticipating an increase in imports.

Known oil and gas reserves of Latin America are substantial. Mexico and Venezuela have lengthy histories as petroleum exporters, although Mexican exports dropped to minor quantities prior to and following nationalization of the nation's oil industries during 1938. Because Mexican reserves were thought to be small, as late as 1972 it was projected that Mexico would become a net importer during the 1980s [13]. In 1973, however, a chain of discoveries began which by the end of 1978 led to estimates of potential reserves of as much as 700 billion barrels [14]. Saudi Arabia's proved reserves, by comparison, are about 150 billion barrels, and those of the entire Persian Gulf area are about 400 billion barrels. Most of the new Mexican finds extend southward from the older producing areas around Tampico and Veracruz into Guatemala and then in a great arc along an ancient barrier reef around the Yucatan Peninsula. The oil is being explored for and developed by Pemex, a company established by the Mexican government when the industry was nationalized. In addition to oil, the Mexican fields contain great quantities of natural gas. The United States would seem to be a natural market for much of Mexico's surplus oil and gas, a matter which is certain to be a major item of negotiation between the two countries during the 1980s.

Because the Mexican reserves had been only slightly developed, Venezuela was producing more than half of Latin America's petroleum output during the late 1970s. About 90 percent of Venezuela's oil is exported, primarily to the United States and western Europe. The major producing area is in and around Lake Maracaibo. A second producing district to the east of Caracas is in early stages of development. The Venezuelan economy is heavily dependent on oil exports. Reserves are limited, however, and in an effort to increase domestic benefits from oil production the nation has begun a program designed to phase out foreign oil companies and to phase in domestic companies.

Colombia, Ecuador, and Bolivia also export oil. Development of a new field in the interior permitted Ecuador to become the second largest oil exporter in Latin America during the late 1970s, whereas the nation was a net importer in 1972.

The only net exporter of petroleum among European nations is Albania, and the quantity exported is small. The Netherlands and Poland are the only net energy exporters. The Dutch export natural gas, primarily from the Groningen field, and the Poles export coal, primarily from Silesia. Romania, once a surplus producer of oil, is now a net importer. In western Europe the greatest potential for oil production is apparently from underneath the North Sea, within which boundaries of territorial rights were established during 1958 among the British, Norwegians, Dutch, Germans, and Danes (Fig. 11-20). Most oil discoveries have occurred along a north–south line which divides the North Sea approximately in half, and the bulk of the gas is in the sector extending westward from the Netherlands toward Great Britain. The British expect to be self-sufficient in oil production by 1980. Because most of the reserves appear to be located off the coast of Scotland, a strong movement is underway to give independent Commonwealth status, along with the oil, to Scotland.

The United States led the world in oil production until 1974, when the Soviet Union became the world's leading producer. The peak year in United States oil output was 1970, with output declining some 15 percent by 1977. Production of natural gas in the United States remains about double that of any other nation, although output peaked in 1973 and has declined since. The United States became a net importer of petroleum products in 1948. At that time Venezuela was the major source of imports, but since then the major sources have shifted to Nigeria, Saudi Arabia, and Canada. During recent years imports from Canada have declined, with sources shifting more and more toward Africa and the Middle East. Canada remains the only major source of imported natural gas for the United States.

The northern Appalachians was the first commercial oil-producing area in the United States. Soon afterward production began in Ohio and in other midwestern states, followed by developments in Texas, Louisiana, Oklahoma, Kansas, and California. Largest output occurs in Texas, which produces about 40 percent of the nation's oil (Table 11-5). Louisiana

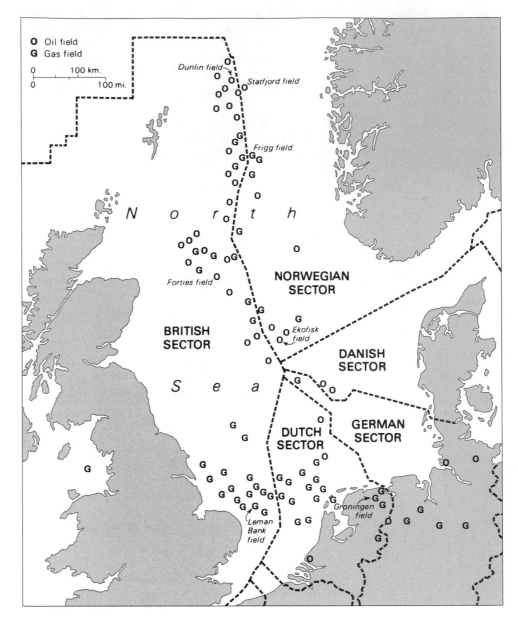

Fig. 11-20. North Sea territorial rights and oil and gas fields. (From Rick Gore, "Striking It Rich in the North Sea," *National Geographic*, 151, No. 4, April, 1977, p. 525.)

TABLE 11–5. Oil and Gas Output for Selected States in the United
States: 1964, 1974, and 1977

STATE	OIL (Million Barrels)			NATURAL GAS (Billion Cubic Feet)		
	1964	*1974*	*1977*	*1964*	*1974*	*1977*
Texas	990	1,262	1,138	6,490	8,171	7,051
Louisiana	549	737	563	4,153	7,754	7,218
California	300	323	350	660	365	345
Oklahoma	203	178	156	1,316	1,639	1,769
Wyoming	139	140	112	232	327	264
New Mexico	114	99	87	874	1,245	1,196
Alaska	—	71	169	—	129	173
Kansas	106	59	58	764	887	781
TOTAL, United States	2,787	3,203	2,985	15,462	21,601	19,942

SOURCE: U.S. Bureau of Mines.

accounts for about 20 percent; California, about 10 percent; and Oklahoma, about 5 percent. Other major producing states are Wyoming, New Mexico, Alaska, Kansas, Mississippi, Colorado, Utah, and Montana.

The leading oil-producing states are also the largest producers of natural gas, although their rank in gas production varies somewhat from their rank in oil output (Table 11–5). The Appalachian region accounts for a larger share of the nation's oil than gas output, and California is less important as a gas than as an oil producer. Both fuels are produced in large quantities in the Gulf of Mexico and off the California coast, and production off the Atlantic Coast—especially near New Jersey and New York—is in initial stages of development.

Alaska is beginning to produce large amounts of oil, and natural gas is soon to follow. The major Alaskan producing region is near Prudhoe Bay in the North Slope fields. The oil is transported through a pipeline which crosses the state and opens onto the Pacific Ocean. The pipeline crosses two major mountain ranges, fault (earthquake) zones, and huge areas of permanently frozen subsoil. Oil is then moved by ocean tanker to ports in California and Washington. Some of it goes through the Panama Canal to Atlantic ports for distribution within the eastern United States. Alaskan natural gas is to be moved through a pipeline across Canada into the western United States, where it will enter the primary national distribution system. Some Alaskan oil, at least for a time, is being sold to Japan because present transcontinental pipelines do not have adequate capacity for moving Alaska's full output into interior and eastern markets and because of the cost and environmental risks involved in shipping the oil by ocean tankers to east coast ports.

Canada's oil and gas production occurs primarily in Alberta around

Edmonton, but output also occurs in the neighboring provinces of Saskatchewan and British Columbia. The oil is moved to markets in Eastern Canada by a pipeline which runs through northern Minnesota to the south of Lake Superior and finally reenters Canada south of Lake Huron. Until recently considerable amounts of Canadian oil were sold to consumers in the upper Great Lakes states, but increasing demands in Canada have virtually eliminated such sales. Gas produced in western Canada also moves eastward by a pipeline which branches into two lines at Winnipeg, one following a route just north of Lake Superior and Lake Huron and the other following the route of the oil pipeline. Large amounts of Canadian gas are also moved by pipeline into the western United States.

Trade

Petroleum. In 1975 the Middle East accounted for 63 percent of all petroleum entering international trade, followed by Africa with 16 percent and Latin America with about 7 percent (Fig. 11-21). The major exporting nations were Saudi Arabia, Iran, Iraq, and Kuwait, which together accounted for 54 percent of the world's exports (Table 11-6). Nigeria has risen rapidly as a petroleum exporter during recent years and in the mid-1970s became

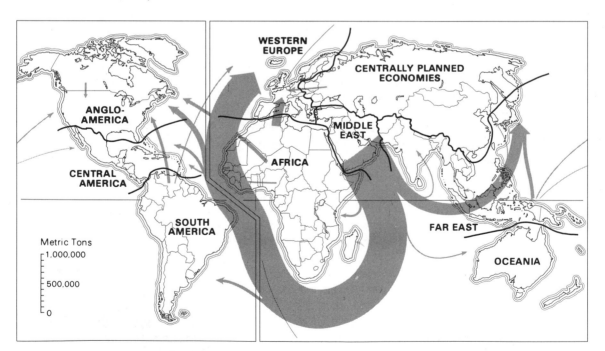

Fig. 11-21. Major international petroleum movements, 1974. (From *World Energy Supplies: 1950-1974, op. cit.,* Table 7.)

TABLE 11-6. Major Petroleum Exporting Nations: 1971, 1974, and 1975 (Thousands of Metric Tons)

NATION	1971	1974	1975	PERCENTAGE OF WORLD TOTAL 1974	PERCENTAGE OF WORLD TOTAL 1975
Saudi Arabia	209,910	394,410	328,194	25.6	23.3
Iran	198,800	268,580	233,720	17.4	16.6
Kuwait	140,000	111,490	90,940	7.2	6.5
Nigeria	72,460	108,760	84,910	7.0	6.0
Venezuela	121,270	92,450	76,720	6.0	5.4
Iraq	79,400	90,880	103,220	5.8	7.3
United Arab Emirates	50,730	81,690	80,380	5.3	5.7
Libya	130,810	72,110	69,180	4.7	4.9
TOTAL	1,003,380	1,220,370	1,067,260	79.1	75.7
WORLD TOTAL	1,266,710	1,542,730	1,409,260		

SOURCES: *World Energy Supplies: 1950-1974,* United Nations, Series J, No. 19, Table 7; and *World Energy Supplies, 1971-1975,* United Nations, Series J, No. 20, 1977, Table 7.

the major source of imported petroleum for the United States. Exports from Kuwait, Libya, and Venezuela have declined, as these nations have chosen to restrict output in order to lengthen the life of their reserves (and perhaps to conserve the oil in anticipation that it will increase in value).

The major importing nations are Japan, the United States, and the nations of western Europe (Table 11-7). Among these nations, imports by the United States have grown most rapidly during recent years. The steep rise in imports during the late 1960s and the 1970s contributed heavily to a negative balance of trade for the United States and caused a resounding shock effect upon many governmental officials and other leaders. The United States had begun to encounter a negative energy supply–demand situation that Europeans and Japanese had faced for decades. The new energy policies adopted by the United States during the late 1970s, therefore, reflected the early stages of an adjustment to shortages of domestically produced energy that Europeans had long considered as standard fare — such as high gasoline prices and use of small automobiles (by American standards). By comparing the quantity of petroleum imported per capita, for example, it is readily seen that Europe and Japan are much more heavily dependent on foreign energy sources than the United States. United States imports per capita are less than half those of any of the other leading importing nations (Table 11-7).

Middle East nations furnished western Europe with approximately 72 percent of its imported petroleum during 1974, and imports accounted for about 98 percent of the total west European oil supply. Africa was the

TABLE 11-7. Major Petroleum-Importing Nations: 1971, 1974, and 1975

NATION	THOUSANDS OF METRIC TONS			PERCENTAGE, WORLD TOTAL		TONS IMPORTED PER CAPITA, 1974[a]
	1971	1974	1975	1974	1975	
Japan	190,830	237,580	219,570	15.4	15.6	2.21
United States	84,130	174,060	202,270	11.3	14.4	.83
France	108,410	130,350	105,640	8.5	7.5	2.49
Italy	117,580	120,200	92,150	7.8	6.5	2.19
United Kingdom	109,660	113,550	87,710	7.4	6.2	1.99
West Germany	101,340	104,460	86,250	6.3	6.1	1.76
The Netherlands	60,250	68,850	52,870	4.5	3.8	5.14
Canada	34,280	41,410	41,430	2.7	2.9	1.84
TOTALS	806,750	990,460	887,890	64.2	63.0	—
WORLD TOTALS	1,266,710	1,542,730	1,409,260	100.0	100.0	—

[a]Based upon 1973 population estimates by the Population Reference Bureau.
SOURCES: *World Energy Supplies: 1950-1974,* United Nations, Series J, No. 19, 1976, Table 7; and *World Energy Supplies: 1971-1975,* United Nations, Series J, No. 20, 1977, Table 7.

source of nearly 23 percent of western Europe's oil, with Libya, Nigeria, and Algeria the chief suppliers. Approximately 77 percent of Japan's imports came from the Middle East in 1974, with Indonesia supplying most of the remainder.

Sources of petroleum for the United States were more widely diffused. The Middle East and Africa each supplied about 28 percent; Canada, about 23 percent; and Latin America, nearly 13 percent. The greater diversity of United States than of European and Japanese sources is declining, however, as imports from Canada and Venezuela (the two major suppliers from the western hemisphere) stabilize or drop and as imports from Nigeria and the Middle East rise. A revolutionary change in the government of Iran during early 1979, and strikes by oil field workers during several weeks prior to the change of governments, resulted in a temporary cessation of oil exports from Iran. Disruption of the Iranian supply led to shortages on world markets, a sharp increase in oil prices, and significant scarcities of gasoline in the United States during the spring and summer of 1979. The Iranian situation further emphasized the vulnerability of the United States and other major energy importers to political and economic disturbances in the highly volatile Middle East.

Natural Gas. Much of the natural gas produced in conjunction with oil in the major oil-exporting nations is burned off at the wells or allowed to escape into the atmosphere. Natural gas is at present uneconomical to transport by measures other than pipeline unless it can be liquified. Liquifi-

TABLE 11-8. Major Exporters and Importers of Natural Gas

| | MILLION CUBIC METERS | | PERCENTAGE OF WORLD TOTAL |
EXPORTERS	*1971*	*1974*	*1974*
The Netherlands	17,400	43,540	39.3
Canada	25,570	27,210	24.6
USSR	4,560	14,120	12.7
Iran	5,620	9,090	8.2
TOTAL	53,150	93,960	84.8
WORLD TOTAL	61,400	110,810	

| | MILLION CUBIC METERS | | PERCENTAGE OF WORLD TOTAL |
IMPORTERS	*1971*	*1974*	*1974*
United States	26,310	27,290	24.6
West Germany	6,500	22,630	20.4
USSR	8,130	11,940	10.8
France	5,170	11,700	10.6
Belgium	6,350	11,590	10.5
TOTAL	52,460	85,150	

SOURCE: *World Energy Supplies: 1950-1974,* United Nations, Series J, No. 19, 1976, Table 16.

cation requires that the temperature of the gas be reduced to $-144°$ C. In liquified form the gas occupies only about one six-hundredth of its original volume. Liquified gas is transported in especially built natural gas tank ships which can hold up to 33 million gallons of the liquid. Although plans are underway for construction of numerous liquification plants and natural gas tanker ships, only a few such facilities were in operation at the time of this writing. The bulk of the world's international gas movements travel overland by pipeline.

The largest exporter of natural gas in 1974 was The Netherlands, which accounted for nearly 40 percent of world exports. Gas was sold primarily to nations bordering the Netherlands, with West Germany, Belgium, and France receiving the largest amounts (Table 11-8).

Canada, the world's second largest exporter, sold gas only to the United States. Iran sold only to the Soviet Union, which in turn distributed gas primarily to eastern and western Europe. The Soviet Union, a net importer in 1971, became a net exporter by 1974. Mexico is a major potential source of natural gas for the United States, but as of mid-1979 negotiations for the United States to import up to 2 billion cubic feet of Mexican gas daily, by pipeline, were stalled over price disagreements.

The only shipments by ocean tanker in 1974 were from Algeria to the United Kingdom, Spain, France, and the United States; from Libya to Spain and Italy; from Brunei to Japan; and from the United States to Japan. By 1976 Japan was receiving 80 percent of its gas imports in liquid form; Western Europe, about five percent. Total ocean movement, however, amounted to only about 12 shiploads [15]. The quantities of gas moving by ocean tankers should increase substantially during the 1980s, most of it going to western Europe and Japan from North Africa and the Middle East. Soviet exports to eastern and western Eurpoe, and possibly to the United States, should also rise sharply.

Electricity

International exchanges of electricity are for relatively short distances across contiguous international borders. The largest transfers are made from Canada to the United States, from the Soviet Union to its eastern European satellites, from Switzerland and Austria to adjoining nations, from Norway to Sweden, and from Sweden to Finland. In almost all cases nations which receive electricity from another nation also transmit electricity to that nation, frequently at some other place along the border.

CONCLUSIONS

The discussion of international energy movements makes clear that three major energy "sinks" exist in the world: western Europe, Japan, and the United States. Energy materials flow into these "sinks" from domestic resources and from the developing nations. The major "fountain" of energy is the Middle East, followed by Africa and Latin America. Mexico and Indonesia appear to be rising "fountains." Of all the major industrial nations, Japan is least capable of meeting its demands for energy from domestic sources, followed by western Europe. Among the developed nations only the Soviet Union appears to have adequate resources for long-term self-sufficiency.

All conventional and experimental energy resources now available to consumers or which may become available within the near future are plagued with financial, environmental, political, or military risks [16]. The risks are almost certain to rise as consumption increases. Oil and gas consumption is threatened by uncertainties over reserves, rising costs, and increasing distances between regions of production and consumption. Increased use of coal threatens escalation of environmental damage from mining and from burning the fuel, as well as adverse economic consequences from the high costs of converting oil and gas furnaces to coal.

Nuclear energy carries the risk of radioactive contamination of the environment and the threat of use of nuclear weapons by terrorists and in wars between relatively minor world powers. Other options such as geo-thermal, solar, tidal, and wind energy and the distillation of oil from shale are handicapped by high costs, lack of suitable technology, environmental hazards, and poor locations of available resources. Expanded use of nuclear energy multiplies the need for internal and international social stability to reduce the threat of terrorist activities and to encourage the settlement of international disputes by arbitration rather than by war. Efforts to provide society with security against the menace of nuclear blackmail by small bands of insurgents may endanger individual freedoms within the democracies or delay the implementation of technically and economically feasible sources of energy.

Increased use of coal will enhance the desirability of strict environmental controls over its mining and burning in order to prevent potentially negative consequences to human health and to the natural environment. An added risk from increased use of coal involves the associated rise in the carbon dioxide content of the atmosphere and the possibility of major changes in world climates.

One of the most significant questions relative to future energy production and consumption concerns the differential effects new energy emphases may have upon the affluent and the developing nations. Most energy technologies have been and will be developed within the advanced nations, primarily to meet their own needs. Although these developments generate positive economic spin-offs for less developed societies, the advanced nations are likely to continue to enjoy the primary benefits from new energy technologies. A few developing nations that possess large reserves of oil and gas may themselves become high energy consumers. There is little reason to believe, however, that current disparities in energy consumption among nations will be substantially reduced. Because their security is threatened by the spread of nuclear technology, advanced areas are increasingly reluctant to share their discoveries with developing nations. Most of the developing areas are deficient in coal resources, and the adverse effects of increased prices of oil and natural gas are almost certain to fall more heavily upon poor than upon affluent nations.

The impact of increasing relative cost of energy is likely to serve as a damper upon economic growth in nearly all parts of the world. Rising living standards and high rates of economic growth during recent decades, especially in the developed societies, have been closely tied to the increasing availability of energy and its decreasing relative cost. Conversion from coal to oil and gas gave sharp boosts to economic growth and living standards because of the greater efficiency with which oil and gas could be produced, transported, and used as work energy. If the world has, indeed, reached the end of a 200-year cycle of almost constantly decreasing energy costs, the probability appears strong that living standards will stabilize or decline in all nations with the possible exception of the major energy exporters. Even the exporting nations may find that their economic advantages are temporary, for as reserves are depleted, they will almost certainly reduce exports. Although rising energy prices may have a lower total economic impact upon the developing than upon the developed nations, the potential for economic and human disasters within the developing areas is probably stronger. This is especially true in areas of high population growth where food supplies are already short and where the margin of safety from massive starvation and unemployment is low or nonexistent. Even the "green revolution," which a few years ago seemed to offer so much promise for decreasing world hunger, may turn out to be a "wolf in sheep's clothing." The new crop varieties which form the basis for the revolution are much more demanding of inanimate energies than the older, less productive varieties.

Urban populations may be especially vulnerable to rising prices and an increasing scarcity of energy. The rapid rise in urbanization among the world's nations has been made possible because of increased supplies and decreased costs of energy. Unless a reversal occurs in recent trends toward higher relative energy prices, therefore, projected increases in urban populations during the next few decades may not materialize.

If we accept as fact that current rates of consumption will deplete world reserves of oil and gas within the next few decades and that the cost of these energy resources is likely to continue rising, an adequate supply of energy can be achieved only by improving the efficiency with which energy resources are utilized and by transferring to alternative energy sources. These choices can be accomplished, however, only through massive investments in research, new technology, and new equipment. These investments, in turn, will probably lead to rapidly rising costs of energy for several decades. Even if the technology for fusion energy or for solar energy collection and storage had already been developed, for example, many years and astronomical investments would be required for conversion to these new energy sources. Thus the central problem comes down to transfer costs, or economic feasibility, rather than technical feasibility.

The vulnerability of the world's nations to economic and social disruptions as the result of rising energy prices is related largely to the degree of dependence on imports and to levels of per capita consumption. Nations which are without significant domestic energy resources but which enjoy high levels of per capita consumption are probably most vulnerable (Fig. 11-22). Although the United States has substantial energy resources of its own, it is also an extremely large consumer of energy. As consumption rises

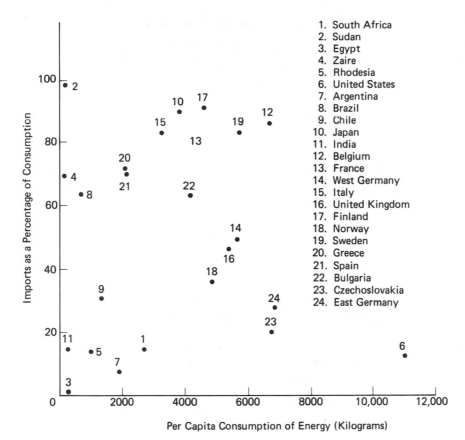

Fig. 11-22. Per capita energy consumption as related to percentage of consumption which is imported, 1974. (From *World Energy Supplies: 1950-1974, op. cit.,* Table 2.)

and dependence on imports increases, so does its vulnerability to economic and social disruptions. Of all large energy-consuming nations, therefore, the United States has the most to gain through energy conservation. If levels of per capita energy consumption in the United States had been comparable to those in Sweden during 1976, for example, the United States could have exported the equivalent of 750 million metric tons of coal or 510 million metric tons of crude oil from domestic energy production rather than importing the equivalent of 436 million metric tons of coal (or 319 million metric tons of crude oil) [17].

Much of what has been presented in this chapter leads to the conclusion that the world's energy situation is in a highly disorganized state. Some groups of scientific experts and government officials are resisting development of nuclear energy, whereas others are pushing nuclear developments as the only way to ensure adequate supplies of energy during the next few decades. We are told on the one hand that oil and gas reserves are nearing exhaustion, whereas others tell us that the world possesses oil and gas reserves yet undiscovered which are the equivalent of five or more times the quantity already discovered. Some experts advocate solar energy as the solution to most of the world's energy problems, whereas others claim that the only solution is for those living in currently advanced societies to return to a form of near subsistence agriculture where virtually no inanimate energy is consumed.

For a number of years the world will struggle through a "sorting out" phase in attempting to solve its energy problems. The problems are extremely complex, and the risks are extremely high. The major problems to be solved are economic and social, for nature itself offers an abundance of energy from numerous sources.

REFERENCES

[1] D. J. Rose, P. W. Walsh, and L. L. Leskovigan, "Nuclear Power Compared to What?" *American Scientist*, **64**, No. 3, 1976, pp. 292-293.

[2] *Ibid.*, p. 294.

[3] Alvin M. Weinberg, "The Maturity and Future Use of Nuclear Energy," *American Scientist*, **64**, No. 1, 1976, pp. 16-21.

[4] Chauncey Starr, Richard Rudman, and Chris Whipple, "Philosophical Basis for Risk Analysis," in Jack M. Hollander (ed.), *Annual Review of Energy*, 1, 1976 (Palo Alto, Calif.: Annual Reviews, Inc., 1976), pp. 629-662.

[5] George A. Cowan, "A Natural Fission Reactor," *Scientific American*, **235**, No. 1, 1976, pp. 36-47.

[6] Earl Cook, *Man, Energy, Society* (San Francisco: W. H. Freeman and Co., 1976), p. 65.

[7] Carol and John Steinhart, *Energy: Sources, Use, and Role in Human Affairs* (North Scituate, Mass.: Duxbury Press, 1974), p. 175.

[8] Elizabeth Drake and Robert C. Reid, "The Importation of Liquefied Natural Gas," *Scientific American*, **236**, No. 4, 1977, p. 22.

[9] K. P. Wang, *The People's Republic of China: A New Industrial Power with a Strong Mineral Base* (Washington, D.C.: U.S. Bureau of Mines, 1975), p. 18.

[10] News Release, U.S. Department of the Interior, Geological Survey, Feb. 26, 1976.

[11] Arthur A. Meyerhoff, "Economic Impact and Geopolitical Implications of Giant Petroleum Fields," *American Scientist*, **64**, No. 5, 1976, p. 536.

[12] *Ibid.*, p. 536.

[13] William D. Metz, "Mexico: The Premier Oil Discovery in the Western Hemisphere," *Science*, **202**, 1978, p. 1262.

[14] *Ibid.*, p. 1263.

[15] Drake and Reid, *op. cit.*, p. 22.

[16] Eric S. Cheney, "U.S. Energy Resources: Limits and Future Outlook," *American Scientist*, **62**, No. 1, 1974, p. 20.

[17] Lee Schipper and A. J. Lichtenberg, "Efficient Energy Use and Well-Being: The Swedish Example," *Science*, **194**, 1976, pp. 1001-1013.

CHAPTER TWELVE

disparities in production and consumption of non-energy minerals

INTRODUCTION

Although during recent years much attention has been focused upon negative social and economic consequences of rising costs and potential shortages of energy, supplies of *nonenergy* minerals are equally crucial to the present status and future welfare of humankind. Through most of human history, but especially since the beginnings of the scientific and industrial revolutions, minerals of all kinds have become increasingly vital components of economic development, social well-being, and international accord or discord.

The centrally planned economies, among which the Soviet Union exerts a high degree of international influence, have pursued with considerable success a policy of self-sufficiency in mineral resources. Mineral supply and demand relationships among the free market nations, on the other hand, have been complicated by a strong sense of nationalism within developing nations, changes in trade arrangements resulting from the end of old colonial empires, the sometimes feisty determination of former colonies to end all vestiges of colonialism, the semi-independence from national laws and regulations of multinational mineral corporations, and widespread emergence of the idea among mineral exporters that by forming international cartels to control supplies and prices they can gain the capital and technology they need for economic development.

Further complicating supply–demand relationships has been an exponential growth in mineral consumption. From 1770 until 1900, during which the world's population increased about 2.2 times, mineral consumption increased approximately 10 times [1]. Between 1900 and 1970 the world's population increased 2.3 times; mineral consumption, about 12.5 times. World mineral consumption today averages more than 6,600 pounds of construction materials, about 3,500 pounds of fuel, 300 pounds of metals, and 340 pounds of nonmetallic minerals per person per year [2]. To supply the average person in the United States, some 40,000 pounds of new mineral materials must be produced annually [3].

The growth in consumption of nonenergy minerals is unevenly spread among the minerals. Aluminum consumption increased more than 1,900 times between 1900 and 1976, whereas tin consumption increased only about 2.5 times. During the same period nickel production grew by more than 100 times; output of nonmetallics such as cement, sand, and gravel, by more than 25 times [4].

Growth in production and consumption of minerals is also unevenly spread among the world's nations. Although the developed nations contain only about 35 percent of the world's population, they produce approximately two-thirds of the world's minerals and consume about 90 percent (Tables 12-1 and 12-2). Quantities of minerals consumed are positively related to incomes. The United States, for example, with about 6 percent of the world's population, consumes approximately as much of the basic metals as all the developing nations, with about 65 percent of the world's population (Table 12-1). The United States and Europe, which together contain about 18 percent of the world's population, consume 50 percent or more of most of the major minerals.

Production of most minerals is more widely distributed than consumption. The United States and Europe produce substantially less of most minerals than they consume, and Japan has to import nearly all of its basic raw materials. Australia is a major net exporter of minerals, especially of

TABLE 12-1. Percentages of Selected Metals Consumed in Selected Developed Areas

AREA	ALUMINUM		REFINED COPPER		REFINED LEAD		NICKEL		REFINED TIN		ZINC	
	1970	*1977*	*1970*	*1974*	*1970*	*1977*	*1970*	*1977*	*1970*	*1977*	*1970*	*1977*
United States	35.1	32.8	25.5	23.4	23.1	21.8	24.9	23.5	25.0	28.6	22.0	19.8
Europe	26.1	24.4	34.0	32.8	34.6	35.5	30.4	28.0	30.0	33.3	31.2	33.7
USSR	12.9	12.1	13.2	15.0	12.6	13.8	NA	NA	07.4	15.9	10.4	16.5
Japan	9.4	11.2	11.3	9.8	5.4	6.7	17.3	14.2	12.5	15.4	12.8	14.2
Rest of World	16.5	19.5	12.0	29.0	24.3	22.2	NA	NA	25.1	6.8	23.6	15.2

SOURCES: *Metal Statistics, 1975* (New York: Fairchild Publications, 1975). *Metal Statistics, 1978* (New York: Fairchild Publications, 1978).

TABLE 12-2. Percentages of Selected Metals or Metal Ores
Produced in Selected Developed Areas

	United States	Europe	USSR	Australia	Rest of World
Bauxite					
1970	3.6	12.9	9.1	15.5	58.9
1976	2.5	8.9	8.3	29.9	50.4
Copper Ore					
1970	24.5	3.3	14.5	2.5	55.2
1976	18.5	4.4	14.3	2.7	60.5
Iron Ore					
1971	10.7	17.7	26.4	8.1	37.1
1976	9.1	11.8	26.7	10.4	42.0
Refined Lead					
1970	18.6	30.7	13.6	5.4	31.7
1976	18.6	28.6	14.6	5.2	33.0
Nickel Ore					
1970	2.2	2.0	16.5	4.5	74.8
1976	1.6	2.9	16.7	10.1	68.7
Tin Ore					
1970	—	1.3	4.6	4.1	90.0
1976	—	1.9	7.5	4.8	85.8
Slab Zinc					
1970	17.0	27.0	11.2	5.2	39.6
1976	8.4	27.2	17.2	4.2	43.0

SOURCES: *Metal Statistics, 1978* (New York: Fairchild Publications, 1978). *Metal Statistics, 1975* (New York: Fairchild Publications, 1975).

bauxite and iron ore. The Soviet Union produces slightly more of most minerals than it consumes.

CLASSIFICATION OF MINERALS

Although some 2,000 minerals are known to exist in the earth's crust, only about 100 are of economic importance [5]. Even fewer minerals are used in large quantities. They may be classified into several broad categories as follows:

Metallic Minerals
    Ferrous (iron)
    Ferroalloys (chromium, cobalt, manganese, nickel, vanadium, tungsten)
    Light metals (aluminum, magnesium, titanium)

Base metals (copper, lead, zinc, and tin)
Precious metals (gold, silver, and platinum)
Electronics metals (cadmium, mercury)

Nonmetallic Minerals
Building stone
Sand and gravel
Fertilizer minerals (nitrogen, potassium, phosphorus)

Mineral fuels (discussed in Chapter 11)
Fossil fuels (petroleum, natural gas, coal)
Nuclear energy minerals (uranium, thorium)

FACTORS WHICH INFLUENCE WORLD PATTERNS OF DEMAND AND SUPPLY

As demands for minerals increase, problems of matching supplies with demands become more complex. Factors which contribute to supply-demand problems involve a combination of interrelated physical, economic, and political circumstances which center around the finite nature of minerals and their uneven distribution in the world.

Exhaustibility, Shortages, Reserves

Perhaps the most disconcerting aspect of any discussion of minerals is their exhaustibility. The problem of exhaustibility is particularly acute with minerals which are completely consumed by use, such as most energy minerals. Other minerals, such as iron, copper, and tin, are finite in nature, but rarely are they completely consumed. They accumulate in and around cities, in junkyards, and in garbage dumps. Although such areas of accumulation are potentially important as sources of minerals for recycling, most current mineral processing facilities are designed to use primarily "new" raw materials rather than previously used minerals, or scrap. Substantial increases in recycling will require a great deal of time, money, and new technology for redesigning plants and for building new plants especially for reprocessing. Shifting sources of supply from traditional mining areas to the scrap heaps of urban areas will also require costly changes in transportation facilities and marketing channels. Major costs may be involved as well in reducing energy consumption associated with recycling and for solving pollution problems associated with some recycling processes.

Although recycling may be a practical method for extending the availability of minerals in short supply or for those with an exceptionally high value per unit weight, it is unlikely to offer an economically feasible alternative to raw ores for most minerals until some time into the future. Known reserves of most minerals are relatively plentiful, and new processes are constantly being developed which enable economic recovery of previously inaccessible or lower grade deposits. Data on *reserves* of minerals are always tentative, as they represent the quantity of known resources that can be recovered at a particular price with a particular technology. A rise in price or improvements in technology may vastly increase the amount of recoverable reserves of most minerals. It is not altogether surprising that reserve estimates seldom forecast supplies sufficient for more than 15 or 20 years into the future. Most of the exploration for and production of minerals thus far in world history have been financed and directed by private corporations which rarely commit investments in activities where earliest returns are to be anticipated in more than that length of time. With the increased instability of economic and political conditions during recent years and the rapidity of technological change, investment cycles have often been shortened rather than lengthened. Thus corporations engaged in production of minerals normally gear investments in exploration toward ensuring supplies for no more than 10 to 20 years into the future.

Shortages of minerals, therefore, when they have occurred, can rarely be attributed to the parsimony of nature. They have resulted from economic and political manipulations or from the inability of producers to keep pace with sudden surges in demand [6].

Substitution

Another opportunity for preventing shortages and extending supplies of minerals is through *substitution*. Seldom is only one mineral suitable for a particular product or a particular production process. Aluminum is now being used in place of more expensive copper in electrical transmission lines, and plastics have been substituted for many products formerly made of metal or wood. As the cost of minerals increases, so does the tendency to restrict their use only to products or processes for which no acceptable substitutes have been discovered. Although substitutes are often helpful in conserving certain minerals, they have sometimes added to problems of pollution or they have contributed to the creation of shortages of other minerals. Production of plastics, for example, requires use of large quantities of energy. Their manufacture contributes to increasingly complex problems of waste disposal, and they have often been responsible for major problems of air and water pollution.

Factors Contributing to Disparities in Production of Minerals

Nature appears to have scattered most minerals through the earth's crust with almost reckless abandon. Some areas are rich in a variety of relatively scarce minerals such as tin, copper, silver, and chromite, whereas other areas with similar geological conditions are lacking in economically exploitable concentrations of any kinds of minerals.

Most minerals are produced far from their major markets. Geological conditions which favor mineral formation often result in surface configurations that are undesirable for human occupance and that make transportation facilities difficult and expensive to build. Many poor nations, lacking the necessary capital and technical ability to develop their own mineral resources, have encouraged development by foreign corporations as a means for generating growth capital.

The mere existence of a mineral deposit, however, is no guarantee that it will be developed. Because huge quantities of development capital are required to exploit most mineral deposits and because consuming industries require dependable supplies, economic and political factors are often more important than physical conditions in determining where mining activities will locate. Although the decision to exploit or not to exploit a mineral deposit is exceedingly complex and based upon numerous variables, the following are usually of substantial importance.

Price of The Mineral. As prices fluctuate, the feasibility of exploiting particular mineral deposits may also fluctuate. A rise in the price of a mineral, for example, may increase the number of deposits that can be economically exploited and lead to changes in geographical patterns of production. A decline in price as well may force the closing of marginal mining operations, especially when the mines are relatively small producers. Following a lengthy period of declining copper prices, for example, the Bureau of Mines, United States Department of the Interior, reported in November, 1977, that depressed prices had led to "a number of mine closures, production curtailments, and a serious level of unemployment" [7].

Geological Characteristics of Deposits. Richness and type of formation of a deposit may affect developmental possibilities. Whether a deposit contains 1 percent, 20 percent, or 50 percent of the desired mineral; whether the reserves are large or small, near the surface or deeply buried, easy or difficult to remove from the host or parent material; and whether undesirable substances or valuable by -products are associated with the mineral in question all have an influence upon the deposit's potential for exploitation.

Technology. Improvements in technology frequently result in expansion of "economically available" resources. Chile once had a virtual monopoly over world supplies of nitrates, used largely in the making of fertilizers and explosives. The monopoly was broken when German scientists discovered methods for extracting nitrates from the atmosphere (pure dry air is composed of 78 percent nitrogen). Loss of the nitrate monopoly had disastrous effects upon the Chilean economy. Germany, on the other hand, once controlled most of the world's potash output — another vital fertilizer mineral. As this mineral became increasingly important to the agricultural industries of such nations as the United States and the Soviet Union, however, exploration and research resulted in discovery of new deposits and in the development of methods for economically extracting potash from low-grade deposits.

Institutional Factors. Institutional considerations are frequently of paramount importance in determining when and where resources will be exploited. Because of the transient nature of international relations, for example, the distribution of mineral production is often subject to dramatic and relatively rapid change. This is true even for minerals whose economically exploitable deposits are locationally restricted and where supplies and prices are subject to substantial control by national monopolies or by international cartels.

International cartels. Although widespread interest in development of international cartels is a relatively recent phenomenon, especially among the developing nations, such organizations among producers of minerals are not particularly new to the world — nor are countermeasures for dealing with such cartels. One of the older international producer organizations was established to control supplies and prices of tin, a mineral which is found in relatively few locations. Partly as a result of efforts by suppliers to keep the price of tin high, major consuming areas were encouraged to recycle the metal and to develop substitutes for it from more abundant metals. The result was that output of tin increased only 2.5 times between 1900 and 1976, the slowest rate of increase in output among the base (nonferrous) metals [8].

The trend toward constantly increasing imports of minerals threatens the developed nations with loss of control over supplies and leaves them subject to prices set by exporter-organized cartels. Taking their cue from OPEC (Organization of Petroleum Exporting Countries), exporters of several vital minerals have formed, or expect to form, their own international cartels to gain control of supplies and prices from the importing nations. International associations of bauxite (the ore for aluminum) and mercury producers have recently been formed, for example, but their effectiveness has not yet been fully demonstrated. It is much more difficult to develop an effective organization (cartel) for control of supplies and prices when sources of a mineral are numerous and widespread, and when the commodity can be recycled, than for a mineral which can be produced in surplus in only a few locations and where the product is consumed by use.

National expropriation of mining operations. In some instances exporting nations have attempted to increase their control over supplies and prices of minerals by nationalizing mines formerly owned by corporations head-quartered in the major importing nations. The huge, privately owned, copper producing operations in Zaire, Zambia, Chile, and Peru have been taken over in whole or in part by the governments of those nations [9]. Other nations have increased their legal or financial control over foreign mineral com-panies, or they have restricted or forbidden further exploration or develop-ment of resources by those companies.

With loss of control over supplies and prices, the importing nations, or companies headquartered in those nations, have tended to move, whenever possible, toward development of domestic resources or toward use of alter-native materials which are available domestically. Price increases brought about by organizations of exporters may have the result of transforming formerly uneconomic deposits in importing nations into profitable mining operations. Thus dependence on imports is reduced and exporters may find themselves saddled with huge stockpiles of minerals which cannot be sold. When lacking adequate domestic resources, importing nations may attempt to discover and secure access to new sources of the materials in areas which are unlikely to join exporter cartels, or they may form bargaining associa-tions among importing areas in order to bring economic and political pres-sures against the exporters. In the case of reusable materials, importing areas have the option to increase secondary production through recycling. In some instances powerful importers may even attempt to stimulate the overthrow of governments in exporting areas and to install persons in power who will give favorable treatment to importing nations or to their business organiza-tions. The extent of action by powerful importers to maintain control over supplies of a mineral depends largely on how vital that mineral is to the na-tion's economic and political security.

Growth of multinational corporations. The distribution of mineral production has also been increasingly influenced by the rapid growth of huge multina-tional corporations. Supplies of minerals from developing areas have often been higher in quality, lower in cost, and more dependable than those from developed areas. Large-scale exploitation of mineral resources in most devel-oping regions is more recent than within developed nations. Labor costs in developing nations are almost always cheaper than in developed countries, labor organizations which tend to strike over wages and working conditions are less likely to exist, and mining operations have encountered fewer incon-veniences and costs resulting from legislative requirements designed to pro-tect the environment. Many multinational corporations have also been able to effect substantial tax savings from their investments in foreign production sites.

The best foreign sources are those in politically stable areas where long-term arrangements for production are obtainable. Most large mineral-producing companies seek to develop sources within numerous nations so as to ensure a stable flow of minerals, encourage maximum competition among supply areas, and assure minimum opportunities for development of monopolistic pricing arrangements.

Other institutional effects. Additional institutional factors which encourage or discourage mining in particular areas include antimonopoly laws, laws requiring that mining be conducted in such a way as to protect environmental quality, and laws that provide subsidies to or tax incentives for particular mining enterprises. In the name of environmental protection mining has been either banned or made prohibitively expensive in some areas, and the use of certain minerals has been discouraged for particular purposes because of environmental or health hazards. Such concerns for environmental and health protection have been associated primarily with the most advanced societies.

Type of economic system is also an important institutional influence in minerals activities. The necessity for profits within free market economies may give way, among centrally planned economies, to primary emphasis upon how the operation meets particular national economic or ideological objectives. Even among the free market economies the degree of direct governmental involvement in mining or of partnership between governments and private mining companies varies greatly. Such cooperative efforts tend to be greatest within nations with the most severe domestic deficiencies in strategic minerals. Governments in Europe and in Japan, for example, have normally been most heavily involved in exploration for, production of, and controlling the use of minerals. Even in the United States, however, governmental involvement in minerals industries has increased as domestic and international circumstances have resulted in diminished security over mineral supplies.

Transportation Costs

Trade in minerals over long distances, including increased imports by industrial nations, has been encouraged by a steady decline in costs of transportation relative to costs of processing and marketing. The growth in size of ocean vessels and the consequent reduction in relative costs of ocean transport have often made it profitable to import minerals from foreign areas even when differentials in production costs are relatively minor. Domestic land transport of minerals over long distances has also been encouraged by decreased costs of movement made possible by use of unit trains, larger motortrucks, pipelines, and other transportation innovations.

PATTERNS OF PRODUCTION AND CONSUMPTION

Although patterns of mineral *production* are subject to rapid change as the result of shifts in international alliances, fluctuating economic conditions, vacillations in trade policies, variations in mineral prices, development of new technology, and discovery of new resources, basic patterns of mineral *consumption* have remained virtually unchanged for several decades. Industrial nations such as the United States, the Soviet Union, Japan, and the nations of western Europe are the major consumers of minerals. Developed nations also furnish most of the investment capital, technology, and expertise for mineral production in developing nations, although the amounts are diminishing. The amounts of minerals produced by developing areas reflect fluctuations in demand within the developed nations. Demand decreases during economic downturns or when nations decide to draw down their stocks of minerals and increases during periods of expanding economic activity or when stockpiles are being built up.

With a few exceptions, nations that export substantially more minerals then they import range from poorly to moderately developed. Those which neither import nor export significant quantities of minerals are often the most poorly developed of all, for they depend on subsistence farming and have little or no means for attracting the investment capital required for economic development.

No nation possesses a sufficient variety of minerals, in adequate quantities, to support a modern industrial economy entirely. Nations which export some minerals must import others, and a few nations must import nearly all their mineral needs. The Soviet Union, among the developed nations, comes closest to self-sufficiency, and Japan is probably least self-sufficient. Several nations in western Europe also depend on imports for nearly all their mineral supplies. The United States occupies an intermediate position, producing large quantities of a great variety of minerals. It is almost wholly dependent on imports for such important minerals as manganese, tin, and chromite, and imports supplement its own large production of many vital minerals such as copper, iron ore, lead, and zinc. Australia has achieved particular distinction since 1950 among the major mineral-exporting nations, especially in exports of iron ore, bauxite, and nickel. The bulk of Australia's mineral exports are shipped to Japan, but substantial amounts also move to western Europe and the United States.

Although the centrally planned economies are largely self-sufficient in mineral production, the Soviet bloc nations of eastern Europe depend more heavily on imports than the Soviet Union or China. Most eastern European imports originate in the Soviet Union, however, as Communist bloc nations do not rely upon supplies of minerals produced in the developing lands.

Most developing nations lack the capital and technology to utilize the considerable reserves of minerals which they possess. To acquire developmental capital, therefore, they export mineral raw materials to the more developed nations. The recent tendency for developing nations to expropriate the holdings of foreign mineral-producing companies, however, has discouraged foreign firms from investing in politically unstable areas where the probability of government takeover of their facilities is strong.

MINERAL COMMODITIES: THE METALLIC MINERALS

Iron Ore

Iron ore is widely produced over the earth, as iron is the fourth most abundant element in the earth's crust (Fig. 12-1). The search for new iron ore deposits following World War II was so successful and production was initiated in so many countries that the resulting surpluses led to curtailment of further exploration [10].

A spectacular transformation has occurred in patterns of iron ore production since World War II. The Soviet Union, in 1976, produced more ore

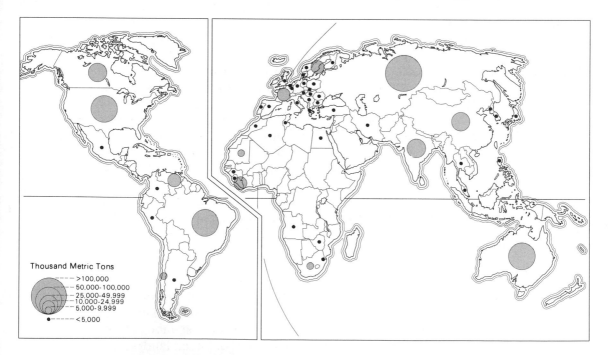

Fig. 12-1. World iron ore production: 1976. [From *Statistical Yearbook, 1977* (New York: United Nations, 1978), Table 56.]

TABLE 12-3. Iron Ore Production: Selected Nations

AREA	PRODUCTION (1,000 Metric Tons)		PERCENTAGE OF WORLD OUTPUT	
	1967	*1976*	*1967*	*1976*
WORLD	338,200	512,700	100.0	100.0
United States	49,608	50,152	14.7	09.8
USSR	90,326	130,890	26.7	25.5
Brazil	14,772	60,596	04.4	11.8
Australia	11,104	58,263	03.3	11.4
Canada	23,610	34,993	07.0	06.8
China	15,400	32,500	04.6	06.3
India	16,024	27,165	04.7	05.3
Sweden	17,595	19,109	05.2	03.7
Liberia	12,575	14,010	03.7	02.7
France	15,997	13,792	04.7	02.7
Venezuela	10,959	11,585	03.2	02.3

SOURCE: *Statistical Yearbook, 1977* (New York: United Nations, 1978), Table 56.

than the entire world produced in 1950 (Table 12-3). In 1950 the United States accounted for approximately 42 percent of the world's ore; in 1976 it produced less than 10 percent.

Prior to World War II nearly all large iron ore-producing areas in the world were located within the developed nations, including the Krivoi Rog deposits of the southern Ukraine and deposits near Magnitogorsk in the southern Urals of the Soviet Union, the Lorraine deposits in France, the high grade Kiruna deposits in Sweden, and several deposits of lesser size in the United Kingdom. Following the war mining began in a number of locations within the developing nations, including Brazil, Venezuela, China, India, and Liberia. Among the developed nations ore production increased rapidly in the Soviet Union, Canada, and Australia, with the Soviet Union far outstripping all others. Canadian deposits were developed to supply markets in the United States and western Europe. During the 1970s Brazil and Australia became the second and third largest producers of iron ore and the world's two largest exporters (Table 12-3). Most Australian ore goes to Japan, with Brazilian ore moving primarily to western Europe and the United States. Significant increases in production during the 1970s also occurred in China and India.

The changing situation concerning iron ore supplies for the United States since World War II illustrates how the complex economic nature of minerals industries affects such factors as domestic self-sufficiency, trading patterns, and policies of taxation. Prior to and during the war the United States was vitually self-sufficient in iron ore production, with about 80 percent coming from high-grade deposits around Lake Superior. Because high-grade deposits in the Superior region were largely depleted by the end of the war, however,

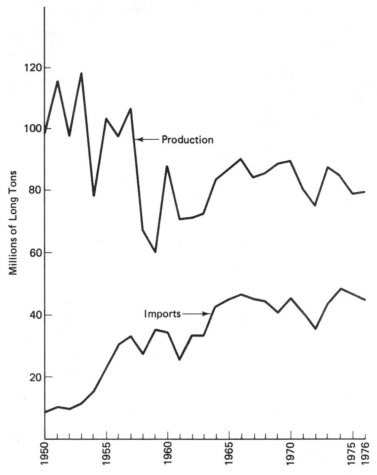

Fig. 12-2. Iron ore production and imports: United States, 1950-1976. [From *Metal Statistics: 1978* (New York: Fairchild Publications, 1978).]

American steel companies sought new sources in foreign areas. Deposits considered acceptable by the steel companies were found in Canada and Venezuela, and the companies quickly proceeded to develop these deposits. Thereafter domestic production declined sharply and imports rose accordingly (Fig. 12-2). During the late 1950s methods were developed for economically exploiting the low-grade *taconite* iron deposits around Lake Superior. Because taconite and similar low-grade iron deposits in the Superior and other regions exist in extremely large quantities, the United States was presented with an opportunity to regain long-term self-sufficiency in iron ore production [11]. Processes of *beneficiation* (concentration) and pelletization of the ore, which were developed largely for the Superior taconite industry, have since been widely adopted in other parts of the world.

Although the opportunity for self-sufficiency existed, however, it was not seized by the steel industries. Huge investments had been made in the Canadian and Venezuelan mining operations, and the industries judged these sources to be safe and dependable [12]. Development of adequate domestic taconite mining capacity would have required additional massive capital investments which the industries opted to avoid. Furthermore, having ready access to foreign iron ore resources, output from which could be expanded on relatively short notice, gave the industries the leverage they needed to secure favorable tax treatment from Minnesota, the state in which most United States iron ore production occurs. The industries also had better access to world markets from Canadian and Venezuelan mines than from those around Lake Superior, and they were able to avoid, in their foreign operations, many of the costs and inconveniences of altering mining processes to safeguard the environment which were being required in the United States.

Besides Brazil, Australia, Canada, and Venezuela, significant amounts of iron ore are exported from Liberia, Sweden, and France. Major importers include Japan, the United States, the United Kingdom, West Germany, and other European nations. The bulk of United States imports are from Canada and Venezuela. European imports are primarily from West Africa, Sweden,

Iron ore mine. (Courtesy, American Iron & Steel Institute.)

Brazil, Canada, Venezuela, and Australia, and Japanese imports are predominantly from Australia, India, and Africa.

Ferroalloy Metals

The ferroalloys are metals used largely to mix with steel to give it special properties, but they also have uses of their own. They include manganese, chromite, nickel, molybdenum, vanadium, and tungsten. Most of the ferroalloys are found in economic deposits in only a few locations. Except for the Soviet Union the major industrial nations are heavy importers of these minerals. The United States is deficient in resources of all the ferroalloys except molybdenum.

Manganese is the most important of the ferroalloys, as some 14 pounds of the metal is required in producing each ton of steel. The Soviet Union is the largest producer, followed by South Africa, Brazil, Gabon, Australia, and India.

Nickel is of particular importance as an alloy in the making of stainless steel. Canada accounts for more than one-third of the world's nickel production, followed by the Soviet Union and New Caledonia. Other significant producers include Cuba, Australia, and the Dominican Republic.

Iron ore pellets. These pellets consist of concentrated iron ore and are ready for use in steel production. (Courtesy, American Iron & Steel Institute.)

Chromite gives steel strength, hardness, and resistance to corrosion. The distribution of production has recently been subjected to international political decisions involving an embargo by the United States and other nations against chromite from Rhodesia. South Africa has approximately 62 percent of known world reserves of chromite, followed by Rhodesia with nearly 33 percent [13]. The Soviet Union is the largest producer, however, followed by South Africa, Albania, Turkey, the Philippines, and Rhodesia.

Cobalt is used largely in the making of heat-resisting steels. Largest reserves are in Zaire, New Caledonia, the Philippines, and Zambia. Zaire accounts for roughly half of the world's output.

Molybdenum adds strength to steel. The United States has about half of the world's known reserves of the metal and accounts for about 60 percent of world production. Canada, the Soviet Union, and Chile are other significant producers.

Tungsten imparts hardness to steel and is an essential alloy which is used in the manufacture of metalworking and construction machinery. It is of particular importance in the manufacture of high-quality tools, drill bits and other cutting edges, as a filament in incandescent lamps, and in electron tubes. China is the world's largest producer, followed closely by the Soviet Union. Approximately 60 percent of known reserves are in southeastern China [14]. Other areas with large reserves include Canada, the United States, South Korea, Brazil, Bolivia, Australia, and Thailand.

Vanadium is most important in the manufacture of steels with high tensile strength, including structural steel, armor plating, and cutlery. The mineral is relatively abundant and because it is frequently found with uranium, copper, phosphate, and even oil, it is produced almost entirely as a by-product of other extractive activities. The Soviet Union possesses approximately two-thirds of known reserves, followed by South Africa, Australia, Chile, and the United States. Although the United States has adequate reserves to meet domestic demands, imports of cheaper ores from South Africa and Chile have been increasing. As a result, South Africa replaced the United States as the world's largest producer of the metal during the early 1970s. Other major producing nations are the Soviet Union, Finland, and Norway.

The Base Metals

The base metals include copper, zinc, lead, and tin. These metals were among the first used by humans, and known reserves remain relatively plentiful. Except for tin, production of the base metals has increased rapidly during recent decades (Fig. 12–3). Prices per pound are normally highest for tin, followed by copper, zinc, and lead in that order.

Copper is the best known and most heavily used of the base metals. Nearly 60 percent of the copper produced goes into the electrical industry,

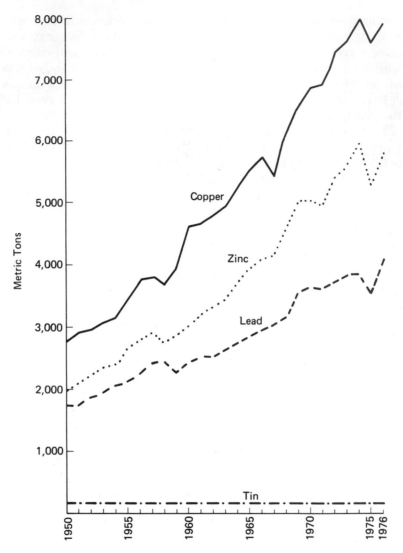

Fig. 12-3. World production of copper, lead, zinc, and tin: 1950–1976. [From *Non-Ferrous Metal Data: 1975* (New York: American Bureau of Metal Statistics, Inc.), p. 129; *Metal Statistics: 1975, op. cit.;* and *Metal Statistics: 1978, op. cit.*]

with most of the remainder used in construction and in industrial machinery. Although the United States is the world's largest producer of copper, domestic output is not sufficient to meet demands and copper is imported from Peru, Chile, South Africa, Canada, and several other nations. Some 40 percent of United States consumption is accounted for by secondary recovery (use of scrap), however, whereas the balance of imports over exports normally amounts to only about 2 to 5 percent of consumption. Arizona

An open pit copper mine in South America, located nearly two miles above
sea level. (Courtesy, ASARCO, Incorporated.)

accounts for 50–55 percent of the United States production. Major producing nations other than the United States, in order of their importance in
1976, were Chile, the USSR, Canada, Zambia, and Zaire (Fig. 12–4 and
Table 12–4). The United States and Chile each contain nearly 20 percent of
the world's known reserves of copper; the Soviet Union, about 8 percent;
and Canada, Peru, Zambia, and Zaire, each contain about 6 percent.

Ownership of copper mines has changed radically during recent years.
Zaire nationalized its mines in 1966, followed by expropriation of large
mining operations in Chile in 1971 and Peru in 1973. Zambia acquired 51
percent of its two largest mining groups, also during 1973. Following nationalization of mining operations by Chile, the United States imports from that
nation dropped precipitously until after 1973 when the Chilean government
concluded compensation agreements with firms whose properties had been
expropriated [15].

Although copper prices fluctuate greatly from month to month and from
year to year and mines often open and close in response to changes in prices,
mines with the highest grade ores do not necessarily have the lowest production costs. The largest mining operations, employing the most advanced
large-scale technology, are those which exploit huge deposits of low-grade
ores. It is these large-scale operations rather than those exploiting the smaller
high-grade deposits that achieve lowest production costs [16].

Zinc ranks third, following aluminum and copper, in consumption

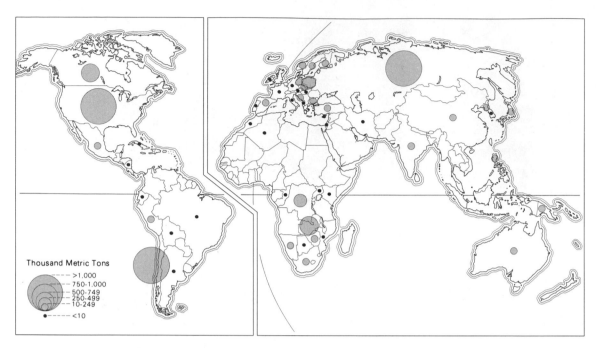

Fig. 12-4. Production of copper ore: 1976. (From *Statistical Yearbook: 1977, op. cit.,* Table 60.)

among the nonferrous metals. It is widely found in the world, frequently in association with other metals such as lead, copper, gold, and silver. Because it has high malleability and ductility and good resistence to corrosion, zinc's major uses are for die castings and as a galvanizing material. In the United States the automotive industry is the largest consumer of zinc, using approximately one-third of national consumption [17].

Most of the world's zinc is produced in the advanced nations, with Japan, the Soviet Union, western Europe, Canada, and the United States accounting for the bulk of the world's supply (Fig. 12-5). The United States is the world's largest consumer of zinc and, despite its large ore reserves, is also the world's leading zinc importer. Domestic output declined by more than half between the middle 1960s and the middle 1970s. Most United States resources are relatively low-grade deposits, the processing of which requires substantial investments to meet requirments concerning sulfur dioxide emissions.

Lead is used primarily in the manufacture of storage batteries and as an additive to gasoline. Its use in gasoline is declining, but as new energy technology, such as that for solar energy, is developed and adopted, it is ex-

TABLE 12–4. Copper Ore: Percentage of World Output Produced in Selected Nations

Country	1966	1976
United States	24.6	19.6
USSR	NA	10.7
Chile	12.6	13.5
Canada	8.8	10.0
Zambia	11.8	9.5
Zaire	6.0	6.0
Peru	3.3	2.7
Poland	NA	3.9 (1975)
Philippines	1.4	3.1
South Africa	2.4	2.6

SOURCE: Harry Jiller (ed.), *Commodity Yearbook, 1978,* (New York: Commodity Research Bureau, 1978), p. 123.

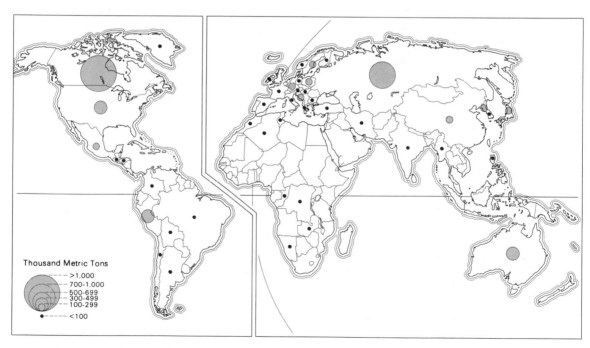

Fig. 12-5. World production of zinc ore: 1976. (From *Statistical Yearbook, 1977, op. cit.,* Table 133.)

Open pit copper mine in Arizona. Revegetation is in progress at the mine site
to stabilize excavated slopes and to improve general appearance. (Courtesy,
ASARCO, Incorporated.)

pected that demand for lead for use in storage batteries (to store solar
energy for use during darkness or periods of cloud cover) will rise sharply.

World patterns of production and consumption of lead are similar to
those for zinc (Figs. 12-5 and 12-6). Much of the world's lead production,
however, is accounted for by secondary recovery (recycled lead). Secondary
lead furnishes nearly one-half of the total lead supply in the United States.

Tin, in contrast with lead and zinc, is produced primarily within the
developing nations and its use has not increased substantially for several
decades. Aluminum, plastics, special steels, copper, alloys, and epoxy resins
have proved to be highly suitable and relatively inexpensive substitutes for
many of the principal uses of tin, such as in containers, electrical equipment,
and solders.

The major tin-producing nations are Malaysia, the USSR, Bolivia, Indonesia, China, Thailand, and Australia (Fig. 12-7). The three southeast Asia
nations of Malaysia, Thailand, and Indonesia account for nearly one-half of
the world's output. Consumption, on the other hand, occurs primarily in the
United States, western Europe, and Japan (Fig. 12-7).

Light Metals

The light metals, aluminum, magnesium, and titanium, have become important only since 1900. Although the basic processes for commercial production of aluminum and magnesium were discovered during the 1880s, their high costs caused them to remain more curiosities than major industrial metals until development of the aircraft industry — with its requirement for construction materials of light weight. Titanium has become commercially valuable since World War II, and its major use is in aircraft construction.

The light metals (especially aluminum) are likely to increase in importance more rapidly than most other metals during the next few decades. High prices for and prospective shortages of energy minerals, together with governmental requirements for the production of more energy-efficient motor vehicles, are forcing manufacturers of transportation equipment to employ the fuel-saving light metals in construction.

Aluminum, among the nonferrous metals, appears to have the best potential for growth in production. From only 7,300 tons produced in 1900,

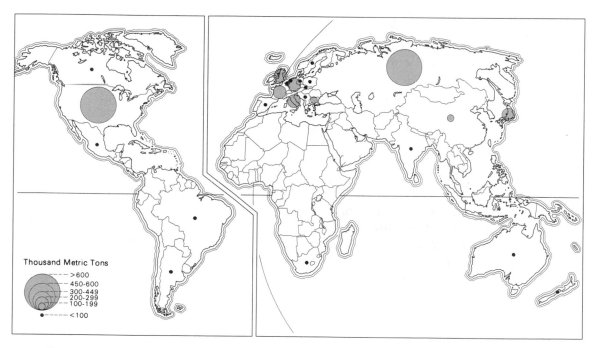

Fig. 12-6. Consumption of refined lead: 1976. (From *Metal Statistics, 1978, op. cit.*, p. 129.

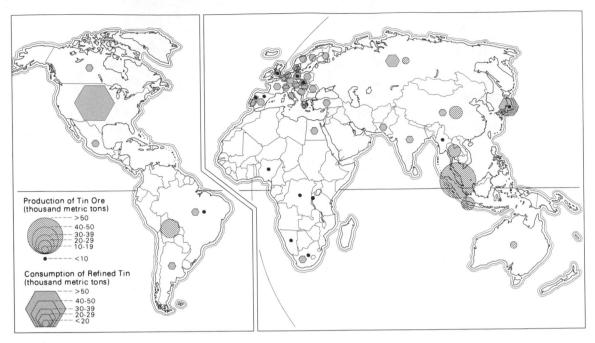

Fig. 12-7. Production of tin ore and consumption of refined tin: 1976. (From *Metal Statistics, 1978, op. cit.*, pp. 231 and 241.)

output had increased to more than 14 million tons in 1976 [18]. Aluminum is the most abundant of the metallic minerals in the earth's crust, and known reserves of bauxite are adequate to last the world more than 300 years at present rates of consumption [19]. Africa has the largest bauxite reserves, followed by South America, Oceania (primarily Australia), Asia, and the Caribbean–Central American region. Bauxite is a *residual* ore; the aluminum becomes concentrated as other surface materials are washed away or carried away in solution, leaving aluminum oxides behind as a residue. Most favorable conditions for bauxite formation are in regions of high temperatures and heavy precipitation. The bulk of the reserves, therefore, are in tropical areas. Materials other than bauxite, such as Kaolin clays, are also high in aluminum content. If the price of the metal rises substantially or if technology enables economic recovery from such materials, most major aluminum-producing areas will have virtually inexhaustible reserves of the metal.

Significant shifts have occurred in major bauxite-producing areas since World War II (Table 12-5). Surinam was the leading source of the ore until the early 1950s when Jamaica became the largest producer. Australia became the leading producer in 1971 and in 1976 produced more than 28 percent of the world's supply (Fig. 12–8). Rapid increases in bauxite production have

Known reserves of bauxite are adequate to furnish the world with aluminum for hundreds of years. (Courtesy, Aluminum Association.)

TABLE 12-5. Bauxite: Percentage of World Output Produced in Selected Nations

Country	1966	1976
United States	4.5	2.6
Australia	3.2	31.1
Guinea	4.6	14.0
Jamaica	22.3	13.3
Surinam	13.7	5.9
USSR	11.7	6.1 (1973)
Guyana	8.3	3.4
France	6.9	3.0
Greece	3.4	3.5
Hungary	3.5	3.7 (1973)
Yugoslavia	4.6	3.1

SOURCE: Harry Jiller (ed.), *Commodity Yearbook: 1978* (New York: Commodity Research Bureau, Inc., 1978), p. 79.

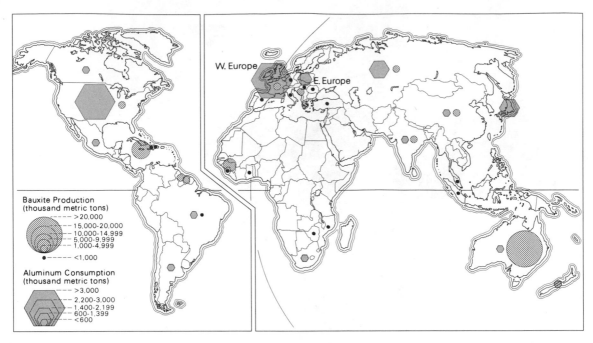

Fig. 12-8. Bauxite production, 1975, and aluminum consumption, 1976.
(From *Metal Statistics, 1978, op. cit.,* p. 24; and *Statistical Yearbook, 1977, op. cit.,* Table 58.)

also occurred in Guinea, West Africa, which furnished approximately 14 percent of the world's supply of bauxite in 1976. Additional major producers include the Soviet Union, Guyana, France, Greece, Hungary, and Yugoslavia. The major importers of bauxite and of alumina (a concentrate of bauxite which has been reduced in weight by 50 to 65 percent) include the United States, Japan, Canada, and nations in northern and western Europe. Huge amounts of energy are required to process bauxite or alumina into aluminum, and most aluminum plants are located near major sources of low-cost energy. For many years most aluminum plants located in areas where hydroelectric energy could be produced in abundance at low cost. This accounts for the large aluminum capacities in Norway and Canada and in the Pacific Northwest and the Tennessee Valley of the United States. More recently, aluminum plants have become somewhat more market-oriented because of high transportation costs associated with location of the industry near huge hydroelectric developments and because most low-cost hydroelectric sites have already been developed and the energy commited for other uses. New aluminum plants, therefore, have often been built where natural gas and coal are available in large quantities, especially when these locations are near major markets. The effect of increasing costs of all forms of energy

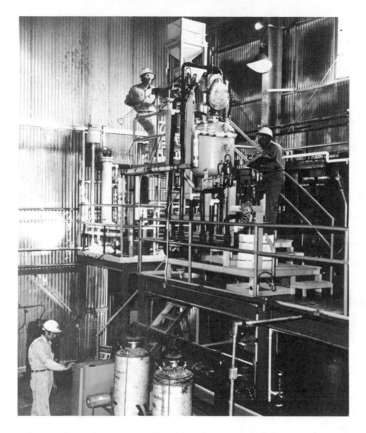

This experimental equipment at Boulder City, Nevada forms part of a co-operative project of the U.S. Bureau of Mines and the aluminum industry to test processes for recovering aluminum from plentiful low-grade domestic minerals. (Courtesy, Aluminum Association.)

and short supplies of natural gas in the major industrial areas may result in further shifts in the locational pattern of aluminum production.

Magnesium and *titanium* have the advantage of great strength relative to their weight, but they are also more expensive than aluminum. Reserves of magnesium are virtually inexhaustible, for it can be economically recovered from seawater. Other sources of magnesium include minerals such as dolomite and magnesite.

Magnesium has a wide range of uses, ranging from flash photography to flares, incendary bombs, and construction, but its primary use is as an alloy with aluminum. Its output has fluctuated widely, with peaks occurring during wartime. In 1943, for example, the United States produced 183,584 tons of the metal, but production dropped to 5,317 tons in 1946. Output rose sharply during the Korean War, with 105,821 tons produced in 1952.

In 1958, production was only 30,096 tons, but thereafter it rose gradually because of increasing United States involvement in the Vietnamese conflict and because of rapidly increasing demand for magnesium as an aluminum alloy in die castings and for other uses [20]. During the late 1970s magnesium output in the United States was probably between 125,000 and 135,000 tons, although actual production data were not reported to avoid disclosing output by individual companies.

The United States produces nearly one-half of the world's magnesium. The Soviet Union ranks second in output, accounting for about one-fourth of the world's supply. Most of the remainder is produced in western Europe.

Titanium is the most expensive of the light metals, costing some six times more per pound than aluminum in 1976. As the ninth most abundant metal in the earth's crust, titanium is relatively abundant, but it is difficult and expensive to separate from its ores — rutile and ilmenite. The major uses of titanium are in aerospace industries, although it has many other uses where a light metal of great strength is required.

Precious Metals

The precious metals are gold, silver, and platinum. Currently they are largely by-products of the production of other metals such as copper, lead, and zinc by large corporations from massive mining operations. The myth of individual prospectors with pick, shovel, pan, and a faithful but stubborn jackass finding a rich deposit of gold or silver and being transformed into instant millionaires has gone the way of wild buffalo herds and the rumble seat in autos.

Gold and silver have been used, historically, as the bases for monetary systems, in the making of jewelry, and as the only universally acceptable mediums of international exchange. Increasing industrial demands for these metals and for platinum, however, have contributed to shortages, rising prices, and efforts by economists and political leaders to find acceptable alternatives which may be used as bases for international exchange. The amount of silver used in coinage in the United States and elsewhere has been radically reduced, and gold coins have become collectors' items. Because of their value as a backing for currency, prices, production, and marketing of most of the world's gold and, to a lesser extent, silver, have been strictly controlled by governments. Until 1974, for example, people in the United States were not allowed to own gold, and the United States government had held a tight lid on gold prices. Since that time ownership of gold has become somewhat freer, and the price has been allowed to climb and fall in response to international economic conditions.

The Republic of South Africa produces approximately 60 percent of the world's gold and has about half of the world's known gold reserves. The

Soviet Union produces about 15 percent of the world's gold, followed by Canada, the United States, and Australia. Many other nations produce small quantities of the metal. Production almost everywhere has been relatively stable for a number of years, with appreciable increases in output occurring only in Australia and the Soviet Union.

Approximately 75 percent of the world's silver is produced in Canada, Peru, the Soviet Union, Mexico, the United States, and Australia. Africa, which accounts for about 70 percent of the world's gold, is of little consequence as a producer of silver. Areas of silver production closely parallel those which produce most of the base metals, for approximately 75 percent of all new silver is a by-product of lead, nickel, copper, and zinc ores.

The principal use for silver in the United States is in the photographic industry, followed by tableware and electric and electronic components. Because demand for silver substantially exceeds new mine production, prices have risen sharply during recent years and major efforts have been made to improve secondary recovery of the metal, especially from photographic chemicals.

The platinum metals (including palladium, iridium, osmium, rhodium, and ruthenium, as well as platinum) are so rare that they are not used as a backing for currency [21]. They are used extensively in the chemical and electrical industries, petroleum refining, production of synthetic fibers, and the manufacture of fertilizers. One of the most recent uses of platinum is as a catalyst in autmobile exhaust converters to reduce pollution from exhaust gases. In 1976, some 41 percent of all platinum used in the United States was consumed by the automotive industries [22].

The Soviet Union and the Republic of South Africa each produce approximately 45 percent of the world's platinum. Other producers include Canada, Colombia, and the United States. South Africa possesses about 70 percent of known reserves; the Soviet Union, about 25 percent. The only exclusive platinum mining operation in the United States, at Goodnews Bay, Alaska, ceased production in 1976. Small amounts of the metal are produced as a by-product of copper production.

Mineral Commodities: Nonmetallic Minerals

Whereas economically exploitable deposits of the metallic minerals comprise only small and scattered portions of the earth's crustal materials, many important nonmetallic minerals such as sand and gravel are extremely common. Other nonmetallics, such as potash (potassium), asbestos, and sulfur, are not so commonly found.

Most nonmetallic minerals are of much lower value per unit weight than metallic minerals. Some of them are produced in extremely large quantities by hundreds of different companies. During 1976, for example, some

4,000 commercial and 700 noncommercial (publicly owned) companies in the United States produced 770 million tons of sand and gravel valued at $1.5 billion, compared with 31 commercial companies producing 50,300,000 tons of iron ore valued at $1.8 billion [23]. Dimension stone was produced in 43 states by some 300 companies in 1976, and lime was produced in 40 states at 167 operations. Virtually all the nation's vermiculite, on the other hand, was produced by one company with operations in Montana and South Carolina, and more than half of the domestic output of mica came from North Carolina.

The nonmetallic minerals are so numerous and their uses so diverse that few generalizations are appropriate to them. Some of the minerals are widely used in industrial processes, some are used primarily in construction, and some are used mainly in the production of agricultural fertilizers. Industrial and fertilizer minerals are least commonly found, whereas most construction materials are widespread and have value because of their locations near places of consumption.

Sulfur is one of the more important of the nonmetallic minerals, for it is used as sulfuric acid in the early stages of nearly all forms of manufacturing. The United States is the world's largest producer of sulfur, followed by Canada, the Soviet Union, Japan, and Mexico (Table 12-6). It is available from a variety of sources, including sulfur-bearing salt domes, petroleum, natural gas, and pyrites. Reserves of sulfur are relatively abundant, as large quantities of the mineral are also associated with oil shale, coal, gypsum, and metal sulfides. Efforts to reduce emissions of sulfur dioxide from power plants, refineries, and smelters provide additional quantities of sulfur and sulfuric acid. Although most industrial nations must import some sulfur, the United States produces a large surplus.

TABLE 12-6. Sulfur: Percentage of World Output Produced by Selected Nations

Country	1968	1977[a]
United States	45.3	20.7
USSR	7.6	16.4 (1975)
Canada	16.2	13.9
Poland	6.8	10.1
Japan	1.7	5.3
Mexico	8.5	4.5
France	8.3	3.9
West Germany	0.6	2.7

[a]Estimates

SOURCE: Harry Jiller (ed.), *Commodity Yearbook, 1978* (New York: Commodity Research Bureau, Inc., 1978), p. 332.

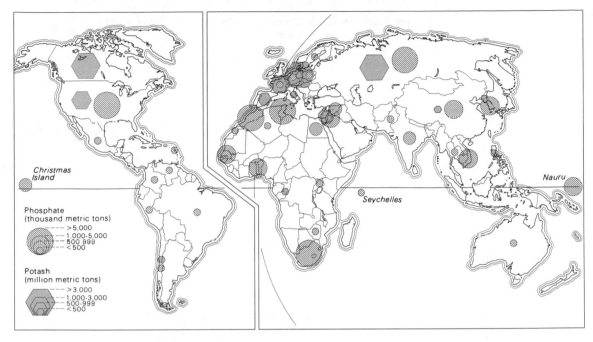

Fig. 12-9. Production of phosphate and potash, 1976. (From *Statistical Yearbook, 1977, op. cit.,* Table 75.)

Fertilizer Minerals

The fertilizer minerals are mainly nitrogen, potash, and phosphate. Nitrogen is a ubiquitous mineral, as it can be extracted from the air. Potash and phosphate, however, are more locationally restricted (Fig. 12-9 and Table 12-7). The United States accounts for 40 percent or more of world phosphate production, with other large producers including Morocco and the Soviet Union. Africa contains most of the known reserves of the mineral, with Morocco possessing about half the world's reserves and South Africa about 20 percent.

More than one-half of the world's reserves of potash are located in Saskatchewan, Canada, and North Dakota and Montana in the United States. Canada and the Soviet Union are the world's largest producers, followed by the United States, West Germany, and France.

Construction Minerals

Minerals used in construction include a wide variety of earth materials such as sand, gravel, limestone, granite, marble, and gypsum. Sand, gravel,

TABLE 12-7. Fertilizer Compounds: Percentage of World Output Produced by Selected Nations

NITROGEN		PHOSPHATE		POTASH	
Country	*1977–1978*	*Country*	*1977*	*Country*	*1977*
United States	24.0	United States	41.1	USSR	25.7 (1974)
USSR	18.6 (1974–1975)	USSR	22.4 (1975)	Canada	21.8
Japan	6.5	Morocco	14.3	East Germany	12.1 (1974)
China	6.7 (1974–1975)	Tunesia	3.1	West Germany	8.6
Canada	4.2	China	3.1 (1975)	United States	8.5
West Germany	3.5			France	6.9
France	3.3				
Poland	3.5 (1974–1975)				
India	3.2				

SOURCE: Harry Jiller (ed.), *Commodity Yearbook, 1978* (New York: Commodity Research Bureau, Inc., 1978), pp. 160–161.

and limestone are the most abundant and widespread in occurrence. Limestone is probably the most widely used of all common rocks and, along with silica and gypsum, is a basic ingredient of cement [24]. Altogether, more than 14 billion tons of sand, gravel, and stone were produced in the world during 1976, or about 7,200 pounds per person. In the United States approximately 15,400 pounds were produced for each inhabitant. Most of the world's gypsum is produced in the developed nations, with the United States, the Soviet Union, Canada, France, and Spain accounting for nearly one-half of the total.

Salt

Salt is obtained primarily from underground deposits, although some is acquired through evaporating seawater. It is required by most chemical industries, which consume more than half of the world's output, and it is an essential ingredient in the diets of all vertebrate animals. The major salt-consuming nations are those with the largest chemical industries, and the leading producing nations include the United States, China, the Soviet Union, the United Kingdom, and West Germany (Fig. 12-10 and Table 12-8). Despite its abundance and low cost, salt is often in short supply in tropical regions such as Central Africa.

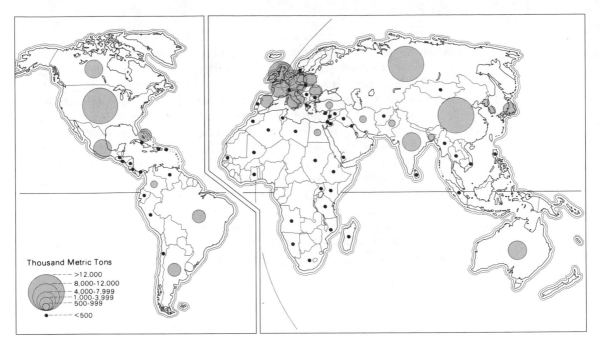

Fig. 12-10. Production of salt, 1976 (From *Statistical Yearbook, 1977, op. cit.,* Table 73.)

TABLE 12-8. Salt: Percentage of World Output Produced by Selected Nations

Country	1977
United States	23.3
China	18.0
USSR	8.5
United Kingdom	4.8
West Germany	4.6
France	3.9
Poland	3.4
Canada	3.2
India	2.7
Italy	2.4

SOURCE: Harry Jiller (ed.), *Commodity Yearbook, 1978* (New York: Commodity Research Bureau, Inc., 1978), p. 302.

CONCLUSIONS

Production and consumption of minerals in the various parts of the world are at least as closely regulated by political and economic conditions as by the relative generosity or miserliness of nature. It would appear, from an examination of known reserves of most minerals, that adequate amounts are potentially available in nature to fill human needs for at least the next hundred years. That the minerals are present in nature, however, does not necessarily mean that they will be available for human use. Economic and political alliances and conflicts, international cartels, powerful institutions such as the multinational corporations, and growing concerns over environmental problems related to production and consumption can and often do interrupt production and trade. It is certain that the patterns of mineral production will change in response to changes in political, legal, and economic conditions. It is almost equally certain that the basic patterns of mineral consumption will not change, at least through the end of the current century.

REFERENCES

[1] Alexander Sutulov, *Minerals in World Affairs* (Salt Lake City: University of Utah Printing Services, 1973), p. 23.

[2] *Ibid.*, p. 23.

[3] *Status of the Mineral Industries, 1977* (Washington, D.C.: Bureau of Mines, United States Department of Interior), p. 2.

[4] Sutulov, *op. cit.*, pp. 31-33.

[5] Charles F. Park, Jr., and Margaret G. Freeman, *Affluence in Jeopardy* (San Francisco: Freeman, Cooper, and Co., 1968), p. 5.

[6] James F. McDivitt and Gerald Manners, *Minerals and Men* (Baltimore: Johns Hopkins Press for Resources of the Future, 1974), p. 10.

[7] *Materials and Minerals: A Monthly Survey*, Bureau of Mines, United States Department of Interior (November, 1977), p. 2.

[8] Sutulov, *op. cit.*, p. 31.

[9] *Metal Statistics: 1975* (New York: Fairchild Publications, Inc., 1975), pp. 19 and 57.

[10] Charles F. Park, Jr., and Margaret C. Freeman, *Earthbound* (San Francisco: Freeman, Cooper, and Co., 1975), p. 51.

[11] "Taconite Build-up on the Mesabi," *Mining Engineering*, 20, No. 9, September, 1968, p. 81.

[12] McDivitt and Manners, *op. cit.*, p. 48.

[13] *Commodity Data Summaries: 1977* (Washington, D.C.: Bureau of Mines, United States Department of the Interior, 1977), p. 35.

[14] *Commodity Data Summaries: 1977, op. cit.*, p. 181.

[15] *Metal Statistics: 1975, op. cit.*, p. 57.

[16] McDivitt and Manners, op. cit., *p. 88.*

[17] *Metal Statistics: 1975, op. cit.*, p. 269.

[18] *Commodity Data Summaries: 1976, op. cit.*, p. 6.

[19] *Ibid.*, p. 17.

[20] *Metal Statistics, 1975, op. cit.*, p. 156.

[21] Park and Freeman, *Earthbound, op. cit.*, p. 85.

[22] *Commodity Data Summaries: 1977, op. cit.*, pp. 126.

[23] *Commodity Data Summaries: 1977, op. cit.*, pp. 82 and 146.

[24] McDivitt and Manners, *op. cit.*, p. 131.

PART FIVE

MANUFACTURING

CHAPTER THIRTEEN
disparities in manufacturing development

INTRODUCTION

Manufacturing has existed in one form or another during most of human history. For hundreds of years it was limited to the making of tools, weapons, utensils, and clothing for home use. As such, manufacturing activities occupied only a part of the daily routine of tilling crops, hunting, and other family responsibilities. Manufacturing did not become a "way of life" until individuals or groups were able to produce surpluses of agricultural or manufactured goods or services that could be exchanged for the goods and services of other individuals or groups.

For centuries manufacturing developed slowly, with occasional advances following discoveries of new technology. Regional variations in levels of product consumption were relatively minor and remained so as long as demands for energy were limited to animate sources.

Development and use of inanimate energy, which led to the industrial revolution and the modern era of manufacturing, began when James Watt patented the first successful steam engine in Scotland in 1769. Since then manufacturing has developed unevenly over the earth, having failed to yield appreciable benefits to the vast majority of Asians, Latin Americans, and Africans. The high levels of productivity and consumption associated with the industrial revolution have been limited primarily to peoples living around the North Atlantic Ocean, with outliers in a few other areas such as Japan, Australia, and New Zealand. Indeed, the 10 percent of the world's people who live in Anglo–America, northwestern Europe, Australia, and New Zealand possess approximately 60 percent of the world's manufacturing capacity [1].

Innovation has always been at the forefront of manufacturing progress. Closely associated with innovative ability is the extent to which a surplus of resources, money, and talent can be provided for investment into creative and imaginative enterprises. Whereas science and technology once advanced slowly, the vastness of recent investments in creative industries by the United States, the Soviet Union, and western Europe have induced an accelerating rate of change. Advanced industrial nations expend from 2 to 4 percent of their gross national products on research and development, and they account for approximately 98 percent of total world investment in technology [2]. The poor nations, by contrast, generally invest less than ½ percent of their gross national products in research and development. For the poor, therefore, technical change normally comes slowly because it must be imported from advanced areas. Modern industrial nations require communication systems capable of constantly reeducating and reorienting the population with respect to continuing changes in technology and culture. In such societies emphasis must be placed upon education not only during the formative years but throughout life.

One result of the rapid development of technology during the twentieth century has been the diffusion of manufacturing into previously undeveloped areas. Much of the manufacturing growth in newly developed areas has occurred as a spin-off from places possessing a more highly developed and more innovative industrial structure. As the advanced nations have invested their capital, labor, and energy into innovative industries with a high potential for profit, the less advanced regions have acquired some of the more stable or mature manufacturing enterprises that are largely unaffected by innovation. Returns on investments in such mature enterprises are frequently higher in the less advanced nations, with their low-cost labor, than in more advanced areas. Industrial growth in the developing nations has also been encouraged by their apparent belief that development of manufacturing is synonymous with improved living standards and the rise of national power. The developing nations view dependence on the old colonial powers for supplies of manufactured goods as an insidious form of modern colonialism which is to be avoided whenever possible, even when goods could be imported at lower cost than they can be produced domestically.

Models For Manufacturing Development

The United States and the Soviet Union have emerged, since World War II, as the two major models for economic development. The democratic political system and reliance upon a free market, as employed by the United States, contrasts sharply with the Soviet emphasis upon central authority and a planned economy. In the United States the profit motive is relied upon to induce savings by individuals and to invest those savings in productive enterprises. In the Soviet Union the state accumulates savings through its taxation policies and makes all major production decisions. Investment and production decisions in the United States are determined primarily by demand from the marketplace (admittedly, the demand is often created through advertising), whereas in the Soviet Union the marketplace is largely ignored [3]. The principal advantage of the Soviet model for the developing nations is that it contains a means through which savings can be enforced, and accumulation of savings is an essential first step in economic development.

Despite differences in methods used for manufacturing development, the industrial structures of the two nations, and the forces which influence such factors as industrial location, are essentially the same. Soviet industrial development is more reflective of national political and ideological considerations, whereas development in the United States is more shaded toward economic considerations. Even in a totalitarian socialist state, however, the decision makers are subject to economic pressures and influences, just as decisions within a democratic free market society must reflect political as well as economic realities.

Neither of these models may be appropriate for many developing nations which lack the basic resources, labor skills, managerial expertise, size, reserve capital, and disciplined populations of the two industrial giants. Because conditions vary radically from one undeveloped country to another, as well as from conditions which have faced the United States or the Soviet Union any time within recent history, each underdeveloped nation must forge its own developmental strategy.

CHARACTERISTICS OF MANUFACTURING: RICH AREAS AND POOR AREAS

Whether manufacturing occurs within the most advanced or the most impoverished nations — whether the type of manufacturing is characterized by extreme simplicity or extreme complexity — certain basic ingredients are required for its successful development. The six major elements required are adequate raw materials, energy, labor, capital, transport facilities, and markets. The nature of these elements may vary substantially from one setting to another. Manufacturing in a primitive setting may involve primarily home-based, handicraft industries using local raw materials and family labor to produce goods for local markets. The mode of transport may consist of human porters, or hand-drawn or animal-drawn carts. Capital requirements are small, with equipment being constructed from local materials by family or village artisans. The manufacturing processes, although they may

The modern Durgapur steel plant in West Bengal, India. (Courtesy, Information Service of India.)

require substantial skills, have often remained virtually unchanged through generations of time. In some instances governmental and international marketing organizations have provided the marketing know-how and capital to introduce the products of these handicraft industries to international markets. Local and national markets for most manufactured products are small, discouraging development of production facilities large enough to allow for high levels of efficiency in output. Some craftsmen depend on sales of handicraft products for their entire income; others use such income to supplement that from farming.

In the advanced areas some handicraft industries exist, but manufacturing takes place primarily in large, corporately owned factories employing dozens or hundreds of workers. Raw materials, markets, or both frequently lie hundreds of miles from the manufacturing plants, and markets are usually highly dispersed. The larger the industry, the more likely it is to be locationally oriented toward markets rather than raw materials [4]. Huge amounts of capital, which may be assembled from many parts of the nation — or indeed, from many parts of the world — are required. Capital in the form of machines is substituted for labor, which is relatively scarce and expensive. The processes used for producing goods are subject to frequent change because of the pace of technological innovation. New products, new materials, and new methods of fabrication are common. Savings in per unit production costs are achieved though increased size of operation (economies of scale).

The types of plants and industrial processes characteristic of manufacturing in advanced societies have also been introduced into the developing nations. Results of such introductions are not uniformly beneficial, however, as goods produced by new processes compete with those manufactured in home-based industries and the machine-made goods are often lower in cost. An additional problem is that the capital-intensive, laborsaving characteristic of modern manufacturing increases output per worker and reduces the supply of jobs in areas where unemployment is already a major problem [5].

In most developing nations a primary object of government encouragement of industrial development is to provide jobs. In such cases the immediate national interest may be best served by construction of several small manufacturing plants that offer large numbers of jobs rather than a huge plant of the most efficient scale of operation. On the other hand, large modern industries stimulate investments and savings, which are basic to economic development.

An additional inhibition against construction of large modern manufacturing firms in developing areas is that they often find it difficult to obtain adequate capital to finance large-scale manufacturing. Domestic markets are too small to justify the minimum-sized plants required for efficient production, indigenous entrepreneurial initiative is lacking, and the labor force is

An industrial area in São Paulo, Brazil. (Courtesy, Consulate of Brazil.)

unskilled and often of low productivity. Local investors are accustomed to quick returns on investments rather than the relatively slow returns associated with manufacturing, utilizing products from allied industries is handicapped by the absence of standardization of sizes and units of measure, and deficiencies in transportation and communications facilities create adverse conditions for assembling raw materials and marketing finished products. Whereas the developed nations have few problems in raising funds for further development, the position of the developing nations is not so favorable. The non-oil–exporting developing nations borrowed heavily during the 1960s and early 1970s to finance industrialization and other development programs. Following the 1973 oil embargo and oil price increases, their accumulated debts rose by almost 50 percent within 2 years [6]. With rising debts the developing nations have found themselves spending larger shares of their foreign currencies in debt repayments, which reduces capital available for internal development.

The technological gap between the developed and developing countries has been growing wider, in part because of cultural and economic hindrances to the transfer of technology from developed to developing areas. New techniques are being developed by advanced nations more rapidly than they can be adopted by developing nations [7]. Limited credit, lack of skills, and small industrial bases have created a "suitability gap" wherein new technologies are simply inappropriate to the economic and social conditions which exist in many developing nations [8].

One factor which has encouraged manufacturing in developing areas is concern among affluent societies about environmental hazards associated with economic development. In most developing nations the central problem is poverty rather than protection of the environment, and undesirable environmental effects of industrialization are overshadowed by the economic benefits it brings. Thus production costs in developing areas may be lower than in affluent areas where expensive modifications must be made to manufacturing plants in order to reduce environmental hazards. Developing areas may also benefit from renewed emphasis upon "natural" rather than "synthetic" products — again as a result of environmental considerations. Synthetic products (especially fibers and plastics) manufactured in affluent nations have during recent decades replaced many natural products formerly exported from developing nations. The developing nations may, however, suffer losses in export of some products as the result of recycling programs in affluent areas.

Patterns of Manufacturing Development

In most parts of the world production of manufactured goods has grown at a faster rate than production of agricultural commodities. The developed nations still account for the vast majority of manufactured goods, but the mix of manufactured products in the relatively poor nations appears to be moving closer to that of the affluent nations. Manufacturing industries in the poor nations are more oriented toward light manufactured goods and textiles than those of the advanced nations, which are more oriented toward heavy industries and metal production (Fig. 13-1). Manufactured foods, beverages, and tobacco products in the poor nations have declined relative to other types of manufacturers and are now comparatively less important than in the more affluent areas (Fig. 13-1).

The composition of manufacturing within the centrally planned economies is essentially the same as that of the developed market economies, although a few exceptions are worth noting. Chemical industries and the paper, printing, and publishing industries are of greater relative importance in the market economies than in the centrally planned economies, whereas food processing, nonmetallic mineral industries (cement production), and metal products occupy a somewhat larger share of the manufacturing mix in centrally planned than in the developed market economies (Fig. 13-1).

World patterns of manufacturing development show a lopsided concentration in favor of the developed nations (Fig. 13-2). Together, the developed market economies and the centrally planned economies accounted for 93 percent of world manufacturing output in 1970 [9]. The only significant shift to occur since the 1950s has been a relative decline in share of manufacturing output in the developed market economies and an increased share in the centrally planned economies.

Manufacturing among the developing nations is extremely uneven in distribution, with six countries accounting for nearly 60 percent of all developing area manufacturing in 1970 (Table 13-1) [10]. Four of the six leaders in manufacturing among the developing nations were in Latin America, which accounted for only 3.5 percent of the world's manufacturing output but for 52.7 percent of all manufactured goods produced within the developing nations. Developing nations in Asia accounted for 2.7 percent of manufacturing; those in Africa, only 0.5 percent. Egypt, alone, was responsible for some 33 percent of the manufactured goods produced by developing nations in Africa.

The enormous disparities in manufacturing output at the world level, as well as among the developing nations, reflects the extremely small influence that developing areas have upon world manufacturing. Nations with small populations and thus small domestic markets are particularly limited in their choices of specific developmental industries unless they are producing for overseas trade [11]. Further limitations to industrial development of low-income areas may occur because industries with high levels of price *elasticity* (industries where demand increases more than proportionally to increases in income) frequently require levels of technology and labor skills which are found only in the more affluent areas. Such industries are those manufacturing chemicals, metal products, electrical machinery, and transport equipment.

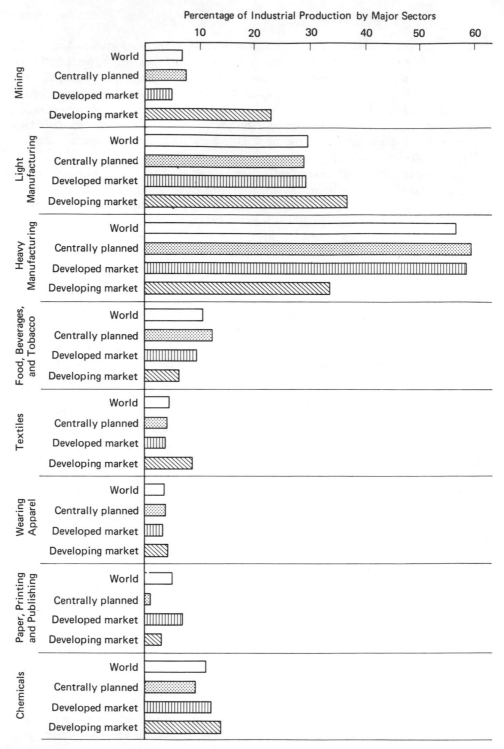

Fig. 13-1. Percentage of industrial production by major sectors for selected areas: 1970. [From *Statistical Yearbook, 1975* (New York: United Nations, 1976), Table 9.]

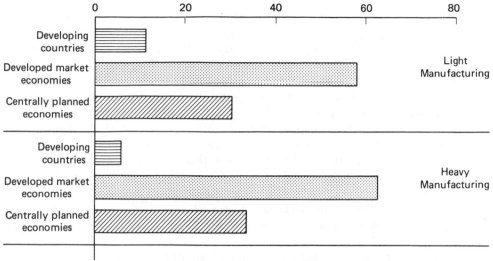

Fig. 13-2. Share of manufacturing output by major commodity group, by region: 1970. [From *Industrial Development Survey* (New York: United Nations, 1973), pp. 5-7.]

TABLE 13-1. Shares of World Manufacturing Output and Urban Populations for Selected Devloping Nations: 1970

Country	Share of Manufacturing Output (Percent)	Share of Manufacturing Output of Developing Nations (Percent)	Share of World Urban Population (Percent)
India	1.0	14.7	8.1
Brazil	1.0	14.3	4.2
Argentina	0.8	11.6	1.4
Mexico	0.7	10.4	2.5
Republic of Korea	0.2	3.4	0.9
Venezuela	0.2	3.2	0.6
Pakistan	0.2	2.9	1.2
Colombia	0.2	2.8	0.9
Indonesia	0.2	2.8	1.6
Chile	0.2	2.7	0.5
Iran	0.2	2.4	1.0
Egypt	0.2	2.4	1.1
TOTALS	5.1	73.6	24.0

SOURCES: *Industrial Development Survey,* **5** (New York; United Nations, 1973), Table 2, p. 8. *World Population Data Sheets,* Population Reference Bureau, 1973.

Per Capita Manufacturing Output

The extent to which regional disparities occur in manufacturing may be illustrated by comparing the value of manufacturing output per person in the population (Table 13-2). In most developed nations per capita manufacturing output is 10 to 50 times that in most developing nations. The value of per capita output in the United States, for example, was some 175 times that in Nigeria, 75 times that in India, and 13 times that in Brazil in 1970. Even among the developed nations substantial differences occur in value of manufactured output per capita. In East Germany, for example, the value of manufactured output per capita was nearly 4 times that in Italy, about 2½ times that of the Netherlands, and twice that of the United Kingdom in 1970. A comparison of centrally planned and market economies in Europe shows no appreciable difference in value of per capita manufacturing output. This may be attributed in large part to a faster rate of growth in manufacturing in the centrally planned than in the market economies during the last few decades.

That disparities in manufacturing development are increasing rather than decreasing is illustrated by a lower growth rate in per capita manufacturing output among the developing than among the developed nations. Between 1960 and 1968, for example, per capita manufacturing output increased only 1.4 percent in Africa, 2.9 percent in Latin America, and 4.3 percent in Asia. This contrasts with a rate of 5.2 percent within the developed market economies and 7.4 percent within the centrally planned economies [12]. Rapid population increase is a major contributing factor to the low per capita growth rates of manufacturing in the developing areas, as are differences in the manufacturing mix. Much of the manufacturing growth in developed areas has come through creation of new products, through improvements in old products, and through new manufacturing processes. The developed areas account for almost all the world's output of highly sophisticated products having a high value per unit weight, whereas the manufacturing mix in developing areas is restricted primarily to products that are widely produced, those in which innovation plays a small role, and those manufactured with unsophisticated processes. The implication here is that the higher the rate of population growth and the lower the capacity for innovation, the more difficult it is to improve levels of individual welfare through increasing manufactured output.

Manufacturing's Share of GDP, Growth in GDP, and Total Employment

Additional measures of the importance of manufacturing to different areas are the share of the total gross domestic product (GDP) accounted for by manufacturing, manufacturing's contribution to growth of the GDP, and the

TABLE 13-2. Per Capita Manufacturing Output and Percentage of Population which Is Urban: Selected Nations

Country	Per Capita Manufacturing Output (U.S. dollars) 1970	Urban Population as Percentage of Total Population	Rank in Percentage of Population Urban[a]	Rank in Per Capita Manufacturing Output
AFRICA				
Algeria	15	50	18.0	23.0
Egypt	37	43	19.5	22.0
Nigeria	6	16	27.0	28.0
Zaire	12	25	24.0	26.5
ASIA				
Burma	12	19	26.0	26.5
India	14	20	25.0	24.5
Iran	44	43	19.5	21.0
Republic of Korea	56	41	21.0	20.0
Thailand	14	13	28.0	24.5
LATIN AMERICA				
Argentina	257	81	2.5	14.0
Brazil	79	58	14.0	17.0
Colombia	68	39	22.0	18.0
Mexico	109	61	10.0	16.0
Peru	57	60	11.5	19.0
UNITED STATES	1,054	74	8.0	2.0
EUROPE				
Austria	514	52	17.0	11.0
Denmark	705	80	4.0	6.0
France	516	70	9.0	10.0
Federal Republic of Germany	764	88	1.0	4.0
Italy	324	53	16.0	3.0
The Netherlands	502	77	5.0	12.0
Portugal	149	26	23.0	15.0
Sweden	869	81	2.5	3.0
United Kingdom	643	76	6.0	7.0
CENTRALLY PLANNED				
Bulgaria	623	59	13.0	8.0
Democratic Republic of Germany	1,249	75	7.0	1.0
Poland	549	55	15.0	9.0
USSR	723	60	11.5	5.0

[a]Note that the ranks of the listed nations in per capita output of manufactured goods corresponds closely in most cases to their ranks in percentage of population which is urban. The Spearman Rank Correlation coefficient for these two variables is 0.778, indicating a strong relationship between the two variables.

SOURCE: *Industrial Development Survey* (New York: United Nations, 1973), Tables 5, 78; and *World Population Data Sheets,* Population Reference Bureau, 1976.

TABLE 13-3. Contribution of Manufacturing to Gross Domestic Product and Manufacturing's Share of Growth in Gross Domestic Product: 1960-1968

Area	Contribution of Manufacturing to Gross Domestic Product (Percent)	Manufacturing's Share of Growth in Gross Domestic Product (Percent)
Developing Nations	17.0	22.4
Latin America	23.3	28.1
Asia	14.6	21.7
Africa	9.7	9.0
Developed Market Economies	29.7	35.3
Centrally Planned Economies	46.3	60.0

SOURCE: *Industrial Development Survey,* IV (New York: United Nations, 1973), Table 3, pp. 6, 7.

importance of manufacturing in the overall employment structure (Table 13-3 and Fig. 13-3). Manufacturing is of greatest importance as an employer and in its contribution to gross domestic product in the centrally planned economies of eastern Europe and the Soviet Union (Fig. 13-3). It is least important in the developing nations of Africa and southern Asia. Additional areas where manufacturing is of particular significance in the employment structure include Japan, Australia, and most of northwestern Europe.

Manufacturing and Urbanism

Because most manufacturing takes place within cities, the percentage of the population which lives in urban areas is an additional indicator of the relative importance of manufacturing (Tables 13-1 and 13-2). That manufacturing is relatively less important in cities of developing nations than in those of developed areas is illustrated in Table 13-1, which shows that developing areas consistently account for a larger share of the world's urban population than of the world's manufacturing output. Urban populations in most developing nations have been increasing more rapidly than manufacturing, and a large proportion of city dwellers is employed in service industries or is unemployed. When the percentage of the population living in urban areas is compared with per capita manufacturing output for a number of developing and developed nations, however, the relationship between the two is very strong (Table 13-2). With a few exceptions, the higher the percentage of urbanites in the population, the greater is the per capita manufacturing output. This relationship lends some degree of credibility to the apparent feelings of a large share of the rural peoples of the world that cities offer economic

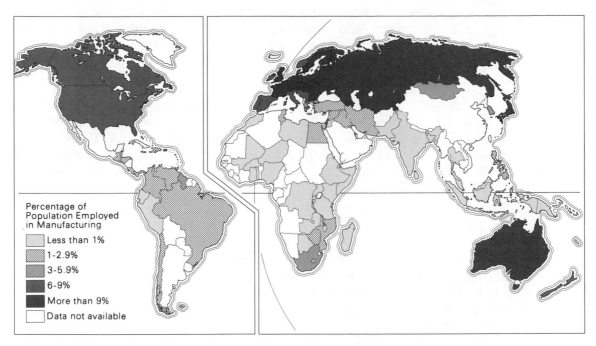

Fig. 13-3. Employment in manufacturing as a percentage of total population. [From *Statistical Yearbook: 1975* (New York: United Nations, 1976), Tables 2 and 80.]

opportunities not present in rural areas. Cities also provide a refuge for displaced agricultural workers, especially in developing areas where farming can no longer absorb burgeoning rural populations.

Modern manufacturing in most developing areas is largely confined to cities of considerable size, whereas in developed nations modern plants are frequently found in small towns and rural areas where labor forces are assembled from great distances. This type of development is often impossible in poor nations that lack a high density network of modern transport facilities.

In most advanced nations the growth of cities and of manufacturing have been associated with rapid social, economic, and technical transformations in the whole of society. Expanding markets, rising manufacturing output, an increased number of jobs, development of new technology, and changes in society are functionally interrelated in what has often appeared to be a chain reaction. In rural areas farms have adopted the machines, chemicals, and other products manufactured in the cities, and growing urban populations have provided the markets for increased farm output. In most poor nations, on the other hand, social, economic, and technical transformations and the expansion of markets for manufactured products is occurring at a slower pace than in advanced areas. Farm mechanization is retarded by the small size of most farms, ignorance, and lack of capital. Rural-to-urban migration within those areas rarely results in an absolute decline in the rural population such as that which happened in the advanced nations; rather it often represents migration out of desperation. Because of rapid population growth in already crowded subsistence agricultural areas, people have no place to go except the cities. Urban populations consist so largely of unemployed and underemployed peoples that markets for manufactured products as well as manufacturing jobs grow slowly if at all. To overcome these limitations to the growth of manufacturing jobs and domestic markets, many developing nations have attempted to secure foreign markets for their manufactured products.

Manufacturing and Trade

The largest markets for manufactured and other goods are within the developed nations, which also seek foreign outlets for their manufactured products. Developing nations seeking to secure export markets, therefore, must structure their manufacturing growth so as to make their manufactured products attractive to markets in other nations, especially those in the more affluent countries. Developing areas, for example, may selectively emphasize development of industries which, because of low returns to investment, have difficulty attracting investment capital within advanced nations. International trade is subject to considerable vacillation, however, for individual nations and groups of nations may invoke barriers to trade through tariffs, import restrictions, discretionary licensing, and quotas. The extent to which such restrictions occur depends on such variable factors as internal economic health, the amount of pressure imports place upon domestic producers, the influence those producers can bring to bear upon public decision makers, and the nature of international relationships among nations.

Manufactured goods represent less than 15 percent of total exports from developing nations, compared with greater than 75 percent for the developed market economies and more than 60 percent for the centrally planned economies. Products imported by developing areas, on the contrary, consist largely of manufactured goods, and imports by developed areas are mostly of raw materials. Manufactured exports from developed and from developing nations have been increasing as have imports. The rate of increase in exports is somewhat higher among developed and centrally planned economies than among developing economies, whereas the reverse is true with respect to imports [13].

Most of the world's trade in manufactured goods is among the developed market economies, and they also offer the largest markets for exports from developing nations. The quantity and number of exports generally increases with growth of gross domestic product [14]. Because the developing nations account for such a small absolute quantity of the world's manufactured goods and manufactured exports, even a large relative increase in production and exports would not match the absolute increase represented by a small rate of growth in the developed nations.

THEORIES RELATED TO MANUFACTURING DEVELOPMENT

Scholars have long sought explanations for the spatial inequalities in manufacturing and other economic activities that characterize the world's economic landscape. Economists, and more recently geographers, have attempted to identify common elements that exist in places possessing similar specialized economic activities and to utilize these common factors in the development of explanatory theories or models. Such theories and models, if successful, not only should be instructive to those who influence the location of economic activity but also should serve as predictive devices for forecasting where future economic activities will develop.

The Classical Economists

The classical economists of the eighteenth and nineteenth centuries included such notable figures as Adam Smith, Thomas Malthus, and David Ricardo. Their theories and ideas had an immense impact upon the thinking of governmental and private leaders in Europe and the United States during the early stages of the industrial revolution. The classical economists concerned themselves primarily with the importance of bringing three elements — land, labor, and capital — together under proper management to produce and market goods and services.

Two common threads which ran through the works of all the classical economists involved predictions of *equilibrium* and *diminishing returns*. Equilibrium refers to a state of balance. The balance may be upset, at least temporarily, by introduction of some external force. Eventually, however, balance will return until upset by another external force, and so on ad infinitum. If the number of automobiles being produced is exactly equal to the number consumers want and are able to purchase, for example, a state of equilibrium has been reached. An increase in production without an increase in demand, however, perhaps because of entry of a new manufacturer, creates a state of disequilibrium. Equilibrium will eventually return because the manufacturers lower prices in order to sell more cars, or they reduce output to demand levels. The classical economists devoted substantial effort to identifying processes through which equilibrium is achieved. Much of their work was concerned with equilibrium in the geographical distribution of economic activities.

The *law of diminishing returns* is based on the concept that certain resources, such as land and minerals, are essentially fixed in amount. As interpreted by most of the classical economists this meant that returns for effort would eventually decline. Let us assume, for example, that a suburban resident devotes 100 hours of labor per year to cultivating his 10 × 20 foot garden plot. The plot yields 100 units of vegetables, or one unit per hour of work. Increasing the effort invested in cultivating the plot to 200 hours per year may yield 200 units of output. If the number of hours devoted to cultivation of the same sized plot continues to rise, however, the number of units produced per hour of labor will eventually decline to less than one. At that point diminishing returns will have set in.

Adam Smith, who published *Wealth of Nations* in 1776, took a more optimistic view of the future of mankind than Malthus and Ricardo. The great economic regulator, according to Smith, was the marketplace. If individuals were allowed, even encouraged, to operate in their own self-interest, in a state of free competition, market demand would serve as an "invisible hand" to guide social and economic forces toward the greatest good for the greatest number of people. The equilibrium which Smith saw was one in which the self-interest of producers, in competition with one another, would provide consumers with the commodities they demanded at lowest possible prices. Diminishing returns would occur in certain industries at certain times; but as long as the market mechanism remained unfettered, it provided the instrument through which returns would eventually begin to accelerate and equilibrium would be returned.

Smith's view that society was on a wavering but generally upward march stood in contrast to the pessimism of Malthus and Ricardo. Malthus' famous treatise, *An Essay on the Principle of Population as it Affects the Future Improvement of Society*, was published in 1798, just 8 years after Smith died. According to Malthus the supply of agricultural land is constant and thus sets limits to the growth of population. Once all the land suitable for cultivation has been occupied by an expanding population, diminishing returns for effort will begin. The inevitable result, as Malthus saw it, was that levels of living would decline to the minimum required to sustain life.

Ricardo was much more an abstract theoretician than Malthus. In his writings during the first quarter of the nineteenth century, Ricardo envisioned society as an arena of great conflict. His major targets were the landlords, whom he sadly believed would be the ultimate winners over the industrialists. Through their competitive struggles the industrialists would find themselves unable to gain in real wealth. The workers would respond to any rise in their own circumstances by producing larger flocks of children who would compete against each other for work, bringing wages back to bare subsistence levels. Only the landlords, who were able to raise rents as the growing numbers of workers and industrialists competed for use of a stable supply of land, stood to gain. The highly pessimistic tone of the theories of

Malthus and Ricardo led to the characterization of economics as "the dismal science."

It was not so much the dismal science of Malthus and Ricardo as the free and unfettered market heralded by Smith that captured the imaginations of capitalists during the late eighteenth and the nineteenth centuries. Indeed, Smith's doctrine of laissez-faire became the theoretical justification behind the efforts of industrialists to block legislation aimed toward improving the working and living conditions of the masses. In reality, however, Smith was not so much opposed to governmental efforts to aid the poor as he was to corporations, monopolies, and mass production. Such developments would interfere not only with free competition but also with the free market which was the cornerstone of his view of a dynamic and forward-moving society.

Beyond the Classical Economists

One of the major weaknesses of the classical theorists was that they failed to realize (and understandably so) the full impact that science and technology would have upon "equilibrium" during the decades that followed. Each time a new product is introduced and each time a new method, process, or machine results in increased returns for effort, equilibrium is disturbed. Because science and technology have grown so rapidly in much of the western world during recent decades, disequilibrium has been a more common condition than equilibrium. Despite the weaknesses in classical economic thought, it formed the basis for the development of modern economics and economic geography.

During the late nineteenth and early twentieth centuries several economists developed theories which emphasized spatial differences in costs of producing and marketing goods. These economists focused not only upon where industries *do* locate but where they *should* locate. They attempted to provide a means for determining *optimum location* for industries through development of a series of abstract models. A basic assumption of most of the models was that the optimum location was the place where an industry could earn the greatest profits. In their efforts to identify such locations one group of theorists assumed that largest profits could be obtained from locations offering lowest possible costs of producing and marketing goods. A second group assumed that maximum profits could be made from locations offering access to the largest market areas. Because neither group of theorists was able to build a model which considered the total complex of forces affecting the location of manufacturing, they frequently postulated (assumed to be true as given) certain unrealistic simplifying assumptions, such as the following:

1. The land surface is a flat plain, with no restrictions to movement in any direction.

2. Physical resources are evenly distributed.
3. Population is evenly distributed.
4. There is only one market center.
5. All buyers have equal purchasing power and an equal propensity to consume.
6. All producers and consumers have perfect knowledge and act rationally.
7. The goal of all producers is to maximize profits in a system of perfect competition, with all buyers seeking to pay the lowest possible costs for all goods purchased.

That these assumptions are obviously in disagreement with reality was fully recognized by those who made them. The assumptions were offered, however, in an attempt to create an economic landscape upon which other variables could be tested. One of the primary objectives of modern "neo-classical" theorists in economics and in geography has been to "relax," or to reduce the rigidity of, many of the simplifying assumptions made by the early theorists so as to give them greater relevance to the real world. Despite their lack of applicability to decision-making processes in the real world, however, the locational principles introduced by the classical economists are not without value. They provide a necessary conceptual framework for an understanding of modern manufacturing processes.

The Least-Cost School

The *least-cost* school of theoreticians, among which the German regional economist Alfred Weber was most prominent, assumed that the best location for a manufacturing industry was at the point which offered lowest total costs of producing and marketing a good. Weber suggested that in the absence of geographical differences in basic production costs, the best location for a manufacturing plant is where total production costs are lowest. Assuming that transport costs are proportional to distance (see Chapter 6), he observed that transportation costs will vary according to the *weight* of materials that must be moved and the *distance* over which they are transported. By combining these two variables an index of transport cost called the *ton-mile* can be derived. In contrast to some earlier theories, a key element of Weber's theory was its allowance for an uneven distribution of some raw materials utilized by manufacturers. *Ubiquitous* materials (those which are universally available, or found everywhere) were classed as *non-localized.* These materials, according to Weber, were insignificant as determinants of plant location. *Localized* materials (those which are unevenly distributed over the earth's surface), on the other hand, exert primary influences upon plant location. Weber subdivided localized materials into pure localized materials and gross localized materials. A raw material whose entire weight becomes a part of the finished good is called a *pure localized* material. *Gross localized* materials are those in which only a portion of the weight of the raw material becomes a part of the finished good or in which some portion of the raw material becomes waste during the manufacturing process. The least-cost location of a manufacturing plant, therefore, could be determined on the basis of the weight of the raw materials relative to that of the finished product. The location which results in the lowest cost is that which involves movement of the lowest total weight over the shortest possible distance (the lowest ton-mileage).

In simplest terms, a manufacturer may locate near the market for his product, near the source of raw materials, or somewhere in-between. To determine which type of location would result in lowest total transport cost, Weber devised a *materials index* (MI), which is a ratio between the weight of localized materials and the weight of the finished product.

$$\text{MI} = \frac{\text{weight of localized materials}}{\text{weight of finished product}}$$

A *pure* material, where there is no waste in the manufacturing process, would have a materials index of 1, as follows:

$$\text{MI} = \frac{100}{100} \quad \text{MI} = 1$$

If all the raw materials used by a plant were *pure*, therefore, transport costs would be the same whether the plant located at the market, at the raw material source, or somewhere in-between. The tendency, however, would be to locate at the market.

If the raw materials used are *gross* localized materials, the materials index will have a value greater than 1, as follows:

$$\text{MI} = \frac{200}{100} \quad \text{MI} = 2$$

The higher the value of the materials index, the greater is the tendency to locate at the raw material source rather than the market. A location somewhere between the raw material source and the market may occur when several gross localized materials, each of which is obtained from a different place, are used in the manufacturing process (Fig. 13-4).

Weber's model has been criticized for being too simplistic, too inflexible, and too heavily based upon unrealistic assumptions to serve as a basis for modern industrial location. Transport costs are not directly proportional to distance, markets are normally spread over large areas rather than existing at single centers, freight rates for raw materials and for finished products are not the same, and the major cost variable is normally not transport cost. Despite its weaknesses, however, Weber's model illustrates some important

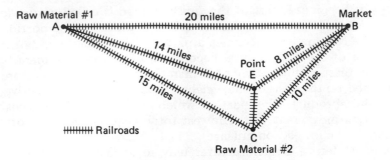

Fig. 13-4. Problem in manufacturing location.

Assumptions: 1. Transport cost = .01 per pound per mile
2. Manufacturer uses 10 pounds of Raw Material #1 and 5 pounds of Raw Material #2 to produce a finished product weighing 8 pounds.

Problem: At which of points A, B, C, or E, would total transport costs be lowest?

Solution:

		Pounds		Cost per mile		Distance Shipped	Total Cost
Point	RM–1	10	X	.01	X	0	$ 0
A	RM–2	5	X	.01	X	15	.75
	F.P.	8	X	.01	X	20	1.60
							$2.35
Point	RM–1	10	X	.01	X	20	$2.00
B	RM–2	5	X	.01	X	10	.50
	F.P.	8	X	.01	X	0	0
							$2.50
Point	RM–1	10	X	.01	X	15	$1.50
C	RM–2	5	X	.01	X	0	0
	F.P.	8	X	.01	X	10	.80
							$2.30
Point	RM–1	10	X	.01	X	14	$1.40
E	RM–2	5	X	.01	X	3	.15
	F.P.	8	X	.01	X	8	.64
							$2.19

The lowest total transport cost occurs at Point E, which is intermediate between raw materials and markets.

considerations in locational decision making, especially with respect to the relationships between raw materials and markets.

The discussion above concerns only a small part of Weber's work and should not be construed as representative of the real complexity of his ideas. The purpose of the discussion, however, and that which follows, is to introduce some of the basic elements of location theory which interested readers can pursue further through independent study or through taking courses with a focus upon theory.

The Market Area School

Recognizing that a location where goods can be produced at the lowest cost may not be an ideal location, other economists developed models based upon the concept that profits can be maximized by gaining access to the largest possible markets. Of central importance to this approach is- the concept of the *range of a good*, or the distance from the point of production that a good can be profitably sold. The greater the distance that a good must be transported from the point of production, the higher the transport cost. As transport cost increases, the producers must either sell at reduced profits or increase the selling price of the good. If we assume that the producer is willing to settle for the minimum amount of profit needed to justify continuation of production, the price charged for the good must increase along with increases in transport costs. As the price of the good rises, its attractiveness to potential customers decreases. Thus the potential demand for the good decreases with increasing distance from the point of production because of increases in its cost (Fig. 13–5). Under such constraints it is to the advantage of a producer to locate near the center of a large population of high density whereby the largest possible number of customers can be reached at the lowest possible cost.

Because it is unlikely that all customers can be supplied with a good from a single production point, additional producers may come into existence. The spacing of the new producers relative to the first producer and subsequent producers must be such that each producer can meet threshold requirements. Otherwise, one or more producers must cease production or relocate (Fig. 13–6). *Threshold* is the level of demand necessary to ensure the producer adequate profits to justify continuation of production.

Several theorists of the market area school have assumed that the ideal market area is one in which a producer has a monopoly over sales. The ideal shape for monopolistic market areas is the hexagon, which assures all consumers access to the good while virtually eliminating competition (Fig. 13–7). When production of a number of different goods is considered, advantages are normally derived from several producers *agglomerating*, or locating near each other. Agglomeration enables the several producers to

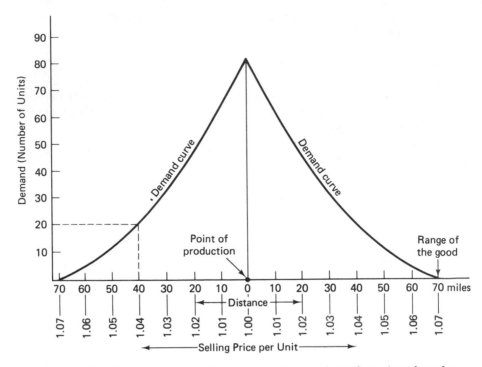

Fig. 13-5. The demand cone. Note that as distance from the point of production increases, the price charged for the good also increases, reflecting increased cost of transportation. As the price of the good rises, demand for it declines. Thus demand for the good at the point of production, where the selling price is $1.00 per unit, is 80 units. At 40 miles from the point of production the price of the good has increased to $1.04, and the demand has dropped to 20 units. At 70 miles from the point of production the price has become $1.07 per unit, and no one is willing to pay any additional amount. The demand at that point, therefore, falls to 0 units. Thus the range of the good is 70 miles.

share commonly useful service facilities and thereby to reduce costs to all concerned. Efficiency is also enhanced through linkages, or the ability of one manufacturing plant (such as a manufacturer of stoves) to use products (such as sheet metal, screws, bolts, springs, and paints) manufactured by other nearby plants. Agglomerations of producers frequently occur in the midst of areas of large demand, and such producers have market-oriented locations. Where a market is large enough to meet threshold requirements of several producers, the producers may agglomerate so as to share service facilities and compete for customers within the same market area. Because cities compress large numbers of people into small areas, they represent major markets for a variety of producers who usually agglomerate within certain sections of the cities. Such situations make for highest levels of efficiency in producing and selling goods.

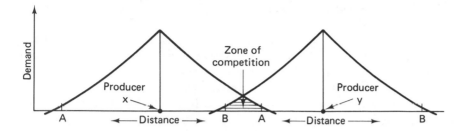

Points A — Range of the good necessary for producer x to meet threshold requirements.

Points B — Range of the good necessary for producer y to meet threshold requirements.

If sales of the good are equally divided by producers x and y in the zone of competition, neither producer can meet threshold requirements and both will fail. If one of the producers is able to dominate sales in the zone of competition the other producer will fail. Both producers can survive only by one (or both) of the producers relocating so as to increase the distance separation between them and thereby to increase the area served with the good, as follows:

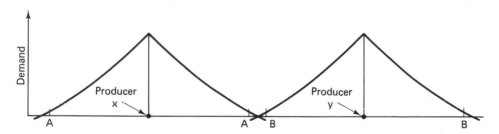

Fig. 13-6. Competition, threshold requirements, the range of a good, and location.

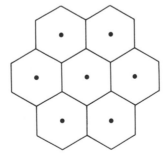

●   Locations of producers
── Boundaries of market areas

Fig. 13-7. Monopolistic market areas. Note that the hexagonal shapes of the market areas allow the entire area to be served with the good without the occurrence of zones of competition. The result is one of monopolistic market areas.

Least-Cost and Market Area Models Combined

In an effort to relax some of the unrealistic assumptions of previous least-cost and market area approaches, D. M. Smith developed a flexible model which attempts to combine the two approaches. Based primarily upon Weber's least-cost methods, Smith's model allows for variable costs of production and marketing, including transport and raw material costs, and for variations in revenue and in levels of entrepreneurial skill. A zone of profitability is identified by use of a *space-cost curve*, which also shows the relative amount of profit which can be obtained by locating at various points within the zone of profitability (the concept of *spatial margins of profitability*) (Fig. 13-8). Changes in revenue, costs, and entrepreneurial skill will alter the zone in which profits are attainable as well as the amount of profit or loss associated with any particular location.

Smith points out that an entrepreneur may consciously reject the most profitable location (Point E, Fig. 13-8) in favor of one which comes closer to meeting his social and psychological needs. These needs may include a particular cultural environment, quality of educational facilities, or aesthetic

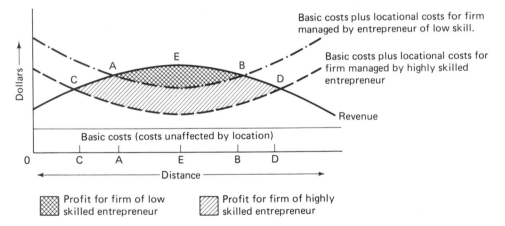

Fig. 13-8. Locational freedom model. The above model is based upon D. M. Smith's models of spatial profitability margins. The profitability of any firm is determined by its revenues minus its costs. The firm shown in the above model which is managed by a highly skilled entrepreneur can successfully locate anywhere between points C and D, whereas the locational freedom of the firm managed by an entrepreneur of low skill is restricted to the area between points A and B. Either firm will earn highest profits at point E, but profits will be higher for the better managed firm. [From D. M. Smith, "A Theoretical Framework for Geographical Studies of Industrial Location," *Economic Geography*, **42**, 1966; and D. M. Smith, *Industrial Location: An Economic Geographical Analysis* (New York: John Wiley, 1971).]

factors. The degree to which an entrepreneur favors a particular location on the basis of social and psychological factors may be termed *psychic income*.

The Information Linkage Approach

Because transport cost is rarely the most significant of the several variable costs that influence locational decisions, and because most companies do not base their locations on the least-cost or maximum profit criteria set forth by neoclassical economists, interest has been growing in the effects of *information linkages* on industrial location [15]. Most locational decisions in the relatively affluent industrial nations are made under a corporate umbrella rather than by private entrepreneurs using their own capital. Thus modern locational decisions must reflect linkages among those who administer or manage the corporation; financiers who furnish the capital for corporate development; stockholders of the corporation; government officials who are responsible for enforcing laws, regulations, and objectives respecting corporate and business behavior; heads of labor organizations; and perhaps numerous others. The final decision, therefore, will reflect the total informational, regulatory, and economic network to which the decision makers have access or to which they must respond. Recognition must also be given to social, economic, and regulatory *trends*, for a location which will yield highest profits today may become unprofitable within a few years. Thus the relative success of location decisions depends on the quantity and quality of information available to the decision makers and their abilities to interpret and use the information correctly [16]. Companies with access to the greatest amount of high-quality information and whose decision makers have superior ability to use the information will normally select viable locations. Others who base locations primarily upon chance factors stand a higher risk of failure.

The Role of Government

Governmental involvement in economic planning has increased enormously since World War II, in developing as well as in developed nations. The growth of government policies and regulations respecting labor, environmental problems, import and export licensing, wages, profits, management and accounting practices, transport rates, and other areas has greatly increased the frequency of contacts between manufacturers and government officials. Government has also become a major source of capital for expansion of old plants and construction of new plants, and government purchases account either directly or indirectly for a large share of the sales of many manufacturing plants. Thus through regulatory procedures, taxation policies, the letting of contracts, and the granting of loans and subsidies, governments can and do exert substantial control over industrial location. Such locational controls are often exercised for social as well as for economic purposes, and they may reflect government efforts toward a redistribution of wealth among social classes or among geographic areas.

In efforts to stimulate economic development, governments may choose any one of several strategies, each of which will affect locational trends in manufacturing. They may, for example, choose the *growth pole* approach to development whereby growth is encouraged in certain selected places with the expectation that economic benefits will diffuse outward from the growth pole. An opposite approach would be to discourage the concentration of industry and to encourage dispersal of facilities in a distributional pattern which reflects the distribution of the population. The British have used this approach to prevent overconcentration in the London area. A third approach involves emphasis upon *social capital*, whereby investments in industrial development are discouraged in favor of expenditures for expanding and upgrading educational and health care facilities. Whereas the growth pole and other approaches that encourage investments in manufacturing are expected to yield short-term economic gains, the social capital approach sacrifices short-term gains in the hope that long-run benefits from emphasis upon development of human resources will exceed those from alternate uses of available capital.

CONCLUSIONS

In regions where industrialization is in its early stages, capital requirements and plant sizes are relatively small. Locational decisions of small private entrepreneurs in such areas, however, rather than being guided by a body of location theory, are most commonly based upon small amounts of relatively low-quality information. Locational strategies in developed nations, on the other hand, are more likely to reflect careful planning by experts who have access to huge amounts of reliable information as well as the most sophisticated analytical devices and techniques. In one sense the greater care afforded locational decisions in developed areas is appropriate, for the decisions involve a more complex economic, social, and political environment.

In developed and in developing areas the location of each manufacturing facility is in many respects a special, or unique, case. In many developing nations the vast majority of companies make no definite location studies and the relationship between location and profitability is poor [17]. Plants are often constructed by local entrepreneurs who have learned the business locally, obtained local financing, and hope to succeed on the basis of personal contacts with governmental officials, suppliers, workers, bankers, and customers. Most such plants are small, as is characteristic of the early stages of industrialization.

Although manufacturing has grown and is growing in many parts of the world, the vast majority of growth is occurring in already developed areas. With a few exceptions there seems to be little chance that the relative contribution of manufactured products by the developing nations will be altered appreciably within the next few decades. Developing areas, for the most part, receive manufacturing industries that are cast-offs from the developed nations because of their low wage structures, lack of skill requirements, low rates of technical progress, or environmental risks. Developing areas do not have adequate capital, skilled workers, entrepreneurial expertise, or innovative capacity to compete effectively with developed areas for a substantial share of the more desirable manufacturing industries.

International patterns of manufacturing are influenced by such additional factors as political stability, quality of national governments, multinational corporations, the existence of international cartels, and the nature or direction of flows of capital. The bulk of the advantages, at least within the next few decades, appear to lie with the already industrialized nations; the developing nations will continue to feed off the crumbs of the affluent. The crumbs, however, may be preferred to nothing at all.

REFERENCES

[1] Gunnar Alexanderson, *Geography of Manufacturing* (Englewood Cliffs, N.J.: Prentice-Hall, Inc., 1967), p. 1.

[2] *Industrial Development Survey*, 5 (New York: United Nations, 1973), p. 33.

[3] Stanislaw Wellisz, *The Economics of the Soviet Bloc* (New York: McGraw-Hill Book Co., 1964), p. 2.

[4] Michael E. Eliot Hurst, *A Geography of Economic Behavior* (North Scituate, Mass.: Duxbury Press, 1972), p. 156.

[5] Amand G. Chandavarkar, "More Growth—More Employment?" *Finance and Development*, 9, No. 2, June, 1972, p. 31.

[6] "Borrowing in International Markets," *Road Maps of Industry*, No. 1818 (New York: The Conference Board, November, 1977).

[7] *Industrial Development Survey*, 5, *op. cit.*, p. 31.

[8] *Ibid*, p. 32.

[9] *Industrial Development Survey*, 5, *op. cit.*, p. 4.

[10] *Ibid*, p. 8.

[11] *Industrial Development Survey*, 4 (New York: United Nations, 1972), p. 30.

[12] *Ibid.*, pp. 4 and 5.

[13] *Ibid.*, pp. 38–43.

[14] *Ibid.*, p. 55.

[15] Alan Gilbert, "Industrial Location Theory: Its Relevance to an Industrializing Nation," in B. S. Hoyle (ed.), *Spatial Aspects of Development* (New York: John Wiley & Sons, 1974), pp. 271–289.

[16] A. Pred, *Behavior and Location*, Part I (Lund: Lund Studies in Geography, Series B, No. 27, 1967).

[17] A. Gilbert, *op. cit.*, p. 283.

CHAPTER FOURTEEN

major
manufacturing
industries

INTRODUCTION

The degree to which manufacturing is concentrated into a few major centers or is dispersed among numerous cities and towns varies greatly from one industry to another. Industries whose products are highly perishable or have a particularly low value per unit weight may be *ubiquitous* in location — or widely distributed over the landscape roughly in proportion to the distribution of the population. Industries of this type include soft drink manufacturers and bakeries. Industries that are likely to be heavily concentrated into a few production centers, on the other hand, are those (1) which benefit greatly from scale economies, (2) which require large amounts of highly skilled labor, (3) whose products have a particularly high value per unit weight, (4) which are heavily oriented toward raw materials, or (5) whose markets are highly specialized. Industries of these types include iron and steel, ore concentration plants, and high-quality machine tools.

Between 50 and 70 percent of the world's production of most manufactured products occurs in North America and Europe (Table 14-1). Manufacturing in the developed nations is highly diversified, although substantial subregional specialization also occurs.

Many areas of concentrated manufacturing originated near water power sites and coal deposits, for these sources of energy, along with wood, powered the initial stages of the industrial revolution. As industries grew and

TABLE 14-1. Percentage of World Population and of Manufacturing Output Accounted for by Major World Regions for Selected Products: 1976 (excluding USSR)

Item	Africa	North America	South America	Asia	Europe	Oceania
POPULATION (1978)	10.3	07.8	05.4	57.7	11.4	00.5
Margarine	08.2	21.3	03.3	11.5	41.0	00.0
Beer	04.0	29.4	05.0	06.8	44.6	02.9
Wood pulp	00.8	52.8	02.1	10.8	24.6	01.5
Paper	00.7	43.3	02.7	16.4	29.8	01.0
Rayon and acetate	00.3	14.0	02.4	21.4	42.9	00.0
Cement	03.3	13.6	04.8	25.5	35.0	00.8
Crude steel	01.2	20.0	01.9	22.4	31.8	01.2
Aluminum	02.4	36.6	01.6	12.1	30.9	04.9
Motor vehicles	—	35.1	02.9	20.9	35.1	01.3

SOURCES: *Statistical Yearbook: 1977* (New York: United Nations, 1978), Table 1, pp. 4, 5. "Population Data Sheet, 1978" (Washington, D.C.: Population Reference Bureau, Inc., 1978).

the demand for energy mushroomed, the ability of wood and water to supply adequate quantities of fuel for industrial growth declined relative to coal. Industrial expansion, therefore, was often most rapid on or near coal fields. By the time petroleum and natural gas became significant industrial fuels during the twentieth century, most present major manufacturing regions were already well-established. Large concentrations of people and markets had developed in the industrial areas, and enormous amounts of capital had been invested there. The major manufacturing areas had also become the foci for transportation routeways. Thus coal fields have continued to serve as locational nuclei for a large percentage of the world's manufacturing output (Fig. 14-1).

Industrial regions not associated with coal are found primarily in areas possessing large reserves of petroleum, natural gas, or metallic minerals; in coastal locations which serve as major import–export points for raw materials and finished goods; or in areas where hydroelectric energy is available in abundance at low cost. Manufacturing regions associated with petroleum and natural gas include the Gulf coastal region in Texas and Louisiana and the Venezuelan manufacturing area around Lake Maracaibo. The Pacific Northwest region in the United States is associated with abundant hydroelectric energy. The southeastern Piedmont manufacturing area in the United States was originally based largely upon availability of water power and low-cost labor. The Scandinavian and northern Italian industrial regions in Europe are associated with exceptionally favorable conditions for hydroelectric power, and the Urals manufacturing region in the Soviet Union is favored by large reserves of a variety of minerals, especially iron ore. Japa-

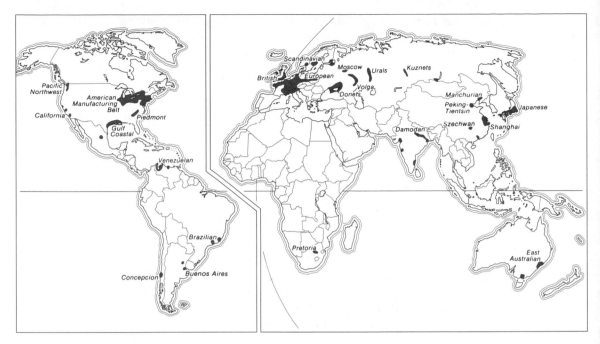

Fig. 14-1. Major manufacturing regions.

nese manufacturing is found largely on or near the coast, and Japan is a major producer of hydroelectric energy.

Although nearby availability of energy and other minerals and access to ocean transportation have been particularly significant influences upon development of major manufacturing regions, many additional factors have played key roles in the creation of the more prominent industrial areas. Factors such as entrepreneurship; availability of capital, labor, and new technology; and just plain good luck or chance have been important in the evolution of each region. Lack of entrepreneurship, capital, technology, and a suitable labor force (and bad luck) have prevented or retarded manufacturing in other areas.

MAJOR MANUFACTURING INDUSTRIES

As a general rule, the more technologically advanced and dynamic a manufacturing industry, the more locationally restricted is its distribution in the world. The more sophisticated products find markets primarily in the advanced nations, and the innovative and entrepreneurial skills, capital, and labor needed to produce them are equally limited in availability. Likewise the total number of products included in the manufacturing mix of a nation is positively related to its stage of economic development. Thus by borrowing some of the concepts and terminology of central place theory, an industrial hierarchy may be established somewhat as follows:

Developing Nations	Moderately Developed Nations	Highly Developed Nations
1. Low order manufactured goods	1. Low order manufactured goods 2. Medium order manufactured goods	1. Low order manufactured goods 2. Medium order manufactured goods 3. High order manufactured goods

Low order manufactured goods are those requiring few special skills to produce and which are commonly considered among the necessities of life. They include food, clothing, and unsophisticated building materials. *Medium order* manufactured goods are those which require modest skills to produce and which are commonly desired by persons of modest means. They include building materials (brick and cement), radios, furniture, and certain forms of wearing apparel. *High order* manufactured goods may be produced only in areas possessing a superior technology and a highly skilled labor force, and their costs and applications are such that only the wealthy and sophisticated are capable of using them extensively. High order goods include those such as aerospace products, large electronic computers, sophisticated research facilities, and specialized metallurgical and chemical goods.

The poorest, least developed nations are those least likely to produce medium or high order goods. Their industries are confined largely to production of goods requiring minimal skills, entrepreneurship, technology, and capital. Nations that have achieved a moderate level of development, such as Argentina, Venezuela, South Africa, and Yugoslavia, normally possess adequate pools of semiskilled and skilled workers and adequate amounts of technology and capital to manufacture medium order as well as low order goods. Highest order goods, on the other hand, are confined almost entirely to the most advanced nations such as the United States and those in northwestern Europe. Besides high order goods, the most advanced nations also produce medium and low order manufactured goods. In producing low order commodities, however, they frequently make use of greater amounts of technology and lower amounts of human labor than developing areas use.

Food Processing Industries

Food and clothing industries are found in every nation, although their characteristics vary a great deal depending on particular conditions of culture and economy (Table 14-2). Food processing in many developing countries remains primarily a household activity. Modern factory methods of food processing utilize products from a number of allied industries, such as packaging materials, tinplate, and glass containers. The absence of such industries in many developing areas has discouraged the construction of modern food processing facilities. Additional handicaps to modern food processing in developing areas are the frequent lack of public utilities, such as purified water, electricity, and transportation facilities, and the absence of adequate marketing, storage, and retail establishments. When a food processing factory must purify its own water; generate its own electricity; and develop its own marketing, transportation, storage, and retail distribution systems, the cost and complexity of the operation may quickly become overwhelming. Lack of processing and marketing facilities aggravates problems of low and unstable production.

In the more advanced nations food processing occurs almost entirely in specialized manufacturing plants. Even where the final stage of preparation is carried out at home, food has usually been partially prepared before reaching

TABLE 14-2. Manufacture of Processed Foods: Leading Nations (1974 or Most Recent Data)

CANNED MEAT		BUTTER	
Nation	*Metric Tons*	*Nation*	*Metric Tons*
USSR	397,733	France	508,200
United States	293,000	West Germany	507,974
Poland	149,588	India	438,600
United Kingdom	137,198	United States	436,230
France	93,700	East Germany	266,300
Denmark	79,884	Pakistan	200,318
Yugoslavia	70,058	Australia	175,497

CANNED OR BOTTLED VEGETABLES		CANNED FISH	
Nation	*Metric Tons*	*Nation*	*Metric Tons*
United States	5,650,855	USSR	677,550
USSR	2,263,441	Japan	374,000
France	1,445,200	United States	352,462
United Kingdom	852,000	Namibia	138,600
Romania	345,300	Spain	117,312
Netherlands	255,500	Morocco	103,089
West Germany	233,818	France	101,200

SOURCE: *Yearbook of Industrial Statistics: 1974* (New York: United Nations, 1976).

the kitchen. Inasmuch as the consumption of food is less elastic than that of most other products, only minor fluctuations normally occur annually in processing industry sales or profits.

Industries most likely to reflect changes in national economic conditions are those manufacturing the most expensive and the least expensive foods. During times of prosperity cheaper goods suffer from decreased sales. Periods of economic depression or recession result in a decline in purchases of more expensive items. Changes in diet and in consumer preference — perhaps initiated through advertising — may have pronounced effects upon individual processing industries. Changes in methods of processing or in form of consumption may also cause shifts in sources of supply in order to take advantage of cheaper or more desirable products. International complications between the United States and Brazil, for example, resulted after the widespread success of instant coffee and a shift in purchases by United States coffee companies from Brazil to Africa.

The beverage industries, including tea, coffee, whiskey, wine, beer, and soft drinks, tend to vary in importance according to the level of consumption in individual countries. Tea, for example, is the favorite drink of the British and Orientals. On the other hand, people living in the United States, France, and the Scandinavian countries consume much coffee. The greatest consumption of wine occurs in regions with Mediterranean climates, and beer and whiskey are most widely used in northwestern Europe and North America.

The drying or fermenting of coffee and tea nearly always occurs in the area of production. Final processing takes place in the country of consumption, thereby providing for individual tastes. An exception to this general rule occurred in 1965 when Brazil began making instant coffee for export in retaliation to United States' purchases from Africa.

The processing of wine, whiskey, and beer is generally completed in the producing country. Soft drinks, relatively low in price and expensive to transport, are usually mixed and bottled within a short distance of consumers. The United States leads in soft drink manufacturing, but in recent years the demand for this product has spread to most of the world.

Textile and Apparel Industries

In spite of the rapid rise in importance of synthetic fibers since World War II, cotton still accounts for about half of the output of apparel textiles in developed nations and 80 percent in developing areas (Table 14–3). Synthetic fiber and apparel manufacturing industries have the advantage of being able to adjust output to changes in market demand more easily than natural fiber industries, and synthetics are more stable in price. Recent increases in prices of coal and petroleum, from which many synthetics are made, have at

TABLE 14-3. Manufacture of Cotton Yarn: Pure and Mixed Leading Nations: 1976

Country	Thousand Metric Tons Produced	Country	Thousand Metric Tons Produced
AFRICA		EUROPE	
Egypt	193.2	France	253.1
South Africa	48.3	Poland	218.5
		West Germany	208.0
NORTH AMERICA		Italy	233.8
United States	1,229.8	Romania	165.0
Mexico[a]	158.3	Spain	72.7
		Czechoslovakia	124.8
SOUTH AMERICA		Yugoslavia	117.4
Brazil	69.7		
Argentina	91.7	USSR	1,583.0
ASIA			
India	1,005.9		
Pakistan	349.7		
China[b]	1,450.0		
Japan	498.3		
Hong Kong	221.9		
Republic of Korea	174.6		

[a]1975
[b]1969
SOURCE: *Statistical Yearbook, 1977* (New York: United Nations, 1978), Table 93.

least temporarily rejuvenated natural fiber industries in some developing areas. Wages in textile and apparel industries, compared with general wage rates, are higher in developing than in developed areas, but absolute wage levels are higher in developed nations [1]. The most important consideration is labor cost per unit of output, however, and in this respect the developed areas normally have an advantage because of the comparatively large sizes of their production units.

The textile industry has been a forerunner in the industrial development of most countries. Skills required by the manufacturing process are minimal and easily taught. Textile manufacturing has normally been a good investment when the nation produces the raw materials or when the industry is able to stimulate the growing of needed fibers. Because their large pools of unskilled and unemployed workers and low wage rates are attractive to textile manufacturers, the developing nations are becoming increasingly self-sufficient in textile production. Some are major exporters to developed areas.

Textile and apparel production is extremely complex when viewed on a world scale because of the great variety of natural and synthetic fibers used by these industries. Output of natural fibers has declined in most of the advanced nations since World War II, but it has increased in a number of developing nations such as India, Pakistan, and Turkey and in several centrally planned economies such as the USSR, Poland, and Romania. Fibers produced from a cellulose base, such as rayon, have also declined in output in several advanced nations which are now emphasizing more recently developed synthetics.

Manufacturing of clothing normally occurs primarily in the nations where they are to be consumed. High fashion garments, or those subject to rapid style changes, are manufactured principally in or near major style centers such as New York and Paris. Coarse fabrics such as jute, which is used as a backing for rugs and for making low-cost twine and bags, are normally manufactured into cloth in the regions where they are produced. India and Bangladesh, for example, manufacture 90 percent or more of the world's jute.

Metals Industries

Iron and Steel. Iron and steel rank first in importance among the metals industries and form the foundations of modern industrial society. Countries with largest per capita output and consumption of iron and steel have the highest living standards and the greatest military and political strength (Table 14–4). The high priority given to expansion of iron and steel production by the Soviet Union since the 1917 revolution was in recognition of the fundamental importance of these commodities to economic development.

TABLE 14–4. Production of Raw Steel in Selected Countries: 1976
(Million Metric tons)

DEVELOPED NATIONS		DEVELOPING NATIONS	
Country	*Output*	*Country*	*Output*
USSR	144.8	China	21.0
United States	116.3	Brazil	11.2
Japan	107.4	Spain	11.1
West Germany	42.4	India	10.2
Italy	23.5	Mexico	5.3
France	23.2	South Korea	3.5
United Kingdom	22.5	North Korea	3.0
Poland	18.0	Yugoslavia	2.8
Czechoslovakia	15.0	Argentina	2.4
Canada	13.7	Turkey	2.0
Rumania	12.2	Taiwan	1.6

SOURCE: *Metal Statistics, 1978* (New York: Fairchild Publications, 1978), p. 195.

Tapping a basic oxygen furnace in a steel mill. (Courtesy, American Iron & Steel Institute.)

Most of the world's iron and steel industries have located where iron ore, coal, and limestone can be assembled at low cost. They are often found near cheap water transportation and in proximity to large markets. During recent years the industry has become increasingly market-oriented as costs of assembling raw materials declined relative to other costs. Less coal is required per ton of steel than formerly, and new processes for beneficiating (concentrating) iron ores have made it possible to develop low-grade ores profitably. Efficient operation of a modern mill also requires local markets capable of absorbing a minimum of about 1 million tons of the metal annually. A chief disadvantage of numerous developing nations is that domestic markets are too small to allow steel industries to achieve *threshold* size or to produce a large enough volume to obtain economies of scale in output. Because steel industries do not require large numbers of highly skilled workers, however, they can be successful in poor nations where markets are of sufficient strength to reach threshold.

The Soviet Union, the United States, and Japan are the leading steel-producing nations (Table 14–4). Most of the steelmaking capacity of the United States is located in the region around Pittsburgh, along the Lower

Steel ingots being poured from a basic oxygen furnace. (Courtesy, American Iron & Steel Institute.)

Great Lakes, and in the Middle Atlantic area. Leading steel-producing areas in the Soviet Union include the Donets Basin, Southern Ural Mountains, and Kuznets Basin. Most of the Japanese steel industry is located on the southeastern side of Honshu Island. British steel industries are concentrated primarily in the Midlands area, the Northeast Coast, South Wales and the Scottish Lowlands. The French steel industry is mainly in the Lorraine District, and the Ruhr District in Germany is one of the outstanding industrial regions in the world.

Aluminum Industry

Aluminum is by far the most important of the light metals. It is a relative newcomer to world industry, for its commercial production dates back only as far as 1886. More than 2,000 uses have been found for the metal, however, and its light weight makes it particularly vital in the manufacture of transportation equipment — especially aircraft. Its principal ore, bauxite, is found in greatest abundance in the tropics and subtropics. The ore is ordinarily concentrated into *alumina* near the mines. Reduction of alumina into aluminum takes place in areas which possess an abundance of low-cost energy and (or) large markets for aluminum. Enormous amounts of electri-

TABLE 14-5. Aluminum Production in Selected Nations: 1976
(Thousand Short Tons)

DEVELOPED NATIONS		DEVELOPING NATIONS	
Nation	*Output*	*Nation*	*Output*
United States	4,251	Spain	236
USSR	1,760	India	234
Japan	1,013	China	220
West Germany	768	Ghana	162
Canada	690	Brazil	149
Norway	670	Greece	148
France	424	Mexico	47
United Kingdom	369		

SOURCE: *Metal Statistics: 1978* (New York: Fairchild Publications, 1978), p. 21.

cal energy are required in the reduction process, and energy is the major cost factor in pricing the finished product. Rising costs of energy and transportation during recent years, however, and lack of availability of additional sites for huge hydroelectric plants have resulted in a shift in new plant locations toward the major markets for aluminum.

The United States produces approximately 30 percent of the world's aluminum, followed by the Soviet Union with about 13 percent, and Japan, West Germany, Canada, and Norway about 5 to 7 percent each (Table 14-5). In the United States aluminum production takes place primarily in the South, the Midwest, and the Pacific Northwest, near major sources of water power, natural gas, or coal. France is the only major producer of aluminum that has a large ore reserve, hydroelectric power, and large markets located close together. The developing nations which produce bauxite are accounting for an increasing share of production of alumina, but they do not possess the market size nor the market sophistication to support more than small aluminum industries.

Metal Fabricating and Assembling Industries

The metal fabricating and assembling industries manufacture an extensive variety of products ranging from watches, machine tools, refrigerators, and washing machines to airplanes, missiles, automobiles, and ships. These industries occur only in the most advanced nations where the necessary labor skills, technology, and markets can be found to support them.

The full range of the metal-fabricating industries is too vast for each one to be considered individually. Because of their great size and importance, however, the machine tool, automobile, and aircraft industries deserve special treatment. Particular emphasis is given to the automobile industry because of its widespread economic and social importance and because of its leadership in developing many of the techniques used in modern manufacturing activities.

Machine Tools. The machine tools industry produces items such as lathes, drills, planes, presses, and cutting and grinding equipment. It is one of the world's most geographically concentrated industries. In the United States, for example, southern New England, Michigan, Illinois, and Ohio account for almost the entire output. Concentration reflects the industry's market orientation and its requirement for highly skilled labor. Competition among manufacturers is based more upon quality than upon the price of the finished product. Automation is reducing the need for skilled labor, but costs of transporting raw materials and finished goods have such relative insignificance in the location of the industry that inertia will probably preclude any major shifts for some time to come. Machine tools industries are virtually excluded from most developing nations because these nations lack adequate supplies of labor with the necessary skills to produce such products and their markets for machine tools are small.

Automobiles. The automobile industry, as the prime example of modern assembly line operation and parts standardization, typifies mass production. The American automobile industry leads all other industries in consumption of steel, rubber, lead, and nickel, and its use of aluminum, zinc, copper, and machine tools is extensive. Products are assembled from many countries for manufacturing the myriad parts which comprise a modern automobile. Parts manufacture occurs primarily in Michigan, but final vehicle assembly often takes place in regional centers. Parts can be shipped much more compactly than assembled autos, which contain a great deal of "dead" space. Consequently, unassembled shipments entail substantially lower transportation charges.

Automobile manufacture is restricted to a few of the more highly developed nations such as the United States, Japan, West Germany, the United Kingdom, France, Sweden, Canada, the Soviet Union, and Australia (Table 14-6). The manufacturing concerns are huge, especially in the United States where frequent model changes require rapid amortization of new machinery. Even where model changes are less frequent, large-scale operations are essential owing to the complexity and magnitude of making and assembling thousands of component parts and because of the vast sums of money involved in advertising and maintaining retail dealerships.

The United States automobile industry is almost as intimately tied to the world of fashion as the ladies' clothing industry. Price competition is played down in favor of style competition. Only in recent years, after governmental pressures to increase the safety and economy of their products, have manufacturers given more than casual attention to passenger safety and develop-

TABLE 14-6. Production of Passenger Cars, Selected Nations: 1976

DEVELOPED NATIONS		DEVELOPING NATIONS	
Nation	*No. of Cars*	*Nation*	*No. of Cars*
United States	8,752,600	Spain	769,000
Japan	5,027,800	Brazil	566,400
West Germany	3,546,900	Mexico	229,000
France	3,388,000	Argentina	142,100
Italy	1,471,300	India	38,000
United Kingdom	1,333,500		
USSR	1,239,000		
Canada	1,137,300		

SOURCE: *Statistical Yearbook, 1977* (New York: United Nations, 1978).

ment of efficient nonpolluting engines and emission systems. The industry is so massive, with such huge fixed-capital investments, that significant changes in body and engine construction require billions of dollars in new capital. Inertia has been a particularly strong force in engine design, leading automakers to sternly oppose governmentally imposed standards for fuel efficiency and pollution abatement.

Concentration of the United States auto industry in southern Michigan has resulted from several factors. Henry Ford and several other pioneers in the industry had made their homes in southern Michigan, but this had occurred largely as an accident of birth or choice prior to the industry's origin. Carriages, which had been manufactured in the area prior to the invention of the auto, formed the basic frame for the earliest automobiles. Furthermore, the skills that had been utilized in carriage construction were easily adapted to early auto manufacturing. Southern Michigan also enjoys proximity to most of the bulky raw materials needed for automobile manufacture. The lower Great Lakes Region is one of the world's fastest growing markets, has access to excellent transportation facilities, and is near the center of population in the United States.

Orientation toward specific raw materials is relatively unimportant, for the auto industry consumes materials primarily as semifinished components. These components are furnished by hundreds of manufacturers in the Great Lakes area. Because the equipment used in assembling automobiles is so highly automated, availability of skilled workers is not a major factor in the location of assembly plants.

Of immeasurable importance to the success of the southern Michigan auto industry has been the high quality of its managerial leadership. The failure during the 1920s of car manufacturers in places such as Chicago, New York, Cleveland, and St. Louis probably resulted from wrong decisions concerning the direction the industry would take in the future. Because they correctly judged the immense appeal that automobiles would have to Americans and were willing to risk the vast sums of capital required to establish large-scale production units, the southern Michigan manufacturers bested those in other areas in the early attainment of sufficient size to gain scale economies in the production of automobiles.

European automakers were not so quick as American manufacturers to adopt mass-production techniques and to standardize auto parts. European cars were built and priced primarily for the wealthy long after Henry Ford and others had begun production of inexpensive models for American consumers. High tariff barriers among European nations, high gasoline prices, and the lower purchasing power of Europeans compared to Americans denied Europe's manufacturers the opportunity to practice the kinds of scale economies available in the United States.

After World War II many economic barriers to trade were eliminated as a result of Common Market agreements. European manufacturers began mass production of small economy-sized, fuel-efficient models and the love affair that had previously characterized American attitudes toward their automobiles was extended to Europe. The experience gained by European manufacturers in making high-quality small cars proved to be a major advantage for them when small cars become popular in the United States during the 1960s and the "energy crisis" led to sharp increases in fuel prices. American automakers, accustomed to producing and marketing increasingly powerful and roomier cars, found themselves unprepared for the sudden surge in demand for the smaller, more efficient models such as the German-made Volkswagon, the Swedish Volvo, and the Italian Fiat. The foremost European automotive producers are centered around Wolfsburg, West Germany; Turin, Italy; Paris, France; and London, England.

Large-scale automobile production has also begun in the Soviet Union. The vastness of the nation and the cost of building all-weather roads and service facilities have retarded the growth of the industry, for Soviet authorities have been hesitant to divert from other activities the enormous amounts of capital and physical resources that would be required to support a massive automobile industry. During recent years, however, the Soviets have shifted significant amounts of capital into automobile construction and have negotiated the establishment of several foreign auto firms in the Soviet Union.

The automobile industry in Japan, like many other industries, has grown explosively since World War II. Japanese manufacturers have successfully captured large markets in the United States and in other countries, at the same time that the domestic market for cars in Japan has grown enormously. Thus Japan's auto production multiplied some 6½ times between 1965 and 1973. As in Europe, the Japanese have had lengthy experience in building small, fuel-efficient, cars. They have enjoyed the further advantage of relatively low-cost labor, although Japanese wages have been rising at a more rapid rate than wages in most western nations during the last two decades.

Aircraft and Aerospace Industries. Although they are relative newcomers on the world scene, the aircraft and aerospace industries rank among the world's largest. Governments constitute the principal markets for these industries, far surpassing purchases by commercial passenger and freight interests. Government purchases are determined primarily by relative values placed upon maintaining air or space supremacy and by the degree of tension in international relations.

Assembly line production does not dominate aircraft and aerospace manufacturing as it does the automobile industry. Designs change so rapidly that obsolescence usually occurs after production of relatively few models of the same type. This is especially true in the production of space vehicles. Furthermore, orders for aircraft fluctuate so widely as a result of changes in international tensions and economic conditions that assembly line techniques can be adopted only to fill large governmental orders. Even the enormous growth in commercial air passenger and freight traffic have not

Fokker Works aircraft manufacturing plant in the Netherlands. (Courtesy, Embassy of the Netherlands.)

appreciably increased orders for aircraft, for most of the newer models have larger passenger or freight handling capacity than prior models. Because of the high cost and relatively rapid obsolescence of aircraft, manufacturers and governmental agencies encourage development of models that can be adapted to several uses.

Like the automobile industry, aircraft and aerospace manufacturing occur only in advanced nations. Nations unable to afford the capital and scientific investment required for modern aircraft production usually purchase their needs for commercial and military planes from the wealthier and more highly developed countries. Aircraft sold to foreign nations are often surplus or outmoded models that the producing countries are happy to dispose of even at low prices.

Aircraft and aerospace plants have greater locational flexibility than those of most other industries, for their success does not depend on proximity to raw materials or markets. As the air and space industries become increasingly complex and innovative, however, with heavy requirements for skilled workers, technicians, and talented scientists, the industries appear to draw closer to places that possess large pools of such personnel.

Parts for planes and spacecraft are made in widely scattered locations, from which they are collected and assembled at a few points. Recent trends are toward increasing concentration of the industry, and several companies have gone out of business or changed to the manufacture of other products. In the case of the supersonic Concorde, England and France joined forces in order to share costs of research and development.

Building Materials Industries

A great variety of substances is used for building materials, ranging from palm leaves, skins, and mud to glass, artificial marble, metals, wood, and stone. Many building products are strictly local in origin and are unprocessed. The use of building materials, however, is almost as ubiquitous as is the use of food. We shall limit the discussion here to two widely used manufactured building materials, cement and bricks. Both industries are market-oriented because they have relatively low unit value and costs of shipping are high. Cement is the most versatile and the most widely used of all construction materials and is produced on a commercial basis in nearly every country in the world (Fig. 14-2). Whereas brickmaking in some regions is largely a noncommercial family activity, cement is nearly always produced on a commercial basis because of the special kilns and high temperatures required in its production. The raw materials for cement production — mainly limestone, clay, or shale and gypsum — are of common occurrence, especially limestone and clay. The industry also uses large amounts of fuel, mostly coal, but the ratio of limestone to coal is about three to one. Thus the localization of the

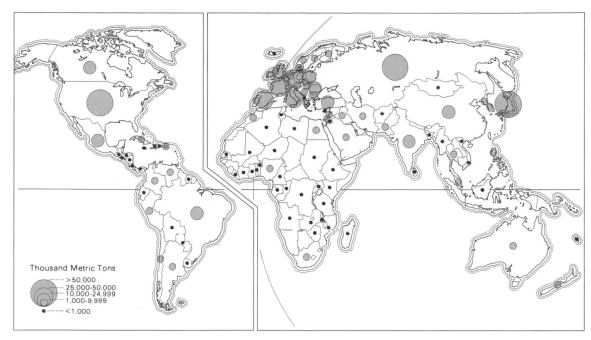

Fig. 14-2. World cement production: 1974. [From *Yearbook of Industrial Statistics, 1974* (New York: United Nations, 1976).]

industry is more dependent on limestone than upon coal. Cement manufacturing does not require great skill, and capital requirements are relatively modest compared to most manufacturing industries.

The Soviet Union is the world's largest producer of cement, followed by the United States and Japan. Most of the remaining output is manufactured in Europe. Disparities in output are indicated in that more than 750 pounds of cement are produced annually per person in the United States, compared with only 44 pounds in India.

Commercial production of bricks is less widespread than that of cement, which is now used in many types of construction formerly utilizing bricks. The principal raw material used in brick manufacturing is clay, and clays of sufficient quality for brickmaking are common. Brickmaking is disproportionately important in several nations with dry climates, where the bricks are often crudely made from a mixture of mud and straw and dried under the sun rather than in artificially heated kilns (Table 14-7). In many such areas the production of bricks is a noncommercial enterprise and data are not collected on their output. As with cement, the Soviet Union is the world's largest manufacturer of bricks, followed by Spain, the United States, Iran, and several European nations. Except in rare instances bricks are used in construction within a short distance of the manufacturing plant.

TABLE 14–7. Manufacture of Bricks, Made of Clay, Selected
Nations: 1974 (Million Units)

DEVELOPED NATIONS		DEVELOPING NATIONS	
Nation	Output	Nation	Output
USSR	33,788	Spain	7,730
United States	7,565	Iran	6,726
Italy	4,976	Yugoslavia	3,241
United Kingdom	4,432	Egypt	743
West Germany	4,367	Brazil	4,124[a]
France	3,389	Rhodesia	274

[a]1966

SOURCE: *Yearbook of Industrial Statistics: 1974* (New York: United Nations, 1976), p. 421.

Chemical Industry

Nearly all industries depend on chemicals, but for some industries almost the entire manufacturing process is chemical-oriented. Products manufactured or processed by the chemical industries include synthetic resins and fibers, explosives, soaps and detergents, pharmaceuticals, paints and varnishes, fertilizers, fuels, and rubber.

Heavy chemicals, such as benzene and methanol; sulfuric, hydrochloric and nitric acids; soda ash; caustic soda; and chlorine are used extensively by the chemicals and other industries. Sulfuric acid ranks first in importance. Large quantities of this chemical are necessary for oil refining and in the manufacture of explosives, textiles, steel, paints, paper, and synthetic fibers.

Fine chemicals, including dyes, analytical chemicals, and synthetic flavorings, are used for specialized purposes. Produced in relatively small volumes, they sell at comparatively high prices. Plastics are an exception, however, for they are used in large volumes for a great variety of products.

The chemical industry is characterized by rapid changes in technology and its growth rate is normally much higher than that of the economy as a whole [2]. Partly because they are heavily research-oriented, chemical industries are often unsuited to any except the most advanced nations. Developing nations often suffer the additional handicap of domestic markets which are too small to enable chemical industries to achieve scale economies necessary to their successful operation. Achieving scale economies is particularly important in the chemical industry, for the relatively short span of use of much of the machinery used in production requires large-scale output in order to raise funds necessary for replacing worn out or outdated equipment. A further disadvantage of developing nations in chemical production is the high percentage of skilled workers, scientists, and technicians required by the industry. Developing nations, therefore, account for only about 5 percent

TABLE 14–8. Production of Sulfuric Acid, Selected Nations: 1976 (Thousand Metric Tons)

DEVELOPED NATIONS		DEVELOPING NATIONS	
Nation	*Output*	*Nation*	*Output*
United States	30,392	Spain	3,730
USSR	20,015	Mexico	2,171
Japan	6,095	India	1,693
West Germany	4,668	Tunisia	1,081
France	3,959	Yugoslavia	934
United Kingdom	3,271	Chile	206[a]
		South Korea	626
		Philippines	280

[a]1974

SOURCE: *Yearbook of Industrial Statistics: 1977* (New York: United Nations, 1976), Table 112.

of the world's chemical production, and they consume substantially more than they produce.

Except for commercial fertilizers, the near universal demand for sulfuric acid in manufacturing and in the processing of raw materials makes it the most widely produced chemical. The United States, the Soviet Union, Japan, and the nations of western Europe account for most of the output of sulfuric acid and for an even higher percentage of production of most other chemicals (Table 14-8).

Nitrogenous fertilizers are also widely produced, although amounts are relatively small except in the same areas that lead in production of sulfuric acid, and in China (Table 14-9). the same distribution of production also holds true for output of superphosphates, but potassic fertilizers are much

TABLE 14-9. Production of Nitrogenous Fertilizers, Selected Nations: 1976-77 (Thousand Metric Tons)

DEVELOPED NATIONS		DEVELOPING NATIONS	
Nation	*Output*	*Nation*	*Output*
United States	9,790	China	3,827
USSR	8,531	India	1,858
Japan	2,399	Spain	883
France	1,462	Mexico	650
Poland	1,548	South Korea	510
		North Korea	270
		Indonesia	250
		Egypt	200

SOURCE: Harry Jiler (ed.) *Commodity Year Book: 1978* (New York: Commodity Research Bureau, Inc., 1978), pp. 160-161.

A portion of the nitrogen fixation plant at Heerlen, the Netherlands. (Courtesy, Embassy of the Netherlands.)

more restricted in location of output. The leading potash producers are the Soviet Union, Canada, East and West Germany, France, and the United States. These six nations accounted for more than 90 percent of world output during 1974.

CONCLUSIONS

Most of the world's manufactured goods are produced by countries located adjacent to the North Atlantic Ocean, and that is where the major manufacturing regions are likely to remain — at least through the twentieth century. The more important relative shifts in manufacturing output since World War II have been toward eastern Europe and the Soviet Union and toward Japan. Recently initiated efforts to modernize China may result in a sharp rise in industrial production in that country, but much depends on China's ability to obtain adequate credit, maintain stability in its leadership, and sustain good relationships with nations that can provide the technology and the markets that rapid industrialization will require.

That developing nations will achieve a major increase in their present share of world manufacturing output is improbable, although absolute growth in industrial production should rise significantly. World population increases are likely to be confined primarily to the developing nations, and more people normally translates into larger markets for manufactured goods. This is especially true when urban populations are growing rapidly, as they are in most developing areas. Whether the increased demand for manufactured goods will be supplied primarily from within the developing nations or from the developed nations, however, remains to be seen.

Manufacturers in developed nations may well look increasingly toward developing areas for markets in the future, for they are facing stable and aging populations in home markets. Expansion of markets within developed nations will depend largely on increases in real incomes and still higher levels of mass consumption than at present. Yet significant opposition to high mass consumption has developed within the advanced nations, along with fears of irreversible damage to the natural environment and scarcity or exhaustion of vital resources. It may be more difficult than previously, therefore, to convince those within the affluent nations that further increases in high mass consumption are desirable.

An additional factor which may have a depressing effect upon growth of manufacturing in developing as well as in developed nations is the increasing cost of energy. Improving the efficiency with which energy is used may offset rising costs to some degree, but other problems such as balance of payments deficits in the major energy-importing nations may discourage industrial expansion. Nations producing a surplus of energy, at relatively low cost, should be in the best position to expand manufacturing if they possess or can purchase the necessary skills, technology, and related resources that are essential to industrial development.

Advanced nations are almost certain to continue their present overwhelming advantage in the more innovative industries that require exceptionally large pools of skilled labor and highly trained scientific talent. Developing nations, on the other hand, could significantly increase their share of world output of goods that come from technologically stable industries requiring minimal labor skills.

REFERENCES

[1] "Industrialization in Developing Countries: Problems and Prospects," Monograph No. 7, *Textile Industry* (New York: United Nations, 1969), p. 55.

[2] "Industrialization of Developing Countries: Problems and Prospects," Monograph No. 8, *Chemicals Industry* (New York: United Nations, 1969), p. 1.

PART SIX
SERVICE INDUSTRIES

disparities in provision of services

INTRODUCTION

Tertiary industries consist of activities that generate wealth without the production of material commodities, or their transformation from one form to another. They include recreational, educational, medical, administrative, and repair services; wholesale and retail trade; banking, insurance, and real estate activities; and the generation and transmission of information. Thus domestic servants, garbage collectors, retail sales clerks, entertainers, doctors, lawyers, educators, computer programmers, truck drivers, and automobile mechanics are all engaged in providing services to the population. Services requiring the highest levels of specialized knowledge or skill are concentrated primarily within the more advanced societies. The importance of such services in the more advanced areas is demonstrated by the revolutionary changes they have wrought in the conduct of business, government, trade, education, medicine, and nearly all aspects of life. Without these services today, it is difficult to imagine how modern societies could function or even survive. Although service industries are important within developing areas, they are normally less sophisticated and require a smaller percentage of the labor force.

Service industries have often been viewed by economists as "nonproductive" because they do not yield tangible goods and they do not transform less useful into more useful commodities. This view is hardly justifiable, however, because without the efficient and dependable operation of sophisticated service functions the tangible goods industries would grind to a halt or find themselves faced with virtually intolerable problems.

CONCEPTS RELATED TO SERVICE CENTERS

Central Place Theory

Most service activity is associated with towns and cities which are often referred to as *central places;* for example, places that provide their surrounding populations with goods and services. They are sites where administrative, sales, medical, and other activities are concentrated. Some goods and services are purchased with much greater frequency than others. Those most frequently utilized by customers, such as food stores, pharmacies, gasoline stations, and banks, are found in greatest numbers. Services of these types are located in even the smallest of towns and villages and they are offered in numerous locations within large cities. According to *central place theory*, services which occur in the most numerous and the most dispersed locations are described as *low order services* [1]. Those which occur infrequently and which are found only in large cities are described as *high order services*. A center which offers only low order services is called a *low order center. High order centers*, however, offer not only high order but a full range of services including those of lowest rank. The important point here is that businesses offering low order services can meet *threshold* requirements (they can generate adequate business volume to assure the minimum profits required for the business to succeed) from a relatively small population base because all or most persons have frequent needs for those services. Threshold requirements for high order services, on the other hand, demand a larger population base because such services are purchased less frequently (because of their high cost or their highly specialized nature) than low order services. The *range* (distance from the service center over which a service is marketed) of low order services is therefore relatively small, whereas the range of high order services is correspondingly large.

Gravity Concept. The gravity concept, or the law of retail gravitation, is based upon a somewhat dubious application of Newtonian physics to the shopping patterns of consumers. The simplest version of the concept states that the amount of trade attracted to a central place is positively related to its size and inversely proportionate to the distance between the place and its potential customers. In effect, a large trade center or shopping mall will attract more customers from a greater distance away than a small trade center or mall. At the same time, the proportion of potential customers who make shopping trips to the large or the small facility will decline with increasing distance from the facility.

An African market scene. (Courtesy, Agency for International Development.)

Efforts to derive "laws" which use the gravitational principle to explain human behavior precisely are probably misdirected, for they imply a substantially more mechanistic character to behavior than is demonstrated in reality. Customers do not always shop at the nearest place where a good or service is offered. Their shopping patterns may be directed by the search for lowest prices, the prestige of a particular store or shopping center, high-quality service, friendly salespersons, a pleasant atmosphere, convenient parking, or the potential for fulfilling several shopping needs in a single trip. Although behavioral patterns are not precisely predictable, therefore, it has been demonstrated that stores or shopping areas with certain characteristics have greater attractiveness to customers then others. A sizable group of service or retail sales establishments in one location, for example, normally attracts a greater number of customers to each firm than would occur if the firms occupied isolated or dispersed locations. A grocery store ordinarily draws its customers from within a relatively short radius, whereas a large department-store normally attracts customers from much greater distances. By placing two such stores adjacent to each other, however, the one adds its drawing power to that of the other. Thus a customer who visits the department store to purchase a tablecloth may stop by the grocery store to purchase some food items to serve on the new tablecloth. The beneficial effect of stores offering different goods and services locating adjacent to each other has been termed *retail complementarity*. Thus the predominant types of retail developments in the United States and parts of Europe during recent years have been neighborhood and regional shopping centers or malls. Neighborhood centers draw customers from a relatively small area compared to regional centers. Their "gravitational" strength is attuned primarily to that of a supermarket, a small variety store, a drugstore, and several specialty shops. Regional centers, on the other hand, base their gravitational strength upon one or more large department stores that carry an enormous array of goods and attract customers from a much wider radius than the neighborhood center. In the regional center, the large department stores complement and are complemented by the attractiveness of grocery stores, banks, and a great variety of specialty shops.

LOCATIONS OF SELECTED SERVICES

Arterial Locations

Most urban areas are built around a systematic arrangement of transportation facilities which provide a basic service to other businesses within and around the city. Once established, the basic transportation pattern is difficult and expensive to alter. Major transportation arteries are influenced by, and in turn influence, the direction, rate, and character of urban growth. Routeways and places where routeways converge often become the foci for locating a great variety of service activities. Many services, such as gasoline stations, automotive repair shops, and motels, are directly related to transport routes and the vehicles that travel them. These and other services such as insurance, real estate and banking firms, grocery stores and pharmacies, laundromats, and restaurants locate along important routes of travel which offer excellent exposure to potential customers or because other businesses have successfully located nearby. Such services are among the first businesses to locate in or near new residential or suburban developments on the outskirts of urban areas. They often form the vanguard services of locational expansion. During and since the 1960s, regional shopping centers, which contain numerous shops offering low order services, have frequently preceded urban expansion. Thus shopping center locations have joined other important catalysts as major influences upon the nature and the direction of growth of urban frontiers.

CBD and Other Locations

Services that confine themselves to the "nerve center" or to the CBD (Central Business District) of an urban area seek to maximize access to transport and communications facilities or to a supply of labor. They usually have relatively small space needs that can be met by structures that are vertical (skyscrapers) or horizontal. Such services include the headquarters of financial institutions and most offices of public administration. Washington, D.C., with its governmental functions spread over much of the city and into bordering portions of Maryland and Virginia, is an exception [2]. Headquarters for some insurance and banking firms, however, have recently moved from CBDs into suburban or even rural settings in order to escape the congestion, pollution, crime, high rentals, high taxes, and other problems of central city areas.

Modern technology has virtually eliminated the necessity to locate within central cities in order to enjoy superior communications facilities. Most airports are located some distance from urban congestion, and development of high-speed interstate highways and urban beltways has often made urban fringe locations more accessible than CBDs to office workers and all ranges of clients.

Personal and professional services are normally concentrated within the CBD and the developing fringes of cities [3]. Professional services, as characterized by large educational and medical facilities, have more consistent locational characteristics than personal services such as recreational and entertainment services [4]. Professional services must normally select locations where rental costs are reasonable but which afford their customers good access. The location of recreational and entertainment services depends on the type of activity and its peculiar market or physical requirements. Nightclubs and cinemas might find that location within or near the CBD is desirable, for example, whereas a golf course would choose a site where land costs are lower than in the CBD and where desirable land surface conditions are available.

SERVICES IN DEVELOPED AND IN DEVELOPING AREAS

Services are vital to the functioning of all nations, without regard to stage of development, political structure, ideology, size, or international prominence. Major spatial variations do occur, however, between and within nations in types of services available. Most of the *developing* nations suffer from a seriously inadequate *infrastructure* (shortcomings in energy-producing facilities, transportation and communications networks, and educational and medical facilities). These shortcomings frequently result in relatively high operational costs and low levels of efficiency in business, manufacturing, and government. National investments in such services as health and education may contribute more to the growth of gross national product (GNP) in the long run than investments in manufacturing and agriculture. A major problem in economic development of the Upper Volta, for example, is the debilitating effect of disease upon the productivity of the labor force [5].

Moreover, expenditures by some of the more advanced nations on agricultural research have permitted significant gains in agricultural output in developing nations such as the Philippines and India. Whatever a nation's relative rank in the development scale, however, it seems clear that "current expenditures on health, education, agricultural extension, family planning, research, management training, etc., may be equally important or even more important than investment in (material) capital" [6].

Services as Percentage of GNP

No consistent difference occurs between developed and developing nations in the percentage of gross national product derived from services (Fig. 15-1). The service industries are consistently weak, however, within the centrally planned economies, and they have declined in relative importance within many OPEC (Organization of Petroleum Exporting Countries) nations (Fig. 15-2). The weakness within the centrally planned economies reflects the smaller emphasis than in market economies upon production of consumer goods and the lower output per production worker than in advanced market economies such as the United States. Mass production and consump-

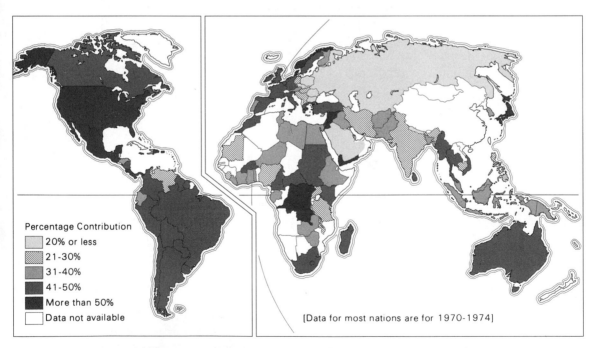

Percentage Contribution
20% or less
21-30%
31-40%
41-50%
More than 50%
Data not available

[Data for most nations are for 1970-1974]

Fig. 15-1. Percentage of gross national product contributed by service industries. [From *Statistical Yearbook, 1975* (New York: United Nations, 1976), Table 188.]

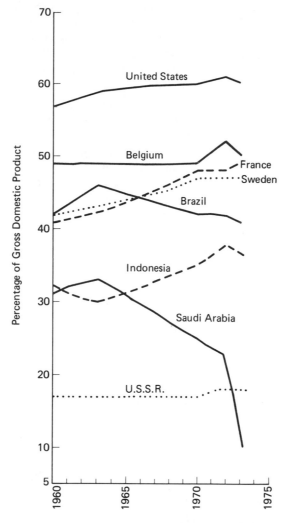

Fig. 15-2. Percentage of gross domestic product generated by service activ-
ties: selected nations.[From *Statistical Yearbook, 1975* (New York: United
Nations, 1976), Table 188.]

tion of consumer goods, which stimulate service employment, are also more
difficult to plan than large-scale output of machines and military hardware
and materials for construction [7].

Because of expanded oil production in OPEC nations since 1960, the
massive inflows of money from oil exports, and efforts of those nations to
modernize their economies, the service sector has declined in its relative
contribution to total GNP in favor of income from minerals exploitation,
manufacturing, and construction. Between 1960 and 1973, for example,

service industry contribution to the gross domestic product in Saudi Arabia dropped from 31 to 10 percent. During the same period, minerals output increased its share of total GNP from 55 to 85 percent. In Venezuela, the service industry contribution declined from 50 to 33 percent, whereas that from minerals exploitation increased from 27 to 59 percent and that from manufacturing, from about 12 to 19 percent [8].

That the prominence of a nation's service sector shows little relationship to the degree of affluence of that nation reflects the varied nature of the service industry itself. Whereas machines have largely replaced labor for many menial tasks within the affluent societies, such is not the case within the poor societies. In affluent areas, for example, service labor is employed largely in banking, insurance, advertising, the professions, the sciences, amenity services (such as recreation, gambling, hairdressing), and automotive services and in government. In poor regions, on the other hand, a large share of service labor is employed as domestics, or as household servants [9].

Services in Affluent Areas

Within most of the affluent societies, service employment is on the rise (Fig. 15-2). Output per man-hour in agriculture and in mining and manufacturing has increased, and these economic sectors have declined in their shares of total employment. The trend toward increased output per worker in the production of tangible goods has been encouraged by a high degree of labor organization (unionization) within these industries, which has had the effect of creating labor scarcity and thus high labor prices. Scarcity and high costs of labor, in turn, have encouraged mechanization of production processes.

Service industry labor, on the other hand, is rarely organized into strong national or international unions. Thus unorganized service workers have not been able to exert as much collective influence upon politicians and legislation or in bargaining with specific businesses or industries as production workers. Members of production worker unions have often voted as blocs, giving them substantial power in influencing legislation concerning such matters as working conditions and fringe benefits. Strong organization and the ability to interrupt production through strikes also gives them great bargaining power with their employers. Lack of organizations of similar strength among service workers has meant that fewer governmental or industry restrictions affect conditions related to their employment [10]. Lack of bargaining power among service workers has usually meant that they are paid less than workers in the tangible goods industries. Service industries have not felt the same pressure to mechanize as the tangible goods industries, therefore, and the service employer rather than a union has been able to exert a greater degree of control over wages and working conditions. Whereas definite limits have been established by legislation concerning how many hours an employer can require production workers to work each week, for example, no similar legislation exists to protect traveling salesman from "unfair" employer practices. A greater degree of laissez-faire, therefore, is found in the service than in the tangible goods industries.

Expansion of service industry employment and income has given rise to use of the term *postindustrial society* to describe the more affluent nations where mechanization, automation, and computerization characterize the tangible goods industries. In such societies output per production worker in some industries has increased by more than 100 times that of the immediate post-World War II period [11]. These nations have created *mass consumption* societies to absorb their huge industrial output. The United States probably entered this phase during the 1920s, prior to the "great depression." Many European nations joined in promoting mass consumption during the 1950s; and Japan, during the 1960s.

Although the rate of increase in productivity among service workers has lagged far behind that of workers in tangible goods industries, that too is beginning to change. The development which is making this possible is the electronic computer, a post-World War II phenomenon. Sharp increases in the capabilities of computers, and even sharper decreases in their costs, followed the introduction of transistors (to replace vacuum tubes) and more recently the development of miracle chips (tiny bits of silicon only about a quarter inch square), each of which has a calculating capability equivalent to that of a computer filling an entire room in the early 1950s. Price reductions quickly follow mass production, as shown by a $10.95 price in 1978 for a pocket calculator which would have sold for $395 in 1971 [12]. In a mass consumption society computers are essential to prevent businesses from becoming buried under mounds of paperwork. Thus computers are performing many tasks formerly performed by service workers, especially in banks, insurance firms, transportation and marketing systems, payroll offices, and other jobs that require storage and processing of information. One service worker today with the aid of a computer can handle thousands of times the number of informational transactions as a pre-World War II worker. And the *Computer Age* is just beginning. Minicomputers are now being installed in automobiles, check-out lanes of retail establishments, doctors' offices, hospitals, telephones, and kitchen equipment, to name only a few applications.

Quaternary services are those which require advanced education and training. They are particularly important to research activities and in decision-making processes. They include services that specialize in gathering, analyzing, and transmitting information, and they have grown at an explosive rate since 1950 in the developed nations. In few other fields has technology made such giant strides in so short a period of time. In perhaps no area other than the processing and transmitting of information has cost of equipment declined so dramatically (relative to its capability), nor its availability and use increased so meteorically. In addition to the national and international organizations whose purposes are to gather, analyze, and transmit news, almost every business expends a substantial portion of its income for the collection and interpretation of information about its products or services, to transmit favorable impressions about those products to consumers, and for research in development of new or improved products or processes.

Whereas many businesses and industries once found central city locations advantageous as nerve centers for collecting, analyzing, and dispensing information, such services are now so readily available within developed nations that they can be accessed at virtually any location. Thus most suburban and rural areas have access to as much information and to as many people, just as quickly, as a center city location.

Evidence of the communications explosion that has taken place during recent years may be seen in the huge increase in number of telephones in use during the 6-year period from 1970-1976 (Table 15-1). The rate of increase in number of telephones during the period was highest in the developing nations, but nearly 75 percent of the absolute increase in number (about 93,930,000 out of 125,525,000) occurred within the developed nations.

In addition to newspapers, telephones, television, and radio, the quaternary services include such widely varying establishments as libraries, census bureaus, educational institutions, public and private research corporations, insurance companies, credit bureaus, churches, and advertising agencies [13]. The list of types of firms that maintain specialized quaternary services seems almost endless, and it grows daily in number and in capability. Fears have arisen, recently, that the information about individuals possessed by in-

TABLE 15-1. Telephones in Use (Thousand Units)

AREA	NUMBER OF TELEPHONES IN USE		PERCENTAGE OF WORLD'S TELEPHONES IN USE	
	1970	*1976*	*1970*	*1976*
WORLD	272,657	398,182	100.0	100.0
Africa	3,342	3,890	1.2	1.0
North America	132,751	173,839	48.7	43.7
South America	6,137	9,127	2.3	2.3
Asia	33,229	60,557	12.2	15.2
Europe	80,776	124,740	29.6	31.3
Oceania	5,422	7,300	2.0	1.8
USSR	11,000	18,000	4.0	4.5

SOURCE: *Statistical Yearbook, 1977* (New York: United Nations, 1978), Table 168.

surance, banking, credit, public revenue, and other such firms may be a serious threat to privacy and to individual rights and freedoms. Thus legislation is being implemented to assure necessary restraints in the use of information in possession of such firms.

Research services are offered in a variety of types of institutions and locations. Most of the research today is carried on in universities and in huge public and private laboratories such as Oak Ridge National Laboratory in Tennessee and the Jet Propulsion Laboratory in Pasadena, California. The types of research carried on at a particular time, and the most prominent research laboratories, are determined to a large degree by specific governmental priorities. Governments invest huge sums in research and determine where those activities are to take place. When the Department of Energy was formed in the United States, for example, it began the dispensing of billions of dollars to promote and to conduct research on energy projects which appeared to hold promise for helping to meet future energy needs — as seen by Department of Energy officials. A few years prior to development of energy as a high-priority governmental concern, billions had been invested in research related to the nation's "man on the moon" program. The geographical allocation of research funds for the moon program had important differences from the allocation for energy research. Other major national research programs in the United States during recent years have been in the areas of disease, urban areas, poverty, military weapons, crime, and agriculture.

Services in Developing Areas

Just as all the affluent market economies obtain more than 40 percent of their gross domestic product through the service industries, so do many developing market economies (Fig. 15-1). In most of South America and in parts of Africa and Southeast Asia, services contribute shares to gross domestic product equal to those of developed economies. In other developing areas services are of lesser importance. Many developing areas possess only rudimentary transportation, communication, and educational systems, and their abilities to form effective bureaucracies are limited by the scarcity of literate persons. Governmental bureaucracies in such countries are often composed of relatives and friends of those in top positions, frequently leading to irrational decisions and corruption [14]. An additional problem within developing nations is the lack of service centers of medium size (50,000–100,000 population) and the concentration of most services in small centers (20,000 population and less) [15]. Thus the types of services normally found in medium-sized centers are restricted primarily to a small number of widely spaced large centers where they become unavailable to substantial segments of the population. Low incomes and high levels of illiteracy inhibit large segments of the population from knowing about or from being able to purchase many of the services which are offered. Limited demand for services may lead to high prices for those which are available, and high cost results in further reduction of effective demand.

Because the labor forces of most developing nations are engaged primarily in agriculture, where the demand for services is substantially lower than in urban areas, most urban-type services exist on a smaller scale in developing than in developed nations. In developing nations which contain sizable numbers of wealthy persons, either foreigners (perhaps those remaining from former colonial governments and businesses or managers, scientists, and technicians employed by foreign corporations) or local entrepreneurs, the number of persons employed in domestic services as housekeepers, cooks, gardeners, and the like may be large. The availability of workers for such services in developing areas is normally quite large because of high levels of unemployment or lack of employment alternatives.

Most small service centers contain some medical, educational, religious, and governmental services, but the majority of service employment is in trading [16]. African traders are often aliens, either Europeans, Arabs, Asians, or migrants from other parts of Africa [17]. In east Africa commerce has long been dominated by Asians. Similarly, in parts of southeast Asia most commercial functions are owned by Chinese. Local entrepreneurs in small trading centers are frequently part-time operators of shops dealing in agricultural commodities. The part-time shopkeepers may also be part-time or full-time farmers who are seeking to enhance their incomes while retaining the security represented by land ownership. Ownership of a shop carries substantial prestige and provides the owner with an entree into the political power structure.

The weakness of service activity in developing nations stems from the nation's lack of a large pool of well-educated persons and persons skilled in specific service functions. The paucity of persons able to operate business machines and medical equipment, and who can teach, results in low levels of productivity among service workers compared to those in affluent areas.

DISTRIBUTION OF SELECTED SERVICE ACTIVITIES

Although nations such as the United States, Mexico, and Zaire may all derive approximately equal percentages of their gross domestic products from service industries, wide differences exist in the degree to which particular services are available. Services in the developed nations tend to be more sophisticated and to require greater skill, knowledge, and capital investments than those in the developing nations. Likewise, persons and facilities engaged in providing services within the developed nations have normally attained a higher level of expertise in their skills than their counterparts in the developing lands.

The percentage of gross domestic product spent for education is generally higher in the developed than in the developing nations (Table 15-2). Although educational expenditures have tended to increase at a faster *rate* in developing than in developed nations during recent years, gross domestic products are so much higher in the developed than in the developing nations that the gap in absolute expenditures continues to widen. In 1976, for example, the United States (with 215.3 million people) spent more than 47 times as much money on education as India (with 620.7 million people). The amount expended on education alone in the United States exceeded the entire gross national product of India.

TABLE 15-2. Availability of Selected Services in Selected Nations[a]

Nation	Daily Newspaper Circulation per 1,000 Inhabitants	Persons per Physician (Thousands)	Percentage of Gross National Product Spent for Education	Number of Radio Receivers per 1,000 Inhabitants	Number of Television Receivers per 1,000 Inhabitants
DEVELOPED NATIONS					
United States	287	0.6	6.7	1,882	571
Australia	394	0.7	5.0	211	274
Belgium	239	0.5	5.1	384	255
Canada	235	0.6	8.1	959	411
Denmark	341	0.6	7.4	331	308
France	214	0.7	3.6	346	268
West Germany	312	0.5	4.1	356	306
Japan	526	0.9	4.3	465	235
USSR	397	0.3	7.5	461	208
Sweden	572	0.6	7.7	380	352
DEVELOPING NATIONS					
Afghanistan	5	20.3	1.3	6	—
Angola	2	15.4	2.2	17	—
Burma	10	5.4	3.4	22	—
Ecuador	49	2.2	3.2	270	37
Ghana	51	10.5	4.6	107	6
India	16	4.1	2.5	24	0.5
Republic of Korea	173	2.2	4.1	144	48
Morocco	21	14.0	5.3	92	27
Saudi Arabia	11	2.5	11.1	28	14
Sudan	NA	11.2	8.0	80	6
Turkey	NA	1.8	5.6	105	12

[a]Most Data are for 1975, but in some instances represent 1970 to 1974.
SOURCE: *Statistical Yearbook: 1977* (New York: United Nations, 1978), Table 169.

In developing societies, those who have an opportunity to obtain significant educational levels are often children of the wealthy class. Occupational status, life-styles, and achievement of wealth in such cases are more a reflection of inheritance than of the level of education attained. Thus the relationship between education and achievement in developing nations is less pronounced than in developed societies where compulsory public education is designed to prepare virtually the entire potential labor force with a degree of literacy that will prepare it for further more specialized achievement following release from school [18]. The mass media in developed societies are utilized to persuade those who have attained basic literacy of the rewards available to those who voluntarily acquire specialized skills and professional qualifications.

Thus the mass media serve a complementary role to the educational system. Mass education makes possible, and is enhanced by, the mass media. The developed nations again are clearly superior to developing nations in facilities for, and in exposure of the population to, mass media (Table 15-1). Whether the particular medium is radio, television, or newspapers, the developed nations on the average have a 10 to 1 edge over developing areas. Africa, as the poorest continent, has the lowest levels of education and of newspaper circulation and the fewest radios and television sets per 1,000 inhabitants.

The principal purpose of media systems is the diffusion of information, ideas, and propaganda. The ideas, information, and propaganda may have political and ideological overtones, or they may reflect social or economic goals. The more effective the "reach" of the media systems, the more rapidly and completely a message can be conveyed to a population; the more literate a population, the greater the effectiveness of the media systems. In developing areas where literacy levels are low and a large percentage of the population is without direct access to any medium of mass communication, the spread of information can be painfully slow. Large informational voids may occur within the population, especially in rural areas where peoples are less likely than urban residents to receive newspapers or to possess radios and television sets. In such instances those who do not have access to media systems may depend primarily on word of mouth for their information. The accuracy of information so transmitted usually deteriorates with each passage from one individual to another. Thus the outcome may be vastly different from that which was intended.

By contrast, the developed societies are capable of direct transmission of huge amounts of information to virtually the entire population almost instantaneously. The same messages may be, and usually are, carried by newspaper, radio, and television. If a person is not reached by one medium, he or she is almost certain to be reached by the other two. Direct transmission ensures a maximum degree of accuracy in the information received by the population. In a matter of minutes, for example, nearly every American

can know about a new soap being placed on the market, that the President wore a pink tie and green socks to a press conference, that an outbreak of a new strain of virus has occurred in Uganda, or that warfare has broken out in some part of the world.

Once a nation has developed a highly skilled labor force through compulsory public education and through stimulation by the mass media toward obtaining specialized skills as a means for gaining access to the "good life," it becomes highly desirable that the labor force be maintained in good health. One expression of the degree of health care afforded by a nation to its citizens is the number of persons per physician (Table 15-2). Whether the health care system is one in which patients seek out and pay for medical care on a private basis, one where responsibility for the provision of health care is vested in government (socialized medicine), or some combination of the two, the availability of health care to the population is closely related to the number of persons each physician is responsible to serve. Ordinarily one could correctly assume that the lower the ratio of patients to physicians, the better the health care. Not surprisingly, the developed areas again provide clearly superior services to those offered in developing areas (Table 15-2).

An educated, healthy, and well-informed populace is normally aware of and concerned about retaining its "rights." To ensure that individual and group rights are maintained, at least in some degree, judicial systems have been established and specialists in the law have emerged to provide for the "judicial care" of the population. Although lawyers have sometimes been criticized for "the fostering of fruitless disputes — which the consumer did not really want," the utility of judicial services can hardly be questioned in a democratic society [19]. The use of courts of law rather than violence to settle disputes is one of the major cornerstones of civilization. Judicial systems in developed societies are usually more formalized and they operate with greater uniformity than those in developing societies. Developed areas have larger numbers of formally trained specialists in the law than developing areas and more consistent procedures of rewards and punishments.

The judicial system, in large part, represents one element in a host of public civil service agencies which operate under the umbrella of government service. The number of government employees has increased rapidly in most parts of the world since World War II, but less rapidly in the developing than in the developed nations [20]. The scale of government employment corresponds closely to levels of government spending, and growth in spending is related to the amount of economic growth and income growth within the national economy. Because of slower absolute economic growth in developing than in developed areas, funds for increasing the sizes of bureaucracies have risen more slowly in developing lands. Increases in government employment are also related to the pace at which the population of a nation is changing from rural to urban. Because urban residents demand more government services than rural residents, rapid urbanization of a population is paralleled by a rise in government employment. During most of the post-World War II period urbanization has been strongest in the developed societies, although the tempo of urbanization in developing areas has increased substantially since the 1950s. Increases in government employment also normally occur during periods of crisis, such as wars and major economic recessions [21]. Following the crisis, the abnormal spending and employment levels tend to become norms. In the developed market economies government employment has also tended to increase along with the rise of giant corporations, under the assumption that big business requires big government.

Distribution, or the movement of goods between producers and consumers, normally involves a complex system of wholesaling, transporting, and retailing functions. In advanced economies where specialists are involved in all phases of the production and marketing of goods, the distance over which goods travel to reach consumers has been increasing, as has the variety of goods available to consumers. The average American and European, for example, has daily access to and makes daily use of goods from all parts of the earth. The cost of moving goods from producers to consumers ranges from 30 to 75 percent of the purchase price. Given the variety of products available for sale in modern supermarkets and department stores, the equally great variety of places from which they originate, the myriad of processes required to make them ready for consumption, and the multiplicity of transport modes used in their movements, it seems almost miraculous that goods usually reach the right places at the right times and in the right amounts.

Wholesalers serve as intermediate owners of goods between producers and the retailers who sell the goods to consumers. The task of the wholesaler is to assemble from producers, or from producers and other wholesalers, an adequate supply of one or more goods to meet the demands of retailers, who must assemble from wholesalers an adequate supply of goods to meet the demands of consumers. With each transaction between producers and wholesalers, among different wholesalers who handle the goods at various stages in their journeys to retailers, and between wholesalers and retailers, the seller must add to the price of the goods an amount sufficient to cover the seller's cost of handling the goods plus some degree of profit. The price paid by the retailer, therefore, reflects charges added to the cost of each product after it is sold by the producer. As the final sellers of products to consumers, retailers have historically absorbed most of the blame for the often wide differential between prices charged by producers and those paid by consumers. Retailers have been the subject of scorn throughout human history. Notable figures such as Aristotle and Napoleon held retailers in as low esteem as many modern shoppers.

Until well into the present century most wholesaling and retailing businesses in the developed nations were relatively small operations. They

African women drawing water from a community well. (Reprinted from *War on Hunger*, a publication of the Agency for International Development.)

were rarely linked by common ownership, and the owners of both types of firms were usually individuals, families, or small partnerships. Following World War I, and especially during the years after World War II, large corporate businesses began to absorb both wholesaling and retailing functions — first in the United States and the United Kingdom and later in continental Europe. The emergence of chains of stores, or numerous stores owned by a single corporation, not only revolutionized retailing but it has brought immense changes also to wholesaling, manufacturing, and production of goods. Thus the large chains which began primarily as retail organizations (such as the Great Atlantic and Pacific Tea Company, or A & P Supermarkets) offer an excellent example of *backward integration*. Thousands of small independent retailers, unable to meet the competition of the corporate chains, were eliminated. The chains became their own wholesalers, dealing directly with producers rather than relying upon independent wholesale businesses. In order to reduce the costs of buying goods, large regional and national chains made regular purchases only from large producers, thus eliminating many small farmers and manufacturers who once sold to small independent wholesalers. Backward integration into manufacturing and farming also occurred through establishment by the chains of detailed specifications concerning the cost and quality of goods they were willing to purchase. Those who refused or who were unable to conform to the standards established by the chains had to secure alternate markets (most often a vain pursuit) or go out of business. Many of today's farmers, for example, use seed, fertilizers, and cultivation and harvesting techniques that are prescribed by the corporate chain which purchases their output. Manufacturers, too, follow similar prescriptions in the production of goods to be sold by the chains. Through such backward integration the producers of goods become subject to the direct influence of market forces.

Not all advanced nations have succumbed to the lure of the efficient marketing techniques of corporate chains. Laws to protect small businesses have hampered large-scale merchandising in much of Europe. Although France has a smaller population than Britain, for example, it has 50 percent more shops [22]. Laws that prescribe operating hours, limit times of bargain sales, and encourage discriminatory taxation often discourage new entry into retailing.

The distribution of goods between producers and consumers in developing nations is in many respects a much simpler process than in developed nations. For the large percentage of the population which is engaged in subsistence farming, the producers are also the consumers. Lack of specialization; inadequate facilities for transporting, processing, and storing commodities; and low incomes limit both the quantity and the variety of goods available to consumers. The majority of goods sold by most retailers is likely to be those which can be produced in the immediate locality. Such conditions are not conducive to the entry of large, integrated merchandising operations, such as supermarket chains, and the bulk of wholesaling and retailing is conducted by relatively small, independently owned businesses. The relatively low demand gives rise to *periodic markets* which function only during certain days of the week, month, or year. When adverse weather conditions or disruptive political or economic circumstances affect the local area, the supply of goods is likely to be reduced and prices to rise accordingly.

In most large urban areas, many of which have coastal locations, supplies of goods and services are likely to resemble those of advanced nations in variety, but overall levels of consumption remain comparatively low. Although some mass merchandising organizations may exist in such cities, the bulk of retailing is handled by small shopkeepers.

Wholesaling and retailing in the centrally planned economies are, in the main, government-owned functions and subject to centralized planning. Government officials decide what is to be produced, in what quantity, and the prices at which the goods will be sold. The character of wholesaling and retailing is determined by *administrative* forces rather than forces arising from the marketplace. The low regard for service activities, as embodied in Marxist philosophy, is also reflected in retailing in that the Soviet Union has only about one-fourth as many retail outlets in proportion to population as the United States or Great Britain [23]. The result is that Soviet citizens spend many of their nonworking hours standing in long lines waiting to purchase desired goods. Private retailing operations in the Soviet Union are limited primarily to the "free" periodic markets on which Soviet farmers may sell goods produced on the small plots they are allowed to utilize as they wish.

CONCLUSIONS

The service industries, regarded by most classical economists as unproductive and therefore undesirable economic functions, have become the dominant sources of employment in most of the developed nations and in many developing areas. Service industries on the whole are much more directly attuned to the specific needs, health, skills, and happiness of people than the tangible goods industries.

If, as many experts are predicting, it becomes necessary to reduce production and consumption of tangible goods to abate depletion of resources and to protect the environment, the service industries offer the only major opportunity for continued growth in employment. Economists, politicians, and planners, therefore, might do well to direct a greater degree of attention than previously to those services which can direct consumer behavior and to those which are capable of providing fulfillment to peoples without increasing the strain upon physical resources.

REFERENCES

[1] W. Christaller, *Central Places in Southern Germany*, translated by C. W. Baskin (Englewood Cliffs, N.J.: Prentice-Hall, Inc., 1966). Central place theory was first formulated by Walter Christaller, a German geographer, in 1933.

[2] L. K. Lowenstein, *Residences and Work Places in Urban Areas* (New York: The Scarecrow Press, 1965), p. 72.

[3] *Ibid.*, p. 89.

[4] *Ibid.*, p. 71.

[5] A. M. Kamarck, "'Capital' and 'Investment' in Developing Countries," *Finance and Development*, 8, No. 2, June, 1971, p. 4.

[6] *Ibid.*, p. 5.

[7] R. Lewis, *The New Service Society* (London: Longman Group Ltd., 1973), p. 5.

[8] *Statistical Yearbook, 1975* (New York: United Nations, 1976), Table 188.

[9] Lewis, *op. cit.*, p. 4.

[10] C. Gersuny and W. R. Rosengren, *The Service Society* (Cambridge, Mass.: Schenkman Publishing Co., 1973), p. 4.

[11] Lewis, *op. cit.*, p. 5.

[12] "Business Thinking Small," *Time*, 111, No. 8, February 20, 1978, p. 51.

[13] R. Abler, J. S. Adams, and P. Gould, *Spatial Organization: The Geographer's View of the World* (Englewood Cliffs, N.J.: Prentice-Hall Inc., 1971), p. 307.

[14] B. F. Hoselitz, "The Recruitment of White-Collar Workers in Underdeveloped Countries," in Jean Meynaud (ed.), *Social Changes and Economic Development* (Paris: United Nations Education, Scientific and Cultural Organization, 1963), p. 173.

[15] D. C. Funnell, "The Role of Small Service Centers in Regional and Rural Development: With Special Reference to Eastern Africa," Chapter 4, in Alan Gilbert (ed.) *Development Planning and Spatial Structure* (New York: John Wiley & Sons, 1976), p. 78.

[16] Funnell, *op. cit.*, p. 83.

[17] *Ibid.*, p. 80.

[18] Gersuny and Rosengren, *op. cit.*, p. 42.

[19] Lewis, *op. cit.*, p. 25.

[20] F. L. Pryor, *Public Expenditures in Communist and Capitalist Nations* (London: Allen and Unwin, 1968), p. 52.

[21] Lewis, *op. cit.*, p. 90.

[22] *Ibid.*, p. 75.

[23] *Ibid.*, p. 28.

CHAPTER SIXTEEN
multinational corporations

INTRODUCTION

At one time the peoples of the earth lived in isolated villages and had little contact among themselves. The economic reality of today, however, is interdependence. As we have moved from isolated villages to a system of world interdependence, the need for international organizations has given rise to institutions which function on a world scale. One of the largest, most influential, and highly diffused international institutions is the multinational corporation (MNC).

In a narrow sense, an MNC is any corporation which conducts business in more than one country. By this definition there are thousands of such corporations, with sales ranging from less than $1 million to in excess of $30 billion. When one realizes that more than 200 MNC's have sales in excess of $1 billion, their potential to affect international affairs becomes apparent [1].

These corporate giants function at an international level and, therefore, interact with governments all over the world. The governments with which MNC's must form a working relationship can be broken into two classes. The *home country* is the country in which the MNC is headquartered. It is here that the operations of the MNC are coordinated. Decisions made in the home country can affect economic activities in several nations, a fact which has generated hostility toward MNC's.

Host countries are those where MNC's base some of their operations but not their headquarters. In these countries an MNC is a foreigner, an outsider come to do business. MNC's are often looked upon as a form of neocolonial-ism for this reason. Thus, some scholars speak of the American challenge, United States-based MNC's dominating the world economy, whereas others point to the European revenge, European-based MNC's using the United States as a host country [2]. MNC's are clearly a part of the world's political economy. To understand today's geopolitics, one must understand the dis-tribution of MNC's over space and time, their goals, and the stimuli which caused them to spread so rapidly during the past 20 years.

THE GLOBAL DISTRIBUTION OF MULTINATIONALS

The distribution of MNC's is best understood in terms of the distribution of home countries, host countries, and the economic activities of the corpo-rations themselves.

MNC home offices are not evenly distributed among the nations of the world. Not surprisingly home countries tend to be the strong free market economies of the world: the United States, Canada, western European na-tions, and Japan. These are nations with a great deal of wealth, and wealth has been both a cause and an effect in the development of their corporate expertise. The United States is, by far, the leading exporter of this corporate ability, followed by the United Kingdom, West Germany, Japan, Switzer-land, France, and other developed nations (Table 16-1). These are the coun-tries which since the end of World War II have used their corporate strength to, depending on the rhetoric you choose, spread technology and wealth or control and exploit the economies of the world.

The majority of foreign investments made by MNC's based in each of these countries are in other developed economies (Table 16-2). Japan is the

TABLE 16-1. Percentage of Direct Foreign Investment by Country of Origin, 1976

Country	Percentage
United States	47.6
United Kingdom	11.2
Federal Republic of Germany	6.9
Japan	6.7
Switzerland	6.5
France	4.1
Others[a]	17.0

[a]All others have less than 4 percent.

SOURCE: *Transnational Corporations in World Development* (New York: United Nations 1978) p. 236.

TABLE 16–2. Foreign Investment by Type of Region, 1974: Selected Home Countries

Country	DEVELOPING		DEVELOPED	
	$(Millions)	*Percentage*	*$(Millions)*	*Percentage*
United States	29,050	26.17	108,194	75.83
United Kingdom	5,059	16.17	26,218	83.83
Federal Republic of Germany	6,015	30.20	13,900	69.00
Japan	5,678	53.47	4,942	46.53

SOURCE: *Transnational Corporations in World Development* (New York: United Nations 1978), p. 292.

only nation which is close to an even split in investment between developed and developing economies. This has occurred because of heavy Japanese investment in the Pacific area, for example, Taiwan, Hong Kong, and Singapore. United States and European foreign investment is oriented heavily toward investment in other developed economies.

The pattern which has emerged is one of *defensive investment* [3]. Nations often place tariffs on imported goods to protect domestic industries, and the tariffs act as trade barriers to market entry. If an MNC wants to attain or retain part of the market in a country, it must circumvent import tariffs by producing in the protected market, hence the term *defensive investment*. The existence of trade barriers acts as a stimulus for multinationalization. The MNC exports the capital and technology necessary to produce a good in the protected market rather than exporting the finished good itself.

Defensive investments are in manufacturing industries and tend to be concentrated in industries which are technologically intensive, for example, drugs, chemicals, computer electronics, and complex machinery [4]. These industries are market-oriented and thus follow demand (and wealth) around the globe. Nations which function as both home and host countries are exporters and importers of manufacturing capital and technology (Fig. 16–1).

Developing countries function primarily as host countries and are less manufacturing-oriented than developed host countries (Fig. 16–1). MNC's need for raw materials, particularly petroleum, has led to a worldwide search for inputs. The investment strategy of extractive MNC's is a function of the spatial distribution of exploitable raw materials. Developed economies will use most, if not all, of their indigenous raw materials, forcing the multinationals to look to the developing countries for raw materials. Energy companies such as Exxon and British Petroleum, for example, have operations in several countries. Firestone Rubber Company has for years operated large rubber plantations in Liberia. Extractive MNC's must regularly seek new resources in order to continue their activities.

Why don't the nations where these resources are located develop their

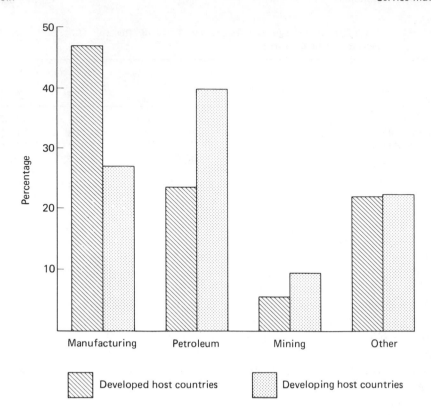

	Petroleum	Mining	Manufacturing	Miscellaneous
Developed Countries	23.6	5.2	47.3	23.9
Developing Countries	39.7	9.3	26.9	24.1

Fig. 16-1. Percentage of direct foreign investment by economic sector, developed and developing areas, 1971. [From *Multinational Corporations in World Development*, U.S. Department of Economic and Social Affairs (New York: Prager, 1974) page 11.]

own extractive industries rather than leaving them for MNC's to exploit? The explanation is that these are *high risk, capital intensive industries*. The search for oil and natural gas, for example, requires highly trained personnel and expensive equipment. It is estimated that the drilling of dry wells in the search for energy sources in the United States alone costs more than $1 billion annually [5]. Only large, well-organized institutions can afford to participate in such businesses. Small firms and governments in developing countries are normally incapable of assembling the necessary capital, skilled managers, and equipment to enter into large-scale production of extractive materials. The MNC, on the other hand, has the fiscal size and trained personnel to overcome what economists call *capital barriers to entry*. The distribution of raw materials coupled with these capital barriers have led to multinationalization in the extractive industries. That many developing countries have more raw materials than they can presently use has led to the concentration of these MNC's in developing nations.

THE UNITED STATES-BASED MULTINATIONALS

American-based multinationals are of importance for three reasons: they are the most numerous of all multinationals (Table 16–1); although most United States foreign investment is in developed countries, American MNC's make up the largest share of investment in both developed *and* developing countries (Table 16–2); and, they best illustrate the trends of the post-World War II dominance of the world economy by the United States followed by the recent counter-invasion by Japanese and European multinationals.

The diffusion of American MNC's after the end of World War II was so great that in the mid-1960s Servan-Schreiber predicted that United States' corporations would soon control the European economy. There were good reasons for his thesis of an American corporate tidal wave engulfing the free world's economy. The growth in the number of American MNC's had been meteoric (Fig. 16–2). From 1960 to 1975, the total number of United States' MNC's increased by 166.4 percent.* Defensive investment coupled with the thirst for new markets led to great gains in manufacturing- and sales-oriented MNC's (191.1 and 175.9 percent, respectively). While the search for raw materials grew in intensity, and cost, the capital barriers to entry dampened growth in a number of extractive industries (84.3 percent). The number of American extractive MNC's actually declined in 1972, 1973, and 1975. The high cost of energy along with a slowing in United States economic growth, vis-à-vis European and Japanese economic growth, no doubt contributed to these declines. However, the trend of expropriation of extractive MNC's is the single most important reason for these declines. Extractive MNC's are involved in a politically volatile business.

TRACING THE GROWTH

Figure 16–2 illustrates the temporal diffusion of American MNC's. In this section, the spatial distribution of new entrants to foreign markets is explored. The reason for studying the pattern of new entrants rather than the number of MNC's in operation is due to data availability. Exits from the

*This figure is based on new entrants to the world market minus exits from the market. Exits due to mergers are not included.

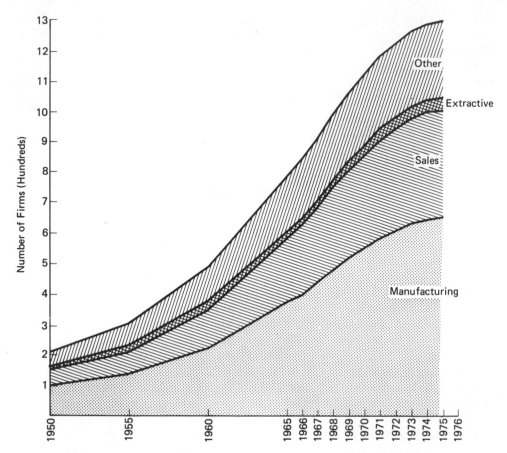

Fig. 16-2. Growth of American-based corporations in foreign areas, 1950–1975, by type of firm. [From *Tracing the Multinationals*, J. P. Curham, W. H. Davidson, and R. Suri (Cambridge: Ballinger, 1977).]

world market, other than by expropriation, can be overlooked without much loss of information.

The overall growth of United States' MNC's has been extensive. The greatest period of expansion was from 1961–1965, when 3,225 new operations were opened abroad. During the next half decade, 4,385 new operations were started. In the first 5 years of the 1970s, the growth "slowed" to the pace of the early 1960s. Since the majority of United States foreign investment has been in developed economies (Table 16-2) and the major growth in manufacturing and sales MNC's (Fig. 16-2), it is no surprise that most of the new MNC's operations were in Europe (Fig. 16-3). During the 1950s, European dominance as a destination for American corporations was not so pronounced. Canada, Central America, and South America were also important markets for the MNC's because of their proximity to the United States. Multinationals, thus, exhibit classic diffusion patterns: Over time,

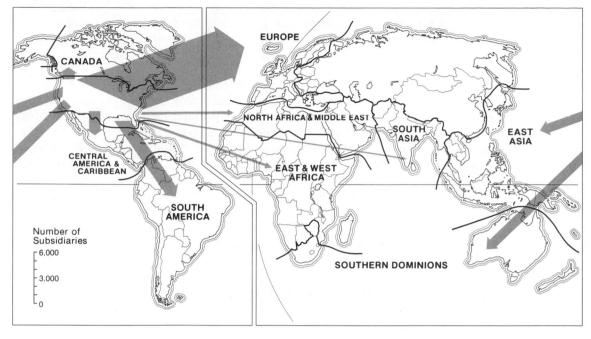

YEAR	REGION		
	Canada	Central America and Caribbean	South America
1951–55	176	121	171
56–60	246	272	301
61–65	345	311	385
66–70	525	395	411
71–75	274	351	295
	1566	1450	1563
	Europe	North Africa and Middle East	East and West Africa
1951–55	288	37	33
56–60	782	43	25
61–65	1469	60	77
66–70	2057	82	131
71–75	1455	96	100
	6078	318	366
	South Asia	East Asia	South Dominions	Total
1951–55	10	57	96	989
56–60	35	93	160	1957
61–65	50	239	289	3225
66–70	37	355	392	4385
71–75	21	370	250	3212
	153	1114	1187	13768

Fig. 16-3. Diffusion of American multinationals into foreign markets, 1950–1975. [From *Tracing the Multinationals*, J. P. Curham, W. H. Davidson, and R. Suri (Cambridge: Ballinger, 1977).]

growth is S-shaped, or logistic; during the 1950s, diffusion over space was a function of spatial separation; during the 1960s, manufacturing and sales multinationals boomed and the spatial distribution of new entrants was determined by a hierarchy based on wealth. From 1960 to 1975, Europe, with its high per capita incomes, became the dominant destination for United States MNC's, gaining over four times as many new entrants as Canada, the second most popular destination. Europe's popularity as a new market for American firms is even' more pronounced for specific industries. Industries based on a high level of technology are oriented to the areas that can afford their products. Two such industries are studied here: the drug industry and the office machines and computer industry.

These industries depend heavily on research. The development of new products is important to them and is costly. Large sums of money are spent on research and development (R & D). Large multinational corporations have adequate financial reserves to fund such research, but they do not use their R & D money capriciously. They finance only those projects which they believe will return a profit. An MNC has an advantage over smaller firms because the cost of product development acts as a capital barrier to market entry. Therefore, when an MNC looks to a European market, its main competitors are usually other large MNC's [6].

Prior to the end of World War II, there wasn't much international competition. In fact, corporate giants often respected each others areas; American firms kept to the United States and European firms protected their own territory. The best example of this was the relationship between the chemical giants DuPont, and Imperial Chemical Industries (ICI). These two corporations, one American and the other British, had an agreement where ICI would give DuPont the American patents for the products it (ICI) developed in the United Kingdom and DuPont would release the British rights to ICI for the products it (DuPont) developed in the United States. Before World War II, DuPont's R & D money led to the development of nylon. ICI soon had fiber of its own to market: polyester. ICI was allowed to sell nylon in its market by giving DuPont the right to market polyester in the United States [7]: a nice neat deal.

During the 1960s, this type of dealing fell by the wayside. In search for more profits, American corporations looked outside the United States, particularly to Europe. As American goods flooded the European marketplace, several countries erected import tariffs. The American MNC's moved their production processes to Europe in an attempt to circumvent the tariffs. The stimulus for defensive investment was present and as Fig. 16–2 and 16–3 show, the American firms responded quickly.

The multinationalization of the drug industry illustrates the dominance of Europe as a destination for high technology American firms. From 1960 to 1975, 392 new American drug subsidiaries set up production overseas, with the bulk of these (162) being established in Europe (Fig. 16–4). The drug industry went to the customers.

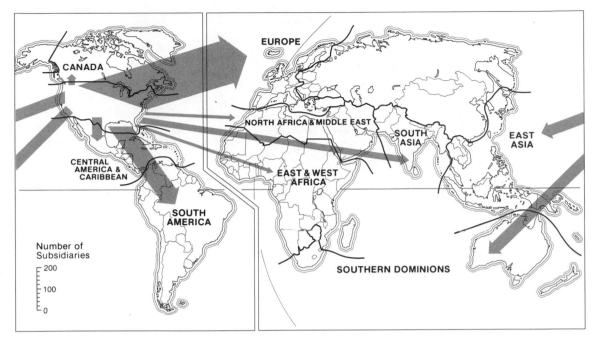

YEAR	REGION		
	Canada	Central America and Caribbean	South America
1951–55	5	3	8
56–60	6	7	20
61–65	9	19	21
66–70	11	14	20
71–75	0	3	17
	31	46	88

	Europe	North Africa and Middle East	East and West Africa
1951–55	16	0	0
56–60	34	0	1
61–65	47	6	1
66–70	78	7	2
71–75	37	2	7
	212	15	14

	South Asia	East Asia	South Dominions	Total
1951–55	1	4	6	43
56–60	11	7	11	99
61–65	7	10	12	132
66–70	6	20	5	173
71–75	2	12	7	87
	27	53	51	3534

Fig. 16-4. Diffusion of American drug multinationals into foreign markets. (From Curham et. al., *op. cit.*)

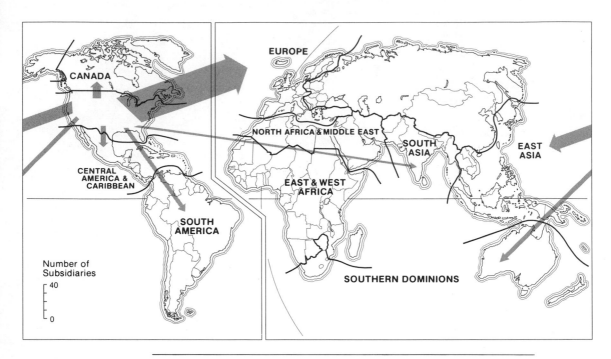

YEAR	REGION		
	Canada	Central America and Caribbean	South America
1951–55	1	0	3
56–60	2	1	1
61–65	1	1	0
66–70	3	2	0
71–75	2	2	1
	9	6	5
	Europe	North Africa and Middle East	East and West Africa
1951–55	2	0	0
56–60	7	0	0
61–65	4	0	0
66–70	21	0	0
71–75	3	0	0
	37	0	0

	South Asia	East Asia	South Dominion	Total
1951–55	1	1	1	9
56–60	0	0	0	11
61–65	1	2	0	9
66–70	0	3	1	30
71–75	0	8	3	19
	2	14	5	78

Fig. 16-5. Diffusion of American office machine and computer multinationals into foreign markets, 1950–1975. (From Curham et al., *op. cit.*)

Whereas the drug industry is oriented to consumers, the office machine and computer industry sells to other corporations. These are quaternary economic activities; that is, they deal in the communication, manipulation, and processing of information. This sector of an economy is usually found in developed countries and is of recent origin. The computer industry's market is other industries, governments, and other large-scale institutions, although this is changing as computers move into the home. The movements of these MNC's are similar to those of the drug industry, with one important difference; the movements of the office machine and computer industry also reflect the location of other MNC's. Quaternary economic activities have agglomerative tendencies. Fifty-eight new foreign operations in the office machines and computer industry were established from 1960 to 1975. As in the drug industry example, the bulk of these (28) went to Europe (Fig. 16-5). The movements to east Asia went to Japan (9), Singapore (2), Taiwan (1), Hong Kong (1), and South Korea (1). Each of these is an important point of multinational manufacturing. Mexico received six firms, while Chile, Colombia, and Venezuela received one each. Each of these, too, is a base for other multinationals. The market orientation of the manufacturing industries has given a spatial bias to the movement of American corporations.

Extractive MNC's are not market-oriented and consequently do not display a strong European bias (Fig. 16-6). Before the development of European offshore oil, Europe received very few of America's new extractive MNC's (28 from 1950–1970). During the next 5 years, 26 new extractive subsidiaries were established in Europe. Canada, Central America, and South America received the bulk of the new subsidiaries. In studying multinational extractive industries, however, the important trend is not so much the appearance of new industries as their disappearance through expropriation.

Before discussing expropriation, it is necessary to examine the causes of hostility between MNC's and host governments. While the governments that MNC's deal with want jobs, taxes, goods, and technology that MNC's have to offer, their relationship is often hostile. Charges made against MNC's include the following.

Driving Out Indigenous Industries. Nonextractive MNC's can use their size and economic resources to underprice local firms in two ways. First, their size and scope of operation may enable them to produce and market goods at a lower unit price than smaller firms (economies of scale). Second, the MNC may participate in the practice of dumping. This occurs when an MNC offers goods in a new host market at prices below production costs. If profits made in other countries are large enough, the MNC can (in the short run) afford to take a loss in the host country market. After driving out local competition, the price can be raised to the level necessary to turn a profit.

Using Inappropriate Technology. The use of cost saving technology is a method for increasing profits, but it may also result in a decline in the size

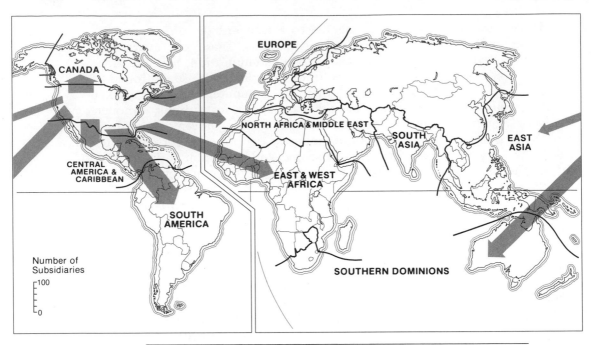

YEAR	REGION		
	Canada	Central America and Caribbean	South America
1951–55	13	6	6
56–60	16	13	14
61–65	15	11	15
66–70	31	13	23
71–75	11	22	14
	86	65	72

	Europe	North Africa and Middle East	East and West Africa
1951–55	4	11	11
56–60	6	7	5
61–65	7	4	5
66–70	11	10	18
71–75	26	3	6
	54	35	45

	South Asia	East Asia	South Dominions	Total
1951–55	0	1	6	58
56–60	0	1	5	67
61–65	0	2	14	73
66–70	0	13	18	137
71–75	0	9	8	99
	0	26	51	434

Fig. 16-6. Diffusion of American extractive multinationals into foreign areas, 1950–1975. (From Curham et al., *op. cit.*)

of the work force. In developing countries where unemployment is chronic, this can lead to resentment of the MNC. Extractive industries may, for example, use labor saving strip-mining techniques to exploit the host country's resources. The "inappropriateness" of the technology depends on which side of the issue one happens to sit.

Producing Inappropriate Goods. MNC's may produce goods which the host country deems inappropriate. Producing goods for high-income consumers in low-income areas is usually the cause for this criticism [8]. The most celebrated case involved the Swiss multinational Nestlé. One of their food products is infant formula; they supply more than one-third of all infant formula in the world [9]. The drop in the total fertility rate in developed countries coupled with the growing popularity of breast feeding led to a decrease in demand for formula. Nestlé then turned to several developing countries where births are booming and advertised formula use as a modern and scientific approach to infant nutrition. Unfortunately, the proper use of formula requires safe water, sterilization of bottles and nipples, refrigeration, and enough money to buy the necessary amount for proper nutrition. Many mothers do not have the means for the proper preparation, storage, and dosage of formula. In an attempt to be modern they water down the formula, and their children suffer from malnutrition.

Avoiding Taxes Through International Organization. MNC's are internationally organized, and they can use this organization for tax advantages. This is done by transferring funds out of countries with high tax rates to foreign tax shelters. Interarms, an American firearms multinational, provides the classic case [10]. To avoid paying high American corporate taxes, Interarms "sold" some of its inventory to a foreign subsidiary, which in turn sold it to other foreign subsidiaries. Each time the price increased slightly, so that when the American home office bought back the arms, the price was over 4 times what they originally sold for. These guns never moved out of the warehouse, but Interarms was able to export much of its taxable American capital to a foreign tax shelter.

Obtaining Cheap Labor Through International Organization. MNC's have many international production possibilities and can, therefore, outmaneuver national labor unions. This was most boldly illustrated when Henry Ford II told British labor unions that they had better behave or he would take his plant elsewhere [11]. Unions have tried international coordination and have met with some success. The United Auto Workers, under the leadership of Walter Reuther, pioneered international labor negotiations by controlling labor activity on both sides of the United States–Canadian border. The International Chemical Workers won pay hikes from the French multinational St. Gobain in America by coordinating their contract demands with French,

Volkswagen assembly plant in Brazil. (Courtesy, Consulate of Brazil.)

Italian, and West German labor unions [12]. The American subsidiary had argued that the American laborers' demands were out of the question because the company did not turn a profit. The union, however, pointed to a large multinational profit and insisted that their pay demands be met. No European union would sign a contract with St. Gobain until the American union reached an agreement with the company. This was a major victory for international labor.

The Question of Ownership.   When an MNC operates in a host country, the question of the degree of host government ownership and control arises, particularly in regard to extractive industries. In defining their relationship, host countries and MNC's negotiate whether the MNC will fully own and manage the subsidiary or whether the government and the company will enter a partnership. Most MNC's wholly own their subsidiaries. Of the 13,795 new American multinational subsidiaries established from 1951 to 1975, 68 percent were wholly owned by MNC's.

Changes in ownership play an important role in extractive industries. At one time petroleum MNC's, for example, stated that they owned the oil and the countries owned the land that was over it [13]. As gunboat diplomacy has faded and cartels such as OPEC have gained strength, this relationship has changed. The extractive industries now have concession rights to the oil. The best example of this changing relationship is in Nigeria. In 1971, the Nigerian government obtained 35 percent of the ownership of foreign companies operating there. They expect majority control by 1982, with full ownership to follow [14].

Hegemony. Multinationals are often accused of being a form of imperialism. They are seen as giants trying to control and manipulate the political economy of the world. Persuasive evidence for this view comes from the behavior of ITT (International Telephone and Telegraph) in Chile. In 1972 it was revealed that this multinational was actively seeking to finance intervention in Chilean politics. As a result of such revelations the United Nations appointed the commission on transnational corporations. The commission's task was to come up with a code of conduct for MNC's [15].

EXPROPRIATION AND COOPERATION

The points of conflict listed above have led to two types of behavior by host countries: expropriation of MNC holdings, and cooperation among host countries when dealing with MNC's.

Expropriation of extractive MNC holdings has risen dramatically since 1970 (Fig. 16-7). Most expropriations have occurred in Middle and South America and Africa (Fig. 16-8). Cuba accounts for all the expropriation in Central America since 1950. Venezuela, Peru, and Chile have accounted for the bulk of South American expropriation. The threat of expropriation has been the major cause in the recent decline in extractive MNC's.

Expropriation is not indiscriminate with respect to industry type. Zaire has nationalized all its copper reserves but at the same time has encouraged manufacturing MNC's to invest there [16]. The manufacturing MNC's have less worry concerning expropriation. The reason for this is that subsidiaries of manufacturing MNC's are often organized as international operations based on vertical integration, that is, any one part of the system is both a supply and demand link in the production chain. What good would it do a country to nationalize an auto assembly plant if it could not get the necessary parts? By practicing *regional specialization*, a manufacturing MNC can insulate itself against expropriation.

Cooperation among host governments takes the form of bargaining pacts. The Andean Pact, composed of Bolivia, Chile, Ecuador, Peru, and Colombia, tries to coordinate its bargaining position with multinationals [17]. This presents a unified bargaining position to MNC's and limits their ability to play one host country against the other. Through cooperation host countries hope to gain the international bargaining power necessary to deal with multinational organizations.

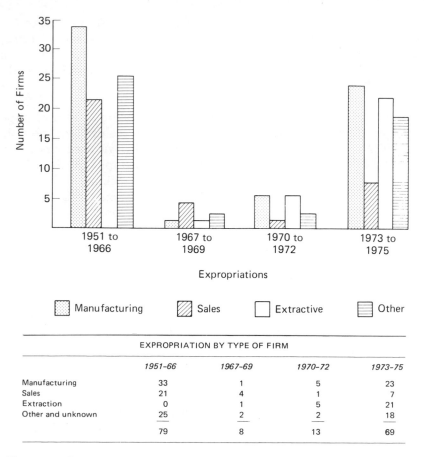

Fig. 16-7. Rate of expropriation of American multinationals, by year and and economic sector. (From Curham et al., *op. cit.*)

EXPROPRIATION BY TYPE OF FIRM				
	1951–66	*1967–69*	*1970–72*	*1973–75*
Manufacturing	33	1	5	23
Sales	21	4	1	7
Extraction	0	1	5	21
Other and unknown	25	2	2	18
	79	8	13	69

When bargaining, MNC's and host countries must determine the degree of foreign ownership, the rate at which indigenous labor replaces foreign managers, and the sectors of the economy in which foreign ownership will be permitted. The first of these goals, ownership, was discussed above. It seems likely that the Nigerian example of gradual takeover will continue, but only in countries which have the necessary cash flow and are important to the wealth of the multinationals. Nigeria's oil is very important to the United States and Europe, so that gradual takeover is an acceptable alternative to expropriation. In poor countries which do not have large enough markets to attract manufacturing and sales multinationals, few restrictions will be put on foreign investment. The Ivory Coast has adopted a policy bordering on laissez-faire toward foreign investment. The belief is that an influx of foreign capital and technology will do more to help the populace than restricted growth [18]. Other host countries see this as a sellout.

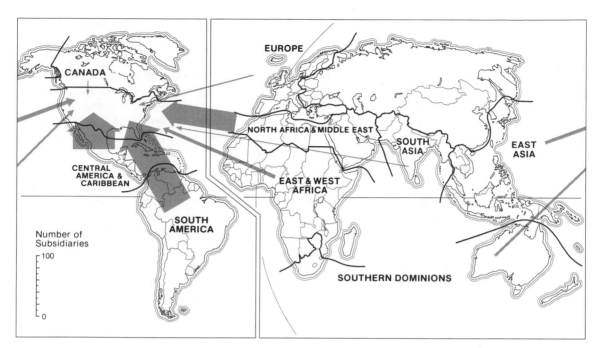

YEAR	REGION		
	Canada	Central America and Caribbean	South America
1951–66	1	71 (Cuba)	0
67–69	0	0	3
70–72	0	0	11 (Chile)
73–75	0	0	39 (Peru & Venequela)
	1	71	53

	Europe	North Africa and Middle East	East and West Africa
1951–66	1	4	0
67–79	1	3	0
70–72	0	2	0
73–75	0	18	5
	2	27	5

	South Asia	East Asia	South Dominions	Total
1951–66	0	2	0	79
67–69	1	0	0	8
70–72	0	0	0	13
73–75	0	4	3	69
	1	6	3	169

Fig. 16-8. Expropriation of American multinationals by region, 1950–1975. (From Curham et al., *op. cit.*)

CONCLUSIONS: LOOKING TO THE FUTURE

Making predictions about the future of MNC's is risky, but certain trends seem to be emerging (Fig. 16-9). Without gunboat diplomacy there will be little growth in the wholly owned extractive MNC's. The threat of expropriation will see to this. What may emerge are multinational cooperatives, business ventures made up of both private and public capital. An example of this is LAMCO, an iron ore company in Liberia owned by the Liberian Government, a Swedish syndicate composed of six companies, private individuals, and Bethlehem Steel [19]. This cooperation between governments and private investors obviously has profound geopolitical implications.

Nonextractive MNC's should continue to grow. The example of the Zairian Government, along with the practice of regional specialization, supports this hypothesis. What will most likely change is their distribution. As markets in developed countries become saturated and where developing countries raise their per capita income, MNC's will find developing countries attractive markets. The differences in investment shown in Table 16-2 may well diminish over the next 10 years.

Although the United States will continue to be the single most important home country, the days of the American challenge are over. Servan-Schreiber's thesis of American corporations dominating the world has not come to pass. A basic belief in migration is that every migration stream gives rise to a counter stream, and this applies to the migration of American corporations. After invading Europe in the 1960s, American corporations have found the Europeans striking back. In 1968, the top 10 companies outside the United States accounted for 38 percent of the sales of the top 10 American companies; by 1973 that figure had risen to 51 percent. The European growth is well-documented [20]. It can be seen as a decline in United States world power, but it is more likely an international adjustment process — an inevitable reaction to the massive exportation of American corporate wealth in the 1960s.

Finally, the relationship between MNCs and host governments is evolving, and hopefully it will mature. Scandals concerning MNC tampering in national elections and bribing foreign officials have led to closer scrutiny of MNC operation by the United Nations and host and home governments. MNC's can no longer portray themselves as heroic knights bringing technology, wealth, and jobs. At the same time, the rhetoric of the political left has been toned down to a point where socialists Rene Dumont and Marcel Mazoyu have stated [21]:

> . . . co-operation has both positive and negative aspects. A blanket condemnation of imperialism is therefore oversimple, and much too easy.

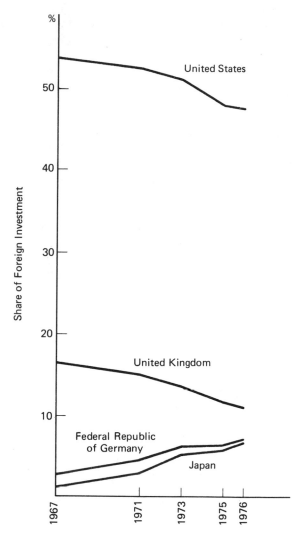

Country of origin	Percentage Distribution				
	1967	*1971*	*1973*	*1975*	*1976*
United States	53.8	52.3	51.0	47.8	47.6
United Kingdom	16.6	15.0	13.5	11.9	11.2
Germany, Federal Republic of	2.8	4.6	6.0	6.2	6.9
Japan	1.4	2.8	5.2	6.1	6.7

Fig. 16-9. Trends in foreign investment, 1967–1976, for selected areas. (From *Transnational Corporations in World Development*, United Nations, 1978, p. 236.)

Multinational corporations are beginning to be seen for what they are: powerful international institutions that can mobilize technology and wealth better than any other organization. Whether this power will be used to create a symbiotic or parasitic relationship among MNC's, home countries, and host countries, depends on how rapidly all sides mature.

REFERENCES

[1] *Multinational Corporations in World Development*, U.N. Dept. of Economic and Social Affairs (New York: Prager, 1974), pp. 143-149.

[2] Jean-Jacques Servan-Schreiber, *Le Defi American* (New York: Antheneum, 1968); Robert Heller and Norris Willatt, *The European Revenge: How the American Challenge Was Rebuffed* (London: Barrie and Jenkins, 1975).

[3] G. C. Hufbauer, "Multinational Corporations and the International Adjustment Process." *American Economic Review*, **64**, 1974, pp. 271-275.

[4] R. Vernon, "Competition Policy Toward Multinational Corporations." *American Economic Review*, **64**, 1974, pp. 276-282.

[5] C. F. Park, Jr., *Earthbound* (San Francisco: Freeman, Cooper and Co., 1975), p. 29.

[6] Vernon, *op. cit.*, note 4.

[7] R. Heller and N. Willatt, *op. cit.*, note 2.

[8] R. M. Moore. "Imperialism and Dependency in Latin America," *Journal of Interamerican Studies and World Affairs*, **15**, 1973 pp. 21-35.

[9] Information supplied by the Public Media Center, San Francisco, Calif.

[10] G. Thayer, *The War Business* (London: Weidenfeld and Nicolson, 1969).

[11] R. Heller and N. Willatt, *op. cit.*, note 2.

[12] L. Turner, *Invisible Empires* (London: Hamilton, 1970).

[13] P. Odell, *Oil and World Power* (New York: Pelican, 1974).

[14] L. L. Rood, "Foreign Investment in African Manufacturing," *Journal of Modern African Studies*, **13**, 1975, pp. 19-34.

[15] *The Economist*, **25**, 1976, pp. 68-69.

[16] Rood, *op. cit.*, note 14.

[17] R. L. Curry, Jr., and D. Rothchild, "On Economic Bargaining between African Governments and Multi-national Companies," *Journal of Modern African Studies*, **12**, 1974, pp. 173-189.

[18] Rood, *op. cit.*, note 14.

[19] S. Amin, *Neo-Colonialism in West Africa* (Harmondworth, 1973).

[20] Park, *op cit.*, note 5.

[21] Heller and Willett, *op. cit.*, note 2.

[22] R. Dumont and M. Mazoyu. As quoted in Curry and Rothchild, *op. cit.*, note 17.

PART SEVEN
EPILOG

CHAPTER SEVENTEEN

geography in an unstable world

INTRODUCTION

World political, economic, and social conditions change constantly and as changes occur, they alter the complex sets of relationships among nations, groups of peoples within nations, and peoples and their natural environments. The degree of change and the forces and phenomena associated with change vary greatly from one part of the world to another. Rapid change is common only within the more affluent nations which have undergone significant industrialization. Change is strongly resisted in most traditional (developing) societies; and when it occurs, it is often associated with major social, political, and (or) economic traumas.

POLARIZATION OF ISSUES

At almost every turn civilization is faced with great debates and mind-boggling choices over changes which will determine or strongly influence human welfare during coming decades. In many instances the great issues of our day are becoming increasingly polarized. Economic growth is good — economic growth is bad. Urban life is superior to rural life — rural life is superior to urban life. *Small is beautiful* [1] — only large-scale operations are efficient. Modern methods and technology must be applied to all agricultural production—modern agricultural methods and technology should be abandoned in all areas. A "soft energy path," emphasizing small-scale energy production, is the best route toward an energy utopia—large-scale energy facilities, including advanced nuclear technology, offer the keys to an energy utopia [2]. Multinational corporations are beneficial to human welfare—multinational corporations are evil. And so it goes for issues of all sorts.

In many instances the question which leads to polarization of issues is the "old way" of doing things versus the "new way." The essence of the debate concerns opposing conceptions of the past and the future. New ways may be justified because evidence indicates that old ways are no longer effective or that new directions are needed to provide hope for a future which is better than the past or the present. Radical social and economic changes are advocated by some groups as essential to the survival of humankind. These same changes are viewed by other groups as fundamentally destructive of any kind of worthwhile future. Nuclear energy, for example, is seen by its opponents as undependable, unnecessary, and (most of all) unsafe. Those who favor nuclear energy, on the other hand, may view those who crusade for solar energy as "impossibly idealistic, impractical, and elitist" [3].

The more important of the basic conflicts that divide humans and that lead to a turbulent world are those related to disparities in levels of living, national security, economic growth, resource sufficiency, educational attainment, self-determination, and environmental quality. These are some of the root causes for a rise in nationalism during a time when cooperation among the world's nations is increasingly vital to human security. Likewise some $400 billion are expended annually on arms when funds for solving problems in the areas of health care, population growth, energy shortages, ignorance, and hunger are in short supply. The magnitude of the danger to world

An unstable world. (Reprinted from *Agenda*, a publication of the Agency for International Development.)

civilization, and even to human existence, has escalated with the development and spread of nuclear weapons. Growing populations and rising mass consumption are placing mounting pressures upon the world's resource base, including the quality of the natural environment. At the same time, fear over the potentially disastrous consequences of new scientific and technical developments has slowed the rate and the extent to which they may be applied in efforts to solve some of the more pressing problems related to resources, population growth, and economic development. Indeed, almost every advance in science and technology leads directly or indirectly to increased demand for mineral resources rather than less.

MANAGEMENT OF PROBLEMS

Another key element in the complex of problems facing humankind is that an institutional structure through which the problems of the modern world can be reasonably addressed has not yet emerged. Nations continue to rely upon huge military expenditures to provide for national security, "on the assumption that the principal threat to security comes from other nations" [4]. Rather than other nations, however, the major threats to security may now be the relationships people have with nature [5]. Natural systems are ignorant of man-made political boundaries, cultural conflicts, military maneuverings, and economic systems. Still, the institutional structures of the world are based predominantly upon political, economic, and cultural concerns and upon precisely drawn boundaries that carve the world into numerous enclaves of peoples whose knowledge and interests are heavily localized.

Despite the "unnatural" fragmentation of the earth into nation states, each of which attempts to operate as if it were a world unto itself, national units are in reality the only vehicles through which strategies for managing the complex problems of the world can be formulated and implemented. Yet the degree of cohesiveness within nations and the capacities to manage their affairs also vary substantially from nation to nation. Even small nations are often unable to control their national territories effectively because they lack a common culture, or language, or tradition or because they lack adequate working capital, borrowing power, skilled workers, or communication and transportation facilities. The basic philosophy of government, that is, whether the political system is democratic or totalitarian or whether the economic system is capitalistic or socialistic, also affects the degree to which particular management strategies may be employed. The Soviet Union, for example, strongly opposes private ownership of land, whereas the United States has fostered private ownership of all forms of property.

Not only have new institutions capable of dealing effectively with worldwide problems failed to emerge, even those which once gave substantial continuity and stability to peoples of the advanced nations are under attack. "God is dead." Nearly half of all marriages end in divorce. Law enforcement agencies have often failed to stem rising crime rates. Medical doctors and teachers have lost some of the high esteem given them by previous generations. The worth of college education is being challenged, especially when it involves a concentration in one of the traditional liberal arts subjects. The "exact" sciences can no longer be regarded as "exact." Politicians are often perceived as being different only in the degree to which they are corrupt.

THE ROLE OF GEOGRAPHY

The polarization of issues and the conflicts that divide humankind are most often viewed within a nonspatial (nongeographical) context. The basic philosophy of laissez-faire, which holds the notion that the best of all possible worlds can be achieved through each individual or group pursuing its own selfish ends seems to have found applications within much of society. Problems and issues are seen through a kind of tunnel vision which disregards peripheral areas, peoples, problems, and issues. Nationalistic policies are followed without regard to the peace, welfare, or security of adjacent areas. An "environmentalist" may pursue the cause of a specific kind of natural environment without regard to the relationship of that environment to the welfare of humankind. Developers pursue growth and development without regard to their negative consequences for the natural environment. Labor unions seek increased benefits for their members without regard to the effects of those benefits upon the national or the world economy, and businessmen seek increased profits without regard to their effects upon the labor force. The poor blame the rich for their economic deprivation, and Americans blame the Soviets for the high costs of their defense establishment. The housewife blames the farmer; the farmer, the middleman; the middleman, the government; and the government blames the opposition.

The geographer attempts to describe and to explain such problems and issues as they differ, or as they are similar, within the context of some part of the earth's surface. It is this particular emphasis that gives geographers an opportunity to play a special role in assessing the state of the world. Although most individual geographers specialize in the spatial functioning of a particular set of phenomena or of some particular area, the goal of the discipline is toward an understanding of the interacting physical and human elements within and among areas. Just as an accountant assesses the financial soundness of a firm through measures of the firm's debits and credits, modern geographers attempt to assess the debits and credits of areas or of selected phenomena within those areas. In either case the debits and credits may or may not be functionally related. Beyond the debit and credit concept, the analogy between the task of a geographer and that of an accountant ceases. The accountant normally deals with a finite problem within the context of a closed system and a limited number of variables. Geographers often deal with infinite problems within the context of an open system and an unlimited number of variables. Although management and control are important in both cases, the conclusions from studying a geographic problem are more likely to involve interpretation and conjecture than conclusions from study of an accounting problem. Furthermore, in an accounting problem the debits and credits may be distinctly labeled as such, yielding a clearly documented report concerning the positive and negative attributes of a firm. In a geographic problem, on the other hand, debits and credits in themselves are subject to interpretation in light of particular management strategies. The rough terrain of the Great Smoky Mountains, for example, may be a negative attribute if viewed within the context of its potential for agricultural and industrial development but a positive attribute for development of the region's potential for recreation and tourism. Similarly, the climate of Iowa may be seen as a negative attribute (a debit) in that it has not been conducive to natural forestation. It is a positive attribute (a credit), however, in that it has been conducive to development of excellent soils for agriculture. That an area is covered with glacial ice or that it is dry does not diminish its worth except within certain prescribed limits of human utility. It is the balance resulting from the total functioning of human and physical elements over time within an area, therefore, which determines the area's viability and whether its viability is increasing or decreasing. To determine the nature of the relationships among specific types of attributes requires inputs from numerous specialists in a variety of fields. Besides the specialists, however, an adequate body of generalists (regional geographers, perhaps) is needed to synthesize the work of the specialists into a meaningful analysis of the overall functioning of the area or areas in question. The task of the generalist, as synthesizer, is likely to be far more complex and difficult than that of the specialist. It requires exceptionally broad and deep comprehension and understanding and a peculiarly cogent ability to distinguish between the important and the unimportant and between associations which are causal and those which are coincidental.

The spatial or areal concerns of geographers have important implications for the management of human societies. The essential questions for humankind, in the long run, will have to do with whether or not human and physical environments are managed so as to yield a positive balance. As population increases, as resources are depleted, and as per capita surface area diminishes, careful management of these phenomena becomes increasingly vital. "We live in a world in which scientific knowledge and technology give us more and more power, over which we have less and less control" [6].

REFERENCES

[1] E. F. Schumacher, *Small is Beautiful: Economics as if People Mattered* (New York: Harper Torchbooks, 1973).

[2] A. B. Lovins, *Soft Energy Paths: Toward a Durable Peace* (Ballinger, 1977). See also, A. M. Weinberg, "Reflections on the Energy Wars," *American Scientist,* **66,** No. 2, March–April, 1978, pp. 153–158.

[3] Weinberg, "Reflections on the Energy Wars," *op. cit.,* p. 158.

[4] L. R. Brown, *Redefining National Security,* Worldwatch Paper No. 14 (Washington, D.C.: Worldwatch Institute, 1977), p. 6.

[5] *Ibid.,* p. 6.

[6] "Conversations with an Author: Dr. Mortimer J. Adler," from an interview conducted by Martin L. Gross, for *Book Digest Magazine,* **5,** May, 1978, p. 27.

index